The Discovery
of the Mind

in Greek Philosophy and Literature

~

Bruno Snell

Dover Publications, Inc.
New York

This Dover edition, first published in 1982, is
an unabridged and unaltered republication of
the work originally published in 1953 under the
title *The Discovery of the Mind: The Greek
Origins of European Thought*. The translation
is by T. G. Rosenmeyer.

Library of Congress Cataloging in Publication
Data

Snell, Bruno, 1896-
  The discovery of the mind.

  Translation of: Die Entdeckung des Geistes.
  Reprint. Originally published: New York´:
Harper, 1960.
  Includes bibliographical references and index.
  1. Philosophy, Ancient. 2. Greece—Intel-
lectual life. 3. Greek literature—History and
criticism, 4. Greece—Religion. 5. Thought and
thinking I. Title.
B173.S6213 1982   182   81-17286
ISBN-13: 978-0-486-242644
ISBN-10: 0-486-242641

Manufactured in the United States by RR Donnelley
24264111   2015
www.doverpublications.com

TABLE OF CONTENTS

TRANSLATOR'S NOTE

The present translation is based on the second edition of *Die Entdeckung des Geistes* (Claassen und Goverts, Hamburg, 1948), with the addition of the essay which here appears as Ch. 7 : *Human Knowledge and Divine Knowledge*. The latter was submitted to the translator by Professor Snell in manuscript form.

Several chapters of the original work had previously appeared in the following publications :

Ch. 1, *Neue Jahrbuecher fuer Antike*, 1939.
Ch. 2, *Das Neue Bild der Antike*, 1942.
Ch. 3, *Die Antike*, 1941.
Ch. 4, *Antike und Abendland*, 1947.
Ch. 5, *Die Antike*, 1944.
Ch. 6, *Die Antike*, 1937.
Ch. 10, *Philosophischer Anzeiger*, 1929.
Ch. 11, *Geistige Welt*, 1947.
Ch. 13, *Antike und Abendland*, 1945.

Thanks are due to Sir Maurice Bowra, Mrs. D. Burr-Thompson, Mr. Casper J. Kraemer, Jr., Mr. R. Lattimore, and Mr. E. V. Rieu, for their permission to quote from their translations.

The translator wishes to express his special gratitude to Professor T. B. L. Webster of University College, London, who read the first draft of the translation and suggested many valuable changes.

T.G.R.

INTRODUCTION

EUROPEAN thinking begins with the Greeks. They have made it what it is : our only way of thinking; its authority, in the Western world, is undisputed. When we concern ourselves with the sciences and philosophy, we use this thought quite independently of its historical ties, to focus upon that which is constant and unconditioned : upon truth; and with its help we hope to grasp the unchanging principles of this life. On the other hand, this type of thinking was a historical growth, perhaps more so than is ordinarily implied by that term. Because we are accustomed to regard the Greek way of thinking as obligatory, we instinctively—or should we say naively?—project it also into thought processes of another order. Since the turn of the eighteenth century our growing awareness of evolutionary patterns may have contributed to the elimination of such rationalist concepts as the ageless, unchanging 'spirit'. Yet a proper understanding of the origins of Greek thought remains difficult because all too frequently we measure the products of early Greece by the fixed standards of our own age. The *Iliad* and the *Odyssey*, which stand at the source of the Greek tradition, speak to us with a strong emotional appeal; and as a result we are quick to forget how radically the experience of Homer differs from our own.

To trace the course along which, in the unfolding of early Greek culture, European thought comes into its own, we must first of all understand that the rise of thinking among the Greeks was nothing less than a revolution. They did not, by means of a mental equipment already at their disposal, merely map out new subjects for discussion, such as the sciences and philosophy. They discovered the human mind. This drama, man's gradual understanding of himself, is revealed to us in the career of Greek poetry and philosophy. The stages of the journey which saw a rational view of the nature of man establish itself are to be traced in the creations of epic and lyric poetry, and in the plays.

The discovery of the intellect cannot be compared with the discovery of, let us say, a new continent. America had existed long before Columbus discovered the New World, but the European way of thinking did not come into being until it was discovered; it exists by grace of man's cognizance of himself. All the same, our use of the word 'discovery' can, I think, be defended. The intellect was not 'invented', as a man would invent a tool to improve the operation of his physical functions, or a method to master a certain type of problem. As a rule, inventions are arbitrarily determined; they are adapted to the purpose from which they take their cue. No objective, no aims were involved in the discovery of the intellect. In a certain sense it actually did exist before it was discovered, only not in the same form, not *qua* intellect.

At this point we encounter two terminological difficulties. The first arises from a philosophical problem: in spite of our statement that the Greeks discovered the intellect we also assert that the discovery was necessary for the intellect to come into existence. Or, to put it grammatically: the intellect is not only an affective, but also an effective object. It must be obvious to anyone that we are here using a metaphor; but the metaphor is unavoidable, and is in fact the proper expression of what we have in mind. We cannot speak about the mind or the intellect at all without falling back on metaphor.

All other expressions, therefore, which we might employ to outline the situation, present the same difficulty. If we say that man understands himself or recognizes himself, we do not mean the same thing as is meant by understanding an object, or recognizing another man. For, in our use of the terms, the self does not come into being except through our comprehension of it.[1] If, on the other hand, we say that the intellect reveals itself, we regard this event not as a result of man's own doing but as a metaphysical happening. This again differs in meaning from the statement: 'A man reveals himself', i.e. he drops his disguise; for the man is the same after the change as before it, while the intellect exists only from the moment of its revelation onward, after it makes its appearance through an individual. If we take the word 'revelation' in its religious significance the same is true once more: the epiphany of a god presupposes that he exists, and that his existence is by no means dependent upon the revelation. The intellect, however, comes into the world, it is 'effected ', in the process of revealing itself, i.e. in the course of history. Outside of history, and outside of human life, nothing could be known of the nature of the intellect. A god reveals himself in all his glory in one single moment, while the intellect grants us only a limited manifestation, always dependent on the individual and his personal characteristics. In Christian thought God is intellect; our understanding of God is beset with grave difficulties, and the reason for this is a view of the intellect which was first worked out by the Greeks.

By using the terms 'discovery' and 'self-revelation' of the intellect we do not mean to commit ourselves to a particular metaphysical position, or to make predictions about a pure intellect existing by itself beyond, and prior to, history. The two terms here convey more or less the same idea. The latter might perhaps be used to advantage in speaking of the early period, when a new understanding was gained in the form of mythic or poetic intuition, whereas the word 'discovery' is more appropriate for the philosophers and scientific thinkers. But there is no firm line of demarcation between the two.[2] There are two reasons why we should prefer the former expression in a historical survey such as this. In the first place, the important thing was, not that a datum be clearly apprehended, but that the new insight be communicable. History acknowledges only what bids fair to become common property. As we shall see, many a commonplace had to be discovered before it could become an ingredient of colloquial speech. Conversely, discoveries may be forgotten, and especially in the world of the intellect discoveries are remembered only at the cost of constant hard labour. During the Middle Ages many ideas fell into disuse, and had to be re-discovered; happily the task was facilitated by the presence of the classical tradition. Secondly, we speak of 'discovery' rather than 'revelation' because, as we shall learn again and again in the course of our survey, man has to pass through much suffering and toil before he reaches an understanding of the intellect. πάθει μάθος, 'wisdom through suffering', holds for the whole of mankind, though perhaps not in quite the same sense as for the single man who has learnt the lesson of his troubles and protects himself against further suffering. Mankind too may learn its lesson, but not by protecting itself against suffering, for that would actually bar them from the acquisition of further wisdom.

The second terminological difficulty which obstructs our way raises a problem of intellectual history. Although we say that the intellect was not discovered, and did not come into being, until after the time of Homer, we realize that Homer conceived of the thing which we call intellect in a different manner, and that in a sense the intellect existed also for him, though not *qua* intellect. This means that we use the term 'intellect' to interpret something—and the interpretation is correct, otherwise we could not speak of discovery—which had previously been construed in another fashion, and therefore existed in a different dress; how, we shall see in our discussion of Homer. This 'something' simply cannot be grasped in our speech, since each language has its own interpretation, fixed in advance by its words. Whenever we wish to explain thoughts which were recorded in another tongue, we come to the conclusion that the foreign word means this—and again that it does not mean it. The stranger the other tongue, and the further we are removed from its thought, the greater is our dilemma. And when in the end we try to reproduce the alien thoughts in our own tongue—and that is the task of scholarship—we have a choice of either resigning ourselves to vague improvisations, or first finding certain approximations and then subtracting from them where they fail to correspond to the ideas which they are designed to represent. This is a negative approach, but in it lies our only hope of staking out the limits of the foreign material. At bottom, of course, we must be convinced that despite these complications the strange thoughts are intelligible to us, and that there is a vital meaning in what we have delimited, although we may not be able to define its precise significance in our own words. We need not be unduly sceptical, particularly when the foreign material is Greek. For here we come face to face with our own intellectual past; in fact, the sequel may show that those very ideas which we shall first emphasize precisely because they are so unusual are in reality perfectly natural, and certainly more obvious than the immensely intricate notions of our own day and age. Perhaps we shall be able to establish contact with Greek thought, not only through the medium of historical recollection, but also because the ancient legacy is stored in us, and we may recognize in it the threads of our own involved patterns of thinking.

If, therefore, in the chapters to follow we shall venture to say that Homer's men had as yet no knowledge of the intellect, or of the soul, or therefore of many other things, we do not thereby mean that his characters were not capable of joy, or reflection, and so forth. We merely want to stress that they did not conceive of these matters as actions of the intellect or the soul; and it is in this sense that they did not know the two. As a further consequence it appears that in the early period the 'character' of an individual is not yet recognized. Here again there is no denying that the great heroes of the Homeric poems are drawn in firm outline; and yet the reactions of an Achilles, however grand and significant, are not explicitly presented in their volitional or intellectual form as character, i.e. as individual intellect and individual soul. Of course there was 'something' which occupied the place later conceded to the intellect, or the soul; but to ascribe the latter to the Greeks without qualification would make us guilty of confusion and lack of precision. For the existence of the intellect and the soul are dependent upon man's awareness of himself. In questions of this sort terminological exactitude is a necessary requirement, even more so than in other scholarly discussions. Experience has shown how easily the issue may become obscured beyond repair.

To isolate the specifically European element in the development of Greek thought, we need not set it off against Oriental elements. Doubtless the Greeks inherited many concepts and motifs from the ancient civilizations of the East, but in the field which we have been discussing they are clearly independent of the Orient. Through Homer we have come to know early European thought in poems of such length that we need not hesitate to draw our conclusions, if necessary, *ex silentio*. If some things do not occur in Homer though our modern mentality would lead us to expect them, we are entitled to assume that he had no knowledge of them, particularly if there are several such 'gaps' of the same order. Sometimes the gaps are counterbalanced by certain positive phenomena which at first strike us as strange, but which,

X   INTRODUCTION

in combination with the gaps, form a consistent pattern.
In addition, the gradual unfolding of the Greek world
permits us to trace, step by step, those seeds which ultimately
produced the European notions of intellect and soul, and
thereby made possible European philosophy, science, ethics,
and finally religion.

Our perspective of the Greek accomplishment is not that
which served Classicism. Instead of describing a perfect
culture, lying beyond the confines of history, we hope to
indicate an achievement whose importance lies in its historical setting. Such an investigation need not terminate in
relativism; it is well within our power to say whether the
product of a particular era is great or small, profound or
superficial, influential or ephemeral. History is not an
infinite flux, an endless oscillation; the human spirit is
restricted within a small range of possible manifestations,
new departures are notably rare, and their forms severely
limited.

The findings of a scientist or a scholar are made in an
atmosphere of peaceful contemplation, whereas the discoveries of the Greeks which constitute our topic, affecting
as they do the very essence of man, take shape as vital
experiences. They assert themselves with a violence which
is not merely arbitrary or accidental; the historical situation
on the one hand, and the forms in which the mind may
understand itself on the other, provide the dynamic setting
for the new self-realization of the intellect. In the course of
our discussion it will become evident that certain basic
mental patterns exercise a varied control over men's minds
and leave their imprint upon the manner in which man
takes cognizance of himself. Both the historical aspects
and the systematic side of this process must be illuminated
in an intellectual chronicle such as this. The difficulties of
our enterprise are obvious, for it is impossible at one and the
same time to demonstrate the system which emerges from
the stream of time, and to trace the history of the various
motifs which together form a system. Under the circumstances, a collection of essays would seem to be the most
appropriate medium, with now one interest, now another
inviting the attention of the reader. The systematic aspects
of our inquiry will be emphasized in chapter 10; in chapters

1–6 they are purposely relegated to the background, to allow the historical features to enjoy the limelight.

I do not propose to furnish a presentation or interpretation of the poets and philosophers, nor do I wish to offer an introduction into the wealth and originality of early Greek art, or any other educational aim, but a close inquiry into the realm of intellectual history. On occasion it will be necessary to use abstract terminology, if we wish to formulate our findings in such a way that their correctness or falseness may be tested only by means of facts, and not by other interpretations. To place our investigation on the firm footing of demonstrability, it seems to me we have no other course but to reduce the problem of the evolution of Greek culture to the question : What did the Greeks at any given time know about themselves, and what did they not (or not yet) know?³ Much that is valuable and important must remain beyond the scope of our discussion, a victim of our chosen procedure. For the mental processes by which a man knows something, by which he recognizes something new, require to be ferreted out and recorded in ways which would not be applicable to his emotions, his religious sentiments, his feeling for beauty, or his ideas of justice. The fundamental facts of his mental operations may be explored only by a long series of patient comparisons. Actually, the issues at stake are often simple, even naive; but the need to elicit and grasp firmly the essential distinctions will at times lead us into regions remote and abstract.

In order to highlight the crucial stages in the intellectual evolution of the Greek world, I have confined myself as far as possible to the citation of a few textual passages; some of them will be repeated several times as the changing context demands. Also I have tried to direct the brightest beams upon the most significant stages. As is to be expected, we begin with Homer's view of man. Since Homer's position is the one furthest removed, and therefore least familiar to us, it has been necessary to describe the strangeness of that epoch in some detail; as a result the first of the present studies does not quite fit into the general framework of the book. It was felt, however, that an explanation of some of the concepts of early Greek thought, i.e. some words of the Homeric vocabulary, was called for. The treatment of some difficult questions concerning the meaning of words is responsible for the fact that the chapter contains more professional scholarship than the later sections. The chapter about the Olympian gods shows that the religion of Homer is, as it were, the first blueprint for the new intellectual structure which the Greeks erected. The historical pattern is first analyzed in the decisive achievements of the great poets: the creation of the lyric, the origin of tragedy, and the transition from tragedy to philosophy; Aristophanes' criticism of Euripides, the last tragedian, illustrates the meaning of this transition. In the following sections, on the Call to Virtue, on Comparison, and on the Creation of Scientific Thought; we shall see how the Greeks produced philosophy with its views of nature and man. The sketches on *Humanitas* and on Callimachus raise the question how the findings of the intellect became the general property of civilization. The last chapter, using Virgil's *Eclogues* as a model, tries to show how what was Greek had to be transformed in order to become European.

Most of these studies have been delivered as addresses in the course of the past nineteen years; some of them have been published in various journals; but they were from the very beginning designed to appear together. Here and there changes have been made, particularly in the oldest piece (ch. 10), and, wherever it seemed necessary, notes have been added to reinforce the text.

CHAPTER I

HOMER'S VIEW OF MAN

Since the time of Aristarchus, the great Alexandrian scholar, it has been the rule among philologists not to base the interpretation of Homeric words on references to classical Greek, and not to allow themselves to be influenced by the usage of a later generation when investigating Homeric speech. To-day we may expect even richer rewards from this rule than Aristarchus hoped to glean for himself. Let us explain Homer in no terms but his own, and our understanding of the work will be the fresher for it. Once the words are grasped with greater precision in their meaning and relevance, they will suddenly recover all their ancient splendour. The scholar too, like the restorer of an old painting, may yet in many places remove the dark coating of dust and varnish which the centuries have drawn over the picture, and thus give back to the colours their original brilliance.

The more carefully we distinguish between the meanings of Homer's words and those of the classical period, the clearer grows our vision of the gulf which lies between the two epochs, and of the intellectual achievement of the Greeks. But aside from the interpretive-aesthetic approach to the richness and beauty of the language, and the historical approach to the history of ideas, there is a third side to the Homeric phenomenon which we might call the 'philosophical'. It was Greece which produced those concepts of man as an intellectual being which decisively influenced the subsequent evolution of European thought. We are inclined to single out the achievements of the fifth century for special praise, and attribute to them a validity beyond time. How far Homer is removed from that stage can be shown from his language. It has long been observed that in comparatively primitive speech abstractions are as yet undeveloped, while immediate sense perceptions furnish it with a wealth of concrete symbols which seem strange to a more sophisticated tongue.

To cite one example: Homer uses a great variety of verbs to denote the operation of sight: ὁρᾶν, ἰδεῖν, λεύσσειν, ἀθρεῖν, θεᾶσθαι, σκέπτεσθαι, ὄσσεσθαι, δέρκεσθαι, παπταίνειν. Of these, several have gone out of use in later Greek, at any rate in prose literature and living speech: δέρκεσθαι, λεύσσειν,[1] ὄσσεσθαι, παπταίνειν. Only two words make their appearance after the time of Homer: βλέπειν and θεωρεῖν. The words which were discarded tell us that the older language recognized certain needs which were no longer felt by its successor. δέρκεσθαι means: to have a particular look in one's eyes. δράκων, the snake, whose name is derived from δέρκεσθαι, owes this designation to the uncanny glint in his eye. He is called 'the seeing one', not because he can see particularly well, not because his sight functions exceptionally well, but because his stare commands attention. By the same token Homer's δέρκεσθαι refers not so much to the function of the eye as to its gleam as noticed by someone else. The verb is used of the Gorgon whose glance incites terror, and of the raging boar whose eyes radiate fire: πῦρ ὀφθαλμοῖσι δεδορκώς. It denotes an 'expressive signal' or 'gesture' of the eyes. Many a passage in Homer reveals its proper beauty only if this meaning is taken into consideration, as is shown by Od. 5.84 and 158: (Odysseus) πόντον ἐπ' ἀτρύγετον δερκέσκετο δάκρυα λείβων. δέρκεσθαι means 'to look with a specific expression', and the context suggests that the word here refers to the nostalgic glance which Odysseus, an exile from his homeland, sends across the seas. To exhaust the full content of our word—the iterative aspect also needs to be brought out—we should have to become fulsome and sentimental: 'he was ever looking wistfully . . . ,' or: 'his fixed glance continually travelled forth' across the sea; all this is implied in the one word δερκέσκετο. It presents us with a suggestive image of a certain attitude of the eyes, just as in our language the words 'to glare' or 'to gaze' describe a particular type—though not the same—of looking. Of the eagle it may be said that ὀξύτατον δέρκεται, he looks very sharply; but whereas in English the adjective would characterize the function and capacity of the visual organ, Homer has in mind the beams of the eagle's eye, beams which are as penetrating as the rays of the sun which are also called 'sharp' by Homer; like a pointed weapon they cut through everything in their path. δέρκεσθαι is also used with an external object; in such a case the present would mean: 'his glance rests upon something', and the aorist:

'his glance falls on an object', 'it turns toward something', 'he casts his glance on someone'. Convincing examples are furnished above all by the compounds of the verb. *I.e.* 16.10 Achilles says to Patroclus: you cry like a little girl who begs her mother to take her in her arms, δακρυόεσσα δέ μιν ποτι- δέρκεται, ὄφρ᾽ ἀνέληται. With tears she 'looks to' her mother to pick her up. But in English 'look' is a broader term than the Greek word; it resembles the Greek βλέπειν which in later prose encroached upon the area of δέρκεσθαι. To sum up, then, the Homeric δέρκεσθαι does not designate the proper objective of sight, the special function of the eye which is to transmit certain sense impressions to the human perception.

The same is true of another of the verbs which we have mentioned as having disappeared in later speech. παπταίνειν is also a mode of looking, namely a 'looking about' inquisitively, carefully, or with fear. Like δέρκεσθαι, therefore, it denotes a visual attitude, and does not hinge upon the function of sight as such. Characteristically enough neither word is found in the first person, with the exception of one late occurrence of δέρκεσθαι. A man would notice such attitudes in others rather than ascribing them to himself. λεύσσω behaves quite differently. Etymologically it is connected with λευκός, 'gleaming', 'white'; three of the four cases in the *Iliad* where the verb is followed by an accusative object pertain to fire and shining weapons. The meaning plainly is: to see something bright. It also means: to let one's eyes travel. The mood of the word comes closest to Goethe's 'schauen' in his verse: 'Zum Sehen geboren, zum Schauen bestellt.' Pride, joy, and a feeling of freedom are expressed in it. Frequently λεύσσω appears in the first person, which distinguishes it from δέρκεσθαι and παπταίνειν, those visual attitudes which are mostly noticed in others. λεύσσω apparently connotes certain sensations experienced in the act of seeing, particularly in the seeing of specific objects. This is further illustrated by such Homeric expressions as τερπόμενοι λεύσσουσιν (*Od.* 8.171), τετάρπετο λεύσσων (*Il.* 19.19), χαίρων οὔνεκα . . . λεῦσσε (*Od.* 8.200) which bring out the joy that goes with the λεύσσειν; the latter is never used in situations of sorrow or anxiety. It is clear, therefore, that this term too derives its special significance from a mode of seeing; not the function of sight, but the object seen, and the sentiments associated with the sight, give the word its peculiar quality. The same is true again of another verb whose subsequent disappearance we noted above: ὄσσεσθαι. It means to have an impression, especially to have a threatening impression, and thus it approximates to the meaning 'suspect'. Once more, as in the previous instances, the seeing is determined by the object and the attending sentiment.

This is by no means the end of the list; Homer contains still other verbs of sight which depend for their exact significance upon the elements of gesture and feeling. θεᾶσθαι, for example, is to look with one's mouth wide open, i.e. ' to gape' or 'stare'. And finally, the words which were later combined to form the principal parts of the verb 'to see': ὁρᾶν, ἰδεῖν, ὄψεσθαι, show that to begin with there was no one verb to refer to the function of sight as such, but that there were several verbs each designating a specific type of vision. Space does not allow us to discuss to what extent original areas of meaning may be carved out even for these verbs.

Another expression of a more recent vintage, θεωρεῖν, was not in origin a verb, but was derived from a noun: θεωρός; its basic meaning is 'to be a spectator'. Soon, however, it came to mean: 'to look on', 'to contemplate'. Whatever the word may have conveyed in its initial stages, in the contexts in which we have it, it does not reflect an attitude, nor an emotion linked with the sight, nor the viewing of a particular object; instead it represents an intensification of the normal and essential function of the eyes. The stress lies on the fact that the eye apprehends an object. Evidently, then, this new word expresses the very aspect which in the earlier verbs had been played down, but which to us conveys the real substance of the operation known as 'sight'.

To sum up: the verbs of the early period, it appears, take their cue from the palpable aspects, the external qualifications, of the act of seeing, while later on it is the essential function itself, the operation common to every glance, which determines the content of the verb. In the later period, the various kinds of sight are modified by the insertion of adverbs and prepositions. παπταίνειν comes to be reproduced, however imperfectly, by περιβλέπεσθαι 'to look around' (*Etymol. Magnum*).

It goes without saying that even in Homer men used their eyes 'to see', i.e. to receive optical impressions. But apparently they took no decisive interest in what we justly regard as the basic function, the objective essence, of sight; and if they had no word for it, it follows that as far as they were concerned it did not exist.

At the risk of interrupting the sequence of our argument, we must now turn to the question of the words which Homer employed to speak of the body and the intellect. Aristarchus was the first to notice that in Homer the word σῶμα (soma) which subsequently came to mean 'body' is never used with reference to a living being;[2] soma is the corpse. But how does Homer refer to the body? Aristarchus[3] expressed the opinion that for Homer δέμας (demas) was the live body. That is true in certain cases. 'His body was small' appears in Homer as μικρὸς ἦν δέμας, and 'his body resembled a god's' is δέμας ἀθανάτοισιν ὅμοιος ἦν. Demas, however, is but a poor substitute for 'body', seeing that the word occurs only in the accusative of specification. It means 'in structure', 'in shape', and consequently its use is restricted to a mere handful of expressions, such as: 'to be small or large, to resemble someone', etc. And yet Aristarchus is right: in the vocabulary of Homer demas comes closest to playing the same role as the later soma.

But Homer has some further expressions at his disposal to designate the thing which is called 'body' by us, and soma by fifth century Greeks. Our phrase 'his body became feeble' would be the Homeric λέλυντο γυῖα ; ' his whole body trembled' would appear as γυῖα τρομέονται. Where we might say: 'sweat poured from his body', Homer has ἵδρως ἐκ μελέων ἔρρεεν; 'his body was filled with strength' is πλῆσθεν δ'ἄρα οἱ μέλε' ἐντὸς ἀλκῆς. Here we have plurals where our linguistic tradition would lead us to expect the singular. Instead of 'body' Homer says 'limbs'; γυῖα are the limbs as moved by the joints,[4] μέλεα the limbs in their muscular strength. The words ἅψεα and ῥέθεα which occur in similar contexts may be disregarded for our present purposes; there are only two instances of ἅψεα in place of γυῖα, both in the Odyssey, and ῥέθεα in this usage is altogether erroneous, as will be shown presently.

Let us continue with our game of translating our speech

into the language of Homer, instead of the reverse which is the usual practice. We find that there are several other ways of rendering the word 'body'. How would we translate: 'He washed his body'? Homer says χρόα νίζετο. Or how would Homer say: 'The sword pierced his body'? Here again he uses the word *chros*: ξίφος χροὸς διῆλθε. On the basis of passages like these some scholars have contended that *chros* is the equivalent of 'body' rather than 'skin'.[5] But there is no doubt whatever that *chros* is the skin, not the skin as an anatomical substance, the skin which can be peeled off—that is δέρμα (*derma*)—but the skin as surface, as the outer border of the figure of man, as the foundation of colour, and so forth. In point of fact, however, *chros* is often used in the place of 'body': περὶ χροῒ δύσετο χαλκόν, he placed his armour about his body—or literally: about his skin.

We find it difficult to conceive of a mentality which made no provision for the body as such. Among the early expressions designating what was later rendered as *soma* or 'body', only the plurals γυῖα, μέλεα, etc. refer to the physical nature of the body; for *chros* is merely the limit of the body, and *demas* represents the frame, the structure, and occurs only in the accusative of specification. As it is, early Greek art actually corroborates our impression that the physical body of man was comprehended, not as a unit but as an aggregate. Not until the classical art of the fifth century do we find attempts to depict the body as an organic unit whose parts are mutually correlated. In the preceding period the body is a mere construct of independent parts variously put together.[6] It must not be thought, however, that the pictures of human beings from the time of Homer are like the primitive drawings to which our children have accustomed us, though they too simply add limb to limb. Our children usually represent the human shape as shown in fig. 1, whereas fig. 2 reproduces the Greek concept as found on the vases of the geometric period.

Our children first draw a body as the central and most important part of their design; then they add the head, the arms and the legs. The geometric figures, on the other hand, lack this central part ; they are nothing but μέλεα καὶ γυῖα, i.e. limbs with strong muscles, separated from each other by means of exaggerated joints. This difference is of course

partially dependent upon the clothes they wore, but even
after we have made due allowance for this the fact remains
that the Greeks of this early period seem to have seen in a
strangely 'articulated' way. In their eyes the individual

FIG. 1　　　FIG. 2

limbs are clearly distinguished from each other, and the
joints are, for the sake of emphasis, presented as extraordinarily thin, while the fleshy parts are made to bulge
just as unrealistically. The early Greek drawing seeks to
demonstrate the agility of the human figure, the drawing of
the modern child its compactness and unity.

Thus the early Greeks did not, either in their language or
in the visual arts, grasp the body as a unit. The phenomenon is the same as with the verbs denoting sight; in the
latter, the activity is at first understood in terms of its
conspicuous modes, of the various attitudes and sentiments
connected with it, and it is a long time before speech begins
to address itself to the essential function of this activity.
It seems, then, as if language aims progressively to express
the essence of an act, but is at first unable to comprehend it
because it is a function, and as such neither tangibly apparent
nor associated with certain unambiguous emotions. As soon,
however, as it is recognized and has received a name, it has
come into existence, and the knowledge of its existence
quickly becomes common property. Concerning the body,
the chain of events may have been somewhat like this: in the
early period a speaker, when faced by another person, was
apparently satisfied to call out his name: this is Achilles,
or to say: this is a man. As a next step, the most conspicuous
elements of his appearance are described, namely his limbs
as existing side by side; their functional correlation is not
apprehended in its full importance until somewhat later.
True enough, the function is a concrete fact, but its objective
existence does not manifest itself so clearly as the presence of
the individual corporeal limbs, and its prior significance

escapes even the owner of the limbs himself. With the discovery of this hidden unity, of course, it is at once appreciated as an immediate and self-explanatory truth.

This objective truth, it must be admitted, does not exist for man until it is seen and known and designated by a word; until, thereby, it has become an object of thought. Of course the Homeric man had a body exactly like the later Greeks, but he did not know it *qua* body, but merely as the sum total of his limbs. This is another way of saying that the Homeric Greeks did not yet have a body in the modern sense of the word; body, *soma*, is a later interpretation of what was originally comprehended as μέλη or γυῖα, i.e. as limbs. Again and again Homer speaks of fleet legs, of knees in speedy motion, of sinewy arms; it is in these limbs, immediately evident as they are to his eyes, that he locates the secret of life.[7]

To return now to the intellect and the soul, we find there too the same perspective. Again Homer has no one word to characterize the mind or the soul. ψυχή (*psyche*), the word for soul in later Greek, has no original connexion with the thinking and feeling soul. For Homer, *psyche* is the force which keeps the human being alive. There is, therefore, a gap in the Homeric vocabulary, comparable to the deficiency in 'physical' terminology which we discussed above. As before, the gap is filled with a number of words which do not possess the same centre of gravity as the modern terms, but which cover more or less the same area. For the area of the 'soul', the most important words are *psyche*, θυμός (*thymos*), and νόος (*noos*).[8] Concerning the *psyche* Homer says that it forsakes man at the moment of death, and that it flutters about in Hades; but it is impossible to find out from his words what he considers to be the function of the *psyche* during man's lifetime. There is no lack of theories about the nature of the *psyche* prior to death, but so far from relying on the testimony of the Homeric poems they are based only on conjectures and analogies. One would do well to remember how little Homer says about the *psyche* of the living and of the dying man; for one thing, it leaves its owner when he is dying, or when he loses consciousness; secondly he says that the *psyche* is risked in battle, a battle is fought for it, one wishes to save his *psyche*, and so forth. There

is no justification here for assuming two different connotations
of *psyche*, for although we shall have occasion to translate it
as 'life', that is not its true meaning. The *psyche* which
is the prize of battle, which is risked, and saved, is identical
with the soul which departs from a dying man.

Of this departure, Homer mentions only a few details.
The *psyche* leaves through the mouth, it is breathed forth;
or again it leaves through a wound, and then flies off to
Hades. There it leads a ghostlike existence, as the spectre
(*eidolon*) of the deceased. The word *psyche* is akin to ψύχειν,
'to breathe', and denotes the breath of life which of course
departs through the mouth; the escape from a wound
evidently represents a secondary development. This vital
breath is, as it were, a semi-concrete organ which exists in
a man as long as he lives. As for its location, and its function,
Homer passes them over in silence, and that means that we
cannot know about them either. It appears as if in Homeric
times the term *psyche* chiefly evoked the notion of an
eschatological soul; at one point Homer says: he has but
one *psyche*, he is mortal (*Il.* 21.569); when, however, he
wants to say: 'as long as the breath of life remains in a man'
he avoids the word and puts it (*Il.* 10.89): εἰς ὅ κ' ἀυτμὴ ἐν
στήθεσσι μένῃ καί μοι φίλα γούνατ' ὀρώρῃ, 'as long as my breath
remains in my breast and my knees are in motion.' Yet in
spite of the mention of breath or respiration, the presence
of the verb 'remain' suggests that the notion of the *psyche*
is also involved, and that therefore Homer has a concept of
the 'breath of life'.

The other two words for the 'mind' are *thymos* and *noos*.
Thymos in Homer is the generator of motion or agitation,
while *noos* is the cause of ideas and images. All mental
phenomena are in one way or another distributed so as to
fall in the sphere of either of the two organs. In several
passages death is depicted as a departure of the *thymos*, with
the result that scholars have attempted to interpret *thymos*
as 'soul', rivalling the *psyche*. 'The *thymos* left his bones' is
a phrase which occurs seven times; 'quickly the *thymos* went
forth from the limbs' is found twice. If we translate *thymos*
as 'organ of (e)motion', the matter becomes simple enough.
Since this organ, prominently among its functions, determines physical motion, it is plausible enough to say that at

the point of death the *thymos* leaves the bones and the μέλη, i.e. the limbs with their muscles. But this hardly implies that the *thymos* continues to exist after death; it merely means: what provided motion for the bones and limbs is now gone.

Other passages in which *thymos* and *psyche* are apparently used without any distinction in meaning are more difficult to explain. *Il.* 22.67 Homer says: 'when someone by stroke or throw of the sharp bronze has bereft my ῥέθη of *thymos*.' At this point the meaning of ῥέθη must be 'limbs'; the concept is the same as in the verse just quoted, viz. that the *thymos* departs from the limbs, and this explanation was already given by the ancients.[9] The difficulty arises when we come to the other passages which contain ῥέθη: *Il.* 16.856 =22.362: 'his *psyche* fled from his ῥέθη and went down to Hades.' This is unique, for ordinarily the *psyche* leaves the body through the mouth (*Il.* 9.409) or through a wound (*Il.* 14.518; 16.505), i.e. through an aperture of the body. The expression 'from the limbs', besides being considerably less plausible and convincing, also presupposes that the soul has its seat in the limbs, a view which is not met with elsewhere in Homer. Now it so happens that the word ῥέθος remained alive in Aeolic, but not in the sense of 'limb'; we take this information from the scholia on the verse cited above,[10] whence we conclude that for Sappho and Alcaeus ῥέθος bore the meaning 'face'.[11] From the Aeolic poets this meaning of the word was handed on to Sophocles (*Antigone* 529), Euripides (*Heracles* 1204) and Theocritus (29.16). As the same scholion tells us, Dionysius Thrax already came to the conclusion that in Homer too ῥέθος must refer to the face.[12] Other ancient scholars opposed him by pointing to the circumstance that in Homer the *psyche* sometimes leaves the body through a wound. In any case, the solution offered by Dionysius is too simple, for as has already been stated, in *Il.* 22.68 we read that the *thymos* takes its leave from the ῥέθη and they must be the μέλη, for if our interpretation of *thymos* as (e)motion is right, it may be expected to escape from the limbs but not from the face, let alone the mouth. *Il.* 16.856, on the other hand, concerns the *psyche*, and here we are not surprised that it should fly off through the mouth.[13]

The whole confusion is easily resolved once we take into

consideration the age of the various passages. *Il.* 22.68 is
undoubtedly very late, probably even, as E. Kapp has pointed
out to me, dependent on Tyrtaeus. The author is someone
who was not conversant with the Aeolic word ῥέθος, and
whose understanding of Homer's language was on the whole
no longer perfect. Confronted with such seemingly analogous
passages as 13.671: 'the *thymos* quickly went forth from his
limbs (μέλη)' and 16.856: 'his *psyche* escaped from the
ῥέθη and went down to Hades', he was quick to equate *psyche*
with *thymos* and μέλη with ῥέθη; and by a further analogy
with a passage like 5.317: μή τις . . . χαλκὸν ἐνὶ στήθεσσι βαλὼν
ἐκ θυμὸν ἕληται he finally formed his own verse: ἐπεί κέ τις ὀξέϊ
χαλκῷ τύψας ἠὲ βαλὼν ῥεθέων ἐκ θυμὸν ἕληται. By the standard
of Homer's own usage, these words make no sense at all.[14]
There are other indications that the concepts of *thymos* and
psyche are easily confused: *Il.* 7.131 reads: 'his *thymos*
escaped from his limbs (μέλη) down to Hades.' It has long
been noticed[15] that the idea of the *thymos* going down to
Hades contradicts the usual Homeric conception. The verse
is contaminated from 13.671 f.: 'quickly the *thymos* went
forth from the limbs (μέλη)' and 3.322: 'grant that he dies
and goes down to Hades.' It is just possible that the con-
tamination is the work of a later poet who did not know the
Homeric usage. But it is more likely that it was brought
about by a rhapsode who confused several sections of verses
in his memory, a common enough occurrence in oral delivery.
In that case emendation would seem to be called for, and as
it happens another part of a verse from Homer furnishes an
easy remedy. In 16.856 (=22.362) we have a reading which
is good and meaningful: ψυχὴ δ᾽ ἐκ ῥεθέων πταμένη Ἀϊδόσδε
βεβήκει, 'the soul flew down to Hades from the ῥέθη.' From
this, 7.131 may be reconstructed: ψυχὴν ἐκ ῥεθέων δῦναι δόμον
Ἄϊδος εἴσω. It is true that there remain a number of passages
in which *thymos* is the eschatological soul which flies off at the
moment of death;[16] but in each case it is the death of an
animal which is so described—the death of a horse (*Il.* 16.469),
of a stag (*Od.* 10.163), of a boar (*Od.* 19.454) or of a dove
(*Il.* 23.880). I have no doubt that the origin of this usage
was as follows: evidently people were averse to ascribing the
psyche, which a human being loses when he dies, also to an
animal. They therefore invented the idea of a *thymos* which

leaves the animal when it expires. The idea was suggested by the passages which exhibit the *thymos* leaving the limbs or the bones of a man. Those passages in turn which speak of a *thymos* of animals contributed their share to the confusion between *thymos* and *psyche*. But the phrase 'the *thymos* flew off' which occurs four times, i.e. with comparative frequency, is always applied to animals—and, incidentally, to no one more than once. This proves that in the early period the two terms were not yet used interchangeably.

Whereas the contrast between *thymos* and *psyche* is clear and emphatic, the line between *thymos* and *noos* cannot be drawn with the same precision. If, as we have suggested, *thymos* is the mental organ which causes (e)motion, while *noos* is the recipient of images, then *noos* may be said generally to be in charge of intellectual matters, and *thymos* of things emotional. Yet they overlap in many respects. To-day, for instance, we regard the head as the seat of thinking, and the heart as the organ of feeling ; but that does not prevent us from saying: he carries thoughts of his beloved in his heart—where the heart becomes the seat of thinking, but the thoughts are oriented towards love; or the reverse: he has nothing in his head but revenge—and here again the meaning is: thoughts of vengeance. But these exceptions are only apparent, for they are easily replaced by equivalent turns of expression: he has vengeance in his heart, etc. The same is true of *thymos*=(e)motion and *noos*=understanding; the exceptions which might be cited by way of argument against these equations are not real. Nevertheless it is only fair to concede that the distinction between *thymos* and *noos* is not as evident as that between *thymos* and *psyche*. Here are a few examples.

Ordinarily the sensation of joy is located in the *thymos*. But *Od*. 8.78 we read: Agammenon rejoiced in his *noos* when Achilles and Odysseus quarrelled with each other for the distinction of being the best man. Agamemnon's delight does not spring from the altercation of the two most valiant heroes—that would be absurd—but from his recollection of Apollo's prophecy that Troy would fall when the best heroes contended with one another. The basis of his joy, therefore, is reflection.[17]

Another instance: generally speaking it is the *thymos*

which rouses a man to action. But *Il.* 14.61 f. Nestor says: 'Let us take counsel . . . if the *noos* may accomplish anything'. In this passage *thymos* would be quite meaningless, for Nestor asks them to consider whether 'counsel', i.e. an idea, may achieve anything. Although the *thymos* is customarily the abode of joy, pleasure, love, sympathy, anger and all mental agitation, occasionally we also find knowledge residing in it. *Il.* 2.409, for example, we are told that Menelaus did not have to be summoned to the assembly, for 'he knew in his *thymos* that his brother was beset by trouble.' He knew it, not because he had been informed, or because his perception was especially acute, but by virtue of his instincts, through brotherly sympathy.[18] Or, in the words of the poet, he knew it through an 'emotion'. Examples of this sort could be multiplied freely. *Noos* is akin to νοεῖν which means 'to realize', 'to see in its true colours'; and often it may simply be translated as 'to see'. Witness *Il.* 5.590: 'She saw (ἐνόησε) Hector in the ranks.' Frequently it is combined with ἰδεῖν, but it stands for a type of seeing which involves not merely visual activity but the mental act which goes with the vision. This puts it close to γιγνώσκειν. But the latter means 'to recognize'; it is properly used of the identification of a man, while νοεῖν refers more particularly to situations ; it means: 'to acquire a clear image of something'. Hence the significance of *noos*. It is the mind as a recipient of clear images, or, more briefly, the organ of clear images: *Il.* 16.688 'The *noos* of Zeus is ever stronger than that of men.' *Noos* is, as it were, the mental eye which exercises an unclouded vision.[19] But given a slight shift which in Greek is easily managed, *noos* may come to denote the function rather than the organ. In its capacity as a permanent function *noos* represents the faculty of having clear ideas, i.e. the power of intelligence: *Il.* 13.730 'To one man the god has given works of war . . . but in the heart of another far-seeing Zeus has placed an excellent *noos*.' At this point the meaning 'mind' shades off into the notion of 'thinking'. The two are of course closely related; in our language we employ the term 'intelligence' to refer both to the intellect and to its activity or capacity. From here it is only a short step, and *noos* will signify also the individual act, the individual image, or the thought. We read, for instance, that someone thinks a *noos*: *Il.* 9.104 and

Od. 5.23. Thus the area covered by this term exceeds the
competence of our words mind, soul, or intelligence. The
same is true also of *thymos*. If it is said that someone feels
something in his *thymos*, the reference is to an organ which
we may translate as 'soul' provided we keep in mind that it is
the soul as the seat of (e)motions. But *thymos* may also serve
as the name of a function, in which case we render it as 'will'
or 'character'; and where it refers to one single act, the word
once more transcends the limitations of our 'soul' or 'mind'.
The most obvious example occurs *Od.* 9.302 where Odysseus
says: 'Another *thymos* held me back;' each individual impulse,
therefore, is also a *thymos*.

What bearing does all this have on our investigation of
Homer's attitude towards the human mind? At first it might
be suspected that *thymos* and *noos* are nothing more than the
parts of the soul, such as we know from Plato's psychology.
But those parts presuppose a psychic whole of which Homer
has no cognizance.[20] *Thymos*, *noos*, and *psyche* as well are
separate organs, each having its own particular function.
We say: 'to look at a thing with different eyes', without
meaning to refer to the organ; the idea that someone provides
himself with another set of eyes would hardly arise. Rather,
the word 'eye' here stands for 'function of the eye', 'vision',
and what we actually mean is 'to see with a different view'.
Homer's 'another *thymos*' must be similarly understood. But
that is not all: the two passages with *noos* cited above (*Il.*
9.104 and *Od.* 5.23) lead us even further, in a most significant
direction. *Noos* as understood in their context no longer
refers to the function itself but to the result of the νοεῖν. νόον
ἀμείνονα νοήσει still lends itself to the translation: 'he will
devise a better thought'. But now thought has ceased to be
the activity of thinking, and has become the thing thought.
τοῦτον ἐβούλευσας νόον presents the same situation. It is
worth pointing out, however, that *noos*, in the only two
Homeric passages where it is to be rendered as 'thought',
appears as the internal object of νοεῖν and βουλεύειν. The
actio verbi of νοεῖν, i.e. the function, obviously remains a
decisive factor.

We have intentionally avoided bringing into our inquiry
the distinction, on the face of it so pertinent, between 'concrete' and 'abstract'. Actually this distinction is for our pur-

poses open to question, and not nearly so fruitful as the
difference between organ and function. It might, for instance,
be thought that because the word ἄθυμος is found in one
Homeric passage, *thymos* must already have possessed an
abstract significance. But if that were so, one would have to
admit that 'heart' and 'head' are abstracts too, for it is entirely
feasible to say that someone is heartless, or has lost his head.
If I declare that someone has a good brain, and I mean his
thinking; or: someone has a soft heart, and I mean his feelings,
I use the name of the organ in place of that of the function.
'Heartless', 'brainless', and ἄθυμος refer to the lack of a
function. The metaphoric use of words for organs, which
may be interpreted as abstraction, has its place on the most
primitive level of speech, for it is precisely on that level that
the organ is regarded, not as dead and concrete, but as
participating in its function.

As soon as we attempt to describe the mental concepts of
Homer by means of the catchwords 'organ' and 'function'
we are bound to encounter terminological difficulties such as
always arise for anyone who wishes to reproduce foreign
idioms and peculiarities within the terms of his own tongue.
If I say that the *thymos* is a mental organ, that it is the organ
of a psychic process, I find myself caught in phrases which
contain a contradiction in terms, for in our eyes the ideas of
the soul and of an organ are incompatible. To express myself
accurately I should have to say : what we interpret as the
soul, Homeric man splits up into three components each of
which he defines by the analogy of physical organs. Our
transcription of *psyche*, *noos* and *thymos* as 'organs' of life, of
perception, and of (e)motion are, therefore, merely in the
nature of abbreviations, neither totally accurate nor exhaus-
tive; this could not be otherwise, owing to the circumstance
that the concept of the 'soul'—and also of the 'body', as we
have seen—is tied up with the whole character and orientation of a language. This means that in the various languages
we are sure to find the most divergent interpretations of
these ideas.

According to some the remark that Homer had 'not yet'
acquired the knowledge of many things lowers his stature.
Consequently they have tried to explain the difference between his mentality and ours by the proposition that Homer

stylized his thinking, that for aesthetic or other reasons he avoided the description of mental processes because such details might have detracted from the grand simplicity of his heroes. Is it conceivable that Homer could deliberately have turned his back upon the notions of 'intellect' and 'soul'? Such psychological finesse, affecting the most subtle particulars, cannot in all fairness be attributed to the ancient epic poet. What is more, the gaps left by Homer's 'ignorance' suddenly fall into a meaningful pattern if they are set off against those of his notions which our modern thinking seems to lack. Deliberate stylization is undoubtedly to be found in Homer, but this is not one of the quarters in which it takes effect. Do we expect Homer to present us with that invention of Goethe's humour, Little Mr. Microcosm? Everything human, and especially everything great, is one-sided and confined within limits. The belief in the existence of a universal, uniform human mind is a rationalist prejudice.

Actually there is further evidence for our contention that we are dealing with an early stage of European thought, and not with stylization. That Homer's conception of *thymos*, *noos* and *psyche* still depended to a large extent on an analogy with the physical organs becomes a matter of absolute certainty if we turn to that era of transition when his conception began to be abandoned. To be sure, the evidence for the use of the words *soma* and *psyche* during the period extending from Homer to the fifth century is not full enough to allow us to trace the origin of the new meanings 'body' and 'soul' in every detail. Apparently they were evolved as complementary terms, and more likely than not it was *psyche* which first started on its course, perhaps under the influence of notions concerning the immortality of the soul. The word denoting the eschatological soul was put to a new use, to designate the soul as a whole, and the word for corpse came to be employed for the living body; the reason for this must be that the element which provided man during his living days with emotions, perceptions and thoughts was believed to survive in the *psyche*.[21] Presumably people felt that animate man had within him a spiritual or intellectual portion, though they were unable to define this element by one term sufficiently accurate and inclusive. As a matter of fact, this is the state of affairs which we shall meet among the early writers of lyric poetry. And it may be inferred that, because the eschatological *psyche* had been correlated with the *soma* of the dead, the new *psyche*, the 'soul', demanding a body to suit it, caused the term *soma* to be extended so that it was ultimately used also of the living body. But whatever the details of this evolution, the distinction between body and soul represents a 'discovery' which so impressed people's minds that it was thereafter accepted as self-evident, in spite of the fact that the relation between body and soul, and the nature of the soul itself, continued to be the topic of lively speculation.

The first writer to feature the new concept of the soul is Heraclitus. He calls the soul of living man *psyche*; in his view man consists of body and soul, and the soul is endowed with qualities which differ radically from those of the body and the physical organs. We can safely say that these new qualities are irreconcilable with the categories of Homer's thought; he does not even dispose of the linguistic prerequisites to describe what Heraclitus predicates of the soul. The new expressions were fashioned in the period which separates Heraclitus from Homer, that is to say the era of the lyric. Heraclitus says (fr. 45):[22] 'You could not find the ends of the soul though you travelled every way, so deep is its *logos*.' This notion of the depth or profundity of the soul is not unfamiliar to us; but it involves a dimension which is foreign to a physical organ or its function. To say: someone has a deep hand, or a deep ear, is nonsensical, and when we talk of a deep voice, we mean something entirely different; the adjective there refers to vocal expression, not to the function of the voice. In Heraclitus the image of depth is designed to throw light on the outstanding trait of the soul and its realm: that it has its own dimension, that it is not extended in space. To describe this non-spatial substance we are of course obliged to fall back on a metaphor taken from space relations. But in the last analysis Heraclitus means to assert that the soul, as contrasted with things physical, reaches into infinity. Not Heraclitus but the lyric poets who preceded him were the first to voice this new idea, that intellectual and spiritual matters have 'depth'.[23] Archaic poetry contains such words as βαθύφρων, 'deep-pondering', and βαθυμήτης, 'deep-thinking'; concepts like 'deep knowledge,' 'deep thinking', 'deep pondering', as well as 'deep pain' are common enough in the archaic period. In these expressions, the symbol of depth always points to the infinity of the intellectual and spiritual, which differentiates it from the physical.

Homeric speech does not yet know this aspect of the word 'deep'. It is more than an ordinary metaphor; it is almost as if speech were by this means trying to break through its confines, to trespass on a forbidden field of adventure. Nor does Homer show himself conversant with the specifically spiritual facet of 'deep knowledge', 'deep thinking' and so forth. The words βαθύφρων and βαθυμήτης are, it is true, formed by analogy with Homeric expressions, but they are πολύφρων and πολύμητις, 'much-pondering' and 'much-thinking'. Just as lyric poetry specializes in compounds formed with βαθυ-, so Homer uses the prefix πολυ- to express an increase of knowledge or suffering: πολύιδρις, πολυμήχανος, πολυπένθης etc., 'much-knowing', 'much-devising', 'much-suffering'. Quantity, not intensity, is Homer's standard of judgment. *Il.* 24.639 Priam laments the fate of Hector: 'I groan and brood over countless griefs'. πολλά αἰτεῖν, πολλά ὀτρύνειν, 'to demand much', 'to exhort much' is a frequent figure, even where the act of demanding or exhorting takes place only once.[24] Our 'much' offers a similar ambiguity. Never does Homer, in his descriptions of ideas or emotions, go beyond a purely spatial or quantitative definition; never does he attempt to sound their special, non-physical nature. As far as he is concerned, ideas are conveyed through the *noos*, a mental organ which in turn is analogous to the eye; consequently 'to know' is εἰδέναι which is related to ἰδεῖν 'to see', and in fact originally means 'to have seen'. The eye, it appears, serves as Homer's model for the absorption of experiences. From this point of view the intensive coincides with the extensive: he who has seen much sufficiently often possesses intensive knowledge.

Nor does the *thymos* provide any scope for the development of a notion of intensity. This organ of (e)motion is, among other things, the seat of pain. In Homer's language, the *thymos* is eaten away or torn asunder by pain; the pain which hits the *thymos* is sharp, or immense, or heavy. The analogies are evident: just as a limb is struck by a pointed weapon or by a heavy stone, just as it may be corroded or torn to pieces, so also the *thymos*. As before, the concept of the spiritual is not divorced from the corporeal, and intensity, the proper dimension of the spiritual, receives no attention. Homer is not even acquainted with intensity in its original sense, as 'tension'. A tension within the soul has no more reality for him than a tension in the eye would, or a tension in the hand. Here too the predicates of the soul remain completely within the bounds set for physical organs. There are no divided feelings in Homer; not until Sappho are we to read of the bitter-sweet Eros. Homer is unable to say: 'half-willing, half-unwilling;' instead he says: 'he was willing, but his *thymos* was not'. This does not reflect a contradiction within one and the same organ, but the contention between a man and one of his organs; we should compare our saying: 'my hand desired to reach out, but I withdrew it'. Two different things or substances engage in a quarrel with one another. As a result there is in Homer no genuine reflexion, no dialogue of the soul with itself.

Besides being 'deep', the *logos* of Heraclitus is also a κοινόν, a 'common' thing. It pervades everything, and everything shares in it. Again, Homer has no vocabulary to express a concept of this sort; he cannot say that different beings are of the same spirit, that two men have the same mind, or one and the same soul, any more than he would allow that two men have one eye or one hand between them.[25]

A third quality which Heraclitus assigns to the mental sphere also diverges from any predications which could be made of the physical organs; this means that it must clash with the thought and speech of Homer. Heraclitus says (fr. 115): 'The soul has a *logos* which increases itself.' Whatever the exact significance of this statement, we gather that Heraclitus ascribes to the *psyche* a *logos* capable of extending and adding to itself of its own accord; the soul is regarded as a sort of base from which certain developments are possible. It would be absurd to attach a similar *logos* to the eye, or the hand. For Homer the mental processes have no such capacity for self-induced expansion.[26] Any augmentation of bodily or spiritual powers is effected from without, above all by the deity. In the 16th book of the *Iliad* Homer recounts how the dying Sarpedon with his last words implored his friend Glaucus to help him; but he too was wounded and could not come. So Glaucus prayed to Apollo to relieve him of his pain and restore to him the strength of his arms. Apollo heard his prayer, soothed his pain, and 'cast strength in his *thymos*'. As in many other passages in which Homer refers to the intervention of a god, the event has nothing super-natural, or unnatural, about it. We are free to conjecture that Glaucus heard the dying call of Sarpedon, that it caused him to forget his pain, to collect his strength, and to resume the fighting. It is easy to say that Glaucus pulled himself together, that he recovered his self-control; but Homer says, and thinks, nothing of the sort: they are notions which we read back into the scene. We believe that a man advances from an earlier situation by an act of his own will, through his own power. If Homer, on the other hand, wants to explain the source of an increase in strength, he has no course but to say that the responsibility lies with a god.

The same is true in other cases. Whenever a man accomplishes, or pronounces, more than his previous attitude had led others to expect, Homer connects this, in so far as he tries to supply an explanation, with the interference of a god. It should be noted especially that Homer does not know genuine personal decisions; even where a hero is shown pondering two alternatives the intervention of the gods plays the key role. This divine meddling is, of course, a necessary complement of Homer's notions regarding the human mind and the soul. The *thymos* and the *noos* are so very little different from other physical organs that they cannot very well be looked upon as a genuine source of impulses; the πρῶτον κινοῦν, Aristotle's 'first mover', is hidden from Homer's ken, as is the concept of any vital centre which controls the organic system. Mental and spiritual acts are due to the impact of external factors, and man is the open target of a great many forces which impinge on him, and penetrate his very core. That is the reason why Homer has so much to say about forces, why, in fact, he has so many words for our term 'force': μένος, σθένος, βίη, κῖκυς, ἴς, κράτος, ἀλκή, δύναμις. The meaning of each of these words is precise, concrete, and full of implications; so far from serving as abstract symbols of force, as do the later terms δύναμις and ἐξουσία which may be used of no matter what function, Homer's words refer to specific functions and particular provinces of experience. μένος is the force in the limbs of a man who is burning to tackle a project. ἀλκή is the defensive force which helps to ward off the enemy. σθένος is the muscular force of the body, but also the forceful sway of the ruler. κράτος is supremacy, the superior force. That these forces were at one time invested with religious awe is indicated by certain formulas: Alcinous, for example, is called the 'force of Alcinous', ἱερὸν μένος 'Αλκινόοιο; compare also βίη 'Ηρακληείη and ἱερὴ ἲς Τηλεμάχοιο. These idioms are difficult to resolve because they have already by Homer's time become fixed and rigid, nor are we in a position to find out whether βίη was the original term, or ἲς or μένος. In all probability metrical considerations have played their part in the choice. A proper name such as Telemachus or Alcinous cannot appear in the nominative case at the place which is usually preferred for the citation of proper names, viz. the end of the verse; and so the poet resorts to circumlocution. It has also been observed that adjectival formulas of the type of βίη 'Ηρακληείη occur in connexion with those names which are not members of the Trojan circle; hence it seems fair to conclude that they were adopted from earlier epics. But since they must have been meaningful at one time or another, it has been suggested[27] that among the so-called primitive peoples the king or the priest is often regarded as the possessor of a special magic force which elevates him high above the rest of his fellow tribesmen, and that the formulas which we have cited originally described the leaders as invested with such a force. This is a felicitous suggestion; we would, of course, be mistaken to look for a belief of this sort in our Homeric poems. The very fact that the formulas have become hardened, that metrical patterns now determine their use, prevents us from exploiting them toward a 'magic' interpretation of the epic poets. The *Iliad* and the *Odyssey* have a great deal to say about forces, but there is not a scrap of evidence to suggest that there is anything mystic about them; all in all magic and witchcraft have left few traces in the poems, except for some rather atrophied survivals. Homeric man has not yet awakened to the fact that he possesses in his own soul the source of his powers, but neither does he attach the forces to his person by means of magical practices; he receives them as a natural and fitting donation from the gods.

No doubt in the days before Homer magic and sorcery held the field, and even Homer's view of the human soul has its roots in such a 'magic' stratum. For it is only too obvious that psychic organs such as the *noos* and the *thymos*, incapable as they are of spontaneous thought or action, are at the mercy of wizardry, and that men who interpret their own mental processes along these lines consider themselves a battleground of arbitrary forces and uncanny powers. This enables us to form some vague opinions about the views which men held concerning themselves and their lives in the pre-Homeric period. The heroes of the *Iliad*, however, no longer feel that they are the playthings of irrational forces; they acknowledge their Olympian gods who constitute a well-ordered and meaningful world. The more the Greeks begin to understand themselves, the more they adopt of this Olympian world and, so to speak, infuse its laws into the human mind. It is true that they continued throughout to preserve a belief in magic, but all those who helped to advance the new era had as little regard for it as Homer, for they pursued the path which Homer had trod. However primitive man's understanding of himself as presented in Homer's speech may appear to us, it also points far into the future: it is the first stage of European thinking.

CHAPTER 2

THE OLYMPIAN GODS

THERE is a German fairy-tale in which a youth wants to know what fear is. He is so stupid that he has never known fear. So his father, unable to cope with him, sends him forth into the world to find this fear and thus satisfy his curiosity. The tale takes it for granted that all men, far from needing to exert themselves, possess an instinctive acquaintance with the terror inspired by the mysterious. To wean ourselves from this fear we would have to go much farther than the hero of the story goes on his quest. The fear of the uncanny controls much of the thinking of a child before it becomes conversant with the order of the universe about it. It looms equally large in the mentality of primitive peoples where it is usually precipitated in the form of religious ideas. It may be asked, therefore, whether he who feels no fear is so very stupid after all; and in fact the ending of the tale shows us what is meant: the fool marries the king's daughter and wins the charmed treasure precisely because he is ignorant of fear. This wise simpleton, one of the ilk of Lucky Hans and Little Klaus, has the right attitude towards life; after many a spook and ghost which fail to produce their effect on him, he becomes terror-stricken when a maid pours a bucket of fish into his royal bed. Among all his dreadful escapades, this was the only one real enough to touch him.

How do men and tribes learn to distinguish reality and fact from spectres and sprites? By what standard do they determine what is natural? The awesome and the mysterious first confront man under the guise of the numinous or the demonic; the primitive seek to control and exorcise them through religion, and consequently the conquest of terror is for them tantamount to a change in religious ideology. This change has already been effected in the creed of the Olympian gods who rule in the Homeric poems, the *Iliad* and the *Odyssey*. They presuppose a transformation so radical in spirit that we find it hard to understand how a faith can be so completely devoid of terror and mystery. The wise fool of the fairy-tale overcomes the ghosts simply because he does not believe in them. It seems that the Greeks too, in discarding their fear of the uncanny, somehow gave up a portion of their faith. In fact, when we consider the religion of Homer and the creed of the Olympian gods which he created, we may well wonder whether this is a faith at all. Our notion of faith or belief always allows for the possibility of disbelief; this is true in the world of ghosts, but is especially valid on a higher religious plane. 'Faith', the *credo*, requires as its opposite a false belief, a heresy; it is tied to a dogma which people must either attack or defend with their very lives. All this was foreign to the Greeks; they looked upon their gods as so natural and self-evident that they could not even conceive of other nations acknowledging a different faith or other gods.

To the Christians who landed in America the gods of the the Indians were of course idols and devils; to the Jews the gods of their neighbours were enemies of Yahweh. But when Herodotus visited Egypt and encountered the native deities, it never occurred to him that he might not find Apollo, Dionysus and Artemis there too. Bupastis translated into Greek is none other than Artemis (2.137), Horus is called Apollo, and Osiris is Dionysus (2.144). Just as the Egyptian name of the king sounds different in Greek, as his insignia deviate from those of a Greek or a Persian king, as a ship or a street does not have one and the same name or appearance in Egypt and in Greece, so also the Egyptian gods are not identical with those of the Greeks, but they are easily 'translated' into the Greek tongue and into Greek ideology. Not every nation calls all the gods its own; Herodotus found some barbarian gods for whom he was unable to cite a Greek name; those gods were to be regarded as barbarian *par excellence*. The Greeks, then, did not think along the same lines as the Jews or the Christians or the Mohammedans who know but one true god, their own, a god who demands conversion of those who would not recognize him. The Greek attitude springs in part from the circumstance that, dispersed as they were over various lands, they worshipped their gods in many shapes and under many names. The Artemis of Ephesus, the goddess with a hundred breasts, scarcely resembles her namesake, the huntress of Sparta. What wonder that in Egypt she exists in yet another guise, and under another name? The gods of the Greeks are a necessary part of the world, and that is reason enough why they should not be linked exclusively with national boundaries or privileged groups. How could there be any gods but those whose existence is self-evident, inherent in nature itself? Who, for instance, would gainsay that Aphrodite exists? Everybody knows that she is as active among all other peoples as she is among the Greeks; even the animals are subject to her rule. It would be downright absurd to maintain that one does not 'believe' in Aphrodite, the goddess of love. It is possible to neglect her, to pay no respect to her, as was done by the huntsman Hippolytus, but Aphrodite is present, and active, none the less. The same is true of Athena and Ares. And could anyone deny that, when all is said and done, Zeus upholds the sacred order of the world? The existence and the power of the gods are no less certain than the reality of laughter and tears, the living pulse of nature around us, the plain fact of our doings whether they be sublime and solemn, or bold and hard, or bright and serene. Every human act betrays the vitality of the ultimate cause behind it.

But, it will be objected, what about the atheists who flourished in Greece? Were not Diagoras and Anaxagoras banished, did not Socrates suffer execution, because they contested the existence of the gods? For an answer we must turn to their trials; they will show us in what sense we may be permitted to speak of religious belief, or unbelief, in Greece.

Almost all the trials for irreligion which we know to have taken place in antiquity occurred during the brief period between the start of the Peloponnesian War and the end of the fifth century, i.e. within a span of thirty years. It was a time, moreover, in which the Olympian gods were no longer crowned with the full splendour of their ancient power. The trials were conducted, not with the youthful intolerance which we would expect from a proud and self-confident religion, but with the restlessness and irritability with which a lost position is defended. About the faith of an earlier generation when piety was owned by all, these trials tell us nothing; nor were they concerned with 'faith', as the Christian trials of heretics were. It need hardly be pointed out that these suits were instigated less for religious than for political motives; the condemnation of the philosopher Anaxagoras was designed to strike at the politician Pericles, and the religious argument was a smoke screen for an attack upon a political enemy otherwise unassailable. But even if we concentrate on the religious controversy which occasioned the trial, the problem of faith never became an issue. These accusations of atheism were never brought against those who subscribed to another religion, but only against philosophers. They were prosecuted, not because they denied a certain dogma—for Greek religion had none, and we never hear of a Greek philosopher challenged to forswear his mistaken creed —but because of their *asebeia*, their transgression against the gods. *Asebeia*, a crime for which the death penalty could be demanded, is an outrage committed against something sacred; anyone who steals dedicatory gifts, who mutilates the statues of the gods, who pollutes a temple, or who betrays the secrets of the mysteries, is *asebes*. But could any of these charges be made good against the philosophers?

To understand what is meant by the accusation of *asebeia* against them, we must look for help from another Greek term. We know the content of the brief against Socrates. According to the usual translation it says: Socrates is a criminal because he does not believe in the gods in which the city believes, but has introduced other deities and novel gods. The word which we have rendered 'believe' is *nomizein*. The law on the basis of which Socrates was condemned must have contained the following clause: 'Anyone who fails to *nomizein* the gods of the city is to suffer the death penalty'. At first sight the translation 'who does not believe in the gods' would seem plausible enough. The Athenians of 399 B.C. understood *nomizein* to mean: to acknowledge the existence of the gods. In their opinion Socrates disavowed the reality of the gods and was plotting, by means of his *daimonion*, that strange voice from within him, to introduce new deities, 'new demons', to replace the old ones. In their eyes, therefore, Socrates was, not a heretic or a dissenter, but an atheist. But such an accusation has no precedent in the religious convictions of an earlier time because the very idea that the gods perhaps do not exist could not have been proposed prior to the middle of the fifth century. The sophist Protagoras was the first to advance it explicitly. Yet long before

Protagoras there was a law which stipulated severe penalties for those who failed to *nomizein* the gods. In that sense, the word means: to value, to respect; we might compare the kindred word *nomisma* which denotes something that has value, that is valid: i.e. the coin, Latin *numisma*, whence our term 'numismatics'. Aeschylus occasionally uses the word, when he wishes to state that someone does not respect the gods, i.e. that he pays no attention to them.[1] The commandment: 'Respect the gods' was interpreted in two ways; first, people should not commit acts of open *asebeia*, religious transgressions; and secondly, they ought to participate in the rites of the official cult. Consequently the friends of Socrates took special pains to assert, in his defence, that he had always carried out the customary sacrifices. It appears, then, that the prescripts which characterized the early stages of Greek religious life were not aimed at the control of opinions, nor did they favour the setting up of dogmas or sacred doctrines. Atheists were persecuted only once, during the brief period when the enlightenment of the philosophers seemed about to destroy the firm structure of human society, and then only in Athens. To enforce their punishment, one word of the ancient law was made to carry a meaning which it did not originally have. No one seems to have noticed the shift; there was as yet no science of semantics which might have saved Socrates. On one other occasion, towards the eve of the ancient world, do we hear of religious intolerance and of religious trials: the persecutions of the Christians. The Christians were hounded, not because their tenets presented a problem to the pagan creed, but because they were unwilling to participate in the official cults, above all in the cult of the Roman emperor, i.e. the ceremonies of the State. They were never called upon to renounce their beliefs, but merely to carry out the prescribed rites. They however refused to do so, religion being for them a matter of conviction and faith.

What then was Greek religion? Was it essentially a thing of cult and ritual? But surely cult, stripped of the element which we call faith, is little more than magic, an endeavour to influence and prevail over the deity by means of hallowed spells and charms; and would not this bring us back once more to the mysterious, the uncanny which the Olympian

religion was supposed to have left far behind? Or is it pre-
ferable to assume that the more profound religious needs of
the Greeks found their full satisfaction only in the mysteries
of Eleusis and Samothrace, or in the Dionysiac, Orphic and
Pythagorean sects which cherished hopes of liberation and
expectations of a blissful life after death?

It is a fact that, beginning with the romantics, there have
been attempts to seek the true religion of the Greeks in those
quarters. Winckelmann and the ' classical' Goethe had
tended to see in the Olympian gods the products of an artistic
imagination rather than the actual objects of genuine reverence. As a result, Creuzer set out to locate the real religious
forces of the Greeks in the sombre recesses of symbolism,
mysticism and ecstatic frenzy; unfortunately he projected
back into the classical and pre-classical periods much that is
characteristic only of late antiquity.[2] Ever since then there
has been a heated debate on the question whether the
Olympian gods, the pan-Hellenic, the truly 'classical' gods,
who reign in poetry and in the visual arts, far removed from
the mysteries, from chthonic darkness and ecstasy—whether
these Olympian gods did not also elicit a response which,
whatever the qualifications, might be called 'faith'.[3] It is
certain that they represent more than merely the free invention of an unconcerned or even frivolous intellect, but we
to-day, accustomed to think of religion and faith in terms
of the Old and New Testaments, find it difficult to picture
accurately the particular attitude which is involved. A Greek
would have thought the bargaining between Gideon and his
God (*Judges* 6.36–40) more than a little peculiar. Gideon is
about to march against the Midianites, and asks God for a
sign that He will protect him: he will put a fleece of wool on
the floor, and on the next morning the fleece is to be damp
with dew, but the floor around it dry. This will be his surety
that God will not forget him. God hears Gideon, and carries
out his request. But Gideon turns to Him once more: this
time the fleece is to be dry, and the floor damp. The grace
of God manifests itself in His willingness to cancel the
natural order of things; before God nothing is impossible.
In the Greek tales, likewise, the hero will at times ask for a
visible token of divine assistance; he will pray for a stroke of
lightning, a bird flying by, a fit of sneezing—signs which

under ordinary circumstances could not be expected to come about just at the desired moment, but which are not impossible, and might indeed occur *agathei tychei*, by a happy coincidence. But Gideon's demand that the natural sequence of events should be reversed, and the readiness of the believer to have his faith reinforced and refreshed by the paradoxical, such things are not to be found among the Greeks. The saying ascribed to Tertullian: 'credo quia absurdum' is not Greek; it goes against the very grain of pagan Greek thought, and deliberately so.[4] According to classical Greek notions the gods themselves are subject to the laws of the cosmos, and in Homer the gods always operate in strictest conformity with nature. Even Hera forcing Helios to plunge quickly into the Ocean remains within the limits set by nature since Helios is envisaged as a charioteer who may well lash his steeds on to a greater speed. On no account must she be thought to have sought to disturb the processes of nature by magical means. Nor is the Greek deity capable of creating a thing out of nothing; that is the reason why the Greeks have no *Genesis* of their own.[5] A Greek god is confined to such acts as invention and transformation; beyond that he cannot go. It would not be far wrong to say that the supernatural in Homer behaves with the greatest regularity; nay more, it is possible to formulate precise laws which control the gods' interference in human affairs.[6]

In Homer every new turn of events is engineered by the gods. The *Iliad* begins with the plague sent by Apollo; Agamemnon is induced to return Chryseis, and his claiming of Briseis as a substitute rouses the ire of Achilles. In this way the *mise en scène* of the epos is established. At the start of the second book Zeus dispatches the false dream to Agamemnon which by its promise of victory sends him off into battle; hence war and disaster are visited upon the Greeks. And so the story continues. At the beginning of the *Odyssey* we witness the assembly of the gods which decides on the return of Odysseus; again and again the gods intervene until ultimately Odysseus with Athena's help succeeds in killing the suitors. Two dramas are acted out simultaneously, the one on a higher stage, among the gods, and the other here on earth. Everything that happens down below is determined by the transactions of the gods with one another.

For human initiative has no source of its own; whatever is
planned and executed is the plan and deed of the gods. Not
only does human endeavour lack an inherent beginning, it
also has no proper end. The gods alone act in such a manner
that they achieve their ends, and even if a god sometimes
cannot realize all his designs—Zeus unable to save his son
Sarpedon from death, or Aphrodite who must suffer to be
wounded in battle—the supreme frustration of the human
race, eventual death, is not for them.

This higher life which the gods live on their exalted plane
endows the existence of men with its meaning. Agamemnon
sets out to conquer, but Zeus has long decided that the Greeks
are to be beaten. All the various enterprises on which men
have set their hearts, which they would carry out even at the
risk of their lives, are piloted by the gods and obey their
slightest nod; it is their designs which are brought to fruition,
and they alone know the end for each thing. This position
of the gods in the Homeric epics is responsible for the coining
of the term 'divine apparatus' (*Goetterapparat*) as if the poet
could use the gods arbitrarily, as a literary strategem to
quicken an action which has slowed down. In the epic works
of later antiquity this machinery of the gods becomes so
lifeless that Lucan does not hesitate to cast it aside,[7] for
which he was much criticized by his contemporaries. The
Homeric poet, however, wields no discretionary powers over
the appearances of his gods. On the contrary, they often
step into the picture at moments when a divine apparatus
is perfectly superfluous; instead of serving to promote an
event which otherwise would be difficult to explain, the
intervention of the gods actually interrupts the natural
sequence of an action, or at least so it would seem to our
more sophisticated taste.

At the very opening of the *Iliad*, when the quarrel between
Agamemnon and Achilles has flared into open view, Agamemnon demands that Achilles deliver Briseis over to him; this
angers Achilles so much that he clutches his sword and
wonders whether he ought to draw it against Agamemnon.
At that critical point Athena appears to him, and to him
alone as we are expressly told. She holds him back and warns
him not to fall a victim to his wrath; in the end it will be to
his advantage to have restrained himself now. Achilles at

once obeys the command of the goddess and places his sword back in the scabbard. The poet, we feel, had no special need of the divine apparatus at this juncture; Achilles simply controls himself, and it would have been sufficient to explain his failure to rush upon Agamemnon from his own mental processes. From our point of view, the intercession of Athena merely confuses the motivation rather than making it plausible. Homer, however, could not do without the deity. We might substitute a decision on the part of Achilles, his own reflection and his own incentive. But Homer's man does not yet regard himself as the source of his own decisions; that development is reserved for tragedy. When the Homeric hero, after duly weighing his alternatives, comes to a final conclusion, he feels that his course is shaped by the gods. Even nowadays, when we try to recapture the past, we may lose sight of our own share in an event in which we were once implicated, and ask ourselves: how did this plan, or that thought, ever come to me? If we take this notion, that a thought 'came' to us, and give it a religious twist, we come fairly close to the Homeric attitude. It is worth pointing out that concepts of this kind recur, somewhat more rigid to be sure, in the philosophical doctrines of Descartes and the Occasionalists, as *assistentia dei*. Homer lacks a knowledge of the spontaneity of the human mind; he does not realize that decisions of the will, or any impulses or emotions, have their origin in man himself. What is true of the events in the epic holds also for the feelings, the thoughts and the wishes of the characters: they are inextricably linked with the gods. In this sense we need not hesitate to speak of a belief in the gods. Goethe frequently emphasized this function of the deity, most tersely perhaps in his conversation with Riemer (Biedermann 1601): 'The god to whom a man proves devout, that is his own soul turned inside out.' From the viewpoint of history, we might reverse this: the soul of a man is the deity transplanted into him. For what was later known as the 'life of the soul' was at first understood as the intervention of a god.

To begin with, then, we have arrived at a rather general truth: primitive man feels that he is bound to the gods; he has not yet roused himself to an awareness of his own freedom. The Greeks were the first to break through this barrier, and thus founded our western civilization. Does Homer perhaps allow us to glimpse some of the trends which ultimately led to this liberation? First of all it must be remarked that Athena, in the scene cited above, enters the stage at a moment when the issue is, not merely a mystery, but a real secret, a miracle: how, that is the question, does the spiritual manage to express itself in the world of appearances? This is the same problem which occupied Descartes. The fathomless depth of the world of the spirit, and indeed its very existence, remains outside the focus of Homer because of his faith in the gods. With his concrete appreciation of things natural —we might almost say, with his common-sense diplomacy— Homer has his gods intercede especially in those cases where a mind, or the passions, or the sense of the action are deflected from their old course.

In the scene which we have described, an unobtrusive feature of Athena's speech allows us to perceive the immense difference between Greek faith and Oriental beliefs. She begins: I have come down from the sky to assuage your anger—if you consent. What noble charm is expressed in these three words. They carry the graceful stamp of an aristocratic society; with chivalrous courtesy the speaker tempers her own claims and gives full consideration to the other person's privileges. The commerce between mortals and immortals is regulated by the most polite sentiments. The Greek god does not burst forth in a storm-cloud to strike man with his thunder, nor is the worshipper awed into a sense of insignificance by the terror which his god inspires in him. Athena says, as if she were speaking to her peer: follow me, if you wish. And Achilles answers, with perfect assurance: yes, even if a man is very angry, it is better to follow the gods. Throughout his poems Homer has his gods appear in such a manner that they do not force man down into the dust; on the contrary, when a god associates with a man, he elevates him, and makes him free, strong, courageous, certain of himself. Whenever a great, a decisive deed is to be accomplished the god steps in and gives his advice, and the man chosen for the deed strides cheerfully ahead. The *Iliad* and the *Odyssey* differ a little in this respect; in the former each single turn of events is determined by the gods, whereas in the *Odyssey* the gods may be said to act as permanent companions. But the two poems are at one in the credit given to the gods whenever some extraordinary performance is at stake. Conversely those acts with which a man would not gladly identify himself are considered folly, delusion, deeds in which the god has no part. Those closest to the god in Homer are not the poor and the meek, but the strong and the powerful; the godless one, i.e. the one who is shunned by the gods, upon whom they do not bestow any gifts, is Thersites. The emotion which a man experiences in the sight of his god is not awe, not even primarily fright or fear, or reverence or respect; all these are still too close to the magic shudder, they involve a more mysterious deity than usually appears in Homer. On the other hand, it goes without saying that the gods are not approached with humility or love, qualities which do not come into their own before the dawn of the Christian era. The peculiar reaction with which Homer's heroes face their gods is put into words in the scene of Achilles: 'Athena stepped behind him and caught him by his hair, appearing to no one but him. But Achilles was amazed and turned around. And at once he recognized Pallas Athena, for her eyes shone greatly.' Amazement, wonder, marvelling—these are the sentiments which the gods continually elicit from their favourites. In many passages of the *Iliad* and the *Odyssey* we are told that a man was amazed when the god or the goddess appeared to him, that he admired the god when he caught sight of him. Do not even the later Greeks exhibit a gesture of prayer which is basically a pose of admiration?

But amazement and admiration, even from Homer's viewpoint, are not of a specifically religious character. Beautiful women and sturdy heroes receive admiration, artfully wrought implements are 'a wonder to behold'. Admiration has always been widely in evidence, but the early Greeks were particularly susceptible to it. It is a response excited by things which are not totally strange to the onlooker, but merely more beautiful and more perfect than everyday objects. The Greek word for admiration, *thaumazein*, is derived from *theasthai* which means 'to look'. Admiration is a look of wonder in one's eyes; it does not affect the whole man, as terror does. The eye lends distance to things, it makes them into objects. With admiration of beauty usurping the place of terror before the unknown, the divine becomes at once more remote and more familiar; it no longer thrusts itself upon man with the former intensity; the power of its spell over him is broken, and yet its presence appears more natural and convincing than before.

The Homeric hero stands free before his god; he is proud when he receives a gift from him, and again he is modest in his knowledge that all great things accrue to him from the deity. And when a man is made to suffer under a god, as Odysseus suffers under Poseidon, he does not bow his head and give way, but gallantly faces up to the struggle, retaining a precarious balance between humility and arrogance. This narrow border is not easily maintained; the god of the Greeks far outstrips the gods of the Jews, the Indians, or the Chinese in inviting his worshippers to equal him. The Greeks have ever been prone to the hazard of insolently overstepping their bounds, and it is from them that Europe has inherited that vain ambition—called *hybris* by the Greeks—which in spite of Christianity, or perhaps precisely because of its teachings, has become the great vice, the antipode of all virtue, the cause of many a harsh atonement. The gods are the *rheia zoontes*, they live at ease; their life is especially vital in as much as they are not touched by the darkness and the imperfection which death engenders in the human life, but even more so because theirs is a fully conscious life. The gods know the meaning and the end of their existence as human beings can never hope to. Even conflict, resistance and failure are part of their life in the sense that they add to its fulness, for life could not be without struggles and the desire to deploy one's powers. The gods would be dead without their jealousies and their ambitions, their victories and their defeats.

Darkness and death have been pushed to the furthest limits of this world. Death is a void, or little more than a void, into which men are submerged. Everything on earth is clouded by the prospect that even the bloom of youth, the strength of maturity will not stave off death, a thought which affects men with the deepest melancholy. Nevertheless they do not permit their anxiety about death to influence their lives, although they maintain the utmost loyalty in the performance of their duties toward the dead. Since all life has its boundaries, even the free life of the gods is limited, if not by a blind fate, at least by a fixed order or universal law such as that which compels all men to die. Likewise the gods pay heed to the just wishes of their colleagues, and though they may grumble and skirmish, Zeus in the end restores the peace and reconciles them with each other over nectar and ambrosia. Now and then he will pronounce dire threats, and remind them of their uncouth and disorderly past. But usually Homer avoids speaking of the battles in which the Olympians once had to contend with Cronus and the Titans and the Giants. No doubt these myths of warfare between the gods reflect a time when the Olympians were not yet in power, when another religion held sway. It is perhaps not permissible to recognize in the fallen gods the actual deities in whom earlier men had believed; but the contrast gives us an indication of what was regarded as the essential contribution of the new gods. The defeated are not devils, malicious, shrewd, or sensual; but they are undisciplined and rude: mere brawn and little else. The Olympians brought about the rule of order, justice, and beauty. For the Greeks, the Titanomachy and the battle against the Giants remained symbols of the victory which their own world had won over a strange universe; along with the battles against the Amazons and against the Centaurs they continue to signalize the Greek conquest of everything barbarous, of all monstrosity and grossness.

Now it is well known that substantial elements of the earlier Greek religion remained alive long after the rise of brighter days; the uncanny and the spooky, the belief in ghosts and magic practices never lost their hold on the people. If we do not find these ingredients in the epics, their elimination must be intentional.[8] The last phase of this trend may still be observed: the notions of *Moira* and the *Daimon*, for example, lose some of their vigour between the *Iliad* and the *Odyssey*. Vestiges of the original beliefs are numerous in Homer. Many of the sonorous epithets which adorn the names of his gods had at an earlier stage undoubtedly served for the magic imprecation of the *numen*; others had referred to a special function of the god which was now no longer compatible with his more refined personality. Apollo is the 'far-shooter', Zeus the 'cloud-gatherer;' some of the attributes even remind us of an earlier theriomorphic religion, such as 'owl-eyed Athena' and 'cow-eyed Hera'. We are accustomed to regard these epithets as characteristic- ally Homeric; but then again we are struck by other expres- sions which are more truly Homeric, as e.g. when Apollo and Athena are simply called 'the beautiful and great gods'. This is where we get an inkling of Homer's enlightened reverence, the blandness of his admiration. But the old belief is not yet long forgotten, and the new Homeric conception of the gods is still young. It may be conjectured that the credit for making Zeus, the lord of the Thessalian Olympus, into the ruler of the other immortals and the father of gods and men, belongs to the nobles of Thessaly, long before the days of Homer. But it would scarcely do to explain that essential, and most typical, feature of Homeric religion, the suppres- sion of all chthonian elements including the worship of Mother Earth, of Ge and Demeter, by contending that the great barons of Thessaly deliberately distinguished their religion from the crude superstitions of the peasants. No, this differentiation had to wait until the colonists in Asia Minor severed their ties with their home soil and its hallowed cult centres. The transparent clarity of the Homeric creed is a fruit of the detached sophistication of the aristocrats in the cities of Asia Minor; in departing from Greece they had left the dark powers of the earth behind them, and were able to raise their sky-god Zeus to his domination over gods and men. The gods do not derive from the cults, nor do they owe their origin to priestly speculation; they took shape in the songs of the poets, side by side with the company of the Achaean heroes. They in turn spring from the echoes, kept alive through many centuries of hardship and misery, of the heroic age of Mycenae; they are moulded by the nostalgia for a paradise lost and a homeland deserted. 'As men are nowadays . . .' Homer says again and again, regret- fully. But, unlike paradise or the golden age, that distant past is not irrevocably lost; it is still, after a fashion, accessible to memory, and is in fact counted as history proper. Conse- quently the great figures of the past are saluted, not with sad longing, or with the sorrow felt in the face of an irreversible loss, but with admiration. This is the emotional matrix which gives us the Olympian gods: they are real and natural, but their distance raises them on a lofty pedestal.

Herodotus, himself born in the land of these poems, testifies that Homer and Hesiod presented the Greeks with their gods. Since Homer also gave to the Greeks their lingua franca of literature, we must acknowledge that it was Homer—using his name in the wide sense which scholarly practice has sanctioned—who created the intellectual world of the Greeks, their beliefs and their thoughts. We are far too familiar with these Homeric gods to appreciate fully how bold an achievement their creation must have been. The Olympians never were the sole rulers; especially in the mother country deities of a chthonic or mystic character managed to maintain themselves, or even to increase their number. The fact remains, however, that Greek art, Greek poetry, all their higher intellectual efforts received their special stamp from the religion of Homer. Soon after the appearance of the *Iliad* and the *Odyssey* Greek sculptors begin to make their statues of the gods large and beautiful; the gods' images have houses built for them, not for the benefit of some secret cult or mystery, but merely as a fair home for a fair statue. In this manner the artists attempt to duplicate in stone the sentiments pronounced by the poet. For three centuries Greek art endeavoured to enhance the beauty and the impressiveness of its gods.[9] Now and then, as during the early stages of Attic tragedy, the dark forces regain their power, and the terror of the mysterious asserts itself once more. But in the great achievements of art the Olympians and their kind always set the tone, and Aeschylus repeatedly made their victory over the demons of old the theme of his works, to bring the action of his drama to a harmonious conclusion.

Although in the Homeric poems the control and the meaning of the plot rest with the gods, the writer is not primarily interested in what happens on the upper stage, to retain our former metaphor. His sympathy is chiefly with the wrath of Achilles, and the wanderings of Odysseus. Nor does the fate of the heroes depend from the outset, as it does in the *Aeneid*, on the guidance of the gods leading everything to its predestined, purposeful end. The human action does not serve a higher, a divine cause, but quite the reverse: the story of the gods contains only so much as is needed to make the happenings on earth intelligible. The natural outlines of mortal life are nowhere distorted. Perhaps this is the most remarkable thing about Homer's world, that in spite of the impact of his divine interventions all that is done or spoken by men is entirely natural and human.

'Natural.' What is the meaning of this word which has more than once slipped into our argument? The cunning simpleton of the fairy-tale who accepted everything 'naturally' would be at a loss for an answer. Modern theories could not but associate the natural with the rational, whereas our present context is a religious one. The natural first sees the light of day in the Homeric poems; its emergence involves an intimate connexion between the life of man and the purpose of the gods. Because these gods do not use brute force and senseless terror in their contact with human life, it is free to unfold itself in accord with its own modest principles. The Greeks faced a meaningful and orderly world with admiration and peace of mind; they recognized the profit which lay in putting to work their hands, their eyes, and above all their intellect. The beauty of the world was enticingly spread before them, promising to reveal its meaning and its disposition. Wonder and admiration, in an even wider sense than contemplated by Aristotle, issued in philosophy.

Hegel once said:[10] 'Religion is the sphere in which a nation gives itself a definition of that which it regards as the True.' Plato, by defining the true as the perfect, the 'idea of the good', merely rings a change upon the basic concept of the Olympian religion. With equal force the plastic art of the Greeks seems to say that the beauty and perfection of this world of appearances ought to be evident to any one who probes deeply enough. And, most important of all, the sciences sprang up from this same belief that our world is reasonable and open to human intellection. Thus the Olympian gods have made us the Europeans we are.

This is not to say that the Homeric creed involves the kind of optimism which we associate with an era of enlightenment. The contrast between optimism and pessimism is too banal to have any bearing on our problem. Actually the Greeks might well be called pessimists. With deep sorrow they confront this life which sees human beings perish miserably like leaves in the autumn; and beyond life the suffering is even greater. But, let the world be happy or sad, it still contains all that is fair within it, and the gods are its children, its most perfect, most beautiful, most real products. The early Greeks justify their own misery on earth by pointing to the ease and the splendour which characterizes the life of the gods. In a similar fashion, the Greek of a later period will derive a vindication of his earthly existence from his admiring contemplation of the fixed courses of the stars. Even Plato and Aristotle who value the theoretical or 'contemplative' life above the practical life because it leads men beyond the material world, infuse their theory with traces of a religious emotion which ultimately stems from the Homeric *thaumazein*. True enough, this progress of thinking towards philosophy was effected at the sacrifice of the gods themselves. They lost their natural and immediate function in proportion as man became aware of his own spiritual potential. Whereas Achilles had interpreted his decision as an intercession of the goddess, fifth century man, proudly convinced of his personal freedom, took upon himself the responsibility for his choice. The deity whose guidance and authority he recognized with ever increasing assurance was formulated as the concept of justice, or the good, or honesty, or whatever else the norm of action be called. Such formulation actually helps to enhance the sublimity of the deity, but at the same time the gods are stripped of their former abundant vitality. The trials of Socrates and other philosophers occurred during this period, and they show how acutely this change was perceived and lamented. Socrates could be justly accused of having discarded the old gods; but in a deeper sense he continued to be a servant of the Olympian gods who had first opened the eyes of the Greeks. It would be absurd to suppose that Apollo or Athena could have regarded the intellect as their enemy, and Aristotle speaks as a true Greek when he says (*Met.* 1.983 a) that the god does not begrudge man his knowledge. A foe of the intellect who wishes to cite Greek views in corroboration of his stand must base himself upon the gloomy concepts of chthonic powers; he may point to some cult celebrated with ecstatic abandon; but he may not call to witness the great works of the Greek genius: the epics, Pindar's poems, or tragedy.

The Olympian gods were laid low by philosophy, but they lived on in the arts. They remained one of the most important themes for artistic production even after people had ceased to believe in them wholeheartedly. In fact they did not attain their perfect form, the form which was to be decisive for all times, until the days of Pericles when we may be sure that the artists were no longer believers in the old sense. Ancient poetry also continues to cull its more important material from the myths of the Olympian gods, and even the triumph of Christianity did not halt this trend. Finally, the rejuvenation which the gods experienced in the Renaissance also lay in the realm of the arts.

The Olympian gods prove that they are meaningful and natural, not only through their intercession in human affairs —to which we have so far given almost all our attention— but through their very existence; through it they furnish a meaningful and natural picture of the world, and it is this aspect of them which has left its imprint on later developments. It is through the gods that the Greeks approach the secret of existence. In their persons the Olympians give clear expression to all that is great and vital in this world. Nothing is concealed; all the forces operating in body and mind are drawn into the portrait of the gods. The resulting picture, far from being sombre and painful, is one of serenity, detachment and pure perfection. No single factor is extolled or placed in a ruling position; everything has its destined place and conspires to make for a purposeful cosmos. But this order is not an impersonal system, devoid of warmth and vitality. On the contrary, the world of the gods teems with a full measure of life, as is shown by the following example. Among the ladies of Mount Olympus Hera, Athena, Artemis and Aphrodite are supreme. We might divide them into two groups: Hera and Aphrodite representing woman in her capacity as mother and loved one; Artemis and Athena typifying the virgin, one lonely and close to nature, the other intellectual and active in the community. It may fairly be said that these four women signalize the four aspects of all womanhood. The four goddesses help to bring out the spiritual peculiarities of the female sex; more than that, they are instrumental in making the notion of femininity intelligible. Four goddesses who stem from totally different cults

have effected this notion by merging their interests and
permitting cross-reference between them. They are the
products of men's meditation on the various manifestations
of the divine; we find in them the first sketch of a logical
system, a prelude to the eventual hypostatization of the
typical and the universal.

The idealizing strain of their theology guards the Greeks
against the danger of viewing the characteristic in the oblique
light of caricature. The Greek goddesses, in spite of their
one-sidedness, are faultless and attractive creatures. With
no effort at all they possess the noble simplicity and quiet
grandeur which Winckelmann regarded as the essence of
the classical spirit. But the original Greek temper surpasses this classicistic ideal. The Olympians have their full
share of the passions, without however sacrificing an iota of
their beauty; they are so assured of their status that they can
safely indulge in their rather insolent moods towards one
another. We find it difficult to understand how the gods of
one's faith could be subjected to Aristophanic jests. But
laughter is part of the meaning, the fruitfulness, the positive
side of life, and it is therefore, in the eyes of the Greeks, more
godlike than the sour solemnity which we associate with
piety. Thus the Olympian gods combine in their persons
three things: vitality, beauty, and lucidity. As the belief in
these gods becomes more questionable—the end of this
process is reached with the Roman poets who transmitted
the gods to the Western world—the gulf between their life,
ever serene and fair, and the reality of man begins to widen.
In Homer the affairs of men are given their full meaning by
the gods, but Ovid conveys to us that everything on earth
is at bottom without rhyme or reason, and that we cannot
look upward and spy the divine splendour save with a touch
of nostalgia. Ovid escapes into that perfect world of yore as
if it were a haven of solace and salvation. The Olympian
gods of his *Metamorphoses* are already 'pagan' in the sense
that their unfettered vitality is no longer pictured with a
simple and unaffected heart. In Ovid, and even before him,
robust strength and hearty buffoonery are replaced by
bawdiness and frivolity. Nevertheless the Ovidian gods are
the legitimate successors of Homer's Olympians, for like
them they compel admiration, for their limpid beauty and

their lively spirit. Perhaps, instead of spirit, we should use
the word *esprit*, for the Ovidian deity is clever and ingenious
as Homer's was not. But Ovid's wit is so pure, his alertness
and charm so persuasive, that the Olympian gods could not
really be angry with him. Take his account of how Apollo
pursued Daphne, the wild and unwilling maiden: running
behind her he offers her his love—he, the god with the
beautiful locks, sees her tresses streaming in the wind before
him—*et, quid si comantur ait*—and he says: imagine her
with her hair done! On another occasion, Ovid tells the
mournful tale of Orpheus who had to leave Eurydice behind
in Hades. Thereupon, he continues, Orpheus invented
pederasty, perhaps because his experiences with women had
been so unfortunate, or again, because he wanted to remain
loyal to his wife.

It is this world of the ancient gods, somewhat cynical but
clever and brilliant, which the Renaissance came to know,
and, as was to be expected, its specifically pagan flavour
became immensely popular: the light-hearted gods stood out
against the foil of an ascetic Christianity. The lords of
Olympus and the classical myths were not among the least
means to help the Renaissance once more to perceive and
admire the beauty and the grandeur of the universe. In
antiquity the failure of this perspective, the decline of the
spirit of wonder, set in long before Ovid; not improbably
it also was a natural consequence of the enlightenment which
had carried men all the way from the primitive terror in the
face of the unknown, to a free admiration of the divine.
Democritus already praises *athaumastia* and *athambia*, the
absence of wonder; the Stoic sages regard it as their highest
aim not to lose their composure, and Cicero as well as Horace
commends the *nil admirari*.[11] But for an expression of the
genuine Greek tradition we must go to the old Goethe
(Eckermann, 18.2.1829): 'The highest to which man may
aspire is wonder.'

CHAPTER 3

THE RISE OF THE INDIVIDUAL IN THE EARLY GREEK LYRIC

IT IS generally agreed nowadays that the various poetic genres which make up the literatures of the West, the epic, lyric poetry, and drama, coexist side by side. Among the Greeks, however, who created the types destined to serve as the vehicles of great poetic inspiration, and through whose influence, direct or indirect, they were spread among the nations of Europe, the genres flourished in chronological succession. When the strains of the epic subsided, the lyric took its place, and when the lyric was about to expire, drama came into its own. In the land of their origin, it seems, the literary types were the result, and the vocal expression, of specific historical situations. The style of writing characteristic of the epic, the exposition of life as a chain-like series of events, is not a mechanism artfully designed; Homer did not, from among several methods of portraying the existence of man, purposely choose this particular one because it seemed most appropriate to the epic. Lessing is mistaken when he credits Homer with aesthetic discrimination for avoiding the description of static scenes and translating everything into the language of dynamic events. Actually this feature of Homer's style is a necessary function of the perspective in which he discerns man, his life and his world. According to his view—and there could be no other for him—a man's action or perception is determined by the divine forces operative in the world; it is a reaction of his physical organs to a stimulus, and this stimulus is itself grasped as a personal act. Any situation is likely to be the result of stimuli, and the source of new stimuli in its turn.

The origin of the Greek epic is shrouded in the darkness of pre-history. The oldest work of which we have any knowledge is at once the pinnacle of Greek epic art; it is the work which goes by the name of Homer, the *Iliad* and the *Odyssey*. When we come to the lyric, however, we are in a position to judge in historical terms, and to ask ourselves how it differs from the older art, the epic, and what new spirit is manifested in it. Perhaps the most striking difference between the two genres, as regards the men behind the works, is the emergence of the poets as individuals. As compared with the grave problem of identity which the name of Homer continues to pose, the lyrists announce their own names; they speak about themselves and become recognizable as personalities.

The era of lyric poetry is the first to introduce upon the stage of European history a number of highly individual actors, with a great variety of roles. Party-leaders, law-givers and tyrants, religious thinkers and, somewhat later, philosophers, plastic artists who are beginning to record their names on their works: all these pierce through the veil of anonymity which covers the earlier period. Literature, i.e. the lyric, evinces the intellectual significance of this development more clearly than any other sphere of art, for it allows the new outlook to make itself known by word of mouth, the only means of explicit expression for things of the mind.

Greek lyric poetry, both the choral works and those designed for solo delivery, has a double origin. On the one hand it is dependent on popular, pre-literary forms which have existed in all cultures at all times, such as dancing songs, cult hymns, working songs and the like, which at particular moments in the life of the society further the execution of common enterprises. At the same time the early Greek lyric reveals the tremendous impact which the epic, especially Homer, had upon it; there is no lyrist who does not betray his debt to Homer in many a crucial passage. It is this which helped the lyric to develop beyond the stage of mere functionalism, in spite of its continued association, on a large scale, with definite and concrete occasions.

The majority of the early Greek lyrics which have come down to us are poems composed for various festivals in honour of gods or men; their purpose is to make the present significant over and above the *hic et nunc*, to lend an air of permanence to the joy of the moment. The ways in which this is achieved, apart from the fixed traditional form which serves as a stabilizing factor, are chiefly two: myths, and maxims. The myths, especially those which had been subjected to the purifying agency of the epic, help to draw a parallel between the events on earth and some divine or heroic paradigm; as a result the affairs of men are endowed with a purpose and meaning. Maxims show the connexion between the particular and the universal, often in the guise of warnings and instruction, and thus spur the mind on to a better understanding of the permanent values, of truth. Included in this type of poetry are almost all the choral lyrics written between the end of the seventh and the middle of the fifth century, from Alcman via Stesichorus, Ibycus, Simonides down to Bacchylides and the greatest of them all, Pindar. They constitute the great age of Greek lyric poetry; their work was of immeasurable influence, both for the Greeks and for us, towards the development of a 'grand' poetic style. Tragedy, and hence all Western poetry in the grand tradition, draw their lifeblood from that source; among German poets, Klopstock, the young Goethe, Hoelderlin, and Rilke looked toward the Greek lyric when they created their hymns. One basic difference which distinguishes the lyric from the epic is to be found in the value which the former attaches to the present. The great deeds of the past are no longer celebrated for their own sake, but because they serve to exalt the present; for the Greeks of the archaic period took an un-bounded delight in the present, in everything that is alive and colourful. The tension between value and fact, between myth and actuality, claim and realization, tends to become more and more evident in the course of the two hundred years during which lyric poetry prevailed; but the present, albeit raised to the level of timelessness, remains, throughout, its immediate frame of reference.

Side by side with the songs of praise there existed another branch of lyric composition, no less important than the first, and indeed somewhat older; a branch which more closely resembles our own conception of lyric poetry because its poets were concerned with their own personal problems. The Greeks themselves did not list 'personal' poetry in a separate class by itself. For them the lyric is a sung poem, whether it be a choral ode of the type we have just discussed, or a monodic song presented by a single person, as those of Sappho, Alcaeus and Anacreon. Actually not a few of these monodies are songs of praise devoted to gods or men: witness the wedding songs by Sappho. But here, more than in the choral odes, the poets show that next to the eulogy which forms their primary theme they consider it an important task to talk about themselves. The same is, however, also true of another type of poetry, contemporary with the lyrics, which the Greeks did not put in the same category because its products were not sung to the accompaniment of the lyre. We do not hesitate to call them lyrics because they more or less coincide with our notion of what a lyric should be. They are poems which were recited to the sounds of the flute; iambs and distichs form their metrical pattern. Ancient tradition names Archilochus as their inventor. I shall use the 'personal lyric ' of the early Greeks—if I may be permitted this somewhat vague expression—to find out what the poets themselves thought to be their distinctive personality, why they talked about themselves, and by what process they became conscious of their individuality. For this purpose I shall select three writers: Archilochus, the poet of colloquial verse who lived in the first half of the seventh century B.C., and Sappho and Anacreon, writers of monodies (Sappho flourished *ca.* 600 B.C., Anacreon died *ca.* 500 B.C.). Our questions are, therefore, addressed to a variety of characters and tempers; roughly two centuries, i.e. almost the whole span of time during which lyrics were composed, extend between the oldest and the youngest poem in our series of examples. In this way, we hope, the common features of the genre, but also the personal peculiarities of the writers, will become fairly evident.

The field which we survey is littered with sorry ruins. To form an estimate of the intellectual accomplishment of the early Greek lyrists from the handful of completely preserved poems by Archilochus, Sappho and Anacreon, and from the passages briefly quoted by later writers, we are compelled to exploit even the smallest detail. Often it is almost by accident that we perceive how a motif or a thought is derived from something older, and that we succeed in isolating what is new and significant. In the end, however, the new ingredients will fall into place to create a harmonious picture; we shall see that the road travelled by the lyric poets follows a definite direction, and that a larger historical trend lies at the bottom of what at first might appear to be variations on a fixed theme, or arbitrary changes wrought upon a traditional motif.

Archilochus read in the *Odyssey* (14.228):

> For different men take delight in different actions.

From this, he proceeds to his own version (41)[1]:

> Each man has his heart cheered in his own way.

This insight into the truth that men have various goals is not yet clearly stated in the *Iliad*. We find that the *Odyssey* displays a more subtle perception of the distinctions between men than its predecessor. Archilochus is fully sensitive to them, and through him this notion becomes a basic component of the mentality of the archaic age. Solon describes in detail how the paths of life differ one from another, and more especially Pindar again and again produces new formulations of the same idea. Simultaneously with this insight the eyes of the writers become sharpened to the changes which each man undergoes in the process of time. In the *Odyssey* Archilochus had found (18.136 f.):

> For the spirit of men on the earth is as the day that
> comes upon them from the father of gods and men.

With these lines in his mind, he addresses the following verses to his friend Glaucus (68):

> Such a mind, Glaucus son of Leptines, do mortal men have
> as Zeus may usher in each day, and they think their
> thoughts in accord with their daily transactions.[2]

Archilochus goes to the *Odyssey* for these general statements concerning the instability of things and the flux by which man is tossed about, and the spell which the world exercises upon him. Archilochus is keenly aware of the vulnerable position of man; other verses corroborate this impression. There is nothing entirely new in this, but along with the more complex perspective disclosed by these phrases we find a more precise appreciation of the self and its distinctive qualities: and that is indeed the beginning of something new.

That one man should contrast his own ideas with those of others is the theme of a poem by Sappho which was found in Egypt on a badly disfigured papyrus (27). With the necessary restorations it says in effect:

> Some say an army of horsemen is the fairest thing on the
> black earth, others an army of footsoldiers, and others a
> navy of ships—but I say the fairest thing is one I love.

> And it is very easy to make this understood by all. For
> even she who surpassed all in beauty, Helen, left the
> noblest of men and destroyed the honoured fortress of
> Troy. She gave no thought to her daughter nor to her dear
> parents, but against her will Kypris led her astray.
> A woman is easily swayed if love casts its light spell
> on her mind; and now I am reminded of far-off
> Anactoria. I would rather see her lovely gait and the
> bright radiance of her eyes than the chariots of the
> Lydians and their footsoldiers fighting in armour.

In the opening and at the end Sappho makes use of the
'preamble', a species of folk poetry emphasizing one thing
above the rest, to distinguish her own aesthetic judgment
from the values of others. Over against the sumptuous sights
which everybody admires, parades of horsemen, soldiers,
and ships, she discloses the unpretentious object of her own
modest desire: the lovely step and the radiant face of her
beloved Anactoria. 'The fairest thing is one I love.'[3] Sappho
places that which is inwardly felt above external splendour.
The notion of Homer and Archilochus, that 'each has his
heart cheered in a different way', had allowed for a number
of excellences or ideals, with no priority given to any one of
them. Sappho tells us which thing has the greatest value:
that which is lovingly embraced by her soul. We find similar
confessions in other archaic writings, but Sappho was the
first to put this into words.[4] On another occasion (152) she
says of her beloved Kleis:

> I would not exchange all the Lydian lands for her,

and Anacreon echoes her thought in the form of a preamble (8):

> Neither would I want Amaltheia's horn, nor wish to
> be king for a hundred and fifty years over rich
> Tartessus.

Anacreon rejects the treasures craved by others, the full
cornucopia of Amaltheia or a lengthy rule over the mythically
prosperous city in the west. The passages in which he pro-
fesses his own preferences are lost, but since he is indifferent
to pomp and ostentation, what he professed must have been
something quite modest.[5]
    The contrast between the showy spectacle admired by all,
and the more substantial qualities which cause little stir, has
no parallel in Homer, but Archilochus comes close to it,

though in a totally different area. The rough man-at-arms
who would have no taste for the delicate notes of Sappho's
Muse, or the ingenious charm of Anacreon, lays down his
estimate of the traits which a good officer ought to possess
(60):

> I do not like a tall general, striding forth on his long
> legs; who prides himself on his locks, and shaves his chin
> like a fop. Let him be a small man, perhaps even bow-legged,
> as long as he stands firm on his feet, full of heart.

In Homer, a like separation between external and internal
values is never made. Odysseus returns to his home in the
guise of a wretched old beggar, and yet remains the strong
hero; but his wretchedness is merely a mask behind which
Athena has hidden her favourite so that he will not be recognized. Appearance and merit are contrasted with one another,
but the inner qualities are not, as in Archilochus, played off
against the surface impression. Archilochus' general is good
precisely because he is not elegant. The beggar Irus (*Od.*
18.3), it is true,

> had neither vigour nor strength, but he was bulky enough to
> look on.

He is brought in as the antithesis of Odysseus. But no one
before Archilochus underlines the paradox that the officer
is enfeebled by his splendour, that he does not use his long
legs except to run away (that seems to be the implication),
that the outer appearance undoes the good within.[6]

As a rule Archilochus formulates his own views, which
run counter to the opinions of the majority, with considerably
less delicacy than Sappho, and even offensively (6):

> One of the Thracians now boasts of my shield which,
> though it carried no blame, I left behind in the
> bushes, against my will. Myself I saved from death;
> why should I worry about my shield ? Let it be gone:
> I shall buy another equally good.

What is a shield to me? My life is worth more. The Spartan
code which requires that a warrior return from battle either
carrying his shield or stretched out upon it, is for Archilochus an illusion which he exposes with cheerful insolence.
Anacreon later derives the same pleasure from exposing a
fraud, though his performance is not as fresh. As Archilochus
removes the mask from the face of the mannered general,

Anacreon unveils the true aspect of the parvenu Artemon who travels in state (54):

> Once he walked on foot, a Cimmerian tarboush on his head,
> with dice of wood in his ears, and about his ribs a
> hairy oxhide which had not been washed since it served
> as the cover of a wretched shield. He used to go about
> with bread-women and whores, making his living by fraud.
> Often he had his neck in the stocks, or bound to the
> wheel; often his back was scourged with the raw-hide
> whip, and his hair and his beard were plucked.
>
> But now he wears earrings of gold, and travels in a coach,
> the son of Kyke, and carries an umbrella with ivory handle,
> just like the ladies.

What right have the poets to pass such personal judgment? By what rule do they determine the properties which meet with their approval? Does the disillusioned cynicism of Archilochus have anything in common with the sparkling wit of Anacreon, or with the passionate intensity of Sappho? Their agreement is, first of all, of a negative sort. The reasons for which they reject the traditional values are not principally moral or legal; the fact that Sappho gets no pleasure from military parades bears no relation to ethics or legal standards. That Archilochus reckons his life more valuable than his shield defies all customary morality—but he does not mean to preach a new set of ethics, or pass judgment from a higher plane.

Sappho's phrase: 'The fairest thing is one I love' sounds as if it opened the door to the arbitrary decision of personal taste over which, as the Latin proverb has it, there can be no quarrelling. Archilochus shows all the symptoms of an uninhibited individualism. But both of them are evidently concerned to grasp a piece of genuine reality: to find Being instead of Appearance.

Even before Archilochus, Callinus and Tyrtaeus in their elegies had taken the martial exhortations which they found in Homer and filled them with fresh vigour; they had, as it were, restored them to the status of actual war songs, with which in the struggles of their days they challenged the fighters to perform deeds of bravery. Here we have the first instance of a return from literature to immediate reality, the kind of harking back which again and again was to propel the creative spirit of Europe toward ever newer accomplishments. Archilochus was the first to perform this return to reality with deliberate intent, and without compromise. He too stands in the literary tradition of the Homeric epic; he speaks its language, and treats its chief topic—war. But he divests war of all its epic grandeur and instead savours it as the strong stuff of life. He speaks of the coarse bread at the front, he describes drinking on the watch (2; 5), he hints at the cruelty of the fight which awaits him (3). Being a mercenary soldier, he has found in his own fortunes what the epic sings of, but without its illusions, and therefore—from his point of view—in greater concentration. We have only fragments of his poetry, and conclusions *ex silentio* are always hazardous; but apparently he touched less on the goals of war, or the bravery which leads to victory, than on the misery and the uncertainties of the battle. In the clash of arms he experienced the naked reality of life in a way which was unheard of, and great. His war song, unlike those of Callinus and Tyrtaeus, no longer serves to encourage the soldiers; it is no longer, so to speak, a battle cry in verse, an aid designed for the closed circle of his comrades-in-arms; such social functions it leaves far behind. Archilochus pursues his own private aims; what is more, his verses aid him not only in his actions—active as he is—but also help him to express his sensations, and to give voice to the trials and tribulations of life.

His words about love all stress the misery of love. Homer knows love as one of the great delights; he names it together with dancing, wine and sleep. Of unhappy love he makes no mention. At worst, love is an ominous illusion; the magic girdle of Aphrodite contains 'love, desire and cunning chatter which rob even the wise of their sense' (*Il.* 14.217). Archilochus develops this theme (112):

> Such a desire of love was entwined in my heart
> and shed a thick mist over my eyes, stealing the
> subtle wits from my breast.[7]

The mist which is poured over his eyes also stems from Homer where it is the symptom of death or unconsciousness. In all likelihood, however, Archilochus does not, like Homer, act the part of a spectator observing the consequences of futile love in others, but he gives us a description of his own unhappy love. The idea occurs in another fragment which certainly refers to himself (104):

> Wretched I lie, unsouled by desire, pierced through my
> bones with harsh pangs, by the will of the gods.

For Archilochus love is a force which all but makes him faint, or die. By the will of the gods, he says, love pierces him; here again we encounter the Homeric notion that the emotions do not spring spontaneously from within man, but are bestowed on him by the gods. This much, however, is new that the love which is barred from happy fulfilment creates a particularly strong reaction in him. This means that love is no longer a part of the tranquil stream of human enjoyments; it undergoes a complete change, and becomes a sensation of death.[8] Love as such the poet continues to connect with the authority of the gods, but when the smooth current of his emotions is suddenly blocked, and he becomes aware of a loss of strength, a helplessness very near death, he seeks the cause in his own personality. We may compare Sappho's experience of love (2):

> That man appears to me to equal the gods who sits before you,
> and by your side hears your sweet speech and your charming
> laughter which has put wings on the heart in my breast.
> When I look at you but once, my speech ceases to obey me.
> My tongue is broken, a subtle fire creeps under my skin,
> my eyes see nothing, and my ears begin to ring. Sweat pours
> down over my limbs, a trembling seizes me from head to toe,
> I am paler than grass, and I appear close to death. But one
> can endure all . . .[9]

The poem is a wedding song for a girl from Sappho's circle; it begins with the traditional eulogy of the man who is to take her in marriage. But for Sappho the wedding means separation. In the verses cited earlier in this chapter she had derived her idea of the nature of beauty from her unhappy longing for a distant companion; her present love is equally unhappy, though the girl is not yet far away, but only making ready to depart. And just as Archilochus had his violent sensation of impotence, of loss of life, so Sappho mercilessly depicts the failure of her senses and her body—how she is brought to the brink of death. The kinship between Sappho and Archilochus is not merely one of accidental and external similarity, for Sappho was well acquainted with the poems of Archilochus. An old epithet defined sleep as the 'looser of limbs', evidently because sleep deprives the limbs of men of their power of motion.[10] In the same vein, Hesiod says (*Theog.* 120):

> Eros, the fairest among immortal gods, the looser of limbs;
> of all gods and men he overcomes the mind in their hearts
> and their knowing counsel. . .[11]

Love, by casting a spell on men, robs them of their quickness and their understanding: an effect which can be observed in others. Archilochus applies the image to his own experience, at the beginning of a poem (118) whose first verse must have read approximately: I am incapable of doing anything.[12] Then he continues:

> Desire, looser of limbs, has overwhelmed me, my friend.

Love makes a man helpless. This idea was adopted for her own by Sappho; we have an instance of it, again at the beginning of a poem (137):

> Once more Eros, looser of limbs, drives me about,
> a bitter-sweet creature which puts me at a loss.

The cadence of her words, and the novelty, at the time, of the thought that the unhappy lover is made to feel inactive and helpless, render it almost certain that Sappho learned from Archilochus how to experience, and to express, her luckless love, which comes so near to death.

Even in these lines Sappho's treatment of love is purely 'mythical': love is not an emotion which breaks forth from within, but the intervention of a deity. But the feeling of helplessness is her own, her personal property in the fullest sense of the word. The love which has its course barred, and fails to reach its fulfilment, acquires a particularly strong hold over the human heart. The sparks of a vital desire burst into flame at the very moment when the desire is finally blocked in its path. It is the obstruction which makes the wholly personal feelings conscious, and annihilates the normal values. At this point we find the new distinction between Being and Appearance, between what others prize and what one's own judgment declares to be essential. And since it is understood that love is not a private whim, not a subjective affectation, but an experience of supra-personal,

of divine dimensions, the lover cannot but find his way to
some reality, through the agency of his individual passion.
For Sappho, impassioned and sick at heart, this reality is
simple and natural, a sensation of having approached to the
very roots of her being: she is favoured with a glimpse into
the uncharted territory of the *soul*.

Because of the purity and the tender sincerity of her
feelings Sappho far surpasses Archilochus, in spite of the
great influence which he exerted upon her. Archilochus
was not the sort of man to dwell on his sensations; he saw
rather in his unhappiness an obstruction which prevented
his happiness. He knew how to defend himself actively
(66):

> One thing which is important I know well: how to return with
> interest the evil which others have done me.

His unhappy love has released in him the harsh strains of
anger and vexation rather than tender laments. Resentment
speaks to us from many of his poems which have no connexion with love—and yet they are not unlike Sappho's love
poetry, at least in one important respect. Here is an example
of his invective, crude but graphic (79):

> ... washed ashore by a wave; I hope that in Salmydessus the
> top-knotted Thracians will seize him, naked, at the dead of
> the night; there he will get his fill of suffering, eating
> the bread of slaves. May the cold freeze him, all covered
> with seaweed from the surf, and may his teeth chatter, lying
> on his face like a dog at the rim of the beach, helpless,
> vomiting sea water. This I would like to see because with
> his feet he trampled under the oaths, the man who once was
> my friend.

Archilochus confesses a desire to see someone fall into the
ocean and be washed ashore in the cold north, to face a life
of misery; at the end we are shocked to hear that the one he so
curses was once his friend. This poem too represents his
reaction to an event which turned out contrary to his wishes;
again his injured feelings are more than subjective resentment;
not merely friendship, but a sense of justice is at the bottom
of his indignation.[13] Justice, like love, is unconditioned; its
claim to be greater than men, to be divine, is even superior.
A sense of justice may manifest itself in many different
ways: exhortation, praise, a decision, and so forth. Archilo-

chus recognizes the principle of justice as soon as an impediment arises in the path of his expectations or demands. To him, justice is not a goal of action, or the foundation of a political order, or any other norm; he speaks out against the injustice which has been done to him. Righteous indignation is the keynote of his temper. In the hands of Archilochus, poetry becomes a dangerous weapon against a disloyal friend. The poem is more than just a curse, more than even the invective of a Homeric hero for whom abuse had been an instrument for victory in battle. Nor is it simply a tool for purposes of litigation, as much of Hesiod's verse is. Archilochus' poem ends—for the last words probably form the conclusion of the poem—on a note of regret: 'the man who once was my friend'. Here his speech ceases to be of help to him in his conflict, and expresses nothing but helpless bewilderment. As in his war songs, the present poem is lifted above the plane of practical utility, and becomes the mouthpiece of his subjective sensations.

In a fable by Archilochus, the fox prays in a spirit of just exasperation (94):

> O Zeus, Father Zeus, Thine is the rule of heaven. Thou
> seest the works of men, whether they be sinful or just;
> likewise sin and virtue among the beasts are Thy concern.

In one verse (96) it appears that Archilochus considers it a fault in a man if he knows no righteous anger:

> You have no gall in your liver.[14]

Righteous indignation, therefore, is based on the same mental conditions as unhappy love. The soul must speak because it is made helpless by the schism between what is and what ought to be. Under the stress of his hard life, Archilochus found solace in the thought that suffering is not permanent, that the gods drag a man down only to raise him up again, and that hence he alternates between joy and grief. This basic insight was then a new discovery (58):

> All things commit to the gods. Men who are stretched low
> on the black earth they often raise up from their misery;
> often again they take those who are firmly established,
> trip them and lay them low. Then great misery comes upon
> the man, he roams about in sore need, and his mind is
> distraught.

When a calamity had struck his city, he wrote (7):

> No one among the citizens, Pericles, will blame us for
> mourning our loss, nor will anyone in the city take
> pleasure in the feast. Such were the men overwhelmed
> by the hissing wave of the sea; and our hearts are
> swollen with groans. But, my friend, the gods have
> ordained sturdy endurance as a remedy for incurable
> suffering. All men at one time or another suffer such
> woe. Now it has turned upon us, and we grieve at the
> bloody wound; but soon it will pass on to others. Quickly,
> therefore, put away your womanish mourning, and endure.

'But I must endure all': thus Sappho began the last strophe
of her poem (2), and struggled to recover her composure.
Again, therefore, she has learnt her lesson from Archilochus:
throughout the sea-changes of life, man must content himself
with patient endurance. The same thought, with one crucial
addition, is featured in another passage by Archilochus (67):

> Heart, my heart, convulsed with helpless troubles, rise
> up, defend yourself against the foe, meet them with
> truculent breast. With firm stance receive the enemy's
> onslaught, and neither rejoice openly if the victory is
> yours, nor crouch at home and wail if you lose. But when
> life brings joy, rejoice, and when it brings suffering,
> do not grieve overmuch. / Understand the rhythm of life
> which controls man.

One must understand the ebb and flow of life, and the
knowledge of this alternation will allow us to bear it. The
same idea forms the general theme of the one and only poem
by Sappho which we have in its entirety (1):

> Immortal Aphrodite of the patterned throne, daughter of
> Zeus, weaver of wiles, I beseech thee, subdue not with
> pangs or sorrows, lady, my heart, but come hither, if
> before at other times thou didst hear my voice from afar
> and hearken to it, and leaving thy father's golden house
> didst come yoking thy chariot. Fair swift sparrows brought
> thee over the black earth, fluttering their multitudinous
> wings, from the sky through the air between, and swiftly
> they came. And thou, Blessed One, smiling with immortal
> countenance didst ask what again is the matter with me,
> and why again I call, and what now most of all in my
> frenzied heart I wish to happen: 'Whom now dost thou wish
> Persuasion to lead into thy affection? Who, Sappho, wrongs
> thee? Even if now she flees, soon shall she pursue: if she
> receives not gifts, yet shall she give, and if she loves

not, soon shall she love, even though she would not.'
Come to me now also, and deliver me from harsh cares, and
all that my heart longs to accomplish, do thou accomplish,
and do thou thyself be my ally.[15]

Among the many beauties of this poem, not the least is
this: that the experience which produced these verses is made
to extend beyond the scope of the present, to a point twice
removed in time. Once before Sappho had called to Aphrodite in her distress, and even then it was not the first time.
The gleam of comfort which illumines the whole poem takes
its brightness from the distance which Sappho has placed
between herself and her suffering; she realizes: this has
happened before; the goddess helped me then; she will do it
again now.

There are other lines which show that Sappho visualized
her sensations *sub specie iterationis;* we have already cited the
beginning of a poem (137): 'Again Eros, looser of limbs,
drives me about.' That the 'again' is a feature typical of
archaic poetry is proved by a fragment of Alcman (101):

> Again love, at the bidding of Kypris, warms my heart
> with its sweet flush.

In Anacreon's love poems the 'again' becomes a sterotyped
formula of opening lines (5):

> Again golden-haired Love throws me his purple ball and
> calls me to play with a bright-sandalled child; but the
> girl—she comes from glorious Lesbos—ridicules my
> hair—alas it is white—and gapes after another.

Or (17):

> Again I stand up and dive from the Leucas-cliff into the
> grey wave, drunk with love.

And (26):

> Again I came to Pythomander when I was trying to escape
> from Love.

Or (45):

> Again Love has struck me like a smith with his great
> hammer, and bathed me in a stream of ice.

And finally (79):

> Again I love, and I love not, I rave and do not rave.

The inventive skill with which Anacreon puts his love on
the boards is indeed masterly, but the exordium 'Again I

love . . .' has lost its original force.[16] Sappho's love is such
that the phrase can only mean: it is my constant fate that I
must love and suffer by turns; that is how she understands
the law of her existence, the rhythm of her feelings. But
when Anacreon repeats five times over: 'Again I have fallen
in love . . .', we suspect his heart is not in it.

Anacreon also imitates the solace with which Sappho
shields herself against the tides of life, but as before he lacks
the depth and the fullness of her emotions; instead he
produces an ingenious if somewhat frivolous variation upon
the theme in a poem addressed to a young Thracian girl,
the only poem of his, incidentally, which is certainly preserved
complete (88):

> Thracian filly, why do you look at me askance, why do you
> cruelly shun me? Do you think I am an ignoramus? Know well
> that I could easily put the bridle on you, and take the
> reins and race you around the goal of the course. But you
> are still grazing in the pasture, cutting your care-free
> capers, for you have not yet had a rider who knows his
> tricks to break you.

Anacreon reduces the radical innovations of Archilochus,
the deeply emotional confessions of Sappho, to the level of
easy pleasantry. With the greatest facility and virtuosity he
lightly masters an attitude towards life which had once been a
profound experience, acquired at great effort and pain. The
towering dark floods which had once threatened the very
existence of Archilochus have turned into insignificant ripples
which Anacreon navigates without strain or danger. But
even this *jeu d'esprit* of Anacreon, with all its playfulness,
has for its foundation the insight characteristic of the older
lyric. 'Know well,' says Anacreon, 'that all may turn out
otherwise.' Aphrodite had told Sappho: 'Now she is fleeing,
but soon she will pursue you;' Archilochus had addressed
his heart: 'Understand the rhythm which controls men.'
Suggestive elements of this typical situation are already
brought out in Homer's most advanced monologue. At the
beginning of the twentieth book of the *Odyssey*, Odysseus,
as yet unrecognized on account of his disguise, lies down to
sleep in the hall of his palace, on the eve of the suitors'
destruction. When he hears the maids jesting and laughing
with the suitors, he is indignant, for as their real master

he ought to command their obedience. He wonders whether he should rush among them and kill them all, or whether he should allow them one more night with the suitors. His heart barks within him, but he apostrophizes it: 'Endure, my heart; you once bore an even baser thing, when the Cyclops devoured your comrades. But still you endured till your guile found a way.' His instinctive desire for just revenge cannot be gratified, and this impediment makes him painfully aware of his own helplessness. The heart reacts violently in its distress and resentment, but it is urged to bear its load patiently, always remembering that on a previous occasion the misfortune had been even greater. This is the basic situation of the poems we have discussed; especially Archilochus' lines are so closely related, even in matters of detail, that he must have known Homer's verses, and been influenced by them. There is a connexion also with Sappho: Odysseus is not completely calmed until Athena appears on the scene and talks to him, like Aphrodite to Sappho, with soothing familiarity. But Homer's recollection extends to only one earlier episode comparable to the present event; Odysseus does not yet know the alternating cycle of life, the rhythm which controls men. When the heart of Odysseus barks, and he addresses it, or when, as we read earlier, the *thymos* in his breast is moved, that is not quite the same as Archilochus' harangue to his *thymos*. Homer's *thymos*, and similarly his heart, is but an organ of spiritual agitation which in its essentials does not differ from other bodily organs.[17] That the lyric poets put the non-physical in a separate category cannot, indeed, be cogently shown by citing the words 'soul' and 'mind', for our fragmentary material does not permit such conclusions, and perhaps the new ideas had not yet crystallized sufficiently to compel the coining of new terms for things spiritual.[18] But a turn of speech here, and another there, allow us to state with some conviction that the lyrists had ceased to interpret the soul only by analogy with the physical organs. Archilochus, in calling his *thymos* 'stirred up with suffering', or saying of his general that he is 'full of heart', uses expressions with which Homer is not acquainted, and which point to an abstract notion of the soul.[19] Sappho and Anacreon furnish even better proof of this transformation. They begin to suspect that the contradiction inherent in all feelings cannot be explained merely by an alternation in time, an unending oscillation between passion and tranquillity, between good fortune and misery, but that the present moment itself contains the seeds of discord. We have already come to know Anacreon's line :

Again I love and love not; I rave, nor do I rave.

The unhappy lover describes his state of struggling helplessness by the paradox that he affirms and negates one and the same thing. He depicts a similar experience when he says that Eros forged him with his hammer and bathed him in the cold stream. For this condition Sappho had found an equally paradoxical but even terser formulation when she wrote of the 'bitter-sweet Eros'. At the time her epithet was no commonplace; the coin which has now become worn with the handling of 2,500 years then bore a clear and fresh design. The epic does not yet feature such emotional discord or tension, because conditions of that sort do not exist in the area of physical operations, in whose image Homer portrays the mental processes. Sappho, with her bold neologism 'bitter-sweet ', discovers the area of the soul and defines it as fundamentally distinct from the body. Here too Archilochus had anticipated her; though we do not have any one passage in which he outlines the dilemma of the unhappy lover as explicitly and succinctly as she does, the phrases in which he attaches the symptoms of swooning or death to the sensation of love betoken an unusual insight into the emotional tension of the soul. For the death-likeness of love is, particularly in Sappho's view, the greatest tension of which the soul is capable.

The early poets conceive of this new mode of feeling as something supranatural; a divine impulse powerful enough to determine their values for them. But that does not mean that this affect cannot, objectively speaking, be led astray. The soul of Archilochus reacts with what amounts to unbridled violence. But this violence is itself a significant trait of the historical situation in which he found himself. At this time a man is not yet fully conscious of his individuality except during the brief moment when his senses are jarred by an emotional upheaval. It is but the 'barking' heart, as Homer calls it, vexation in love, or the fire of a righteous wrath, which begin to focus his eyes upon the individual in him. The less immediate landmarks: his experiences and achievements, his fate and his character, do not yet assert themselves as the traits of a unique personality; rather they form the kind of pattern which leaves no alternative but to recognize the operation of a universal force. This, the law of eternal change, is also a discovery of the lyric writers; it is not of the same order as the discovery of individual feeling, but it acts as its complement. The new individuality is paralleled by a new universality; the new capacity of the senses is braced by a new rational understanding. They are intimately and necessarily connected; the eternal ebb and flow is emotionally experienced, and the result is knowledge. Life, elusive and quick, is caught and held fast in the meshes of this law of alternation; its abundant vitality, however, goes unchecked.

The intellectual arena within which the early Greek lyric moves has its boundaries very narrowly defined. It is true of all Greek culture that the total course of a human life is seen, not as an individual life, but in terms of general categories. This has been called the 'classical conception' of life. It is, of course, characteristically Greek that the eruption of personal feeling in the early Greek lyric is unhesitatingly based upon the recognition of constant change. For all that it is remarkable that even in the field of action the lyric poets do not as much as suspect the individual character of their deeds.

In Homer the outstanding feats of a man are said to spring, not from his individual character or from his special gifts, but from the divine force which flows through him. To formulate this more pointedly: There are personal fates, but no personal achievements. Thus when Archilochus wishes to describe his double life as a soldier and a poet, he says (1):

> I am the servant of Lord Enyalius, and also I know the
> desirable gift of the Muses.

Similarly Sappho sees herself in the power of her deities, Aphrodite and Eros. The mythical form begins to be shed as the individual experience, with its intensity and its contradictions, finds recognition as a personal matter, and again when the order and meaning of events is no longer, as in Homer, safeguarded through constant divine intervention, but receives its sanction from the timeless and autonomous cycle of change. But neither advance suffices to enable man to acknowledge personal achievement. He may be aware of an individual sensation, but that leads merely to helplessness, to *amechania*. His insight into the flux, on the other hand, his rational illumination of the rhythm of the world, qualifies him for endurance and patience rather than for positive action. Even in the *Odyssey* these features are already more prominent than in the *Iliad*; but Odysseus who 'endured many troubles in his soul', the 'long-suffering ', was also the *polymechanos* who always knew a way out, and who overcame his helplessness by means of ingenious deeds.

Likewise when the lyrists speak of perfection, they have in mind not a goal of action but an ideal of sensation: that which appeals to the senses, which produces a joyous reaction of the emotions, is of the highest value. Again and again, down to the times of Pindar and Bacchylides, the good is pictured as an object of glittering beauty. The divine is radiant and luminous, perfection is a bright flame, greatness lives on in a blaze of glory; the poet reveals this splendour and projects its rays beyond the barrier of death. The songs of praise offer a wider scope for these images than the 'personal' lyrics; as an example we may cite one of the few comparatively well preserved poems by Sappho, a wedding song (55) which for the greater glory of the occasion recounts a mythical marriage, that of Hector and Andromache. The opening lines of the poem are lost; in its present state it begins with a herald arriving in Troy and announcing that the newly-wed couple had just completed their crossing from Thebes, the home of the bride, and landed on the Trojan shore.

> Quickly the herald approached . . .
> the speedy messenger, Idaeus, and brought the good news:
> 'To-day imperishable glory comes to Troy and Asia. Hector
> and his friends are bringing the radiant-eyed maiden from
> holy Thebes, the rich city on the Placus, delicate
> Andromache, with their ships across the salt sea, with a
> wealth of golden chains and purple robes, and a variety
> of things pleasant to see and pleasant to the smell, and
> countless silver cups and ivory goods.' These were his

words, and immediately the dear father rose from his seat.
The news was spread through the spacious city of Ilus.
At once the daughters of Ilium attached the mules to the
well-wheeled cars, and the whole crowd of women and tender-
ankled maidens sat in them, but the daughters of Priam
travelled apart from the others. And the men strapped
the horses to the chariots, and the young men came with them
in a body. The great mass of the people rolled mightily
along, and the drivers drove their horses weighed down
with ornament . . .

The next few verses are lost. Then she continues:

. . . like the gods
. . . this thronged crowd
drove speedily . . . to Ilium.
The sweet-piping flute mixed with the lyre
and the rattling of castagnets; brightly the
maidens sang a sacred song, the divine sound
reached the aether . . .
along all roads . . .
mixing bowls and platters . . .
myrrh and cassia and frankincense rose in the air.
The women raised a cry, those who were older,
and all the men raised a delightful song, triumphant,
calling upon the far-shooting Lord of the Lyre, and they
sang of Hector and Andromache, like to the gods.

This is the earliest poem of those that have come down to
us to give us some idea of the significance of myth in Greek
festival poetry.[20] Myth and reality are so closely interwoven
that the mythical situation appears to extend into the present.
The tale of Hector's wedding ends with the striking up of the
wedding song, and it is the singing of the wedding song which
we witness when Sappho's composition is heard. Though as
a rule in a hymeneal the bride and groom are likened to the
gods, in this instance they are equated with the figures of
myth whom Sappho describes less for their great deeds and
fortunes than for their splendour and shining perfection.
Even the wedding gifts are more important than the action,
precisely because they are so precious in appearance. Thus
the tale leaps from one bright station to the next, and the
climaxes glow with the brightness whose lustre survives the
day.
How little Anacreon measures life by the goal of action,

how little he appreciates its purposive structure, he betrays
with startling clarity in a poem of his old age (44):

> My temples have turned grey, and my crown is white.
> Charming youth is no longer here, and my teeth are decayed.
> Of sweet life not much time is left.
> Therefore I often groan, shuddering at Tartarus.
> For the abyss of Hades is frightful, and the descent to it
> Grievous. And once you have gone down, there is no coming back.

In this bit of autobiography, his eyes are centered upon his
helplessness; his 'will to life' sees itself hemmed in. Experience, i.e. the senses, decide what is valuable and what is not.
Youth is sweet, old age is full of fear and troubles. The
waning of young manhood, the approach of old age are
common themes among the archaic writers (Homer's heroes
had not even remarked on the contrast between the various
epochs in their own life), but the whole of a man's history is
not yet integrated into a meaningful unit.

There is, however, another side. If we look beyond the
Ionic-Aeolic sphere—Achilochus was born in Paros, Sappho
in Lesbos, Anacreon in Teos—we find that the sixth century
also produced thoughts about the life of man which form a
very different impression. Solon, the great man with whom
Attica takes her place on the literary stage, says: 'I grow older
every day, but every day I learn more'. As an active statesman who steers a middle course with his legislation, he is
stirred by the problems of human action and human behaviour.
This is not the only verse in which he comments on the
direction and the purpose of his life. And so he paves the
way for Attic tragedy. When Archilochus speaks of justice,
his reference is purely negative, to an outrage committed
against justice, or to the state of equity which the gods
continually restore. Justice as an observance, as the doing
of what is right, is not yet part of his vista. Sappho and Anacreon do not think about justice at all.

The lyric writers are imaginative enough to contemplate
many situations which do not occur in actuality, and to
experience fully the discrepancy between what is possible
and what is real, between their hopes and the cruel present,
between Being and Appearance. Nevertheless they do not
picture perfection in the guise of an ideal for which a man
strives, or which one might adopt as a model for the transformation of the world. That life on earth is imperfect and

sorrowful is known even to Homer; even his heroes share in the deep-rooted imperfection of man. But his gods endow everything under their sway with its particular essence, and ensure its continued existence. These gods also sustain the world of the lyrists; any rebellion against them is out of the question until man, on his own initiative, begins to wonder whether his life could not be more meaningful, and the gods more perfect; and above all, until he asks about the role of justice among men.

In the expression of their private sentiments and demands the early lyrists try to reproduce those moments in which the individual is all of a sudden snatched out of the broad stream of life, when he senses that he is cut off from the ever-green tree of universal growth. Such are the moments which furnish man with his first glimpse of the soul. This new personal soul is not yet by any means the foundation for all feelings and emotions; it is merely the source of the reactions which set in when the feelings are blocked. Love is not a passion which wells up from within, but a gift of Aphrodite or Eros. Only the emotional discord released by unhappy love is truly personal. In spite of the wilfulness of Archilochus, or the profundity of Sappho, they do not lose themselves in the abyss of their own sensations. When Sappho declares: 'The fairest thing is one I love,' she may mean that men have different views of what is beautiful, but simultaneously she insists that each individual person is certain of his own judgment. Emotion never relaxes into uncertainty, but always maintains a steady course towards a concrete goal dictated by desire or ambition.

This also explains why the archaic poets, as has long been recognized, never express themselves, like the moderns, in solitary monologues, in spite of their newly-found knowledge that they stand alone in the world. They always address themselves to a partner, either a deity—especially in prayer— or an individual or an entire group of men. Though the individual who detaches himself from his environment severs many old bonds, his discovery of the dimension of the soul once more joins him in company with those who have fought their way to the same insight. The isolation of the individual is, by the same token, the forging of new bonds.

In a poem by Sappho (98) whose opening lines and con-

clusion are lost we are to assume that Sappho has remained
in Lesbos with Atthis, a maiden whom she greatly loves,
while another girl, Arignota, has had to leave their circle
to return to Sardes, the capital of Lydia.

> . . . from Sardes often
> . . . she sends her thoughts hither, thinking how we
> used to live together, when she compared you to a
> noble goddess, and she rejoiced most in your song.
> But now she shines among the Lydian ladies as the
> moon, when the sun has set, with her rose fingers outshines
> the stars about her, and pours her light on the salt sea,
> and also on the flowery plains. Fair dew is sprinkled over
> them, and the roses bloom and the tender grass and the
> blossoms of the honey plant. And often when she wanders
> through the fields she remembers her desire for gracious
> Atthis, and her tender heart is ravished with baleful grief.
> 'Come here' she cries to us with a loud voice, but the
> silencing night does not allow the sound to reach us
> across the sea.

We know from other poems by Sappho that Atthis gave
her much cause for jealousy, and Arignota was especially
fond of Atthis while she was yet a member of Sappho's
group. Now that Sappho has remained behind with her
beloved Atthis she draws a nostalgic picture of Arignota in
Sardes during a summer night under a full moon, thinking
of her friends on the other side of the sea and longing to be
back with them. In spite of their separation in space, Sappho
voices a feeling of companionship which is realized in the
realm of memory and love and has to do with the soul.
Evidently Sappho also seeks a closer friendship with Atthis
by pointing out to her that they belong together; together
they are thinking of Arignota, and she sends her thoughts
to both of them. Literally the first sentence says: 'Often she
has her mind here from the direction of Sardes.' This is the
sort of formulation which for Homer would have been
impossible. For Sappho, the mind is capable of dissociating
itself from its place, and so a community of thought and
feeling is entirely feasible. These concepts have become
common coin in our world, but Homer does not yet have
them. He knows, of course, what longing is. Odysseus, for
instance, desires to return home from the island of Calypso:

> But Odysseus longs to see the smoke rising from his land,
> and then to die.

Nothing but the objective aim of the desire is named; we

are touched by the lines, apart from the euphony and the
picturesque concreteness of the Greek, because Odysseus is
content to die after achieving so moderate a wish.

   In another poem, again lacking beginning and end, Sappho
similarly remembers a girl who is gone. She tells how she
consoled her at her departure by reminding her of all the
beautiful things which they experienced together (96):

> . . .
> Truly I wish I were dead. She cried much when she left me,
> and said: 'Alas, how terrible is our fate. Sappho, very
> much against my will I am leaving you.'
> I answered her: 'Go with good cheer, and remember me;
> you know how much we have loved you. If not, then I am
> willing to remind you of what you have forgotten, how dear
> and fair were the times we have been through together.
> For in my company you have adorned your locks with many
> wreaths of violets and sweet roses; you have dressed your
> delicate neck with many woven garlands of hundred flowers;
> with many a precious scent, with royal balm and the juice
> of myrrh, you have anointed your fresh skin in my presence;
> stretched on a soft couch, you have quenched your desire
> in our circle of maidens. There was no dance nor festival
> nor game at the seashore in which we did not take part;
> there was no grove where in the spring the song of the
> maidens did not swell up in harmony.'

   In this instance it is memory which connects the lovers
with one another across the distance. Again human beings
are brought together by something non-physical, something
that lies in the realm of the soul. But they do not abandon
themselves to sentimentality, or rebel against the world.
Theirs is a memory of the things of this world, sensuous,
radiant, and fair. Memory allows the pleasures of the world
to survive, it lends permanence to the joy derived from them,
and establishes harmony between those who have relished
the pleasures. It has been said[21] that this type of reminiscing,
as practised by Sappho, is as it were a consolation which
lasts for ever; and we have been referred to a scene in the
Odyssey in which someone who is about to depart asks to be
remembered. But there is an important, albeit subtle distinction. When Odysseus leaves the land of the Phaeacians,
Nausicaa says to him (8.461):

Farewell, stranger, so that you will remember me when you have reached
your homeland, for you owe your salvation to me more than anyone.

Remembrance in this passage is the gratitude which one person owes to another for a good deed. In Sappho's poem, the lovers are joined together by one and the same memory, with no one-sided obligation turning the scale. The pure reflexion that memory is but an evocation of past beauty attunes the two souls to each other. In the Arignota-poem the 'thoughts sent hither from Sardes' coincide with Sappho's own desire, delicately unvoiced as it is; so also here: a memory joins two souls in unity.

This longing which bridges the distance, such unifying recollection of beauty, is not to be found in Archilochus or Anacreon, and yet they present the same phenomenon transposed into masculine terms. The archaic period witnessed the rise of a number of institutions, above all the symposium, designed for men of like minds to meet with each other. Wine alone may join men together—though on occasion it produces the opposite effect—but the symposium, with its poetry and its music, is an even better guarantee of companionship. The sympotic lyric, beginning with Archilochus, occupies an important place in archaic poetry. One song by Anacreon (43) stresses the significance of 'fair songs' at the banquet:

> Come, my boy, bring me the cup, that I may drink
> bottoms up. I'll mix ten measures of water with
> five of wine, for I do not want to carouse again
> with a lack of decorum. Let us not again behave
> like Scythian drunks with roaring and stamping
> of feet, but drink politely to each other with
> fair songs.

Since the symposium of this period cultivates solidarity and sociability, the poems recited at the bout often deal with the question how to tell a true friend, and how to determine what a man feels in his heart. Theognis says (1.499):

> In the fire the experts test silver and gold, but the
> mind of a man is laid open by wine, even the mind of
> an understanding man, who drinks beyond measure; so he
> is disgraced even if he was wise before.

Appearance or Semblance is to be unmasked, and the true mind of the boon companion must be revealed, for men wish to meet over their cups in a harmony of souls. How seriously this solidarity of feeling was sought after is also proved by the fashion of pederasty which during this early period was particularly cherished, and which played its dominant role at the symposium.[22]

On the political scene, too, men of the same outlook band together. For the first time in history political parties are formed; about their struggles we are informed by Alcaeus, the contemporary and compatriot of Sappho, and by Solon of Athens. Solon tried to allay the contention of the parties, and to strengthen and unite the State through the forces of law and statute. At the time of the lyric the Greek *polis*, the City State, becomes established; in place of the old feudal society there emerges a new community which rests upon law and order. It should not surprise us that the cognizance of individuality and the communal establishment of the polis are contemporary events; for to be a citizen is not the same as belonging to a mass of retainers. The law is the new link which binds men together.

In the religious sphere, too, those of the same disposition find their common meeting-ground. Within the sects of the Pythagoreans and the Orphics which became powerful during this same period men cling to a new hope and a new faith, based on common experience. The very fact that these sects concern themselves with the soul of man is symptomatic; their conception of the soul was a product of the new age.

Nevertheless it is the lyric writers who give us the clearest picture of the spirit of innovation which thus burst upon the world. For they use words, and they are explicit; and from them we learn what the new discovery was—a discovery of hitherto unmapped areas of the soul.

We have shown that Homer was not yet capable of understanding the soul as basically opposed to the body. We did this by pointing out that he lacked the terminological tools to define the three predicates which Heraclitus ascribes to the soul: 'tension', which included both intensity and depth, 'spontaneity', and 'solidarity' or 'joint possession'. The individual character of the lyric writer's experience led both to the discovery of the discord in his soul, and also to the knowledge that intellectual and spiritual possessions are held in common. Archilochus, Sappho, and Anacreon, it is true, do not acknowledge the spontaneity of the soul except within a comparatively small area of their experience. Violent affections they still regard as sponsored by the gods, and only the distress of the soul is claimed as man's private property. What is more, the areas of the will and of action are not yet opened up. But since the discoveries of the lyrists are matched in the creations of the visual artists as well as of the thinkers and the politicians, we may assume that these achievements of the great personalities are part of a larger historical process. History is a tissue made up of fate and achievement; on one side the garment shows only its warp, but if it is turned we may notice only the woof.

CHAPTER 4

PINDAR'S HYMN TO ZEUS

THE city of Thebes where Pindar was born boasted a richer
store of myths and tales than any other place in Greece. Here
Semele had given birth to Dionysus the dispenser of wine,
and Alcmene had nurtured Heracles who cleansed the world
of its monsters. The citadel had been ruled by Cadmus who
brought with him from Phoenicia the art of writing, the
source and foundation of all civilized life. He had sown the
dragon's teeth from which the Spartoi, the ancestors of the
Thebans, were sprung, and he led Harmonia in marriage.
The unfortunate Labdacids had sojourned in this little
town: Laius, Iocaste, her son Oedipus, and his children
Eteocles, Polynices, Antigone and Ismene. The narrow lanes
of Thebes produced the seer Tiresias; Niobe lived there,
the wife of king Amphion versed in song; it was from here
that Trophonius and Agamedes set out for Delphi to build
the temple of Apollo—these are just a few of the mythical
personages who dwelt in the city of Thebes, some of greater,
some of lesser renown such as Ismenus son of Apollo, and
the ash nymph Melia.

In Greece heroic tales are attached to the places which had
been important centres of Mycenean times. Over Mycenae
and Tiryns which, during that earlier age, had been the most
powerful bastions in the land, Thebes had this advantage
that her position remained strong long after other citadels
had fallen. Some cities, like Athens, may have outstripped
her in the end, but they were at first of so little significance
that the stories associated with them had no chance of
winning a large and loyal audience. Even a figure like
Theseus in the last analysis remained an exclusively Athenian
hero.

To the lyric poet of the archaic age the ancient stories
afforded an easily accessible source upon which to draw for
the embellishment of a festival, and if these stories were those
of his own land he was able to weave them into poems
which his listeners might relish for their old associations as
well as his new interpretation. Already as a boy Pindar

felt that this unimposing home town of his, the walls along
which he walked day after day, the springs from which he
drank, a street here and a square there, were profoundly
linked with the past, with the age of the gods and demi-gods.
From childhood on he lived close to memories fondly
cherished, not only by Thebans, but by all the Greeks. By
force of circumstances, therefore, he grew up in an atmosphere of spiritual riches, and this to a poet is probably far
more valuable than the quality we call genius or talent.[1]
Later in his life he exploits his great treasure with a sense of
pride; fully conscious of the wealth of this heritage he steps
before his countrymen and asks: which sample from the
multitude of our myths shall I give you? A hymn to Zeus,
preserved only in fragments, begins (fr. 29):

> Shall we sing of Ismenus, or of Melia of the golden distaff,
> Or of Cadmus, or the strong race of the Spartoi,
> Or Thebe with the dark-blue headband,
> Or of the daring strength of Heracles,
> Or the joyful majesty of Dionysus
> Or the wedding of white-armed Harmonia?

This poem stood at a conspicuous place in the edition of
Pindar brought out by the Alexandrian grammarians; it
introduced the first book of his works. The extant pieces
had been divided into 17 books, with the poems about the
gods—such as the pæans addressed to Apollo, and the dithy-
rambs to Dionysus—preceding the songs in praise of
mortals. But the leading position was taken by the hymns,
and among them the place of honour was granted to the
Hymn to Zeus, a composition of great fame. Later, in the
middle ages, the religious works of Pindar were lost one and
all; only a few fragments were preserved in the writings of
other ancient authors. Fortunately, enough verses from the
Hymn to Zeus are extant through quotation to give us an
insight into some of its major motifs. In fact we now have
roughly 30 lines of it; it has been possible to assign to the
Hymn two considerable portions of text on the grounds that
their metrical scheme agrees with the sections which have
long been known to belong to the poem. Since certain basic
views of Pindar have here found an unusually clear and
impressive voice, we shall not go wrong if we spend some
time near the ruins and reflect on them.

Because Pindar and his audience take it for granted that his poem should relate a myth, he at once begins with the question: of whom among the figures of myth shall I sing? Likewise the second *Olympian* ode starts: Which of the gods, what hero, what mortal man shall we celebrate? In the Hymn to Zeus he names a large number of Theban celebrities; we may compare the first part of the 7th *Isthmian* written in honour of a Theban: he mentions successively the tales of Dionysus, Heracles, Tiresias, Iolaus, Adrastus, and the conquest of Amyclae by the Theban Aegeids, tapping the inexhaustible well of his native tradition in order, as he puts it, 'to gladden the heart of Thebe, blessed city, with her native splendours'. In the Hymn to Zeus too Pindar proposes to display his abundant resources for the praise and the delight of Thebes. He composed the song for a festival of Zeus in his city, and coached a chorus of his fellow-citizens for the performance. The long series of hallowed domestic names which he proclaims in honour of Zeus and Thebes progresses from those less important, from Ismenus and Melia, via Cadmus and Thebe to Heracles and the god Dionysus, terminating in the marriage of Cadmus and Harmonia. This was the crowning episode; another fragment (32) tells us that Cadmus listened to Apollo as he intoned his music; the occasion cannot be any other than the wedding of Cadmus. For by analogy with the presence of the gods at the union of Peleus and Thetis—for that visit there had of course been special reasons, seeing that Zeus had originally intended to marry Thetis himself—the Thebans were convinced the gods had come to attend the nuptials of Cadmus and Harmonia. Pindar himself says once (*Pyth.* 3.90 ff.) that the weddings of Peleus and Cadmus were graced by the gods who took part in the feast and brought gifts, and that the Muses contributed their songs and dances.[2] As regards the Hymn to Zeus, we are merely told that Cadmus heard the music of Apollo, not that he listened to the singing of the Muses. But already in the *Iliad* (1.603 f.) Apollo's function at the table of the gods is that of leading the Muses in dance and song, and accompanying them with his lyre. The same must be true in the Hymn to Zeus. Now the writer who informs us of Apollo's attendance at the wedding of Cadmus also reports that Pindar recited a tale of the events

and of the changes which in the course of time had fallen to
the lot of mortals.[3] Moreover a verse of this poem (fr. 33) says
that Chronos, Time, is the ruler of all the blessed gods, and
stronger than they. By combining the two notices it has
justly been concluded that Apollo, along with the Muses,
regaled the wedding guests of Cadmus with a great mythical
account which told of the origin of gods and men. We shall
presently become acquainted with a number of pieces which
have plausibly been assigned to this section of the song.
Pindar thus follows up an invention of his compatriot Hesiod
who had written in his *Theogony* (lines 36–55):

> Come, let us begin with the Muses who gladden the great mind of
> Father Zeus in Olympus with their songs, telling of the present
> and of the future and of the past, in tuneful harmony.   Untiring
> the sweet voice flows from their lips, and the house of Father
> Zeus, the loud thunderer, laughs as the lily-like chant of the
> goddesses fills it; the peaks of snowy Olympus resound, and the
> houses of the immortals.   And with their undying song they tell
> first of the earliest awesome race of gods, whom Earth and wide
> Heaven produced, and the gods who were born of them, givers of
> boons.   And then, the beginning and end of the song, they chant
> of Zeus, the father of gods and men, how he is the best of the
> gods, and greatest in strength.   And again they gladden the
> mind of Zeus in Olympus singing of the birth of men and of
> sturdy Giants—the Olympian Muses, daughters of aegis-wielding
> Zeus. They were born of Mnemosyne who had embraced their father
> in Pieria where she reigned on the slopes of Eleuther, to be a
> forgetting of ills and a respite from troubles.

Here the Muses sing of the birth of gods and men in the
presence of Zeus and the other gods. Similarly we should
imagine that Pindar's Apollo did not present his great
mythical poem alone, but that he was supported by the
Muses, precisely like Pindar himself who supervised the
performance of his ode as the leader of a chorus. What is
more, the humorist Lucian tells us in his satirical essay
Menippus the Sky-Man how his hero came to Mount
Olympus and witnessed a performance by the Muses of
Hesiod's verses and our Pindaric hymn. Evidently he was
under the impression that the Muses played as active a role
in Pindar as in Hesiod. And finally we shall see that Pindar
had a particular reason for featuring the Muses in this
poem.

Another fragment reads (30):

First the Fates led heavenly Themis, of the good counsel, in
a golden chariot from the springs of Ocean along a gleaming
lane to the forbidding steps of Olympus, to be the foremost
wife of Zeus the Saviour. She bore the undeceiving Horae of
the golden distaff, rejoicing in fruits.

Apparently Pindar thus began to enumerate the various
marriages of Zeus. Here too he follows Hesiod (*Theog.*
886 ff.) who names seven wives of Zeus in due succession.

Reared as we are in a culture which prizes monogamy we
experience some difficulty in appreciating the earnest conviction with which Hesiod depicts these unions of Zeus.
He considered it his task to make a systematic collection
of all the genealogical tales which had been handed down as
true; in this way he hoped to sketch a complete canvas of the
growth and organization of the divine forces operative in
the world. This meant that he had to accept stories from
various quarters which were not always in perfect agreement,
and in his enthusiasm to reduce everything to a neat order he
did not realize that this very order made for the emergence
of some embarrassing features. He was able to make his
peace with the many unions of Zeus because of his 'mythical'
thinking. In his mind the profound religious idea that Zeus,
the highest god, is the source of the infinite wealth of Being
and Life takes shape as a picture of Zeus blessed with an
abundance of children. Pindar was no more frivolous than
Hesiod; what he took from his predecessor he accepted as
traditional, and therefore true, at least in its general outlines.
Still, he had an aim of his own. It appears that he subtracted
from the number of the marriages, but it is difficult to make
out the details of his version, and we do not know what
other spouses of Zeus he mentioned by name. Among the
seven wives Hesiod assigns second place to Themis; Pindar
introduces her at the beginning; in both accounts she is
the mother of the Horae. In fifth place Hesiod has Mnemosyne, the mother of the Muses; Leto who bore Apollo and
Artemis is sixth, and finally, in seventh position, he names
Hera. The lead is taken by Metis, Reflexion, who thus
precedes Themis, the goddess of law and order, and guardian of sacred conventions. In omitting Metis and moving
Themis up to first rank, Pindar may have been prompted by

the desire to shorten this catalogue of amours.[4] But this can scarcely have been his only reason for the change. Since he bestows the epithet 'of good counsel' on Themis, it may well be that he left Metis, Reflexion, out because, as he saw it, reflexion coincides with the rule of law, because it is of the very essence of law that an action should not be rash and irresponsible but based on careful deliberation. Zeus acceded to the reign after the fall of Cronus and the conquest of the Titans; afterwards law and order came into the world, a step which is symbolized by his marriage with Themis. With his policy of wise reflection he keeps wilfulness and violence in check throughout his empire, in the manner of an exemplary king. In Hesiod Themis is the daughter of Uranus, Heaven, and Gaia, Earth, i.e. she is descended from the old elemental powers. She is the sister of Oceanus—that is why Pindar has her fetched from the springs of Ocean; Pindar has her conducted by the Moirae, the Fates, who in Hesiod's version had been the daughters of Zeus and Themis herself. We gather from this that Hesiod regards the Moirae—he groups them as sisters with Law, Justice, and Peace—as belonging to the new order of Zeus, whereas in Pindar, as goddesses of necessity,[5] they date back much farther. He clearly defines the order of Zeus in terms of justice and propriety, in contrast with rigid necessity. We do not find it easy to understand these speculations, much less to savour them as poetry. But at any rate it is evident that Pindar wishes to bring out the beneficent quality of Zeus's rule, for he expressly calls him the 'Saviour', and in another fragment of the poem he speaks of the Titans (fr. 35) who had first, after their defeat by Zeus, been enchained in Tartarus, but were now freed from their prison, 'released from those shackles by your hands, O Lord', i.e. by Zeus.

Nor is this the only passage in which Pindar refers to the liberation of the Titans (cf. *Pyth.* 4.291); prior to him no one seems to know of it, but his contemporary Aeschylus put the redeemed Titans on the stage. No doubt Pindar thought of their release as occurring after a long period of suffering and waiting, and not before the various Olympian gods had appeared on the scene. As regards the latter, he seems to have devoted a detailed account to their successive appearances. We still have two fragments, one dealing with the birth of Apollo (fr. 147), the other with that of Athena (fr. 34). The one presupposes a union between Zeus and Leto who must, therefore, have been named as one of the wives of Zeus; the other ought to require the presence of Hephaestus who with his hammer struck the forehead of Zeus to allow the armed goddess to spring forth—that is what Pindar says (*Ol.* 7.35[6])—and it also involves the marriage between Zeus and Hera, the mother of Hephaestus. But the fragment says literally: '(Zeus) who, struck with the sacred mallet, produced blond Athena'. Perhaps the omission of the name Hephaestus is intentional, for Pindar no less than Hesiod certainly regarded Hera as the last wife of Zeus, and it was their marriage which was to form the climax of the whole tale. The mention of Themis, the first mate of Zeus who introduced the statutes of justice, had already pointed ahead to the ultimate union, that with Hera, which was to initiate the last phase of the divine drama, the age in which the Olympians put the final touch on the organization and the beauty of the world. In this last epoch peace was so firmly secured that Zeus was able to set free even the Titans.

In the course of the government of Zeus all confusion and deformity that exists in the world is gradually being reduced to harmony and order. That is the significance of the lofty myth which begins with the age preceding Zeus when violence and necessity prevailed. We need only point to the fact that the myth was sung at the wedding of Cadmus and Harmonia; Cadmus who introduced the beginnings of civilization into Thebes marries Harmony—and thus discipline and order extend their rule also to the earth.[7]

This idea, which underlies Hesiod's myth too, is more or less generally acknowledged in Greek literature, particularly in the classical writings of the 5th century. But Pindar gives the tradition a special twist, in his own inimitable style. A late rhetorician reports as follows: 'Pindar tells the story that Zeus, on the occasion of his wedding, asked his fellow-gods whether they lacked anything. Whereupon they bade him to create some gods who would beautify with words and music all the great deeds and institutions for which he was responsible.'[8] The assumption is that all the gods, except of course those whose creation is requested, are already in existence, and that the world has by now reached its final

state of beauty and order. The wedding in question, therefore, must be the last, i.e. that of Hera. But who are the gods
who are to make their belated appearance now? Apollo
perhaps? It cannot be he alone, since the petition mentions
more than one. Also, the birth of Apollo could not very well
be dated after Zeus's assembly of the gods and the establishment of order in the world, for he is more than merely a god
of song. No doubt in Pindar, as in the other authors, Zeus
married Leto, the mother of Apollo and Artemis, before his
union with Hera. In Hesiod Leto is the sixth consort of
Zeus, and thus the immediate predecessor of Hera.

So the Muses alone are left. This also involves difficulties,
for according to the popular version the Muses are daughters
of Zeus and Mnemosyne who in Hesiod appears as the fifth
wife of Zeus. It is not very likely that Pindar had the gods
ask Zeus at his wedding with Hera to produce the Muses,
and that Zeus answered he would do their bidding by entering
into yet another union. With all due respect for Zeus's
career as a husband, a conversation of this sort would not
have been the most discreet conduct under the circumstances.
More probably Pindar tried to forget that on other occasions
he had called Mnemosyne the mother of the Muses (*Isthm.*
6.75; *Pæans* 6.56; 7 b. 11), and omitted the union of Zeus
with Mnemosyne, like that with Metis, thus avoiding specific
commitment. It is less probable[9]—but of course we are
groping in the dark—that he substituted another mother,
i.e. Hera, or another father. The scene itself is perfectly
clear: everything has been arranged, the gods have sat down
at the wedding banquet; Zeus asks: Is anything still missing
in this beautiful world? And the gods reply: Divine creatures
who will praise its beauty. If we had this episode in Pindar's
own language instead of the dry prose of the orator, it would
surely be among the most famous in Greek literature. Pindar
could not have expressed more fittingly what poetry means to
the world. On the day when the world attained to its perfect
shape he affirms that all beauty is incomplete unless someone
is present to celebrate it. Pindar frequently says that the great
deeds stand in need of a singer so as not to lapse into oblivion
and to perish—a thought which is rooted in the ancient
tradition that a great name and a great deed are rendered
immortal by song. But he deepens the thought by implying

that the great deed requires a ' wise' poet who will lay bare its special significance. The beauty and order of the world certainly do not depend upon song for their immortality, but they do depend on the wise singer to have their meaning made clear to men. This meaning which the singer teaches by virtue of his praising skill does not lie concealed in some far-away region, behind or above Appearance, but is open to the view of all; only most men do not perceive it and need to have it pointed out to them.

The singer instructs through praise. As an example of this, let us consider the two fragments of the Hymn to Zeus which we have not yet discussed. They must be counted as parts of this poem because of their metrical correspondence with the first fragment. They contain an invocation of Delos, the island in the Aegean where Leto gave birth to Apollo and Artemis. The myth reported that the island, after floating upon the sea without peace for many years, finally came to a halt with the birth of the two deities. Pindar also alludes to the fact that Delos was sometimes called Asteria, the Isle of the Stars.

> Hail, daughter of the sea, built by the gods, a
> shoot most desirable to the children of Leto with
> the glittering locks; motionless miracle of the
> wide earth, which mortals call Delos, but the
> blessed on Olympus the far-shining star of
> dark-blue earth . . .
> . . . For previously the island
> was tossed on the waves by the blasts of manifold winds.
> But when the Coeus-born, feverish with her imminent labour,
> set foot on it, then four straight pillars rose from the
> foundations of the earth, of adamantine bases, and
> supported the rock with their crowns. There she gave
> birth to her blessed offspring, and looked upon them . . .

These verses are of course from the great Theogony which the Muses sing at the wedding of Cadmus and which is climaxed by the marriage of Zeus and Hera; but it remains impossible to determine exactly how they are to be fitted into the poem. Unfortunately the fragments of Pindar's poetry cannot ever be restored to their original order because Pindar did not choose to tell his tales in neat chronological sequence. On the contrary, bold changes and sudden transitions are a special mark of his art. The invocation of a

deity with which the fragment opens—for Delos is saluted
as a daughter of the sea—should be located at the beginning
of a poem, according to our knowledge of similar apostrophes
in Pindar and the other early lyrists.[10] But the first part of
the entire Hymn to Zeus, so we are informed by unimpeach-
able evidence, consisted of the catalogue of Theban mythical
figures.[11] This, however, should not prompt us to suspect
that the metrical correspondences on the basis of which we
assign the fragment to the Hymn are deceptive; they are far
too striking to be explained as accidental agreements. We
should rather assume that it was the song of the Muses
which began with the invocation. It is even possible that the
poem contained several performances by the Muses, for
Homer likewise (*Il.* 1.603 f.) has his Muses intone alternating
songs before the gods, to the accompaniment of Apollo's
lyre. One of the verses from the Hymn to Zeus which has
come down to us (fr. 147): 'In the course of time Apollo was
born,' does not seem to tally with the invocation of Delos; so
perhaps the birth of Apollo was discussed twice, which would
not be at all unusual in Pindar. At any rate, whatever the
place and function of our fragment: the spirited encomium of
the splendours of Delos, the striking and novel description
of matters which were by no means unknown, are good
examples of Pindar's art of praise. Briefly he states that
Delos had been a plaything of the waves and the winds; then
he makes use of a vigorous image to show how the island came
to rest: four pillars spring up from the bottom of the sea and
shoulder the weight of the rock on their capitals. And after
this solemn, this grandiose scene he breaks off and, simply
and unaffectedly, reports that Leto, after ushering her
divine progeny into the world, bent her looks upon them.
Both the miraculous setting of the floating island and the
history of Leto are not merely facts which happened; they
are instruments which Pindar uses to make our eyes dwell on
some image, such as the towering pillars, or the blissful look
which the mother casts on her divine twins. The two images
are meaningfully related to each other; like the island Leto
too has found her peace, after being driven all over the earth
by the jealousy of Hera. But there is also a contrast: on the
one side the massive columns, on the other the enraptured
eyes of the mother[12]—and yet both of them radiant with a

celestial light. Throughout the poem, throughout the whole of Pindar's work, we encounter this wealth of agreements and allusions. At the wedding of Cadmus the Muses sing of the wedding of Zeus, so that the content of the ode is related to the occasion on which it is sung. This is, of course, a common practice among the festival compositions of the archaic period; Sappho, for instance, has given us a wedding song which deals with the wedding of Hector (cf. above ch. 3), and Pindar brings his consummate skill to bear on the practice in his victory songs (cf. below ch. 5). But in our passage the pattern of correspondences is even more subtle than usual. The unions of Zeus have resulted in the establishment of beauty and order in the world: the mortal marriage establishes Harmony on earth. We have already noticed that Pindar sings before a Theban audience, and his topic is taken from Theban myth; this is another type of parallelism which we meet constantly in his poems. The Muses deal with the birth of the gods, and they finish their song with an account of how they themselves were born; that is their way of justifying their existence—or should we say the existence of Pindar and his art? Finally, men give the name Delos to an island which the blessed gods on Olympus call the 'far-shining star of the dark-blue earth'. Pindar is profoundly serious about the ancient name 'Star-isle'. On more than one occasion he says that an island is a gleaming star (e.g. *Pæan* 6.125). It is of course quite true that under the southern sky the earth gleams brightly while the sea reposes in livid darkness. But in this instance he responds to the challenge of the name, and so to speak puts the whole wide world on its head, by devising an unheard-of relationship between sky and earth: when those in heaven look down upon the earth, our earth, particularly the sea, becomes their sky, and Delos flashes up as their brightest star.[13] Descriptions of nature are rare in Pindar's work, as generally in the classical poetry of the fifth century, but this one surely stands among the boldest and grandest of all literature. His nature is not, as we to-day would expect it, invested with a soul. He does not empower it to experience sensations. It is viewed with the greatest objectivity, but from a very particular vantage point. Nature has become the stuff of a mythical image; in characteristically Pindaric fashion, reciprocity and corres-

pondence have become the key factors in his vision, so that
we are confronted with a truly Heraclitean proportion: those
in the sky regard the earth as those on earth regard the sky.
This is not the only place where Pindar betrays a kinship
with Heraclitus' doctrine of energetic tensions, of the
pregnant correlations by which all living things are at once
separated and united. In the final analysis even the idea that
the great deeds and the beauty of the world require song to
praise them is founded on the knowledge that the individual
thing is limited, imperfect, in need of completion, and that
even greatness perishes, while song is indestructible, and
beauty depends on the 'wise' for its manifestation. And
evidently it is up to the wise man to show that the world
discloses its greatest beauty in the wealth of its correlations,
through its correspondences and contrasts: nay, that the
essence of this beauty resides in the agreement and balance
of its parts.

One picture which Pindar draws fits his own technique
admirably (*Nem.* 7.77): 'The Muse is joining together gold
and white ivory and the lily-flower which she has taken from
the dew of the sea.' Piece after piece he moulds his song
from precious materials, continually changing his design,
until he has fashioned a mosaic rich with gold, ivory, and
white coral—the 'lily-flower taken from the dew of the sea'.
More than once he calls his writing a weaving of chaplets.
The strands of a garland disappear and emerge again into
view, tracing a complex pattern of parallels and contrasts;
just so the fibres of Pindar's poem, though far apart and
distributed over its length, require to be perceived together.
A rather superficial example will perhaps help to make this
clear. In a triumphal song we expect certain data about the
victor, such as his name, the name of his father, and his
home. Pindar is fond of introducing these details in such a
way that the victor may first be referred to by the name of
his father, later in the poem he is called by his own, and in the
end he is merely identified by the name of his country. In
this fashion Pindar is able to provide the necessary information unobtrusively and without repeating himself. He has
very much the same approach towards other factors which
form the stock-in-trade of a victory ode: staples such as
myth, maxim, and so forth. They emerge, they vanish to

make room for another motif, they rise to the surface once
more, as if by chance and without immediate provocation:
and all the time they are the strands without which the whole
design would not be harmonious. Pindar elects to create
this ornate tapestry because he wants to represent reality
and nothing else; it is no concern of his to trace an orderly
process pedantically from beginning to end, nor does he
mean to 'get somewhere', to develop an idea or a programme.
The very structure of his poetic designs confirms the message
of his senses that all things are inextricably woven into a
whole; the literary form he uses is a faithful mirror of the
world which he sees. For all that, the individual parts are
not subordinated to the whole so as to play an inferior role.
They are not like the scenes, or even the sentences, of a
tragedy which are each determined by the plot of the whole,
no matter whether they quicken or retard the action (that,
incidentally, is the reason why it is so much easier to assign a
tragic fragment its place in a lost drama). We recognize in
this an archaic element for which there are many analogies in
the plastic art of the pre-classical age. The makers of black-
figured vase paintings, for example, show a tendency to
weave the figures into the composition without leaving any
space unused. Their interest in creating an ornamental, a
heraldic pattern is stronger than their desire to construct an
organic group, autonomous in its relation to the background.
This holds good even for the nude human body; each organ
is stressed in its individual perfection, beautifully shaped and
strongly marked off against its neighbour. They are vigorous
limbs which radiate an intense vitality, but they are anything
but properly integrated into the balanced ensemble of a
body. Their shape is in no way affected by the pressure or
pull of other limbs, or by a burden or resistance exerting its
weight from without (cf. above ch. 1).

Pindar remained loyal to this archaic manner although his
creative activity lasts down to the middle of the fifth century.
Throughout the fifty years of his life which are open to our
view there is no trace of a stylistic development, such as was
the achievement of his contemporary Aeschylus in Athens.
It is a logical consequence of Pindar's mode of thinking that
his poems are crowded with geometric figures, such as ring
composition, figure-eight-loops, parallelisms and mirror

images. The decorated character of his art is most fully
revealed in its metrical form. Never again has the world
seen poetry which equals that of Pindar in keeping its far-
flung variations under the strictest control by means of
measure and number. Therefore the demands which it
makes on the metrical skill of the author are beyond compare.
Without the Greek text we cannot, unfortunately, discuss
Pindar's verse, for it rests on conditions which are foreign to
our own sense of rhythm. In our tongue a verse is based on
the regular alternation of stressed and unstressed syllables.
In Greek, on the other hand, a verse is formed by the orderly
succession of long and short syllables, to which our ears are
not attuned. The most we can do is to arrange the long and
short syllables in a metrical scheme, and then to point out
certain variations. But the rhythmic cadence which filled
these skeletons with life must remain a mystery to us. It is
as if we spotted correspondences and variations in the notation
of a Bach fugue without subjecting them to the test of our
hearing for which they are after all meant.

Pindar's metrical art is his own creation. Some of his
contemporaries tried, without fully succeeding, to imitate
his verse, but in the end it died with him. He refines the
play of responses and variations which had been introduced
by the earlier choral lyrists; at the same time he boldly
magnifies its scope until he accomplishes a towering edifice.
Large strophic formations are multiplied according to rigid
rules; each subdivision begins with lines similar to those
which the older poets had already used, but in the sequel
they undergo kaleidoscopic changes through extension,
shortening and rearrangement. Pindar did not turn off into
the Attic route: that led to a totally different destination.
The choral odes of early tragedy begin to use the variation
of a particular type of line to pass on to other types, to release
themselves from the tight fetters of a rigid metrical scheme,
and thus to achieve an organic strophic structure while
allowing themselves a freer development of themes. In later
tragedy and in the new dithyramb this ultimately led to the
creation of extended compositions in free metrical form. In
all Greek lyric poetry, and particularly in choral poetry, the
metric design was carried by music which—at least as far as
the older period is concerned—has disappeared to the last

note. Thus we shall never have more than a vague idea of the special quality of Pindaric metres. Only this much we may know, that like his thinking they recalled the texture of tapestries, and that therefore they were magnificently appropriate to the vision and thought of the poet.

But we have not yet said our last word about the art of Pindar. His is not a disinterested toying with forms; he does not unveil the correlations which exist in the world merely because he is delighted with the intricate pattern of reality, but because he has discovered in them a higher meaning. As the Muses at the wedding of Cadmus sing of the wedding of Zeus, they magnify the festival of the mythical king of Thebes. As in the sky the final marriage of Zeus led to the perfection of order among the gods and in the world, the same order found its place on earth through the union of Harmonia with Cadmus. And the Pindaric chorus, by singing of this in the presence of the Thebans, reinforces the greatness and the sanctity of their city, and puts them under an obligation to obey this noble tradition, and to maintain the hallowed order. The wise poet espies the element of divine splendour which, coming from Zeus, illumines the mythical Cadmus and casts its lustre even upon the Thebes of his own time. He points to it, and that is his praise. The transitory world participates in the divine, and it is the task of the poet to make this known.

Pindar describes Delos as a star in the sky of the gods, not to create a mood, or simply to voice a private aesthetic response, but in order to celebrate the island. On other occasions when Pindar calls an island a 'radiant star' that is praise enough; how much greater is the glory of Delos whose radiance exists for the gods ! When Heraclitus stresses such mutual correlations between gods and men, we witness a disinterested intelligence at work; in Pindar, everything is geared to the practical demands of life, to the active concern of praising. The two men differ also in another respect. Pindar retains an immediate intuition of the divine; he is able to reproduce its brilliance, and to grasp it, directly and spontaneously, as a mythical fact. In the thought of Heraclitus the deity shows a tendency to become abstract, to detach itself from the world of the senses. An 'invisible' harmony ranks higher in his scale than the agreements which meet his eyes. Pindar and Heraclitus, however, have this in common that the divine, the One, forms their objective; Heraclitus ponders over it and seeks to understand it, while Pindar approaches it with pious contemplation, and is content to praise it. One is a philosopher, the other a poet.

In these days a Christian poet who intones his *Te deum laudamus* is unable to regard the works of God with the same candour and simplicity which were Pindar's privilege. Hoelderlin imitates Pindar in giving praise a central role to play in his hymns—there are, of course, also echoes of the Christian Praise of the Lord in his work—and Rilke, following in the steps of Hoelderlin but once more under the influence of new Christian impulses, thinks of the poet as one 'elect to acclaim'. But the object of their praises does not stand clearly revealed before their eyes; in fact both of them declare that the poet ought to make a concerted effort to seek out this object. It is obvious, therefore, that we cannot expect them to sound the simple and unbroken strains which we hear in the panegyrics of the archaic age of Greece. Pindar owes it to the transitory conditions of his hour that his praise is as pure and as perfect as that of no other poet of Europe. The effulgence of the divine, he feels, is reflected in the appearances of the world; his sensuous delight in the multiplicity of things is not yet obscured by the knowledge that the essence which really matters is located beyond the visible world, and that it can be known only by reason. As a result his intuition is strong and lucid, his expression lively and straight. To be sure, he has his problems; he no longer takes it for granted that the divine is readily discerned in the phenomena about him. Wisdom is required to point it out and to establish its value; only a soaring flight of the mind will contrive to place the divine within our grasp. This conviction is the source of the stately eloquence which distinguishes Pindar's style above that of all the other poets of his time, and which gives his eulogies their peculiar greatness. Though the voice of this genre of poetry is about to be stilled, its flame burns brighter than ever before.

Not all things participate in the divine to an equal degree. But the wise man descries it in the outstanding examples of each kind all around him : among treasures it resides in gold, among the fish it is found in the dolphin, in the eagle among the birds, in the king and the victor among human beings. The fifth *Isthmian* begins: 'Mother of Helios, Theia the many-named: for your sake men have made the great strength of gold to be a thing prized above other possessions',[14] and, so he continues, 'by the honour which you bestow men win respect and glory in all sorts of contests'. Here he endeavours to seek the divine in the principle which is responsible for the value of precious things: a mythology which is Pindar's very own, although we might again refer to Hesiod.[15] This principle he calls Theia, which simply means the divine. We seem to have reached the borderline where intellectual abstraction begins, but Pindar's Theia is 'Mother of the Sun'; the sun, it appears, diffuses his radiant warmth because of her, and the divine finds its purest expression in the sun. At the same time Theia has 'many names'; she reveals herself in many ways, and we need a variety of designations to praise and invoke her.

Sappho (fr. 65 a), in a poem of her old age, had confessed that her joy in the beauty of this world drew its strength from her love of the sun. In the course of the more than one hundred years which separate Pindar from Sappho this archaic type of piety, the willingness to identify the divine with brightness and light, had fallen into decay in the rest of Greece. Pindar and his ancient faith make a rather isolated stand in a world that had largely changed. At times, therefore, he feels the urge to defend himself, to indulge in demonstration. Occasionally he is moved by an impulse not unlike the zeal of an apologist to enter into theological and mythological speculations of the sort which his compatriot Hesiod had brought into currency at the beginning of the archaic age. Austerity and a sense of purpose provide the link between the two Boeotians, one the forerunner, the other the accomplisher of pre-classical poetry, that rich and colourful art.

Hesiod stands on the threshold between the era of the epic and the age of the lyric. A new awareness of reality is the chief factor which separates him from the epic. Under the impact of his hard life as a peasant and herdsman the world of the heroic tales, the songs of his rhapsodic profession, came to be shrouded in a cloud of questions and doubts, and he turned his eyes towards the more concrete forms of his immediate surroundings. He ceased to look for the divine in the restricted aristocratic society of the Olympians who interfere in the actions of kings and heroes as they see fit. Instead he sought to obtain a more exact and systematic knowledge of the divine as a power affecting all. The result of this shift is his theogonic scheme. But he continues to subscribe to the epic tradition in one important respect: he describes his system as one that has come into being, not as one that exists in the present.

His Muses sing of the present, the past, and the future, of the birth of the gods, and the coming into being of a living and meaningful world. In Pindar also the Muses sing of this epic event, how the world gradually came to be put in order; but their real function is one which accords with the lyric rather than the epic: to praise the beauty of Zeus's works.

In the course of the years between Hesiod and Pindar the archaic lyrists became conscious of the tensions of the soul, of the intricate interrelations in matters of the mind, and of the limits restricting the old values. Pindar does not, unlike most writers of archaic lyrics, speak of his private sensations, or of the intellectual links between him and other men, nor does he enlarge upon the values which he rejects. All he does is to state objectively what he considers most precious, what he associates with the divine, how that which is limited partakes of that which is universal and lasting, how man has a share in what is higher than man. Thus although there are no direct ties between his speech and that of his predecessors, the world which he pictures is fully instinct with the new dimension discovered by them. The seeds sown by the lyrists before him (cf. above ch. 3) are brought to fruition in the festival poetry which stems from the cult hymn: and that is his particular achievement. His deity has the very same qualities which Archilochus and Sappho predicated of the soul to distinguish it from the body: tension, intensity, and the capacity to merge separate objects under its force. This means that Pindar's deity is no longer a power of, so to speak, historical efficacy, a power which at any one moment activates one particular event. Instead he visualizes it in the form of pervasive splendour and eternal meaning, 'going through all things' as we might say with Heraclitus, and manifesting itself in a counterplay of opposites. The suitable mould in which to express this new concept is no longer the epic but the lyric ode, as is notably proved by Pindar's Hymn to Zeus.

While Pindar was at work in Thebes, Attica produced a view of the world which differed appreciably from his. Tragedy makes the claim that there should be justice on earth; consequently the tragedians demand more of men, and also of the gods, than is usually fulfilled. In their world praise could not but lapse into silence. Pindar deliberately keeps away from such thoughts which he considers presumptuous. On occasion he may comment that some trait of the tradition which he reports appears to dim the glory of the divine, but he never permits himself to question the beauty and order of life, whatever the weaknesses and vanities of our earthly existence. Never does he feel called upon to play the reformer. With noble insouciance he takes the world as he finds it; its celestial threads of gold cannot be completely blacked out by its shadows. All that matters is to 'turn the brightness outward' (*Pyth.* 3.83), to insist on the beauty which has enveloped him so generously from childhood on. This is the way for a poet to prove his worth; and few of the poets who came after Pindar could vie with his genius for doing just this.

CHAPTER 5

MYTH AND REALITY IN GREEK TRAGEDY

'THE historian relates the events which have happened, the poet those which might happen.' This famous statement by Aristotle (*Poetics* 9.2) is based on the assumption that historiography and poetry had, in spite of their common root, grown into two separate branches, as indeed they did in the fifth century. Aristotle further holds that poetry is more philosophical than history, since poetry deals with the universal, history with the unique. Again it is the fifth century which produces the earliest traces of the notion of universality. Aristotle's assertions, regardless of the truth contained in them, at once prompt the question how the early Greeks understood the relationship between poetry and 'the things which have happened.' As regards the Homeric epic, the answer is easily given; and, as was only to be expected, it does not conform with the Aristotelian proposition. Early man demands of his serious epic poetry that it speak the truth. Whenever critics make themselves heard their argument is that the poets lie: e.g. Hesiod *Theog.* 27; Solon fr. 21; Xenophanes 1.22; Pindar *Ol.* 1.28. It follows that, since the epics are made up of myths, we must conclude that these myths, apparently even their detail, were accepted as reality. There is of course no doubt that the drama—which is uppermost in Aristotle's mind—cannot be judged by the same standards. The simple fact that a play is dependent upon the conditions of its performance would seem to preclude it from being accepted as reality. For if the poetic myth were to pass for truth, the performer would have to be acknowledged as the actual hero of the tale.

But is it not a fact that in the very beginning the actor and the character represented were one and the same? Greek tragedy originated from the choral song, and we know, through some remarkable pieces of evidence, that even the early choral odes often contained some dramatic elements. Mythical events were communicated to the people as an immediate present experience. The result was a relationship between myth and reality, between poetry and truth which differed radically from that found in the Homeric lays. It is our task to study this relationship; only so can we hope to understand the complex nature of Attic tragedy.

We possess a pæan by Bacchylides which he wrote for a chorus of his fellow-citizens, the Ceans; they performed it in Delos, at a festival instituted by Theseus. Bacchylides relates how Theseus, journeying to Crete with the youths and maidens from Athens, picked a quarrel with Minos the king of Crete, and how, in order to prove that he was sprung from Poseidon, he leapt into the sea and emerged with a purple garment and a wreath. According to the tradition Theseus returned to Delos after overpowering the Minotaur in Crete, and there led the Crane Dance which thereafter became the main feature of an annual celebration. The close of Bacchylides' poem runs thus:

> The maidens (in the company of Theseus) shouted with joy, . . .
> and the young men near by sang the pæan with graceful
> voice. Delian Apollo, cheer your heart with the choral songs
> of the Ceans and grant them a god-sent increase of good things.

The youths and maidens with Theseus merge with the chorus of the Ceans for whom Bacchylides wrote the ode; at the end of the poem the chorus is in the same situation as the mythical beings with whom the song concerns itself. The song of the mythical chorus becomes the song of the performing chorus. Here is the germ of drama, the source of impersonation: the transformation of myth into present reality. It leads us into the darkest recesses of the remote past. On the other hand, the actual representation of the Crane Dance has given way to the reproduction of Theseus' tale in song. The epic element which thus enters into the choral presentation completely alters the function of the myth. The original myth can no longer be duplicated in the ritual act; instead of a reality which might again and again be conjured up in the sacred ritual of the festival, we now have a myth transfixed into singularity, a unique event reported in terms of 'history'. And yet, the event retains a special significance for the festive occasion on which the song is performed. Thus it appears that two entirely separate strands, that of the epic tale and that of the sacred act, have become interlaced to form a new complex pattern.

There is reason to suspect that Bacchylides' poem does not

compound myth and reality in as pure a mixture as some choral poetry which came before it. Its plot concerns an experience which Theseus had on his crossing to Crete, before he met with his great adventure. In all probability there were some older choral odes on the subject of the Crane Dance in Delos which related his victory over the Minotaur, his salvation of the youths and maidens, and his landing at Delos; a comprehensive tale of these events would have formed a more natural introduction to the pæan in honour of Apollo. A wedding song by Sappho, presumably a choral ode, permits us to catch a brief glimpse of that earlier method of connecting myth with reality. It deals with the marriage of Hector, and ends upon the hymeneal hymn with which the Trojans saluted the young couple.[1] Such a myth is designed to endow the ephemeral world and its affairs with meaning and splendour; the myth enhances the reality of the present, owing to the proud persuasion of the singers that their celebration is like the earlier celebration of Hector.

This division of the world into two levels of myth and reality, with the one reflecting the values of the level above it, is another legacy of the epic. The choral lyric absorbed it along with the narrative technique of the epic; but the use to which it put this motif was as novel as its previous status had been vague. For in the epic even the human world belongs to the realm of myth, with this distinction that the accomplishments of the heroes are under the constant surveillance of the gods who direct and decide all.

To begin with, tragedy was a dance and choral song in praise of Dionysus, performed by singers who dressed up as animals. Their disguise originally stamped them as divine creatures; for the duration of the dance, therefore, the world of myth and material reality became one. Thus drama and the choral lyric go back to closely related archetypes; what distinguishes them is the manner of their evolution into definitive literary genres or, to put it differently, the reception which they accorded to the myths of epic poetry. When, at the close of Bacchylides' poem, the Cean chorus takes on the personality of the youths and maidens accompanying Theseus, this transformation is but an echo of the older form; for the song itself it is of no great importance. Drama, however, maintains a firm hold on this very transformation; the chorus impersonates the figures of myth, it plays a role, it becomes an actor. The choral lyric, thanks to its inheritance of the narrative form from the epic, may extricate itself from the rigid bonds of the sacred occasion. Thus Bacchylides may place in the centre of his poem, and embellish with charming colours, an episode from the journey of Theseus which bears no relation whatever to his landing at Delos and his Crane Dance. The ancient form is preserved only to this extent that the chorus deals with the myth of the journey; however, instead of acting the myth out, they merely describe it. The word, not the person, serves as the agent of communication. By comparison with the epic, of course, the lyric is not wholly out of touch with the present. Regardless of the apparent lack of connexion which often exists between narrative and occasion of performance, it is the avowed purpose of the great choral poetry of the fifth century to impart a deeper meaning to the reality of human affairs. The victory songs of Pindar, for example, either point to the place or type of the contest, or they refer to the victor's ancestors or home-town. Or again, the poet concentrates on parallels and lessons from other areas of life which throw light on the subject at hand. In this, it is not his intention merely to formulate ideal situations and ethical paradeigmata; he desires to make the special situation of his client fully understood, and so he links it with the mythical past, with an era of greater validity, until the victor of whom he sings, but also the singers, find happiness and strength in the shelter of a hallowed tradition. Since reality may be illumined from more than one side, the possibilities of using myths in choral poetry are varied and plentiful. A wedding, for instance, is comparable to any one among numerous mythical weddings, an occasion of sorrow to divers heroic deaths, and so forth. Many different situations provide a suitable setting for the spirited play of myth.

The case of drama is entirely different. When the rich reservoir of mythical tales, fashioned by countless epic and, somewhat later, lyric poems began to be channelled into tragedy, the bond between myth and reality was destined to be disrupted. Attic tragedy was tied inseparably to a single sacred transaction, the worship of Dionysus. Unlike the lyric, tragedy stoutly maintained the dramatic role of the chorus, the acting out of myth. Consequently, when the performers invaded other fields of cult or myth and ceased to be servants of Dionysus, the meaning of the ceremonial act was lost. We know that this step met with some resistance, on the grounds that tragedy 'no longer seemed to have any business with Dionysus,'[2] but in the dramas of Aeschylus such scruples have long been overcome, with the result that there is no trace of the original connexion with the worship of Dionysus. Even the satyr play with its chorus of sileni, except of course for the mythical disguise, the satyric costume, shows no restrictions with respect to subject-matter or plot.

This, however, does not involve a return to the epic representation of myth. Drama cannot simply imitate reality, but it must mould its material in deference to the demands of the stage. The action must be assembled in various scenes which in turn are as nearly as possible located at one place and enacted in consecutive time, for the Greek stage has no curtain. The plot is developed in dialogue form, with no more than three actors; that was the maximum number of men at the disposal of the Attic tragedian. Finally, because the play is held to a limited playing time, the writing has to be brief and concise, with the utmost concentration on essentials.

The result was that, as the drama detached itself from the pressure of reality, it became more closely attached to its own material: to the rules of the play, to the laws of artistic creation. The business of understanding and defining reality is now relinquished to scientific prose writing whose origins belong to the same age as those of tragedy. And the theorists who engage in reflexions concerning tragedy—we do not hear of such writings before the end of the fifth century —no longer assume that it is the task of tragedy to speak the truth and to copy reality. On the contrary, 'deception' is said to be the proper concern of the dramatist,[3] and a slavish imitation of real life is considered a cause for reproach.[4]

The twofold emancipation of tragedy, both from the reality of what is represented and from the ritual occasion, turns drama into 'play'. This is clearly shown even in the development of the satyr play which because of its chorus of satyrs preserved a somewhat more direct connexion with the cult of Dionysus. We have recently acquired some knowledge of two satyr plays by Aeschylus; prior to this find we were familiar with only two specimens of this art form, both by later authors. In one of the new plays, the *Isthmiastai*, the satyrs are put into the grotesque situation of training for the Isthmian Games. They have deserted Dionysus and joined the service of Poseidon in whose sanctuary they are now hanging up their masks as votive offerings. Their father Silenus makes an abortive attempt to win them back to their old obligations by means of invective and threats. But when the contest takes place, they fail miserably. As someone, perhaps Palaimon, the old man of the sea who is associated with the foundation of the Isthmian Games, shows them the javelins with which they are to begin the pentathlon they decide to have nothing further to do with agonistic matters. At the end of the piece, we may assume, they returned to the service of Dionysus.

If this reconstruction of the plot is correct, the ultimate triumph of Dionysus is appropriate enough to the external situation, the cult of Dionysus. But whatever dramatic force the play has is due to the fact that the satyrs are placed in an alien sphere: the Isthmian contests. The tales about Dionysus were quickly exhausted, and were incapable of furnishing as much fresh material as was needed for the performances. So the satyrs were abruptly transplanted into myths with which, from the point of view of tradition, they had nothing in common. An even better example of this development is provided by the other recent find, the *Diktyoulkoi*, or *Fishermen*. The play deals with the story of Danaë. After bearing Perseus, the son whom Zeus had given her, she is driven out by her father who locks her and her child up in a chest and casts them into the sea. The play opens with the entrance of two fishermen who set their net in the orchestra (this seems to indicate that there was a depression in the middle of the dancing area). There they make a catch so heavy that they are unable to pull the net ashore. Upon their call for help, the chorus of satyrs appears on the stage, and with their assistance a large chest is drawn up from the water. In it they find Danaë, asleep or unconscious, together with the babe Perseus. One fisherman, Diktys, runs off to procure help while the satyrs are to guard the two strangers salvaged from the sea. But Silenus, the father of the satyrs, immediately falls in love with Danaë and proposes marriage. In her despair Danaë hurls reproaches at Zeus for placing her in this predicament and threatens to hang herself, if she is not saved from these 'monsters'. Silenus shows little concern; to the infant Perseus he describes the wonderful life in the woods which is in store for him, and as for Danaë he feels that she must be very happy to have once more found a man of such beauty as himself, especially after her tedious widowhood on the high seas. The chorus prepares to move off the stage, but in the final section, which is not preserved, the satyrs including Silenus were presumably chased away, and Danaë was taken to the city. It is evident from this that Aeschylus used a fable in which the satyrs and Dionysus originally had no legitimate role to play. For the fourth play of a tetralogy, however, the chorus of satyrs was obligatory. Somewhat artificially, therefore, but with considerable skill and a strong sense for dramatic possibilities, Aeschylus introduces the satyrs by having his fishermen, unable to pull the net in by themselves, shout for help. In later satyr plays the appearance of the Dionysiac satyrs is similarly contrived. The poet must transform the tale to do justice to the stage.

It is only natural that this requirement released a powerful impulse to invent free versions of the old myths, and since three, if not six, new satyr plays were performed in Athens each year, more and more myths were attracted into the Thespian orbit. The same is true of tragedy which had to furnish three times as many plays as the satyr piece; and since tragedy had done away with the satyrs in its chorus its plot came to be completely cut off from the cult of Dionysus.

Let us stop here, and once more survey the function of myth and reality in early Greek poetry. With our examples still fresh in our minds we might perhaps attempt a further analysis of the differences between the various literary types. The epic tells myths, it accepts them as reality and arranges them on two levels, one existing on earth and the other in heaven, whereby the meaning and the value systems of human life are made to depend on the gods in the sky. If we look more closely, we detect two other levels of reality which likewise serve the purpose of illuminating the mythical events that take place on earth: the paradigms from the past

which the heroes cite in their speeches when they see the
need for thought and reflection, and the Homeric similes
taken from the reality of the poet's everyday life which
illustrate stages of the epic action. The mythical models
transpose us into a world which stands half way between the
gods and the heroes with which the epic is concerned, while
the similes inject a dose of the poet's own reality into the
world of the epic. These intermediate levels of simile and
paradigm are the first important steps along the road which
ultimately led to the 'conclusion by analogy', the indispensable tool of subsequent empirical thought.[5]

The choral lyric and the drama are based on the ritual
dance in which the divine world coincides with present
temporal reality. This reality, however, differs appreciably
from the reported events of the epic. It is not something that
has occurred in the past and may now be faithfully—or
falsely—chronicled, but a mythical truth which is revived
by being enacted. The play, for the performers and the
audience, 'is' the mythical occurrence; but then again in a
certain sense it is not, because everybody knows that the role
of the hero is now taken by some other man. Once more,
and with greater urgency than the epic, tragedy confronts us
with the question: what is mythical reality? If we were to
look at the problem with modern eyes, we would define it as
an event full of 'significance', a significance which may always
become alive again; to paraphrase Aristotle: an event which
involves the universal, not merely the particular.

Even though the developed choral lyric takes over the
narrative element of the epic it persists in its correlation of
the present with the mythical past. Myth is employed to
ennoble the reality of the hour, to disclose the deep meaning
which it contains, and this is possible only because the myth
is still considered just as 'real' as in the days of the epic, in
spite of its increasing tendency to assume the character of a
special, a higher reality. Drama, as we have seen, removes
itself from immediate contact with the reality of the present
by severing its ties with the ritual situation. Simultaneously,
by becoming a play and an illusion, it robs the myth of its
standing as a piece of reality. Thus the drama lacks the
twofold system of reference which characterizes the epic
and the choral lyric: all bonds with reality, historical or

present-day, seem cut, and myth turns into an isolated
organism which exists only by grace of the dramatic play.
A free exercise of the imagination had of course not been
unknown; there were the popular yarns and extravagant
folk-tales whose influence may to some extent be detected in
the satyr plays. But what about serious drama? If someone
looking at a tragedy asked: is all this true? the answer could
only be in the negative. But does that mean that it is all a
lie? Certainly not. The standard of truth and falsehood which
was appropriate to the epic is wholly out of place here. A
new perspective of reality appears to be in the making.

During the early days of tragedy this change in the relation
between artefact and reality is noticeable also in the products
of Athenian art. B. Schweitzer[6] has drawn our attention to
the fact that in the statuary inscriptions of the early period
the image is quite simply identified with the person portrayed:
the statue is the man. Thus we may read on a figure: 'I am
Chares, the ruler of Teichiousa'. In Attica, however, the
usual phrasing is: 'I am the image, the grave stele, or the
memorial stone of such and such a man.' Here we have proof
that in Athens the work of art is no longer naively declared
to be one with the model. That means that the visual arts
are conceived as a sphere apart; art, instead of being identical
with reality, dissociates itself from its domain. It imitates
reality, represents it, signifies it—and thereby becomes a
different sort of reality itself. The process is the same as in
the realm of tragedy; it is not until art has broken with
reality that we get an expansion of the circle of subjects, a
freer variation of themes. Not until this moment was art
able to unfold itself without impediment. On the other hand
—and again the parallel with tragedy is obvious—sculpture
needed to travel a long way before it reached its objective
of totally unhampered invention. For, to repeat ourselves,
serious art may no longer be interested in portraying reality,
but neither does it lie. Although the myths of tragedy
gradually turn into a jungle of new plots, the 'play' at first
retains as much as possible of the ancient 'reality'; it retains a
certain proximity to fact, and therein it differs from the
sailors' yarns and from comedy. It would be difficult to say
why the writers should have been so serious about their task
unless their efforts were aimed at a reality of some sort.

Perhaps one might even say that both tragedy and art need to pass through this emancipation to attain the real, for in literature as well as in sculpture and painting a straight path leads from this decisive break to realism. The new concept of reality which is thus brought into the world is not easily understood. It is an embarrassing fact that we are no longer able to apply to the arts such terms as 'true' and 'real' without running into complications. Now, if we wish to designate the relationship between artefact and reality we must resort to terms as vague and shifting as: the work of art should be 'appropriate' to, or 'commensurate with' reality.

Should we suspect that this idea of the 'real' is one which can be communicated *only* through play-acting? Tragedy, unlike earlier types of poetry, is not so much interested in events, whose representation may be either true or false, but in human beings. They appear in a completely new light. To comprehend the revolutionary change which the interpretation of man has undergone in tragedy we might profit from a comparison not with choral poetry but with the personal lyric of the early period in which men discuss their own selves, just as in tragedy they express their individual feelings, thoughts and desires.

A happy chance has preserved for us an early drama by Aeschylus. I call it a happy chance, because for centuries one and only one manuscript which contained the play was in existence. The play was composed in the nineties of the fifth century, about one-and-a-half decades before the battle of Salamis. It therefore belongs to the pre-classical, the archaic age. It still consists principally of choral odes, and for long stretches it is more akin to a cantata than to a drama. The chorus is formed by the daughters of Danaus; with their father they are on their way from Egypt to Argos, fleeing from their cousins the sons of Aegyptus who want to force them into marriage. Upon their landing in Greece they hope to find shelter in Argos, the home of their ancestress Io. She had been loved by Zeus and pursued by the jealous Hera; in the end she rested in Egypt to give birth to a scion of Zeus who was to be the grandfather of Danaus and Aegyptus, and the great-grandfather of the Danaids and the Egyptians. The chorus of the Danaids enters the stage with a frightened prayer to Zeus to afford them the protection which is due to defenceless strangers. Trembling with fear they lament their misfortunes.

Pelasgus, the king of Argos, comes in and inquires what they wish. When they demand protection from him, he immediately knows that this means war with the Egyptians for his city; but at the same time he realizes that he may deny shelter to the suppliants only at the cost of incurring the wrath of Zeus. In their panic the maidens threaten to take their own lives at the altar should the king fail to protect them: a terrible stain would thus be imposed on the city. The king resolves to intercede on behalf of the suppliants and goes off to the city in order to present the case to his people. After a prayer of the chorus Pelasgus returns and announces that the citizens have voted to grant the desired safeguard.

The choral songs of this tragedy are sustained by *phobos*, fear, a motif which is by no means peculiar to this early Aeschylean tragedy. For although our knowledge of the plays by Phrynichus, the predecessor of Aeschylus, is very sketchy, from the little that has come down to us we are able to conclude that he too used songs of fear and lamentation as key-elements in his plays. Both Aeschylus and Phrynichus made a special effort to create an air of passion and near-hysteria by means of female choruses and oriental indulgence.

Helplessness is a fundamental motif in the early Greek personal lyric; under its pressure the early lyrist was induced to describe his inner life, his soul, the depth of his sensations. It is one of the achievements of the tragic chorus that it emphasized this helplessness. Its song pierces the heart with an even shriller sound, for Phrynichus and Aeschylus have chosen to treat not merely disappointed expectations, suffering and resignation, but the central topic of life and death. The reason for this increase in emotional intensity is of course in part that pointed situations such as make up the stuff of tragedy are inaccessible to the lyric writer. The lyrists sing of the distress which comes to them from their own experience of reality; should this distress become so poignant that their very lives are endangered, they would cease to write poetry. Again, the dramatic projections of fear and suffering are much harsher than anything that the epic has to offer, for in a drama we are directly confronted with a human being in sorrow. Literature, when reduced to play, has often gained in seriousness. Nor does the chorus, oppressed with suffering, find the solace which enabled the archaic lyrists to rise above their grief—the thought that man's life alternates between joy and sorrow in conformity with an eternal cosmic rhythm. At a moment when life itself is likely to be blotted out any prospect of things changing for the better is automatically eliminated. In drama the nearness to death on which the lyrics brood acquires a greater degree of reality than in poetry, because certain realities cannot be represented as human experiences unless reality is left behind. But the fear of the tragic chorus differs from the helplessness of the lyric poet in more than just the degree of its intensity: it appears that Aeschylus introduces an innovation, which sets him apart also from Phrynichus.

The Danaids are weak maidens. Because the sons of Aegyptus insist on infringing their rights with brutal force, the chorus elicits far more than the share of sympathy which the choruses of Phrynichus could call forth, far more than the emotional interest and compassion which the lyric was able to rouse; for an infraction of justice offends the audience much more acutely than sorrow or misfortune. Aeschylus dramatizes an incident which should not be permitted to happen, an event which ought to be erased from history if our faith in the order of the world is not to be shaken: an event which cries for active intervention. Like other misfortunes, this mishap also challenges a man to reflect upon his soul and to sound it, and to find something in himself which transcends the merely personal. But it is not enough merely to uncover or to acknowledge this spiritual fact, to appraise it and to call it justice: here knowledge demands action.

This action is realized in Aeschylus's *Suppliants*, and thus the play ceases to be a lyrical cantata and becomes a tragedy. When the chorus of the Danaids urge Pelasgus to help them, and threaten suicide, the king says:

> Now we must think deeply about salvation, as a diver descends
> to the depth, his eyes firmly fixed, and with sober mind.

For a moment Pelasgus stands sunk in thought. Meanwhile the chorus sings the verses: 'Think, and become our protector, reverent as justice bids,' words which with the force of hammer blows impress upon him the necessity of a decision. When the king has ended his soul-searching, he sets out for the city to obtain a verdict from the people. It is true that the scene does not contribute a great deal to the action, but Aeschylus has given it all the grandeur which his style could furnish. There is, consequently, a discrepancy between the solemnity of his diction and the meagreness of actual results which could easily appear ridiculous—one is even reminded of scenes from *Punch and Judy*; but we must keep in mind the novelty of the whole enterprise, and its fateful importance for the evolution of Greek, nay of European thought. Nowhere in early poetry does a man go through a similar struggle to arrive at a decision, nowhere does he, as in this scene, reflect 'downward into the depth' of his soul in order to make up his mind. For the first time in literature someone toils hard for the sake of responsibility and justice, for the purpose of warding off evil. This is the birth of concepts destined to lie at the heart of all drama thereafter, concepts which have become increasingly important even outside the province of tragedy. In this scene the tragic situation of the chorus, the fact that justice suffers injustice, is made to bear significant fruit; the shocking calamity in which the maidens find themselves is created for the express purpose of prompting deliberate action. The plot is so contrived that Pelasgus stands between two claims: he is to choose between the welfare of the city and the rightful demands of the suppliants. He is forced back upon his own thinking; he must decide for himself which is the greater claim, the claim of justice. What little we know of the tragedies of Phrynichus indicates that a dilemma of this nature, obvious and necessary as it seems to us—at least it makes a direct appeal to our imagination—did not yet have a place in his work. In the two tragedies with which we associate his name the catastrophe broke in the course of the action, and all the chorus could do was to greet the disaster with songs of trepidation and wailing. A saving act was not envisaged, nor did the question of justice come up for discussion; the spectators were never roused beyond a feeling of compassion, the same response which the archaic lyric had called forth. It is true, of course, that the concrete acting out of the tragic events must have touched the hearts of the audience to the quick.

Pelasgus is strongly contrasted with the barbarism of the Egyptians, and also with the oriental excitability of the Danaids. He is a Greek, moderate and rational. In the other Aeschylean tragedies the contrast between non-Greeks and Greeks is likewise formulated as a struggle between excess, mannerisms, gaudiness on the one hand and modesty and frankness on the other. This contrast is partially connected with the change of style toward the classical ideal; the exuberance of the archaic age gives way to simplicity and even severity. Aeschylus's concentration upon Greek values, therefore, involves a consciousness of the difference, not only between the West and the Orient, but also between his own present and the immediate past. He recaptures the essence of the ancient Greek spirit. His new achievements, the emphasis upon self-reliance, and the grand simplicity of independent action, take the form of a return to a basic Greek heritage.

The Homeric scenes in which a man deliberates what he ought to do are deficient in one distinctive feature which makes the decision of Pelasgus what it is: a wholly independent and private act. In Aeschylus, the hero's choice becomes a problem whose solution is contingent on nothing but his own insight, but which is nevertheless regarded as a matter of compelling necessity. Homer's scenes of reflection and resolution are usually cast in a stereotype form. A man speculates whether he ought to do this or that; finally, when he decides, the resolution may be described in one of two ways: either Homer says that it seemed better to the man to choose such and such a course, or we learn that a god intervened and directed the hero's decision. This is what usually happens in the *Iliad*. Sometimes—and this we find occasionally in the *Odyssey*—somebody else enters the scene and helps to bring about the choice. The formula: 'it seemed better to him' means literally: 'it seemed more profitable, more remunerative to him.' The decision is made on the grounds that one alternative is recognized as the more advantageous procedure. Evidently this has little to do with subjective choice, not to speak of an internal struggle. And where the final voice is given to a deity the decision is of course wholly determined from without.[7]

Aeschylus is at great pains to represent the characters in his tragedies as independent agents, acting upon the bidding

of their own hearts, instead of merely reacting to external
stimuli. This may be seen in another play which has recently
been found, together with the satyr plays mentioned above:
the *Myrmidons*. The papyrus fragment which we have is
the first to acquaint us with an Aeschylean tragedy in which
the poet dramatizes a Homeric subject.

Achilles is angry at Agamemnon and stays away from the
battle. As a result the Trojans succeed in defeating the
Greeks and advance to the line of the ships. In the scene
which has been preserved Nestor's ship has already caught
fire and Antilochus, son of Nestor, has been sent to Achilles
to ask him to renounce his resentment and to re-join the fight.
Meanwhile the followers of Achilles, the Myrmidons, have
risen against their prince, charging him with treason if he
should continue to absent himself from the battle. They
actually threaten to stone him to death, which is the customary punishment for treason. Aeschylus was the first to
introduce this motif into the story, and when it came to light
in the new papyrus the reaction of scholars everywhere was
one of great surprise. The extant conversation between
Achilles and Antilochus suggests the reason why Aeschylus
invented the threat of the Myrmidons: it induces Achilles to
harden his heart even more against helping the Greeks. Is
he to give in 'from fear of the Achaeans?' Are they accusing
him of treason who is more distinguished, and has achieved
greater honours, than all other princes taken together? Thus
Aeschylus sees to it that Achilles resolutely, and deliberately,
persists in his retirement from the war. In the epic his
wrath toward Agamemnon which alone motivates his in-
activity is, as has justly been said, like a strange force attacking
him against whose superior strength he has no means of
defending himself.[8] Aeschylus, on the other hand, shapes the
action in such a way that Achilles' return to the battle is
prevented by causes which lie entirely within himself; he
remains in his tent because of his own wilful determination.

We know that in the end Aeschylus had Achilles go forth
to avenge the fallen Patroclus, a step which won him glory
and an early death, in the place of a long but undistinguished
career. Even before the papyrus was found it had been suspected that Aeschylus here represented a choice, a deliberate
act of decision on the part of Achilles, and that Aeschylus

must have been the inventor of this famous motif. For Homer does not yet speak of such a dilemma; his Achilles merely knows that it is his fate either to die as a young man in a blaze of glory, or to live a long and obscure life. But Plato later gives us to understand that Achilles intentionally elected the more heroic alternative. In the plays of Aeschylus, as we learn from the words of Pelasgus and many others, personal decision is a central theme. Since the new scene of the *Myrmidons* shows us that even at the beginning of the trilogy Achilles acts with deliberate intent, we are now fully entitled to expect the same psychology also at the climax of the tragedy, during the crucial moment in the life of Achilles. In all likelihood this great decision occurred in the second part of the trilogy when Achilles goes back into the fray. In the third part, when Priam arrives to seek the corpse of his son Hector, we may presume that Achilles' heart was heavy with the knowledge of his imminent death, and that this knowledge gave to his reconciliation with Priam a majesty all its own. In my mind, at any rate, there is no doubt that Aeschylus put the finishing touches on the character of Achilles which has remained authoritative to the present day.[9]

It was Aristotle who first said that the *Iliad* provided material for no more than one tragedy. Aeschylus who exploited the wealth of its subject-matter for a single trilogy was constrained to narrow down the broad and unhurried stream of its incidents. Tragedy must dispense with all the detail, minute and yet significant, which naturally grows out of the plot, and which Homer may arrange and fit in at his own leisure. In order to bring everything into line with the one great deed of Achilles, Aeschylus suppresses a good many of the manoeuvres whereby Homer had carefully prepared us for the momentous turnabout of Achilles. Homer allows us to tarry and watch Achilles slowly but irrevocably glide into his fate; Aeschylus hurries the plot, and in addition he devises new motifs such as the stoning. Fully conscious of the implications of his stand Achilles persists in his defiance; and so when finally he puts an end to his stubborn dissent and decides to resume the fighting, his change of mind is more than just another turn in the dramatic plot. The difficulty of his decision is increased by the actions of his mother Thetis who appeared in the second part of the trilogy and, though bringing him his new weapons, warned him not to go into the battle since it would mean his early death. No doubt Aeschylus stressed this motif also over and beyond the treatment it had received in the epic. It must be admitted that the strong emphasis which Aeschylus places upon the act of Achilles to some degree detracts from its probability. How often does it happen that a man is knowingly confronted with such an alternative, either to die a glorious death or to live a long life, and that his choice of death is made so difficult for him to boot ? It is only fair to acknowledge that other Aeschylean scenes too have something exaggerated and unnatural about their crises. Pelasgus is forced to determine the fate of the suppliants and the fortunes of his city, both at one and the same time. Orestes undertakes the gruesome obligation of killing his mother. Does not tragedy by its nature rest upon such scenes of excess, upon parricide, the murder of children, the killing of brothers, and incest?

Aeschylus presents these pointed situations because he is less interested in what happens than in what is done, and because he feels that the essence of human action is to be found in the act of decision. A chemist combines in his test-tube several substances which are rarely or never found together in nature, in order to form a clear and precise idea of their reactions. Likewise the dramatist constructs his actions with a view to isolating the quintessence of action.[10]

Tragedy is not a faithful mirror of the incidents of myth; instead of accepting them as historical reality, as they are accepted in the epic, tragedy traces the ultimate causes in the actions of men, and consequently often pays but little attention to concrete facts. Nor does early tragedy strive to recreate the reality of everyday life in poetic terms. The writers are totally unprepared to undertake a lucid revelation of patterns and causes of behaviour. Aeschylus was the first to show clearly that when a man acted some mental process was involved, and as is usually the case with fundamental discoveries, he started out by greatly emphasizing the essentials of the process. By using the artificial situations of his tragedy he tried to uncover, as clearly as he could, the hard core of human action. Under ordinary circumstances, in the confusion of real life, a thousand motifs are intertwined;

of the basic form of genuine action, i.e. the free decision, only a pale reflexion rises to the surface. But tragedy has the power to construct such an archetye of action; it does so by placing a man half way between two claims almost equal in urgency, and having him choose the noble alternative of death, in full view of the commands of justice and fate.

To be sure, the epic does not indiscriminately reproduce all the features of a myth; the lyric also says only what is significant. But tragedy, in underscoring certain themes, differs fundamentally from the other genres because its concept of what is essential—and that means also, of reality —is not the same as before.

Since, as we have seen, action is stripped of its accidentals and featured in its purest form, the implication seems to be that what is regarded as reality exists only in thought, as an idea. Action in the specific sense in which Aeschylus understands it is an ideal situation. It involves not merely the reaction to a previous fact, but also a commitment for the future. Decision, justice, doom, all those notions which are of the utmost importance for Aeschylus as well as for subsequent tragedy, impinge most compellingly upon a man's mind when he is about to act. The weight of responsibility is felt fully only in the face of action. Pure justice exists only as an objective, or in the will to act; when a deed has already become a fact and belongs to the past, it always admits of a variety of explanations. Finally it goes without saying that the fear of doom is oriented solely toward the future. Action of this sort, however, which is yet in the process of being realized cannot claim to be an empirical fact; it can be grapsed only through an ideal situation. Characteristically enough the motif of stoning which Aeschylus introduces does not further the action of Achilles but militates against it. It is invented to render his choice of the noble alternative more difficult than ever. The noble has no cause, it is teleologically determined by its goal; causes come into play only to block or embarrass the noble choice.

Pelasgus, Achilles, Eteocles, Orestes, all the Aeschylean heroes cannot be made to swerve from their course of action, however powerful the motives operating against it may be. It might be argued that their situations, artificial and laboured as they are, have no meaning for a normal and inoffensive human being. And yet, the man who feels free to do what is just will find in these figures of the stage models for his own life, and will read their actions as ideal formulations of his own hopes and aspirations. For here we have, in its clearest and most typical form, an exposition of what happens to a man who makes a crucial choice. A tragedy offers no scope for dividing the world into two levels, one producing the values by which the other operates. The characters of Aeschylean tragedy are no longer protected by the gods' heavenly radiance which suffuses the things of this world with its lustre and makes them significant. No, man himself controls the significance of what happens, in accordance with his personal understanding of the principles of justice. When Homer makes the meaning of human events depend upon the actions and the words of the gods, these words and deeds are facts and may thus be objectively described; and if he reports them in keeping with the truth, the listener who shares the poet's belief in the reality and function of the gods immediately perceives the significance of the events related. The heroes approach the splendid majesty of the gods with unquestioning simplicity, with the result that they experience no difficulty if there is anything noble or gentle which they wish to say or do. Homeric man is sheltered by a world without blemish, which speaks to him in unambiguous terms, and to which he replies in the same manner. His deity is transcendent, for it is greater than man; but its nature is fixed and its existence permanent since it is independent of man's understanding.

When we turn to Aeschylus, the world of the gods has become a more complex matter. In the *Oresteia*, two deities address their claims to Orestes, Apollo who orders matricide, and the Erinyes who will punish him for it. Under the burden of this twofold ordinance from the gods, man stands all alone. Even though Athena at the close of the *Eumenides* restores the balance, we have travelled a long way from the unencumbered simplicity of Homer. And though the Zeus of Aeschylus is an unassailable guardian of justice, he has retired to a plane high above the world of pressing realities. Instead of guiding the course of events through his actions or his words, he has as it were attained to the status of an ideal: Zeus and the idea of justice are about to merge into one.

Now that man has been made to shift for himself, justice still provides him with a firm foothold, at least in the work of Aeschylus. All the same it is impossible not to notice that this same freedom may also turn into a burden which will gradually wear him down. The deity speaks from a greater distance; man begins to ponder the mystery of the divine, and the more independent he makes himself, the more isolated he becomes. The characters of Sophocles' plays are already lonelier than those of Aeschylus. Oedipus, Antigone, and Ajax are, like their predecessors on the stage, conceived as 'acting' men; they act in accord with definite ideas of their own—but in the Sophoclean context that means that they act in deliberate opposition to the world around them. In the end action turns into self-destruction.

Euripides' characters continue the process of detaching themselves from the ensemble of the old world order. With growing concern the poet attempts to understand those matters which Aeschylus had declared to be the great realities: the human spirit, the idea, the motives of action. The brightly shining world of the heroes, with its splendid deeds, its radiant glory and all its other eye-filling qualities has lost its visual appeal; the new questions, such as: what induced them to act? was their action just? have nothing aesthetically pleasing about them. And because Euripides conducts his inquiry of human motives with a growing perception of the gulf between Being and Appearance, only a faint trace of the ancient splendour is likely to remain.

Being and Appearance had first been distinguished by the archaic lyrists who recognized that qualities of the soul are more essential than external values; they had, however, not yet taken the additional step of applying this distinction to human action and its motivation in particular. The philosophers also had learned to differentiate between Being and Semblance; but the new concept of Reality which thus emerged was valid for an appraisal of the external world of the senses rather than for the discussion of spritual and intellectual problems. They sought to locate Being in the stream of Becoming, to find a constant and essential verity behind the 'mere Appearance', and produced a Reality which transcended the senses, intelligible only through the mind.

A connexion between the notion of Being and that of
Justice may be found as early as Aeschlyus; conversely he
links Appearance with *hybris*. In the *Seven Against Thebes*,
for example, the enemies of Thebes betray their sinful
arrogance with a show of boastful insignia, while the one
whose thought is just would 'rather be more than seem'. In
the days of Euripides this contrast begins to make itself felt
in various ways, by way of a criticism of knowledge, or of
myths, or of morality. It determines his whole orientation
of thought, and even his attitude towards what we would call
'reality', in the most superficial sense of the word, is influenced
by that distinction.

We should not be surprised that Euripides has but little
respect for the material value of things, and that wealth means
nothing to him. These 'external' values had already been set
aside by the older lyrists. But Euripides has completely lost
all capacity for the sensuous enjoyment of display and riches
for which archaic poetry had been noted to the very last. If
brilliant finery and regal array were typical of Aeschylus, the
characters of Euripides are distinguished by rags. The drab
working day has become more real than solemn ostentation.
Apart from empiricist notions of philosophy we may detect
in this attitude also the influence of a social scepticism; this
in itself is of course striking proof that fifth century Athens
has ceased to put its faith in a deity which manifests itself
in the splendour of appearances. Euripides' social views also
add to our impression that considerations of justice increasingly determine the search for the greatest reality. Another
point: in Aeschylus the stage-props very nearly become co-
actors in the tragedy. We would say that the murder-axe of
the *Agamemnon* or the carpet on which the returned king
steps are symbols, and it is true that under this flag certain
meaningful adjuncts have made their way into modern
drama too. But in the mind of Aeschylus there is not yet
room for such a derivative category; for him these things
have a direct significance: they are half alive. Now it is only
to be expected that those who are in possession of the new
concept of reality must regard the Aeschylean stage as a
scene of unnatural sorcery. Objects are dead, and only man
can act.

The new discoveries become most effective in the interpretation and representation of human action. As the human soul is gradually acknowledged as the real seat of life, the projection of man's inner life increases in volume; because the reality of human existence is now largely associated with the soul of man, drama increasingly turns to the tracing of psychological motivations. The greatness of Euripides' achievement in exploring this area is universally appreciated. In his plays the human being is made to stand apart from the variegated tapestry of divine and earthly forces, and instead becomes himself the point whence actions and achievements take their origin. His own passions and his own knowledge are the only determining factors; all else is deception and Semblance. But who is to probe the depth of this human nature? Who is capable of sinking the plumb-line into his own soul? Knowledge of man and knowledge of self become the chief tasks of reflection, just as knowledge of nature becomes the business of research. Reality is no longer something that is simply given. The meaningful no longer impresses itself as an incontrovertible fact, and appearances have ceased to reveal their significance directly to man. All this really means that myth has come to an end. The poet is no more inescapably confronted with vital and real figures, with their peculiarities clearly defined and the significance of their deeds fixed. And so Euripides feels called upon to instil fresh life into the figures, to make them credible once more. Any arbitrary reinterpretation of the story was furthest from his mind; most likely he thought that his best chance of recapturing its essential substance lay in an analysis of its mental and psychological motivation.

His is a logical continuation of what Aeschylus had begun. The reality which constitutes the artistic goal of tragedy resides in the realm of the mind; in order to emphasize this truth Euripides is compelled to go even further than those before him in stylizing events and stripping them of their accidentals. Like Aeschylus he creates exaggerated situations which build up to a climax of decision and action; but with a view to investing them with a more natural colour he places them in a more realistic setting and garnishes them with intricate psychological motives. Again, as in the case of Aeschylus, the isolation of certain types of action in their purest form causes Euripides to resort to 'play', i.e. to an artistic reality which is far removed from factual reality. It may even be said that factual reality furnishes later tragedy, close as it seems to the ordinary world by comparison with Phrynichus and Aeschylus, with even less material than before. Attempts to write historical tragedy were early abandoned by the Greeks, since history was less susceptible to intellectual elaboration, and to play, than myth. Thus myth remained the proper domain of artistic reality, particularly after myth had lost its standing as factual reality.

In tragedy myth severed its connexion with a particular concrete situation. The human situations which it expresses are no longer, as in the archaic lyric, fixed in time and place by victory, marriage, or cult; they are universal situations. It is evident that this broadening of the perspective marks a tendency toward philosophical generalization. Before long the problem of human action which is the concern of tragedy was to become a matter for intellectual cognition; Socrates insists on solving the problem through knowledge of the good. That is the ultimate abstraction of the real, its transformation into a teleological concept. Where a divine world had endowed the human world with meaning, we now find the universal determining the particular. Euripides has not yet reached that stage; he is a poet and not a philosopher; he perceives reality in terms of living shapes, not as concepts. But his work shows us how to interpret Aristotle's word: that poetry is more philosophical than history.

CHAPTER 6

ARISTOPHANES AND AESTHETIC CRITICISM

IN the year 406 B.C., immediately after the death of Sophocles and Euripides, Aristophanes in one of his most impressive comedies made the astonishingly correct prediction that tragedy had died with them. And indeed tragedy lay dead for about two thousand years. In his play, the *Frogs*, Aristophanes also tells us what, in his opinion, caused tragedy to expire. At the end of the comedy, the chorus sings:

> Right it is and befitting
> Not, by Socrates sitting,
> Idle talk to pursue,
> Stripping tragedy-art of
> All things noble and true.[1]

The art had in fact been stripped of its very existence, and it cannot be denied that philosophy was responsible for its destruction. Of this Aristophanes, with his extraordinary insight, was fully aware. Socrates whose name he mentions in this connexion was the most prosaic of all Greeks. Only as a very old man, when shortly before his death he made a last conscientious appraisal of his life, he tried his hand at the writing of verse, much as if he wished to fill a gap in the sum total of his experience before the end overtook him. Socrates managed to side-track the young Plato from the composing of tragedies, and to make him into a philosopher and a writer of prose. But the poet whom Aristophanes has in mind when he describes him as sitting by Socrates and spelling the ruin of tragedy is Euripides. The plot of the *Frogs* leads us into the underworld, where we come upon Euripides engaging in a mighty contest against Aeschylus for the place of honour among poets. In a mixture of burlesque and grandiose exaggeration Aeschylus appears as a crude unsophisticated bard, heroic and belligerent, of whom it is said (822 ff.):

> There will his shaggy-born crest upbristle for anger and woe,
> Horribly frowning and growling, his fury will launch at the foe
> Huge-clamped masses of words, with exertion Titanic uptearing
> Great ship-timber planks for the fray.

But Euripides who peopled his stage with beggars and strumpets knows how to defend himself (826 ff.):

> But here will the tongue be at work, uncoiling, word-testing, refining,
> Sophist-creator of phrases, dissecting, detracting, maligning,
> Shaking the envious bits, and with subtle analysis paring
> The lung's large labour away.

The criticism which Aristophanes levels against Euripides is for the most part rather superficial; in no other fashion could his comedies have managed to reach the Attic theatregoer and shake him out of his inertia. He does not flinch from inventing the most infamous allegations, and summarily condemns everything *modern*. Innovators and reformers of diverse loyalties are shown in his plays as a promiscuous band of gossips, knaves, and corrupters of young men. Whatever the differences between Euripides, Socrates, and the Sophists, in Aristophanes they are indistinguishable; their only activity consists in cleverly lining their pockets through the teaching of various tricks which are destined to wreck the healthy morality of the solid Athenian citizen, and to subvert the traditional structure of the State.

Aristophanes was unable to save the young generation. The best of them sat with Socrates, and while he was, in the eleventh hour, sensible of a void in his life, they were no longer troubled by such thoughts. Disregarding a handful of well-meaning dilettanti and a few vain virtuosos, the year in which the *Frogs* had its premiere became the turning-point after which the Greeks ceased to write stately verse. For one whole century prose reigned supreme. Plato, Aristotle, Theophrastus, Epicurus write their philosophical works, and Isocrates and Demosthenes lead oratory to its glorious heights. The only poetry of the fourth century which exerted an influence upon subsequent generations was the New Comedy, the bourgeois comedy of manners which Menander and his associates put on the stage, and which was far removed from that sublime poetic ideal for whose return Aristophanes clamoured.

And yet, though the further development of poetry ran counter to the wishes and inclinations of Aristophanes, the ideas which he offered in the *Frogs* did not fall on sterile ground. They continued to live, albeit in a sense which

Aristophanes did not desire, or even deem possible. Not poetry itself, but the judging of poetry, and aesthetic discussion, were affected by his pronouncements; even to-day's literary criticism is indebted to his influence. Some time passed, however, before the fundamental significance of his remarks was appreciated, and it was not until very much later that his peculiar orientation met with its share of approval.

There is some doubt how many of the ideas which are of interest to us here were formulated by Aristophanes himself, and which are the views of his contemporaries, or perhaps even the common heritage of his age.[2] For myself I am inclined to believe that the personal contribution of Aristophanes in these matters was very substantial.

In his earliest dialogues Plato uses certain phrases which remind us of the *Frogs*. In the *Gorgias*, for instance (501 ff.), it is taken for granted that tragedy aims only at the gratification of pleasure (*hedone*), and it is therefore characterized as an adulatory art (*kolakeia*) whose objective cannot be genuine virtue (*arete*). Here Plato echoes Aristophanes, though naturally he modifies his thought. Both of them measure tragedy by the standard of morality. This moralization of poetry we owe to Aristophanes; its first exposition as a doctrine, as a deliberate programme, occurs in the *Frogs*. Even in his earlier plays he holds Euripides up to ridicule, but it is in his *Frogs* that his criticism becomes a matter of principle. He accuses him of corrupting the Athenians, poisoning the patriotic spirit of the citizenry, and advancing the cause of immorality. The long dead Aeschylus, solemn and respected, is introduced for the sake of contrast. He had answered to a moral demand: that genuine poetry make better men of us (1008 ff.). The Sophists also claimed to be able to make men better, but according to the view of Aristophanes they merely corrupted the youth. This judgment he transfers to Euripides; as he expresses it in the *Frogs*, it is the task of poetry to make men into valiant and useful citizens, but Euripides served to dissipate and destroy them. Aristophanes found it easy to equate the poets and the Sophists for the reason that the latter themselves, forced to canvass the public under a cloak of moderation and respectability, sought to connect their programme of adult education with the training given to the young. The children were taught from the writings of Homer, Hesiod, Orpheus and Musaeus; these were the writers, Hippias says in the introduction to one of his treatises (fr. 6), whose teachings it was necessary to summarize, to deepen, and to expand. We may assume, of course, that elsewhere he mentioned other writers in addition to the four.[3]

Hippias, to be sure, does not yet regard it as the fundamental purpose or the chief function of the poets that they make men better. This version of the idea is coined by Aristophanes: the poets were teachers—Orpheus of the mysteries and rites, Musaeus of medicine and oracles, Hesiod of agriculture, the divine Homer of honour and glory (1032 ff.) —and for adults they still play the same role as the schoolmaster does for the children (1055). Even to-day Aristophanes is the key witness of those who hold that education is the basic concern of the arts, and of all culture in general. Plato makes this moral precept his own; his appointment of Socrates to be the judge of what is good would no doubt have startled Aristophanes. Against this philosophical axiom Plato, in the *Gorgias*, sets the empirical finding that tragedy merely appeals to the pleasure of the senses (*hedone*);[4] with that he opens the door to endless discussions which via Horace continue well into the eighteenth century: the debate whether the proper task of poetry is *prodesse* or *delectare*, to profit or to please.

When Plato, with the moralization of poetry as his point of departure, eventually bans all poetic art from his State, he simply accepts the consequences of those ideas which first emerge in the *Gorgias*. Obviously Aristophanes is under no such constraint; he has no desire to preach a gospel of aesthetics, but merely to set off against a superior foil the poetry which he has come to hate. He chooses the charge of immorality because it is ruder and more effective than most others. It is evident, therefore, that Plato could not abstract a true theory of art from the *Frogs*. All he could get from it were certain hints and suggestions. Nor does Aristotle, in his *Poetics*, pay specific attention to the play.[5] Years passed before the theorists began to take note of a distinction which Aristophanes had made to bring into sharp focus the contrast between Aeschylus and Euripides.

At the beginning of the Hellenistic age the century of prose gives way to a new type of poetic art which is if possible even more foreign to the sublime aspirations of Aristophanes than the comedy of Menander. It is an art founded on taste and wit, and it tries its utmost to avoid the suspicion of dramatic pathos. Callimachus, the leader of the Alexandrian poets, expressly refuses to 'thunder like Zeus' (*Aetia* 1.1.20). When he says further that he seeks 'delicacy' (*lepton*: 1.1.24) he uses terms which Aristophanes had employed in the *Frogs*. There Aeschylus is the one who 'thunders' (814) while Euripides 'minces delicate words' (829, 876; cf. also 1108, 1111). Aristophanes derived his criteria of poetry from the greatness and might of Aeschylus, and in order to measure the 'magnitude' of the poet, he had humorously arranged for the bringing in of measuring rods and rulers (799). Callimachus, in contrast, deliberately forgoes the grand style of the ancient poets and scoffs at the new writers who hope to recapture the forms of the past. Nor is he interested in external 'magnitude'; he wants his verses measured by their art, not by the Persian mile (*Aetia* 1.1.17). Aristophanes makes his Euripides pride himself—the comedian himself would of course chide him for it—on having reduced, 'made lean' (*ischnos*: 940), the swollen art of Aeschylus. Callimachus confesses (*Aetia* 1.1.23) that Apollo advised him in the early stages of his writing: 'A sacrifice ought to be as fat as possible, but a poem should be tender and delicate.' This distinction of Callimachus, an exact reversal of the notions of Aristophanes on which it is no doubt modelled, acquired great importance for the programme of Hellenistic poetry. More particularly the Roman poets defended their delicate, highly limited art by pointing to the formula of Callimachus, whenever they were reminded not to neglect the ampler dimensions of the epic. In some Roman quarters the Callimachean distinction between delicate and grandiose poetry was in practice confounded with Aristotle's discrimination between the various forms of life, the *bioi*; consequently the renunciation of grand poetry was identified with the withdrawal from the active life of a soldier or a politician, while the cultivation of the delicate style was held the equivalent of a life of artistic sensibility (cf. Tibullus 1.1; Propertius 2.1). Such developments may be traced back to Aristophanes, though their distance from him is great. Similarly in the field of rhetoric Aristophanes is the source whence the genres of diction, the grand and the simple, were originally obtained.

For many centuries the principal design of Aristophanes failed to enlist supporters; no one was interested in his attacks upon Euripides. The tragedian who seemed so enigmatic to his own age, who experienced one disappointment after another in his struggle for recognition, was in the fourth century celebrated as the classical exponent of drama, and thereafter occupied the throne while Aeschylus was almost forgotten. It is true that in the days of Aristophanes Aeschylean plays were once more admitted to the stage; his voice speaks to us through that last exaltation of the pathetic style of which we have any knowledge, the *Persians* of Timotheus. But despite the position which Aeschylus gained in general education, his direct impact upon writing came to a halt.

Euripides, on the other hand, surpasses the other two tragedians by the influence which he brought to bear upon our culture throughout Roman times, and which has again become a potent force since the Renaissance. Until Lessing it was he who was regarded as the pinnacle of Greek tragic poetry. Then came Herder who looked for the essence of poetry in its popular character, its elemental power, its divine spark, and so the evaluation of the Greek dramatists was once more reversed. His hero was Aeschylus whose choral odes he was the first to re-read with ardent enthusiasm; he worshipped him as the untutored genius through whom the unbroken vigour of the spirit of the people had found its voice. This paves the way for a new conception of the origin and decline of Greek tragedy. Previously it had been the custom to trace a gradual unfolding of the dramatic form, an ever closer approximation to its ultimate perfection, or, to use Aristotle's terms, the fulfilment of its own nature. Instead it became the fashion to lament the tragedy of Euripides as the final corruption of an art whose pristine vitality was divinely inspired. No doubt about it, here we have the reappearance of ideas with which we had become acquainted in the *Frogs*, and in fact August Wilhelm Schlegel, the man who was chiefly responsible for propagating this thesis, makes direct use of Aristophanes' comedy.

In the year 1808 Schlegel gave a course of lectures on

dramatic art and literature. He admitted that he could not but censure Euripides severely for his many shortcomings, and particularly for his 'ethical non-conformism'. 'He makes no effort to demonstrate the immense superiority of the heroic age over the men of his own day. On the contrary he strives to fill in, or bridge the gulf between his contemporaries and that wonderful generation of old, and to spy upon the gods and heroes in their nightshirts, a method of observation against which not even the greatest are said to be immune.' 'Euripides elects to remind his spectators again and again: look, those giants were men, they had the same weaknesses, and were actuated by the same impulses, as the least among you. Consequently he loves to depict in detail the foibles and the moral imperfections of his characters; more than that, he dramatizes them by means of naive confessions on the part of the characters themselves. They are not merely vulgar, but they boast of their vulgarity as if it were a necessity.' 'Let us distinguish in him two different personalities: the poet whose creations were dedicated to a solemn religious occasion, who stood under the protection of religion and was therefore obliged to give it its due; and the sophist with his philosophical designs, seeking to expound his non-conformist views and doubts in the midst of the wonders and miracles of religion whence he drew the material of his plays. While shattering the very fundament of religion he acts the part of the moralist; to make himself popular with his audience he projects into the heroic age the fashions and social etiquette which were typical of his contemporaries.'

Schlegel's attitude towards Euripides may be put into three words: he indicts him on the charges of realism, rationalism, and immorality. These are the very charges which Aristophanes had flung at him. Schlegel himself shows clearly enough that his judgment was inspired by Aristophanes. The same notes are struck in Nietzsche's youthful pamphlet on the *Birth of Tragedy*. Because of the influence of Schopenhauer and Richard Wagner, Nietzsche often shifts his emphasis, or brings an argument into clearer focus. But his appraisal of Euripides is directly dependent upon Schlegel—though there are but few mentions of his name, and those polemical—and thus ultimately on Aristophanes. 'The feat on which Euripides in the *Frogs* of Aristophanes prides

himself, namely that with his household remedy he helped
the tragic Muse to lose some of her pompous corpulence, is
especially noticeable in his tragic heroes. Actually the
spectator saw no one on the Euripidean stage who was not
his own double, and he delighted in his own eloquence and
his cleverness.' 'Hitherto in tragedy the tone had been set
by the demigod, and in comedy by the inebriate satyr, i.e.
the demi-man. With Euripides the voice became that of
bourgeois mediocrity upon which basis he placed his political
hopes. And so the Euripides of the *Frogs* takes special pride
in having portrayed the common life, the well-known weekday activities which any one may understand and judge.
Moreover, he says, because of the wisdom with which he has
impregnated the people, everybody is able to philosophize,
to administer estates and to conduct law suits. . . As a poet
Euripides feels superior to the mob, but there are two members of his audience whom he respects. . . Of these two, one
is Euripides himself: Euripides the thinker, not the poet.
His critical gifts were extraordinarily developed, and it might
be said of him, as of Lessing, that his critical genius managed,
not to create, but at least to promote a secondary artistic
impulse. . . Euripides undertook to publicize the counterpart
of the 'unknowing' poet; his aesthetic tenet, viz. "only that
which is known is beautiful" runs parallel to that of Socrates:
"only that which is known is good". Thus we may regard
Euripides' aesthetic theory as Socratic in nature. And
Socrates was that other spectator; he did not understand the
older tragedy, and so he did not esteem it. Together with
him Euripides dared to come forth as the herald of the new
art. If Euripides was responsible for the death of ancient
tragedy, his Socratic attitude toward aesthetics supplied the
murder weapon. And in as much as the struggle was directed
against the Dionysiac element of the older art, Socrates, it
appears, was the enemy of Dionysus.'

Nietzsche, it is evident, repeats the same three accusations:
realism, rationalism, and moral corruption. The bias of
Schlegel is manifestly present in his words, but as we search
further we once more come upon Aristophanes. Especially
the comic writer's notion that anyone who sits by Socrates
ruins tragedy is poignantly developed by Nietzsche. He
differs from Schlegel in but one characteristic point: in his

view Socrates is not immoral, but very much of a moralist, and it is precisely because he is a moralist and a theorist that he paralyses and kills the sacred tradition. For Nietzsche morality is a corrosive poison.

During the last generation or two the discussion of aesthetic problems has been strongly affected by Nietzsche's early work. His criticism of Euripides in particular is of some importance to us, for it provided the impetus for the modern notion that poetry may corrupt. Earlier in this chapter we had been content to show that there was such a thing as an Aristophanic influence upon the discussion of aesthetics; the adoption of certain ideas and suggestions from him had been more or less superficial and, as it were, accidental. But now the scene has shifted; his basic views about Euripides have attained to the status of general truths. Euripides, as seen through the eyes of Aristophanes, has become the representative of decadent poetry as such; and for Nietzsche the rise and fall of Attic tragedy is the master sample of the rise and fall of great art in general. All this compels us to ask: what are the facts about this Aristophanic Euripides, with his alleged rationalism, his realism, and his destructive influence?

Herder and Schlegel and the scholars who turned scientific historians in the wake of the romantic revolt, revived the debate concerning the origins of tragedy because they were convinced that the great and vital forces were to be found long before the age of Socrates, and far removed from the intellectual climate for which he stands. Those who speak of the rise of tragedy devote their discussion almost exclusively to the irrational powers which were active in its creation. It has been shown how early tragedy was closely linked with the popular festival of the Dionysia in Athens, and that primitive religious concepts presided at its birth; fertility magic and ritual mummery produced the satyrs' choruses which formed the germ of tragedy. Nietzsche seeks the essence and the grandeur of early tragedy in the spirit of music and in the mythical forces to which he attaches the names Dionysiac and Apollonian. In such and similar attempts we perceive a fine sympathy with the elemental power of inchoate tragedy. Such a view, however, usually fails to take into account one rather important item. The popular character and the religious function of tragedy would never, by themselves, have sufficed to make tragedy what it is, to advance it beyond the stage of a masked procession such as may be found anywhere and at any time. For the popular religious festival which is so prominent among primitive societies to achieve the unique quality which has given Attic tragedy its importance far beyond its own time, something else was needed. This indispensable element which explains why we continue to occupy ourselves with tragedy is none other than the very principle in which Aristophanes discerned the undoing of tragedy. It is the Socratic 'knowledge', the element of reflexion. It attended at the birth of tragedy, and if we encounter it also at its demise, we should in all fairness refrain from crying 'murderer'.

Attic tragedy succeeded to the status of great literature because it was able to rise above its ancient cult foundation. The whole ghostly business of goat choruses and phallic processions receded before topics and problems which sprang from a totally different sphere. To be sure, Attic drama never turned profane, for almost without exception its subject-matter continued to be myth. But it was the type of myth which had been fashioned by the Homeric poets on the colonial soil of Asia Minor, far away from the sacred precincts of the mother country where cult and magic held their ground in primeval gloominess. In the poems of Homer god and man meet as free and amicable partners. The gods are the pilots of fate without throwing men into confusion or fear, without forcing them down on their knees before their invincible power. With eyes wide open men look out into a world of sense and clarity, a world in which the one who is alert and uses his reason fares best. We may even say that the Homeric poems establish the Greek, nay the European view that the world is a natural thing. Among primitive societies the 'natural' is unknown; Rousseau was mistaken when he thought he could find it there.

These natural gods and men of Homer made their entry into the Athenian orchestra when the myths which had first been moulded in non-dramatic literature were admitted to the choral performances of the Dionysiac festival. The way in which tragedy approaches the relationship between god and man differs from that of the Homeric epic in only one respect. But this one difference is all the more crucial: for the first time in history man begins to look at himself as the maker of his own decisions.

In Homer a man is unaware of the fact that he may think or act spontaneously, of his own volition and spirit. Whatever 'strikes' him, whatever 'thought comes' to him, is given from without, and if no visible external stimulus has affected him, he thinks that a god has stood by his side and given him counsel, either for his benefit or for his destruction. It follows that Homer's men act with perfect assurance, and that they do not know what it means to be burdened with scruples or doubts. Nor do they feel the weight of a personal responsibility for right or wrong. In the tragedies of Aeschylus, on the other hand, the agent, conscious of his individual freedom of choice, makes himself personally answerable for his actions. This is most clearly shown in Aeschylus' last tragedy, the *Oresteia*, which I would like to use here as an appropriate foil against which to understand the Euripidean problem under discussion.

Orestes is under an obligation to avenge his father; this means that he must slay his mother. He performs this deed only after experiencing the cruel difficulty of his decision to the full. This is the discovery of the contrast between freedom and fate, between duty and doom, a discord which sunders the world of men from that of the gods. Orestes stands between two divine commands, and in the last play of the trilogy the tragedy actually issues into a struggle between two hostile camps of gods, the Erinyes who desire to punish Orestes for the murder of his mother, and Apollo who eventually clears him of his guilt.

With two deities making irreconcilable claims on him, the human agent is forced to confine himself to his own resources. Values which previously were unambiguous are cast in doubt; man becomes irresolute and incapable of spontaneous action, and finds himself pressed to consider in his own terms the problem of right and wrong. The new direction in which he is thrust is as human and as natural as anything he has known. It is a proud awareness of his freedom, a sense of autonomous action, which necessarily frees him of his old religious and social shackles. And this brings us to the very heart of the difficulty which Euripides presents to Aristophanes.

Two Euripidean tragedies may briefly serve as examples. In one of his earlier plays—it should be admitted that practically all the plays which we have were written during the second half of his creative life—a scene of crisis and decision forms the core of the dramatic plot, exactly as in Aeschylus' *Oresteia*. Here we have palpable proof of the manner in which the Aeschylean motifs were developed and transformed. Euripides' *Medea* is wholly written around the monologue in which Medea makes up her mind to murder her children. With consummate artistry and with expert timing Euripides has constructed the scenes at the beginning of the play in such a way that they lead up to the monologue; the latter thus becomes the receptacle for all the motifs on which the poet had set his heart.

Medea, the barbarian woman from Colchis on the Black Sea, has followed Jason to Greece in return for saving him from certain destruction when he came to her country to recover the golden fleece. But now an unheroic conflict has sprung up between the two. In Corinth where they have gone with their two children Jason is offered the chance of marrying the daughter of the king, and because no legal marriage ties bind him to Medea—she is not a Greek citizen—he leaves her and the children and weds the princess. This is his opportunity once more to live a normal life as the member of a community, and perhaps eventually to become king of Corinth.

Euripides takes great pains to point out that Medea stands alone, that she has no stake in those bonds and affiliations which protect a man and offer him support. She has betrayed her home and her family, she has left them and put her trust in a purely private association, the love between her and Jason. Jason does not commit a transgression in the conventional or juridical sense; but a higher law, more natural and more human in spirit, decidedly favours Medea. She disposes of no legal claim which would stand up in court; unlike Sophocles' Antigone, she cannot even refer to a divine injunction to defy the arguments of her opponent. The one and only source of her anger is a purely personal feeling of what is right; she is a barbarian, and so this feeling turns into a furious wrath.

Jason may reason and plead that his actions have been

ARISTOPHANES AND AESTHETIC CRITICISM

entirely sensible, and even profitable for all concerned. But in the face of the ardour and earnestness which characterize Medea's sense of justice—a more genuine sense of justice than Jason's, Euripides will have us know—Jason's figure dwindles into nothingness. From the very beginning Medea appears as an extraordinary, a strange and mysterious woman beside whom the reasonable and well-intentioned Jason must strike us as shabby and commonplace. This is how Euripides draws the hero of the Greek myth and the barbarian witch; because he took the sacred tradition and redistributed the light and the shadow in it, it is possible to understand how Aristophanes could accuse him of dragging the hallowed figures of the past through the mire. But Euripides does not do this because of an ignoble desire to humble the mighty, but on the contrary because he had a moral design. The perspective of Nietzsche was clearer than that of Aristophanes or Schlegel. The fond ideals of religious tradition are unmasked and demolished so that a truer justice may be discovered, and its claim staked out. And who would fail to be impressed with the justice of Medea's case? Who would deny that Euripides has here uncovered a new and powerful truth? And who finally would be so rash as to strike from the ledger of history this revolutionary thought which was to be of the greatest significance to the course of western culture?

The criticism which Euripides directs against Jason is not confined to this particular case; it is a radical critique which applies equally to all myths and their treatment of right and wrong.

The action of Euripides' *Medea* is set off when Creon, the new father-in-law of Jason, in his fear of the witch Medea decides to drive her and her children from his kingdom. Prudent and self-assured as she is, Medea easily succeeds in winning the sympathies of the chorus, and obtaining from Creon a postponement of her exile for one day. Now she is ready to accomplish her revenge. Somewhat unexpectedly king Aegeus enters the scene and offers the exiles a haven in his city of Athens. Thus Euripides sees to it that Medea's subsequent deed will not appear to be an act of complete desperation, the irresponsible act of a lonely woman who does not know where to turn. Deliberately, and with careful

planning, she will take vengeance upon her enemy Jason.
Prior to the monologue Jason has two scenes; on the first
occasion he offers Medea some money, generously as he
thinks, to defray the expenses of her journey. Medea's
answer betrays her burning hatred for him, and with cold
disdain she rejects his proposals. At his second appearance
Medea pretends to give in; she commends her children to
him. They are to plead her case with gifts for the new bride,
gifts which are poisoned and will bring death to the girl.
When the children obtain permission to stay in Corinth
Medea feels that the time has come to carry out her gruesome
revenge. She decides to kill her own children in order to
destroy Jason completely. For a father lives on in his children,
and so, after the removal of the new wife who might have
given him more sons, the children whom Medea herself
has borne to him will have to die. This is the point at which
Euripides introduces the great scene of decision, the monologue in which Medea takes one last account of what she
proposes to do, and in which she affirms her resolution to do
away with her children. It is significant that she arrives at
her decision by way of a monologue. Before Euripides the
genuine monologue had not existed in tragedy. Aeschylus'
Orestes, in the greatest hour of his need and doubts, had
turned to his friend Pylades. Medea is alone; there is no one
but herself to consult about her fate. Instead of the demands
and warnings of some superhuman authority giving her guidance, she is torn between the conflicting impulses of her heart.
The sentiment which dominates her heart is the passion of
revenge, but at the same time she realizes that there is a
better force in her which would prevent the horror (1078 ff.):

> I know what crimes I am about to commit, but my anger
> is stronger than my reason, anger which causes the
> greatest afflictions among men.

These verses reveal the first emergence into consciousness
of a new morality which in days to come was to reign supreme.
A morality of psychological and individualistic colouring, it
appears in the guise of a purely internal impulse, in the
negative form of a moral inhibition or scruple. It is not an
accident that the later moral philosophers are particularly
fond of citing these words of Euripides. After the monologue

Medea carries her work to its swift conclusion. She murders the children and is carried off in triumph. Jason remains behind a broken man.

Euripides' *Hippolytus* has this in common with Aeschylus' *Oresteia* that the dramatic conflict finds its parallel in a struggle between two deities. But the two plays differ in an essential point; the divine engagement in Euripides is not ignited by the special situation of the plot, but it is an eternal war of universal proportions. Instead of two deities taking contrary views of a certain action, the contest is between two human beings who are assisted by their divine protectors. What is most important, in Aeschylus Apollo holds the field against the Erinyes, i.e. the purer faith triumphs over the hoary superstitions, and the sombre plot is brightened by a meaningful end. In Euripides, however, the two chief agents perish, and the two deities continue to face each other across an irremediable breach.

Statues of Aphrodite and Artemis flank the background of the stage, and between these goddesses the play is enacted. Aphrodite speaks the prologue: she promises to take her vengeance upon Hippolytus who has led the chaste life of a huntsman, honouring Artemis and slighting Aphrodite. Hippolytus upon his return from the hunt salutes the image of Artemis, only to pass by the image of Aphrodite without so much as a nod.

Phaedra, the stepmother of Hippolytus, has fallen violently ill and is carried forth from the palace. Her sickness, as she later confesses to her old nurse, is nothing but passionate love for her stepson. Aphrodite has sent her this love, to impose her punishment on Hippolytus. With the meticulousness of a physician Euripides describes the love of Phaedra as a grave sickness of the mind, involving the most vehement physical suffering. It is true that this situation stems from the goddess, and actually expresses her essence as the goddess of love; but this, so to speak, transcendental aspect of the plot is of no significance for the rest of the play. The psychological fact that Phaedra is passionately in love with Hippolytus, the individual turmoil of her soul, the desires which spring from this confusion, the obstacles which bar the way of these desires—this is the material utilized for the dramatization of the story. The goddesses Artemis and Aphrodite are all but reduced to the function of symbols, illustrating a variety of psychological types; as for the human agents, however, their inner life and their intellectual scope are enormously enriched. Only now, in fact, are we in a position to speak of characters and individuals in tragedy. Personalities such as Medea or Phaedra have well-nigh become instructional models for those who want to throw light upon the human psyche.

It cannot be denied, however, that Aristophanes was justified when he complained that all this made for the profanation of myth. But there had been earlier moves in this direction. The people of Aeschylus are not altogether dependent on the gods, but are to a degree responsible for their own actions. Euripides goes further and locates his arena of conflicts in the human heart alone. Men like Aristophanes may lament that a beautiful world has thus collapsed, but for most of the Greeks this profanation of myth was not a sacrilegious act; faith in the Christian sense was unknown to them, especially in matters of the Homeric religion which by and large controlled the great works of literature. The Greek myth was not destroyed by the opposition of non-believers, or the fanaticism of heretics; it underwent a logical transformation in accordance with its own laws. The divine gave way to what was considered more natural—or should we say, in the spirit of this religion, to what was considered more divine? Men gradually succeeded in depriving the gods of their power over the natural world and claiming it for themselves, for they had discovered that the human mind was itself divine. Theirs were gods who had long ceased to work with miracles, which demand faith because they shock human reason. Though Aristophanes pictures Euripides as indulging in wickedness with his natural, his all too natural interpretation of the characters of myth, Euripides for his part aspires to serve a moral interest with his exposés. The objective of the *Hippolytus* is by no means merely an analysis of the passion of love as such, but a scrutiny of the moral conflict of Phaedra which is no different from that of Medea. The call of morality is voiced against blind impulse, and once more the ethical reactions, scruples and inhibitions and a bad conscience, come into play.

> We know and recognize what is right, but we do not act
> on it, for we are in the grip of passion.

These words from the great monologue of Phaedra (380 f.) are analogous to those of Medea.[6] Some may consider it immoral that Euripides' characters are without a firm footing, that they are tossed wildly about by their own inclinations and drives. But it is not true, as Aristophanes would have us believe, that they derive a perverted pleasure from their lack of moral direction. Medea and Phaedra are both afraid; inescapably they move towards the eventual catastrophe without being able to save themselves. And yet they have their share of human greatness, and never once do we withdraw our sympathy from them.

When Phaedra's nurse has coaxed her secret out of her, the queen wants to commit suicide. It is then that the fatal trap closes on them. The nurse, a versatile woman who wears her morality lightly, and is thus a pronounced antagonist of Phaedra, attempts to help her mistress in her own way. Practical, sensible and unscrupulous as she is, she hopes to remedy the situation by disclosing Phaedra's love to Hippolytus. Is it not likely that a little pandering will make everything turn out all right? But Hippolytus flies into a rage at his stepmother's depravity. Phaedra feels that she has been betrayed and that her good name is forever lost. So she takes her own life, and in doing so drags Hippolytus down with her. The catastrophe is brought to pass for no other reason than that both of them are extremely sensitive to the prescripts of moral behaviour.

But immorality is not the only count on which Aristophanes indicts Euripides. He also calls him a clever sophist, and accuses him of splitting hairs and other cunning manipulations. And yet it was Euripides who first placed the accent on the irrational forces in man. Medea and Phaedra are great women because they are passionate; it follows that Euripides ·cannot be a one-sided champion of reason and enlightenment, On the contrary, it might well be maintained that Euripides reduces reason and reflexion *ad absurdum:* in both plays reason plays a negative role, doubly negative indeed, for on the one hand it acts merely in a warning and deterring capacity, and secondly it does not succeed in that function, unlike the *daimonion* of Socrates which is also confined to a repressive role. Moreover the 'reasonable' figures in the two dramas, Jason and the nurse, are contemptible and immoral precisely because they are reasonable. Still it would be wrong to define Euripides in terms of a contrast between reason and irrationality. Aristophanes has some justice on his side when he places Euripides among the company of the Sophists and Socrates, for his moralizing is largely that of a philosopher and dissenter. His discontent, his scepticism shatters his faith in the gods and in the ancient meaning of life, and tinges his creative temper with nihilistic overtones. In his later plays the characters have a hollow ring, their action is devoid of any significance or higher mission. In the *Iphigenia in Aulis* the brothers Agamemnon and Menelaus easily unmask the idealistic motives which each alleges to the other; the principles which really control their actions are egotism, lust for power, and—cowardly fear of the other. With biting cruelty Euripides has shown us the true nature of these Homeric heroes who now find themselves isolated in a world stripped of the gods, a world that makes no sense. With no illusions left to support them, they totter and threaten to fall. This is the gain which has accrued to man from his newly-found independence: he has no firm ground to stand on, and is helplessly exposed to the hazards of life.

Of all the characters that Euripides brings on the stage in this late work, Iphigenia herself is the only one capable of a great deed. The innocent young maiden who has never before taken a step of her own understands that her death is necessary for the success of the great venture which the Greeks have launched against the barbarians—the Trojan War. Of her own free will, and with the burning enthusiasm which the task requires, she offers herself as a victim. There are other plays in which Euripides dramatizes an ethical impulse in young and inexperienced people. Moral fortitude, he seems to say, is not a matter of calculation, it is not linked with the wisdom of experience or an understanding of the issues of life. Nor is it based upon the recognition of an existing custom or tradition. It springs from a fresher soil: the private sensation of an individual emotion. We see, therefore, that the negative moral sentiments, the bad conscience and self-restraints and inhibitions, are counterbalanced by a positive feeling, a moral enthusiasm, which is likewise grounded in the individual workings of the soul.

Iphigenia sacrifices herself for all of Greece and the struggle against the barbarians. Her spirit of devotion did not become a political actuality until long after Euripides' death; at the time of the Peloponnesian War when the *Iphigenia in Aulis* was written it was but a utopian dream. Iphigenia's deed transcends the situation of the moment; it is an idealistic sacrifice carried out with idealistic fervour. All this is far from sophistic, nor is it lacking in morality. True enough, the image of Aeschylean vigour which blocks Aristophanes' field of vision has little in common with this Iphigenia, a pure embodiment of the moral principle as discerned by Euripides. The ethical quality of her action does not flow from the prestige of the State or the gods, nor from the pious honouring of ancient injunctions, but from the simplicity of her heart, chaste and untarnished in a confused and senseless world. Aristophanes, on the other hand, finds his ideal in the proven valour of the citizens who fought at Marathon; this is as far as he will go, and it is in deference to those heroes that he distorts the features of Euripides. Even his portrayal of Aeschylus, striking as it is, shows the traces of a somewhat crude simplification. For is it correct to see in him merely the warrior-poet, the artless primordial giant? Euripides creates a new crisis for morality, for by rooting ethical convictions in the sentiments of the individual heart he puts morality at the mercy of subjective vacillation. The old values are shrouded in doubt; men begin to flag; once more, albeit on a different level, we witness the process which we have come to know in the early lyrics. Just as then the bulwark of traditional virtues had crumbled, so now the Athenians lose that equilibrium which from the time of Solon and his laws had been their greatest treasure. The dramatic conflict of forces is resolved into a discussion between human beings whose lives are themselves unresolved and problematic. Tragedy shades off into the dialogue of moral philosophy; what had once been presented by living figures comes to be reasoned out and discussed in the abstract.

Tragedy thus fulfils the destination of Greek thought, for the same trend is true also of the other great genres of literature; they pave the way for scientific reflexion. The epic issues into history, theogony and cosmogony are continued in the natural philosophy of the Ionians which probes into the *arche*, the basis and beginning of all things, and lyric poetry promotes the inquiry into the meaning of life. Tragedy passes over into Attic philosophy which concentrates on the actions of man, i.e. on the good. Plato's dialogues furnish a sequel, on a more theoretical plane, to the discussion in which the tragic figures had been engaged. The transition from drama to philosophy takes the characteristically Greek shape of a renewed interest in the 'natural', of an attempt to step once again 'into the depth of the self'. In as much as myth is no longer recognized as reflecting the natural form of man's existence, the focus of contemplation is narrowed upon man himself. The humanization of myth which runs its course from Aeschylus to the late Euripides proves to us that the inherited myth is increasingly rejected as unnatural. The questions of the day are no longer solved by reference to the distant personages of a half-divine world, to their exceptional situations and quarrels which are on the whole foreign to the natural problems of human life. Socrates who progresses, or returns, to the domain of natural man, documents his speculations with examples from ordinary human affairs. With the tools of natural reasoning and common sense he proceeds to answer any questions that may arise. As a result, of course, the questions themselves are tinged with a philosophical shade. 'We know the good, but we do not perform it' says the Phaedra of Euripides. Socrates seeks to fortify this knowledge of the good, and to have men yield to its authority. He takes thinking seriously because it is the unique and natural gift of man, and because it adds new strength to the feeble resources of the individual.

It is, of course, difficult to see how this theoretical interest in the good could have sustained the creation of tragedies or any other poetry. Attic tragedy breathed its last with Euripides, and Socrates bears the blame for its death. But at the same time he brought about the birth of something new: Attic philosophy. The judgment of Aristophanes is correct, but let us not be mistaken about him. He is a romantic reactionary who refuses to give up what is already lost, and, instead of welcoming the new, mourns the passing of the old.

His moral objections, however, are entirely unjustifiable. It will not do to accept a traditional code as the only possible morality, and to take it for granted that a decent citizen may do nothing except what is sanctioned by the established rules of religion, State, and family. Aristophanes fails to understand that a man's opposition to the traditions, and his appeal to another authority—be it reason or the voice of conscience—are fully as moral as obedience to custom; some have since considered it an even higher type of morality. As long as this new notion of justice is a matter of genuine conviction it will manifest itself not merely as an isolated sentiment, but as a persuasion common to many. Schlegel goes beyond the position of Aristophanes because his attitude against Euripides is one of general principle. Socrates' destruction of tragedy means to him the crushing of art by the intellect. We need not close our eyes to the questionable aspects of this intellect which Aristophanes attempts to resist; it extricates itself from its old nexus, it soars high above the ground and refuses to be brought into line. But this awakening of the intellect is the path of history. And when Schlegel extends his criticism to the formal characteristics of Euripidean art he gives away the psychological motives which underlie his hatred of the sophist tragedian. For him Euripides is a poet of dissolution and decay even in the manner of his writing: 'Usually he sacrifices the whole to its parts, and in these again he is after exotic charms rather than genuine poetic beauty.' Thus Schlegel discovers in Euripides those very defects which constitute his own weakness. He desired nothing more fervently than to be a poet, but his real gifts were his culture, his critical judgment, and his wit. The artist in him was unable to keep pace with the critic, and for the sake of scoring a clever point he was likely to neglect everything else. The whole romantic age was oppressed with the notion that thinking blocks the current of life, that man is cut off from the happiness of a naive existence by an undue vigilance of the mind. In his speculation art is seen as a state of innocence from which man is abruptly torn by the force of knowledge. Some think that the wound can be cured only by the weapon which has struck it, by knowledge itself. This is Hegel's opinion, and Kleist also subscribes to it at the conclusion of his tale of the *Puppet Theatre*: 'Thus we should have to eat once more of the tree of knowledge in order to lapse back into the state of innocence.' Others who feel that their productivity is thwarted by their knowledge allow themselves to conceive a violent hatred of the intellect, of enlightment and non-conformism. In Schlegel's eyes, Euripides is the prototype of poetic libertinism.

Nietzsche holds the same grudge against Euripides. In his later writings where he stigmatizes the degeneration of the modern mind, we may always detect the shades of Socrates and Euripides as they were represented by Aristophanes and Schlegel. One sign of the decadent style, he says in *The Case Wagner* 7, is the liberation of the parts at the cost of the whole; this is a variation upon Schlegel's condemnation of Euripides, and like Schlegel Nietzsche unwittingly condemns himself. For his antipathy toward Euripides is actually directed against one side of his own personality. With the merciless scalpel of his critique he cut through the illusions, the dreams and hopes on which men support themselves; there remained to him a longing for naive health and vigour, a craving for genuine art which, like Schlegel, and Herder before him, he regarded as a creation from the recesses of myth. 'Without myth all art loses its organic vigour and its creative strength,' Nietzsche says in the *Birth of Tragedy*. This myth is 'decomposed' by the efforts of the 'critical-historical spirit of our civilization'. In this way he broadens Aristophanes' criticism of Euripides over and beyond the measure proposed by Schlegel, and establishes it as a general cultural law. At the same time he shows unmistakeably that his enmity toward Euripides feeds upon the sufferings of his own life, upon his longing for the youth of humanity, and his dissatisfaction with the historical pattern of all nature.

Goethe was not tortured by any such bias against the intellect and, especially when he had reached old age, was by no means inclined to exaggerate the importance of the bloom of youth in art. He did not take it in good part that Schlegel, this 'poor herring', disapproved of Euripides. 'A poet,' he said to Eckermann, 'whom Aristotle praised and Menander admired, whose death prompted Sophocles and the city of Athens to don mourning, must amount to something. If a modern like Schlegel wishes to point out mistakes in an ancient of such stature, let him do so on his knees.'

To conclude, here is another quotation from Goethe concerning Euripides, and Aristophanes' criticism of him;

Goethe entered these words in his diary just a few months before he died. 'I am really amazed that the scholastic nobility does not comprehend his virtues, that they rank him below his predecessors, in line with that high-toned tradition which the clown Aristophanes brought into currency . . . . Has any nation ever produced a dramatist who would deserve to hand him his slippers?'

CHAPTER 7

HUMAN KNOWLEDGE AND DIVINE KNOWLEDGE AMONG THE EARLY GREEKS

'HUMAN nature has no knowledge, but the divine nature has.' Statements similar to this saying of Heraclitus (fr. 78 Diels) are made by a number of pre-Socratic philosophers, as also by Socrates, Plato, and Aristotle. They were preceded in this view by Homer, and at the opposite end of the historical development the Christians may be cited to the same effect.[1] We may suspect, however, that if any of them were to say what he meant by divine knowledge and its human counterpart, what he considered the limits and the trustworthiness of human understanding, they would find themselves embroiled in a heated debate.

Homer's incantations: 'Sing, goddess, of the wrath' and: 'Tell me, Muse, of the man' show us the bard whose words do not flow from his own genius or from his individual experience, but who is inspired by a deity. The belief that a superhuman voice issues from the poet is indeed widespread; it is found not only on a primitive level, among shamans and dervishes,[2] but also on that higher plane which we associate with the sublime sensations of our own poets. Usually this inspiration involves a kind of ecstasy. Homer, however, has left us remarkably few traces of the notion that the Muses cause the poet to lose control of his wits. The most explicit invocation occurs at a point in his poems which would hardly seem a suitable occasion for emotion and pathos. This is the prelude to that most sober section of the *Iliad*, the *Catalogue of Ships*:

> Tell me now, Muses that dwell in the palace of Olympus—
> For you are goddesses, you are at hand and know all things,
> But we hear only a rumour and know nothing—
> Who were the captains and lords of the Danaans.

The goddesses are superior to man for the simple reason that they are always at hand, and have seen everything, and know it now—both notions are contained in the *iste* of line

485 and in the *idmen* of line 486[3]—while he absorbs nothing but hearsay. Homer continues:

> But their multitude I could not number or name,
> Not if I had ten tongues and ten mouths,
> And an unbreakable voice, and a brazen heart within me,
> If the Muses of Olympus, the daughters of aegis-bearing
> Zeus, did not put into my mind all those that came to Ilios.

To enumerate the ordinary soldiers of the army the poet would require even more, and more capable, organs. And even then he would not succeed without the Muses; it is their task, as daughters of Mnemosyne, Memory, to enlarge the recollection of the poet.

All this is simple enough, and it represents in comparatively plain terms what the generation of Homer had to say on the subject of knowledge. The Muses who are omnipresent provide the poet with what we would call a mental picture. Dark rumour is transformed into a product of the Muses, it becomes poetry; everything comes alive, and the poet, as it is said of Demodocus in the *Odyssey* (8.491), sings 'as one who has been present, or heard the tale from an eyewitness.'[4] What we would ascribe to the imagination, to an intellectual effort or an act of sympathetic identification, Homer likewise traces to actual experience. Consequently the uncomplicated views which he holds concerning knowledge always apply in the same stable ratio: the wider the experience, the greater the knowledge. The eye-witness commands a better knowledge than the recipient of hearsay. The experience of the Muses who were always present is complete; that of men is restricted. Provided the Muses share their experience with the singer, he needs to contribute only an adequate performance of his physical organs.

Over and above his confidence that he is inspired by the Muses, the singer of course prides himself on his own achievement. In the *Odyssey* Phemius says: 'No one has taught me but myself, and the god has put into my heart all kinds of songs' (22.347). This is a characteristic statement; whenever a Homeric hero reflects upon the source of his particular gifts, he refers them to the gods.[5] Even the *Catalogue of Ships*—in all probability a late piece of Homeric poetry, notwithstanding the unitarian support it has received of late —conforms with the traditional concepts.[6] As a matter of

fact there is no reason why we should consider plain language
a sign of late authorship. It is only natural that the poet
found it difficult to picture to himself the forbidding number
of leaders and ships, and that because of this he calls upon the
Muses to assist him.[7]

Hesiod, at the beginning of his *Theogony*, has a somewhat
different description of his relation to the Muses. They
address him on Mount Helicon (lines 26 ff.):

> Shepherds of the fields, wretched things of shame, mere bellies,
> We know how to say many false things as if they were true,
> But we know, when we will, how to utter true things.

Hesiod had just mentioned his own name; it was he whom
the Muses taught 'fair' song, and they honoured him above
the idle paunches of his fellow herdsmen.[8] They bestow
upon him the sceptre of laurel, and they inspire him to sing
of 'things that would be and that had been before.'[9] It is not
enough now that Hesiod expects the Muses to present him
with a clear picture of the facts; for such a picture is of
necessity confined to the short moment during which the
singer relates one particular event. No, he stresses that once
in days gone by the Muses on Helicon had taught him the
art of song. His whole status as a poet is a special gift and
grace of the Muses. Still he maintains that he wishes to
report true things, by which he understands the total aggregate of concrete reality. He knows that he has been chosen,
that he is superior to all other poets, and yet his song is a
boon from the goddesses. The Muses themselves say that
they know many false things which resemble the truth. This
seems to be Hesiod's way of referring to those singers who
learn from the Muses all sorts of matters which cannot
possibly be known with any degree of accuracy. His own
art has a different objective; the Muses tell him the truth.
Clearly they have summoned him in a novel and startling
way; in fact we may say that they are not the old Muses at
all, for they bear features which are ordinarily associated
with the Nymphs, the maidens of the wild who unbalance the
minds of men. Those who have been 'caught by the Nymphs',
the *nympholeptoi*, are afflicted with madness, they are beside
themselves.[10] Hesiod is the first of the poets to regard himself as a stranger among men. Neither with the Homeric
singers nor with his native shepherds is he fully at home; and

so he attempts to unite the two worlds in himself. This is the reason for the novelty of his message; a fresh start is ever caused by the meeting of contraries.

As Hesiod saw it, the presentation of the heroic lays of the past was not true in the sense that it was worthy of the Muse and her teachings. In his surroundings, the only 'past, present, and future' which mattered to him were to be found in the struggle by which man ekes out his livelihood oppressed on all sides by the powers of darkness and light.[11] This is what the Muses helped him to understand. The songs of others appeared to him as folly or lies.[12] There is, thus, a correlation between these two facts: Hesiod looks upon himself as a special type of man, and his truth is of a special perfection. He is subjective in the sense that he has his own understanding of what objective truth is. His knowledge, *in fine*, stands half way between the divine knowledge of the Muses and the human knowledge of the fools.

About the year 500 B.C. Xenophanes echoes the motto of the invocation of the *Catalogue of Ships* (fr. 34)[13]:

> And as for certain truth, no man has seen it, nor will
> there ever be a man who (has seen, i.e.) knows about the
> gods and about all the things I am saying. For if he succeeds
> to the full in saying what is completely true, he himself is
> nevertheless unaware of it (i.e. he has not seen it); Semblance
> is fixed upon all things.

Men have seen little, and therefore know little—this much Xenophanes retains from Homer. But he defines more accurately the contrast between what is reliably known and what is not. No one knows the *saphes*, what is clear, evident; only *dokos*, Semblance or Appearance, shows itself to man, and is spread over everything. Homer distinguished between the exact knowledge of the eye-witness, be he god or man, on the one hand, and hearsay on the other; Xenophanes feels that human knowledge is in its very essence deceptive. This new attitude towards knowledge emerges very neatly in fr. 18:

> Truly the gods have not revealed to mortals all things
> from the beginning, but by long seeking do men discover
> what is better.

Here we have the new notion that men acquire their knowledge through their own striving, that even though they may never arrive at complete enlightenment they always have it in their power to search out better things. Hesiod found himself standing between divine and human knowledge; with Xenophanes for the first time man's own initiative, his industry and zeal, become crucial for the acquisition of knowledge, and for the bridging of the gulf between men and gods.

Xenophanes is a rhapsode. At an earlier time the soldier Tyrtaeus had proclaimed bravery, the special virtue of his own particular caste, as the only true virtue, over against the false virtues of other orders and occupations. The statesman Solon had similarly celebrated justice as the cardinal virtue. In the same fashion Xenophanes arrays the virtue of his calling, wisdom (*sophia*), against the standards of other groups (fr. 2). Being a singer in the Homeric tradition, however, he realizes that human knowledge is obscure; and yet, like Hesiod, he feels that he has raised himself above the level of his class, and that his message is true in a special way. Even before him Archilochus and Sappho had discovered that by their own strength—not, as Hesiod, with the help of the deity—they were able to arrive at a number of personal value judgments. All these trends meet in Xenophanes and add up to something new: wisdom is the highest goal of man; our knowledge as such is obscure, but it is illumined by searching.

The knowledge which Xenophanes seeks is not that of the other rhapsodes. Ever since Homer, men had striven to shed some light on the mysteries of the world order; by about 600 B.C. these efforts had developed into a search for uniform principles whereby men hoped to eliminate the obscurities and uncertainties which beset their various fields of vision. Tyrtaeus and Solon posited one virtue, Sappho pitted the one thing which she esteemed best against the values of others (fr. 27 a), Thales regarded water as the one fundament and essence of all things. Anaximander and Anaximenes were engaged in similar speculations, and Xenophanes carried them further. He also inquires into the true nature of the world. Both Sappho's questions and those asked by Thales ultimately resulted in the distinction between the genuine and the spurious, the essential and the fortuitous. Xenophanes combines this with the rhapsodic tradition that

man's knowledge is fallacious: 'mortals assume (*dokeousi*)
. . .' he says when he makes mention of a false view (fr. 14);
'Semblance (*dokos*) is fixed upon all things' (fr. 34) whereas
the deity alone sees clearly. Deceptive semblance in the
external world, and false assumptions among men—both are
expressed by the Greek word *dokein*—correspond to one
another. Thus Xenophanes touches upon an idea which was
to become of great consequence for Parmenides. More of
this directly.

Xenophanes deviates from the course of Thales, but follows
in the tracks of Hesiod, in that he tries to locate his essence
or Being in the realm of the deity, and not in the domain of
matter. Here he makes his most fruitful discovery: 'There is
one god ' (fr. 23).[14] He attempts to detach himself from any
allegiance to a multitude of anthropomorphic gods; he is the
first to have a revelation of the divine as a comprehensive
unity. Yet the god whom he thus grasps continues to
resemble himself as well as his ideal. The divine comple-
ments the human as the rhapsode understands it; since
wisdom is the highest attainment of man, it plays the same
role for the deity. Only man's knowledge is imperfect, but
the wisdom of god is faultless. 'He sees as a whole, thinks
as a whole,[15] and hears as a whole' (fr. 24). Gross anthropomorphism is left far behind; the deity is conceived as possess-
ing none of the human organs of perception such as ear and
eye. With its whole being it absorbs its experience, and the
very fullness of this experience constitutes the essence of its
divinity.

Xenophanes despises athletic prowess among men (fr. 2)
because wisdom alone merits the designation of virtue.
Similarly he imagines a god who operates 'without toil,
merely by the thought of his mind' (fr. 25).[16] He hinges his
theological speculations, not upon the omnipotence of the
god,[17] but on his cognitive capacity. In fr. 25 we read
literally: the god 'makes everything tremble' without toil, by
means of his thought. We are reminded of the scene in the
first book of the *Iliad* in which Zeus nods assent to the
request of Thetis and thereby causes the towering Olympus
to shake and tremble. It is clear, therefore, that Xenophanes
is not concerned with the god's purposeful direction of the
world, but that he emphasizes the tremendous effect which

is produced by the god's mental activity. And there is something else to remind us of Homer. In the fragment (34) which recalls the invocation from the *Catalogue of Ships* Xenophanes says: occasionally a man may say something that is completely true (literally: 'that has completed itself'), and yet he has no exact knowledge, in contrast to the god. This is Homeric phraseology; a word or thought 'completes itself'[18] i.e. it is concretely realized. The expression is chiefly used of wishes and hopes which look toward the future, but, speaking more generally, it applies to any word which 'comes off' or 'hits the facts'. The godhead always achieves its *telos*,[19] that is its primary characteristic. Instead of deriving divine wisdom from divine omnipotence, Xenophanes has his god proceed from thought to 'completion'; knowledge comes first, power is its consequence.

Xenophanes says: '(The god is) not at all like mortals in body or mind (*noema*)' (fr. 23). Clement of Alexandria who cites these words concludes from them that Xenophanes already conceived his god as incorporeal. Other notices, however, prove that he followed the older physical speculations according to which the earth, the ocean, and probably even the cosmos were seen as perfect rounds; he regarded his god as a sphere which comprises everything within itself and rests motionless (21 A 31.3—9 Diels). Though he was the first to regard human knowledge as the fruit of personal endeavour, he himself failed to attain the pure intelligence which he was seeking. It is important, however, that he no longer views the gods in the human shape which forces itself on the naive mind. His active desire for knowledge led him beyond such impressions as are but passively received. In proportion as he endows man with a greater share of mental activity, his deity loses its capacity for action; his god 'always remains in the same place, not moving at all, nor is it fitting for him to change his position at different times' (fr. 26). Thus his god differs markedly from the gods of the *Iliad* who come down to the earth and interfere in the lives of men. At the same time, while man's mental activity, his questioning and searching, is stepped up, his practical interests gradually recede behind theoretical considerations, and man strives to identify himself with this newly-discovered god who sees and knows without moving.

How man may obtain a portion of the divine knowledge through his search—for it is evident that Xenophanes himself trusts to soar above the usual false assumptions of men—we are nowhere shown; there is no telling whether Xenophanes failed to speak of it or whether our tradition has not preserved his words. Those who succeeded him made this topic their special concern.

At approximately the same time as Xenophanes, Hecataeus broadcast his own concept of truth in opposition to the views held by the rest of mankind. Here is the opening phrase of his *Histories*:

> Hecataeus the Milesian speaks thus; this is my account,
> as it seems true to me.   For the stories of the Greeks, as they
> appear to me, are numerous and foolish.

'As it seems true to me . . .'—the 'paradox which lies in these words does not appear to have worried him. He made light of such theoretical difficulties as this: how it was possible that what 'seemed' to him could also be 'true'. He has an immediate and clear-cut understanding of the reason why the stories of the Greeks strike him as foolish: they relate matters which do not tally with ordinary experience. His knowledge is the solid and dependable knowledge of an eye-witness, firmly sanctioned by the tradition of the Ionian epic. But he no longer believes that a man may derive his knowledge from the gods. Man makes himself independent and sets out on his own to discover what is true. Once Hecataeus has eliminated the miraculous from his design, its place is soon taken by plausible constructions whenever his knowledge falls short. Thus we have his rational explanations of myths, or his notions concerning the earth: it is a circular disk of perfect symmetry, floating upon the ocean, and subdivided into equal portions of Europe and Asia. In the end Hecataeus suffered the fate of the over-confident. His successors, beginning with Herodotus (4.36) gave his accounts the same scoffing reception which he had accorded to the stories of the Greeks. But it remains his particular achievement that he placed knowledge, as it was understood by him, in a position whence it could be advanced and augmented. Like Xenophanes, only more concretely, he holds that knowledge consists of the data gained from inquiry and search. This search is not forced upon him as it was on Odysseus who saw the cities of many men, nor does he pursue it at leisure like Solon who is said to have been the first to travel round the world for the sake of *theory* (Herodotus 1.29). He goes on his journeys in conformity with a well-organized plan in order to arrive at a maximum of knowledge, a systematic picture of the earth and of the customs and deeds of men. The ardour with which he devotes his life to *theory* surpasses even that of Solon—and that means that his theory makes him all the more active.

This enthusiasm for investigation lives on in Herodotus. For him, experience forms the one and only basis of knowledge. He distinguishes between what he has seen himself, what he has heard from eye-witnesses, and what he has learned merely as rumour, and thus completes the pattern which had first been sketched in the invocation of the *Catalogue of Ships*.

This delight in a wealth of experience which was so prominent in archaic Greece, and which was not to be extinguished until the days of the classical period, met its first adversary in the person of Heraclitus, with whose pronouncement concerning the ignorance of humankind we opened this chapter.

> Much learning (*polymathie*) does not teach anyone to have
> intelligence (*noos*); for else it would have taught Hesiod
> and Pythagoras, and again, Xenophanes and Hecataeus (fr. 40).

Heraclitus rejects the very thing which the Homeric singers and Hesiod had praised as the divine knowledge of the Muses, and which had subsequently become the prime objective of human inquiry. True enough, Xenophanes also, much as he yearned for experience throughout his long life, and despite his definition of the god as one who knows by experience, had at the same time sought to discover the One, the essence of things in this god. But Heraclitus turns off in a completely new direction. On the one hand he interprets the divine substance more abstractly as Mind, and on the other he points to this as the ultimate goal of human knowledge. In the place of extensive searching he demands an intensive approach: 'Wisdom is one thing: to understand the intelligence which steers all through all things' (fr. 41). The deity no longer has a great memory which it shares with men, nor does the investigation of men dissipate itself in several directions. Heraclitus himself assumes that the 'philosophic' men, i.e. those who love wisdom, must inquire into many things (fr. 35); he actually says (fr. 55): 'The things of which there is sight, hearing, knowledge: those are the things I prize'—apparently in preference to mere speculation concerning objects which cannot be perceived. But 'eyes and ears are bad witnesses for men if they have barbarian souls' (fr. 107), i.e. if the soul does not understand the language in which the senses render their account. All experience, necessary as it is, remains without value unless it leads to an intensive understanding of the *logos*, the fundament of which speech is only the superstructure, and whose objective existence is implied in every word that hits the mark.

Heraclitus glories in his superior knowledge no less than Hecataeus, but his measuring-rod is not the experience of men, but rather his conviction, which he shares with Xenophanes, that he partakes of divine knowledge, that his comprehension of the role of the deity in the world transcends the opinions held by the mass of the people. This divine element is anchored in the depth of the soul. Anyone may manifest its effects in his speech, provided his words are based on the *logos* common to all. The exploration of Heraclitus, therefore unlike that of Hecataeus and Xenophanes, does not content itself with the course of experience, the road which leads to the external world. He says: 'I searched into myself' (fr. 101). The idea of divine knowledge has ceased to be that of the Muses who are present everywhere and have seen everything; nor is it that of the god of Xenophanes who is all experience. Similarly the folly of men which Heraclitus ridicules differs from the ignorance criticized by his pre-decessors. Men are not awake, he says, they resemble those who are in deep sleep (frs. 1; 73; 89), or they may be likened to the drunken (fr. 117); they are like children (frs. 70; 79; 121) or like the beasts, a charge which recurs time after time (frs. 4; 9; 13; 29; 37; 83; 97).

Thus man occupies a place half way between god and beast The universal living principle on which the world depends is both of an intellectual and of a vital nature. In its intellectual aspect it exhibits several different degrees of perfection; there are echoes of the perfect *nous* of the deity, and the inferior intelligence of man. As a vital principle it comprises both man and beast; we may compare the early notion according to which the *thymos* of a lion may reside in a man. This is how Heraclitus manages to establish his contention that the relationship between beast and man corresponds to that between man and god. For the understanding of this *logos* he does not propose a mystic communion, nor does he demonstrate a methodical approach. He urges men to be watchful, and to pay heed to what nature has to say (fr. 112). In as much as the *logos* pervades everything it manifests itself in the individual also; and yet it 'is set apart from all things' (fr. 108) since it transcends the particular. The mysterious essence, the vital tension, reveals itself through significant particular events which man uses as symbols to apprehend the divine.

The physician Alcmaeon, a disciple of Pythagoras, began his treatise *On Nature* with these words: 'Concerning things unseen the gods have certainty, whereas to us as men conjecture (only is possible)' (fr. 1). Here the ancient distinction between two types of knowledge, the human and the divine, has become associated with the contrast between things visible and invisible; the assumption seems to be that men have some intelligence of the visible world, while the 'non-apparent'—that is the literal meaning of Alcmaeon's term—may be ascertained only by the gods. As in Homer and in Xenophanes, to know is basically to see; it is concerned with what is distinct and clear, the *saphes* which we have already encountered in Xenophanes. Alcmaeon differs from Homer and Xenophanes in that at the opposite pole he places, not that which is known only from hearsay, or what belongs to the realm of assumption and semblance, but the non-evident, or better still the not-yet-evident, for he points to a path by which a man may at least come closer to the invisible. This is Conjecture, the drawing of conclusions from clear indications. That is not the procedure of Heraclitus, although in his thought too the visible signs are a means of attaining to the invisible. But for Heraclitus they are symbols in which the wise man catches a glimpse of the profound secrets of life, while Alcmaeon proceeds from the rich stock of sense experience to approach the invisible, not by intuition, but by an orderly method of analysis. His criteria are psychological and physiological, as befits an empiricist. He examines sense perceptions and the 'intelligence'; according to his view both men and beasts possess *to aisthanesthai*, sensuous perception, but man alone has *to synienai*, intelligence. He discovers the function of the brain; it transmits the sense perceptions which in turn make for recollection and assumption (*mneme* and *doxa*) and, when these have become solid and firm, for knowledge (A 11 Diels = Plato *Phaedo* 96 B). Like Heraclitus he places man in the middle between the deity and the beasts. But Heraclitus recognizes only one understanding; beast, man, and god have it in varying degrees of perfection, degrees which may be expressed in the form of a proportion. Alcmaeon, on the other hand, distinguishes three different kinds of knowledge. The beasts with their sense impressions grasp only the appearances; divine knowledge comprehends even the invisible; whereas man is able to combine his sense perceptions and to make conjectures about the invisible. In this manner the quest to push beyond the limits of ordinary human knowledge, the great adventure of the mind which Xenophanes had set under way, is directed into a fixed channel. A physician, accustomed to diagnose an illness from its symptoms, Alcmaeon succeeded in formulating the universal value of his medical procedure. Later doctors, Empedocles and the Hippocratics, went further and produced from it the so-called inductive method, thereby laying the groundwork for the empirical sciences.[20]

The empirical sciences did not come into full flower until comparatively recent times. That nothing of the sort was achieved in antiquity must in no small measure be blamed on the influence of Parmenides who cast aside human knowledge, i.e. sense experience, and sought a direct access to divine knowledge. He too regards man as 'knowing nothing' (fr. 6 line 4). From Xenophanes he inherits the belief that men have only apparent knowledge (fr. 1 line 30) Like Alcmaeon he offers his own solution how man is to extricate himself from his obscure knowledge and reach the truth; but his solution is radically different. It is not man's own struggle, his objective quest and purposeful striving which brings about intelligence; no, the truth is a gift of the deity, it comes to men through revelation. Here

the concepts of Homer and Hesiod come into their own once
more. Not unlike Hesiod Parmenides describes at the
beginning of his work how the deity conducted him to the
realm of knowledge. But Hesiod's report, with its down-to-
earth vigour, becomes in his hands a solemn and dramatic
recital based, as is proved by a number of analogies with a
poem by Pindar,[21] on the model of choral poetry. Hesiod
relates in detail what happened to him at Mount Helicon
when the Muses spoke to him and gave him the branch of
laurel. Parmenides proclaims in the strains of grand poetry
(fr. 1):

> The mares which carry me convey me as far as my desire
> reaches, since they have set me on the great speech-
> course of the goddess who conducts the knowing man
> through all cities. Along this way I travel.[22]

Thus the journey proceeds towards the light and the
revelation of truth.[23] For Parmenides these events constitute
a revelation more profound than that which was granted to
Hesiod on Helicon. The Heliades, the divine maidens who
escort him, take him up to the goddess who discloses to him
the true Being. It also bears god-like traits: it 'has no coming-
into-being and no destruction' (fr. 8 line 3). Along with these
Homeric attributes of the gods which the natural philosophers
consistently predicate of the cosmos and its first principle,
Parmenides also introduces characteristics which Xenophanes
had ascribed to his deity: 'It is whole of limb and without
motion . . .' Parmenides, to a greater degree than Homer and
Hesiod, not to mention Xenophanes, experiences a deep
religious emotion in the face of this revelation that man is
able to obtain divine knowledge and to comprehend the
highest being. It is not unlikely that the Eleatic thinker was
affected by the religious currents of his native southern Italy.
At first his religious awe may seem surprising in a man who
confines the understanding of truth to the operation of the
pure intellect. But according to Parmenides man succeeds in
thinking the One Being, not along the lines laid down by
Alcmaeon who proceeds step by step from sense perceptions
to the invisible, but, as he himself has found out, by a kind of
grace. The goddess greets him at the portals of light (fr. 1
line 26): 'Welcome, since no evil *moira* has dispatched you
on your journey by this road.' It is his fate, the happy lot

which he has drawn for himself, to be thus able to attain to a knowledge which surpasses human knowledge. But how, then, could he have started his journey as a 'man who has knowledge' (fr. 1 line 3)? In the *Odyssey* the bard Phemius regards himself as his own teacher, without however failing to see in his art the gift of the Muses (cf. above). In the same spirit of apparent unconcern Parmenides is proud of his own knowledge, and still attributes his enlightenment to the deity.[24] The goddess, on her part, does not insist on blind faith as a condition of her revelation, but says: 'Do not trust sense experience . . . but judge by means of the *logos* the much-contesting proof which is expounded by me' (fr. 7). This revoices a thought which in a somewhat different form occurs as early as Homer: that the deity, so far from silencing the thinking of men, actually helps it to express itself in speech. Man requires a certain disposition to receive the truth (fr. 16): 'For according to the mixture of much-erring limbs (organs) which each man has, so is the mind (*noos*) which assists mortals.'[25] Parmenides holds that each man is to a greater or lesser extent susceptible to the truth. Since like Heraclitus, or even Hesiod in his meeting with the Muses, he assumes that most men are foolish and impervious to divine knowledge, he chooses to explain the variety of human understanding in downright anatomical terms which strongly remind us of Alcmaeon's ideas. The mind endows man with thought and divine knowledge, whereas sense perception merely transmits human appearances. He also tried to explain 'how appearances had to become plausible' (fr. 1 lines 31 f.), but concerning this there is only 'likely' speech (fr. 8 line 60).

The deity introduces Parmenides to *pure* thought; with it he comprehends the pure Being. Alcmaeon advances— inductively, we would say—from the perception of the senses, from human knowledge, to the invisible; Parmenides receives a divine instruction to put aside as illusion all sense experience and the process of becoming which the senses apprehend. The goddess shows him no path which leads uninterruptedly from human to divine knowledge, but from the intuitive recognition of Being as such she deduces the truths concerning thought and Being, Being and non-Being, and so forth. Thus Parmenides gives us the discovery of the intelligible world as an independent entity.

At this point we need not pursue further the two methods of inquiry proposed by Alcmaeon and Parmenides. They are joined in a peculiar combination in Plato's *Symposium*. Diotima in her speech first outlines the ascent from the mass of appearances to the thought which creates unity from the particulars. But on the highest level she has a revelation of divine knowledge; as in Parmenides, the One, the Immutable is the ultimate goal. Still, however strongly we may be reminded of Alcmaeon and his successors on the one hand, and of Parmenides on the other, Socrates' influence has seen to it that Plato's perspective is entirely changed.

Empedocles contributes nothing new to the subject under discussion. He too starts with the basic assumption that the sense perception of man is incomplete (fr. 2): the sense organs are narrowly limited, and there are many vile things which thrust themselves on them and blunt the thoughts;[26] during his life a man sees but little, he dies quickly, and is certain of only a few things which he happens to have encountered along the way. Who would maintain that he has found the Whole? Men cannot see it, nor hear it, nor grasp it with their minds (*nous*).[27] Then follows an invocation to the gods (fr. 3) on the strength of which he raises himself above 'mortal intelligence' (fr. 2 line 9), and a prayer to the Muse, with the request to impart to him as much knowledge as men are permitted to entertain. Here we sense the influence of Parmenides. But immediately Empedocles turns back, resolved to utilize his senses to the fullest, and thus to inquire into the secrets of nature more or less in the manner of Alcmaeon.

Once we leave Empedocles' book *On Nature*, however, and look into his *Purifications* we find him strike a totally different chord. He plays the part of a priest-physician rather than a philosopher or a scientist: 'I go about among you as an immortal god, no longer a mortal' (fr. 112). As in the case of Parmenides, only more strikingly so, we here discern the authority of the religious concepts of *Magna Graecia* where Orpheus, the son of the Muse Calliope, was honoured as a divine singer, whose mysteries were believed to provide a knowledge of heavenly bliss. Among the early Greeks this is the most extreme instance of a man claiming the gift of super-human knowledge and lifting himself above his fellow men.

But the notion that divine knowledge was to be acquired in the mysteries was widely held; we may add that, side by side with the motifs which we have mentioned, it occurs in Plato's *Symposium* where Diotima instructs Socrates in the mysteries of Eros.

This is as far as the old epic distinction between divine and human knowledge may be safely traced. It was clearly not without influence upon the form in which the pre-Socratic thinkers became cognizant of their problems and put them in words. Socrates, however, found a new point of departure. And yet he too, if the reports of his teachings do not deceive us, discussed the two kinds of knowledge. But his conception of them differed from that of his forerunners.

Xenophon says of Socrates (*Mem.* 1.1.11 ff.) that he did not concern himself with such questions as how the cosmos came into being, or what needs led to the creation of the celestial phenomena. He preferred to devote his attention to human affairs. Men, he felt, would never be able to discover the truth about these things, and it was evident that each investigator had his own ideas about them. In the final analysis, what use was a knowledge of the laws of nature? It would not enable anyone to make rain, or the winds, or the seasons. In human affairs, on the other hand, in the areas of piety, of beauty and justice a man of knowledge might well acquire supreme virtue. In Plato's *Apology* Socrates states (20 D) that his knowledge is only human, while others—and here he is thinking of those, among others, who speculate on problems of natural philosophy—possess a superhuman knowledge.[28]

We consider it strange that Socrates should put questions of natural science under the heading of divine matters, whereas he classifies ethics as a subject pertaining to the human sphere. One of the reasons is, of course, that the stars and other natural phenomena, the chief objects of scientific speculation, were held to be divine in popular thought.[29] But an equally significant explanation is furnished by the frequent claims of the earlier philosophers that they were able to transcend human knowledge. Whenever he makes mention of such *divine* knowledge Socrates employs irony; among the victims of his irony are the poets,[30] not without some justice, as we have seen. Socrates breaks with the tradition which we have traced beginning with Homer, and, as Cicero puts it, restores philosophy from the sky to its place on the earth. He rejects myth and fabulation with the same determination as his contemporary Thucydides, and like the historian he attempts to attain to the truth through the channels of human understanding. The distinction between human knowledge and divine knowledge, which had first been formulated in the area of sense perception, had helped to separate Being from Appearance, whatever the individual nuances of this separation in Heraclitus, Alcmaeon, and Parmenides may be. The efforts to reconcile the two domains of divine and human knowledge had produced the rudimentary techniques of induction and deduction. All this was once more subjected to a final change when Socrates in his dialogues tried to rest his own proposals on the authority of human thought, and human speech, and nothing else.

CHAPTER 8

THE CALL TO VIRTUE: A BRIEF CHAPTER FROM GREEK ETHICS

For justice, this is ever true,
Is but the wrong which we don't do.

WITH these words the German comic poet Wilhelm Busch takes his stand beside Socrates and Moses. For the moral commandments of the Old Testament, those regulations which transcend the sphere of ritual and tradition, cannot be said to prescribe the good; rather, they forbid evil. Similarly the *daimonion* of Socrates, the moral voice of the most moral of all Greeks, never said: 'Do this,' but merely warned: 'Do not do this.' And what is our own position? A code of laws contains precise definitions of all types of crime, misconduct, dereliction and transgression. But even the most skilful jurist would find himself checkmated if he had to furnish an unambiguous statement of what is good and right. Nor is the quandary of our theologians, our philosophers and our jurists more perplexing than the difficulty which haunts their colleagues of the fourth faculty. An honest physician will admit that he has some knowledge of some diseases, but that he is altogether incapable of saying what health is— except in terms of negatives. When he is called in to cure a sickness, he confines himself to removing the disturbances; for the rest he depends upon nature—whatever that may be —coming to its own aid. But who would be content to accept as a definition of *x* the demonstration that the opposite of *x* is not present, particularly if *x* is of momentous importance? Socrates had his *daimonion*, his warning voice, to make him secure and confident in his actions; yet he went further and mustered all his resources to discover the positive nature of the good. And though in the end he was forced to confess his ignorance, he bequeathed to us a large number of remarks concerning virtue and the good.

The speculations of Socrates were not without precedent. The terms virtue and good and evil had travelled through the mouths and minds of many thinkers before they became securely established in the vocabulary of Socrates. Along the way, their meaning had undergone certain changes; other concepts had intruded themselves and enriched their complexity. For Socrates, therefore, 'virtue' or 'the good' is loaded with a welter of connotations; it signifies a perfection of the self, as well as justice, and utility, and the greatest happiness; it also denotes the true Being as contrasted with Appearance, it is divine, one needs to know and understand it; it is a prize for which under certain conditions a man must be prepared to render up his life: all in all a great variety of concepts, whose relevance to the problem of morality was not established all at once. Thus even the basic principles of Socrates' thought presuppose a lengthy development of moral reflexion.

As the interest in discovering virtue grew stronger, the objective seemed more and more difficult to realize. At the beginning of Greek thought, men had very decided notions of what was expected of them. But when human behaviour became an object of detailed investigation, many practices which had earlier been regarded as highly estimable did not withstand the pressure of the new criticism. The pre-philosophical efforts to define morality culminated in the figure of Socrates, the reputed founder of moral philosophy, blandly confessing his ignorance. We may object to the method of his analysis, and say that it creates nothing but uncertainty. But his question: what is 'truly' moral? cannot be blotted from the record, nor do we deprive it of its sting by reserving all our praise for instinctive, non-reflective action. Socrates is part of the stream of history; the edifice he builds stands on old foundations. Even before his day, as we shall see, the so-called 'natural life' desired by some did not exist. The moral convictions which gave his predecessors what vigour they had were by no means so positive and palpable as to provide them with a concrete standard of action. Then, as now, the good was harder to define than 'the wrong which we don't do'.

The intellectual development of Greece from Homer onward is, generally speaking, clear enough; to trace the chief threads of its skein is not too difficult a task. Let us organize them into a system of ethical motifs, or a kind of genealogy of morals, by taking the motifs found in Socrates, tracing them to their sources, and determining how their initial function compares with their later use, or at least with the use that was later intended for them. We must also inquire whether the original motifs, in spite of the new context in which we find them, still retain a measure of their original force. We should not ask whether Socrates is affected by the moral theories of the pre-Socratics or the early poets, although this problem is not entirely irrelevant to our theme. Instead we should endeavour to find out what ethical notions govern the everyday lives of the people—as in sayings and proverbs—how one ideal relates to another, how they grow and decay and change.

Again, we are not bent on a history of moral conduct. We do not want to know whether, or to what extent, poetic characters such as Achilles and Odysseus, or historic figures like Solon and Socrates, were moral beings, whether they lived up to the conditions of a virtuous life. The problem which we propose to raise is considerably less difficult and ambitious: in what form did the moral imperative present itself to the Greeks? What, in successive periods, were their notions about virtue? What reasons did they advance for a moral behaviour, and how did they convince themselves of its necessity?

Early Greek literature contains hardly any products in which moral reflexion constitutes the principal theme. Moreover, the topic does not find a place for itself until most of the literary genres are well under way. Thus a strictly chronological procedure, beginning with the moral system of Homer and showing how it was transformed by his successors, would tend to cut across certain basic affinities. It would seem better, therefore, to arrange our survey along more systematic lines.

The first call to virtue in Greek literature is sounded in the opening book of the *Iliad*, in a scene which throws much light upon early thoughts concerning human conduct. When Achilles flushed with anger is about to assail Agamemnon with his sword, Athena restrains him and warns (line 207):

> I have come from the sky to put an end to your *menos* (i.e. your passionate impulse), if you obey me ... Forget the quarrel, and do not draw your sword.

Even the ancients interpreted this as a command to use forbearance,[1] but Athena employs no such 'moral' terms.

She bids Achilles to stop his impulse, and to put his sword back in the scabbard. And Achilles obeys. The basic phenomenon which here comes into play may be designated a 'moral inhibition;' elsewhere Homer describes it as the 'curbing' or 'taming' of an agitated soul-organ or its function. The word 'taming' indicates that Homer regards the emotions as something wild and bestial; is it not because of his capacity to control himself, and to yield to his inhibitions, that man stands on a higher plane than the beasts? Athena does not confront Achilles with a positive goal, but she blocks the perpetration of an evil deed. If the situation is such that a passion needs to be inhibited, positive action can only be evil, inaction must be the good. This is the meaning and truth of such commands—or rather interdicts—as: thou shalt not kill, thou shalt not steal, thou shalt not commit adultery.

Athena, however, does not issue a direct order of this sort, although the requirements of the scene would lead us to expect a full deployment of her power to call a halt to the fury of the man. There are other passages in Greek literature where the deity brings her full might to bear on a mortal's obedience, but in this scene Athena does not command. She merely gives Achilles something to think about. With this appeal to his own understanding we have come upon a new element which was to be of great significance for the course of Greek ethical thought. At this point, however, morality is not yet an issue. Athena continues:

> For I say to you—and it will surely be fulfilled: three
> times as many beautiful gifts will in the end accrue to you
> in recompense for this insult. But you hold yourself
> in check and obey us.

Achilles, it seems, in obeying the goddess and curbing his anger, has but his own advantage in mind. This inducement has little to do with morality, and yet it would have been a grave crime if Achilles had assaulted the leader of all the Greeks with his sword. His decision not to do so was a moral matter, whatever else may be involved. We might say that his equation of the good and the advantageous rather narrows the scope of his morality, but then this equation is very common among the early Greeks. The formula : 'It seemed more profitable to him . . .' often terminates Homer's description of a man deliberating with himself.[2] Evidently

the moral gains in plausibility if it can be shown in the guise
of an advantage; more than that, this is the specific form in
which an act may be recommended as practicable.

The notion of profit is remarkably prominent among the
early Greeks. It is found not only in proposals concerning
particular situations, but even in prescripts of a more general
character. Here again the moral as such is at first not emphasized. On the other hand, the Greeks were decidedly averse
to warnings in the form of terrifying injunctions; they had
no taste for the Lady Force and her power to punish. It is
only to be expected, therefore, that the Seven Sages of the
early archaic period, who were credited with a number of
exhortatory statements, should appeal to a healthy profit
motive rather than preach ethics. The sage Chilon, for
example, does not hesitate to propose the jejune motto: 'To
offer security means trouble.' This saying dates from a
period when money was a new acquisition, responsible for
such predicaments as the providing of bail, whose consequences were not easy to foresee. His advice, therefore, is
not so much a moral judgment as a suggestion to consider
the consequences of a certain act. But the very idea that the
agent should not allow himself to be confused, that he should
try to penetrate with a clear eye the dark recesses of future
results, is itself a corner-stone in the edifice of ethics. We
have a wealth of proverbs from that period, full of warnings
against trouble: Be sober! Mistrust others! Be alert! Know
when the time is right! and many a legend about the Seven
Sages is designed to illustrate this principle. Proper action
requires knowledge. To Chilon also is attributed the famous
maxim which sums up the attitude behind all these sayings:
hora telos—see the end, consider the consequences. This
insight was achieved in the sober climate of a practical
mentality, such as is common among people who work for
a living. As men acquired a greater confidence in their own
capacities, and as they learned how to utilize them for their
own benefit, they began to take a greater interest in planning,
in calculations and predictions. In the precepts all action is
frankly modelled upon the bread-winning life, and the good
is equated with the profitable. As a result, the good becomes
predictable, it is sized up and weighed on the scale: Achilles
is offered the prospect of a triplication of his gifts.

Where there is profit, happiness cannot be far off, especially in a society which has as yet no knowledge of 'internal' happiness or bliss. In early Greece the happy man is *olbios*: he is in a state of plenty. His existence is not narrowly circumscribed; he basks in the sunshine of prosperity and splendour: he is *eudaimon*, i.e. he has by his side a good demon who helps him to succeed in everything he undertakes. When Hesiod entreats his brother Perses to be virtuous and promises him a happy life as a reward he is evidently thinking of wealth and prosperity, or, in other words, of his material advantage. In the archaic period, however, that man is *eudaimon* and *olbios* who in an instant of glory is lifted above things human and touches upon the world of the gods; this splendour, this broadening of the human circuit, is the desire of all. There is no need for exhortations to happiness; everyone tries to achieve it. We may call it moral, this early striving for a happiness which is comprehended as a divine effulgence and the helpful presence of a demon. But instead of being autonomous the morality is couched in religious concepts. And perhaps it should also be pointed out that the Greeks found fairly soon that happiness could also be deceptive and brief.

The words for virtue and good, *arete* and *agathos*, are at first by no means clearly distinguished from the area of profit. In the early period they are not as palpably moral in content as might be supposed; we may compare the German terms *Tugend* and *gut* which originally stood for the 'suitable' (*taugende*) and the 'fitting' (cf. *Gatte*). When Homer says that a man is good, *agathos*, he does not mean thereby that he is morally unobjectionable, much less good-hearted, but rather that he is useful, proficient, and capable of vigorous action. We also speak of a good warrior or a good instrument. Similarly *arete*, virtue, does not denote a moral property but nobility, achievement, success and reputation. And yet these words have an unmistakable tendency toward the moral because, unlike 'happiness' or 'profit', they designate qualities for which a man may win the respect of his whole community. *Arete* is 'ability' and 'achievement', characteristics which are expected of a 'good', an 'able' man, an *aner agathos*. From Homer to Plato and beyond these words spell out the worth of a man and his work. Any change in their meaning, therefore, would indicate a reassessment of values. It is possible to show how at various times the formation and consolidation of social groups and even of states was connected with people's ideas about the 'good'. But that would be tantamount to writing a history of Greek culture. In Homer, to possess 'virtue' or to be 'good' means to realize one's nature, and one's wishes, to perfection. Frequently happiness and profit form the reward, but it is no such extrinsic prospect which leads men to virtue and goodness. The expressions contain a germ of the notion of entelechy. A Homeric hero, for instance, is capable of 'reminding himself', or of 'experiencing', that he is noble. 'Use your experience to become what you are' advises Pindar who adheres to this image of *arete*. The 'good' man fulfils his proper function, *prattei ta heautou*, as Plato demands it; he achieves his own perfection. And in the early period this also entails that he is good in the eyes of others, for the notions and definitions of goodness are plain and uniform: a man appears to others as he is.

In the *Iliad* (11.404—410) Odysseus reminds himself that he is an aristocrat, and thereby resolves his doubts how he should conduct himself in a critical situation. He does it by concentrating on the thought that he belongs to a certain social order, and that it is his duty to fulfill the 'virtue' of that order. The universal which underlies the predication 'I am a noble' is the group; he does not reflect on an abstract 'good 'but upon the circle of which he claims membership. It is the same as if an officer were to say: 'As an officer I must do this or that,' thus gauging his action by the rigid conception of honour peculiar to his caste.

Aretan is 'to thrive'; *arete* is the objective which the early nobles attach to achievement and success. By means of *arete* the aristocrat implements the ideal of his order—and at the same time distinguishes himself above his fellow nobles. With his *arete* the individual subjects himself to the judgment of his community, but he also surpasses it as an individual. Since the days of Jacob Burckhardt the competitive character of the great Greek achievements has rightly been stressed. Well into the classical period, those who compete for *arete* are remunerated with glory and honour. The community puts its stamp of approval on the value which the individual sets on himself. Thus honour, *time*, is even more significant than *arete* for the growth of the moral consciousness, because it is more evident, more palpable to all. From his earliest boyhood the young nobleman is urged to think of his glory and his honour; he must look out for his good name, and he must see to it that he commands the necessary respect. For honour is a very sensitive plant; wherever it is destroyed the moral existence of the loser collapses. Its importance is greater even than that of life itself; for the sake of glory and honour the knight is prepared to sacrifice his life.

Up to this point we have uncovered three separate motivations in the calls to virtue: the profit instinct, the search for happiness, and the drive for achievement and glory. Socrates himself made use of all three in the construct of his moral disquisitions. Before he could use them, however, he had to reinterpret and qualify them substantially; for profit, happiness, and honour, as they are generally understood, are highly egoistical: in short, they are immoral.

Actually their defects are so glaring that even in the early period they did not escape criticism. The refashioning of these motives, their adaptation to the new moral objective, begins soon enough. Extend the time range after which a profit is expected, and the notion of private benefit becomes invested with a moral, not to say almost philosophical complexion. Chilon warns: 'Consider the end'; once the end is projected into the far-distant future, this statement turns into a call to virtue, especially if we are told that it is better to forgo a present advantage in order to increase the gain in days to come. Nowadays our businessmen for whom such problems are very real have found that honesty guarantees the best results: 'Honesty is the best policy'. In Greek it would be difficult to find parallels to such proverbs, except perhaps for the advice of Theognis (753 ff.): See to it that you earn your money justly; in the end you will be glad to have followed this suggestion. The belief that the good is profitable, and more particularly that the evil is disadvantageous, also affected the concept of punishment. In the early period this is especially striking: no matter whether the punishment is imposed through self-help or through the agency of the State, or even that of the gods, it is always regulated by the categories of profit and damage. The institution of the fine is the most obvious case in point, and it is significant that this businesslike arrangement becomes the model for many other types of legal transaction. Whether we are dealing with 'an eye for an eye' or with the custom of blood feud, the 'just' penalty is reckoned in figures, and the amount of damage dealt out to the delinquent—the damages —must be commensurate with the amount of damage perpetrated by him. As profit was amenable to prediction and calculation, so also the measures and degrees of justice. It is true, of course, that the idea of punishment and retribution rests on more than merely utilitarian considerations. The primary motivation is furnished by profound moral needs. Human action is feasible only provided the world makes sense, and it does make sense that injustice should reap no rewards. The good man is requited, and the wicked is punished (if not himself, then his children who perpetuate his self; and if not in this world, then in Hades, as Sisyphus and Tantalus found out to their sorrow). This conviction, it appears, confines within utilitarian limits a thought which is basically so profound and so comprehensive that it needs to be confined in this manner. Deeply rooted in the hearts of men, therefore, we find the hope—Kant (*Krit. d. prakt. Vern.* 1.2) feels that men could not exist without it—that good and evil are given their due reward. And if, as it sometimes happens, this ideal is not realized in this world, men are sorely troubled, and again and again they turn to ponder the meaning, or the lack of meaning, of a cosmos in which the good is not always, at least in the long run, profitable too.[3]

The long-range view and duration are likewise stressed in the more thoughtful passages concerning happiness. As we have seen, the early period knows only the kind of happiness which is of this world and cannot be clearly distinguished from material gain. Where a moral 'inhibition' comes into play, it is preferably advocated in the form that momentary happiness ought to be sacrificed to one of lasting value. Passions and desires have a disturbing effect on permanent happiness, and pleasure, *hedone*, is a questionable acquisition because it is short-lived. Solon is credited with the saying: 'Avoid the pleasure which creates displeasure.' Or we may read in the so-called Golden Sayings of Pythagoras (line 32): 'Look after your health and be moderate in drink, food, and sports.' Theognis (line 839) admonishes us: 'Maintain the mean between thirst and drunkenness,' and Eryximachus in Plato's *Symposium* (187 E): 'Pleasure ought to be roused in moderation, otherwise we lapse into sickness.' Everybody knows that some choice dishes will not agree with him, and that a bitter drug or a painful operation may make him healthy. By means of these examples, or variations upon them, we are unceasingly told that it is wrong to follow the pleasure of the moment. 'Health is the best thing,' says an old Attic drinking song (Plato *Gorgias* 451 E). Health is a 'lasting' happiness, modest perhaps, but the highest by far, because it safeguards a maximum span of life. The notion of measure and that of the golden mean spring from such rules as these. From the earliest times the aspirations of the soul are guided and restrained by the image of health. 'Healthy thinking,' *sophronein*,[4] is the name which the Greeks give to self-control, while the instincts and emotions are termed *pathe*, sufferings. *Sophrosyne*, moderation, is the knowledge which governs our health and well-being, and thus our happiness; it is an appreciation of organic nature with a bent toward the practical. In its own domain it has a function similar to the calculation of profit, which we might call a practical appreciation of definite quantities, i.e. of dead objects and their mathematically constant relations. In the case of *sophrosyne* also knowledge is the court of appeal before which morality must render its account. In the counterplay between emotion and restraint we are reminded of Athena's words to Achilles: Bridle your passions by thinking ahead of the future. The concept of *sophrosyne*, however, helps the moral 'block' to divest itself of its religious garb, and so the genuine Greek confidence in the power of the intellect finally comes into its own. With the contrast between self-control and the passions we have, so to speak, a continuation of the old Homeric distinction between the mind as creator of images and the mind as (e)motion. But in the archaic and the classical periods *sophrosyne* nowhere called for a radical rejection of the passions as irrational or sinful. Human health which provides the pattern of *sophrosyne* is very much dependent upon the proper functioning of the emotions. Thus the exhortations to self-control which we have cited enjoin moderation; they do not forbid all pleasure.

But what is health? We have already stated that it is difficult to say, unless we follow Plato's Eryximachus in defining it as a harmony of the various tendencies in the body. Eryximachus subscribes to Empedocles' doctrine of the elements; the 'right' mixture of the four elements produces health, whereas an excess of one over the others brings about sickness. His emphasis on the harmonious tension of opposites, however, is ultimately based on Heraclitus. The Greeks were profoundly impressed with the harmonious character of health and fitness; the ideal of harmony, order and measure is propagated in countless positive admonitions. Nevertheless there remained the difficulty of defining and clarifying the ideal itself; the negative statements, naturally enough, are more concrete and persuasive than the positive demands. *Meden agan* (nothing too much), for instance, undoubtedly conveys more meaning to the active man than its corollary *metron ariston* (measure is the best thing). For to define the nature of order, harmony and measure is fully as difficult as to say what health is, and it is easier to describe the infraction of a norm than the norm itself.

Where morality is measured by the standard of happiness, the writers are wont to refer to well-being, *eu prattein*, and the sensations connected therewith. In this fashion morality is brought under the aegis of aesthetics, and we might well say that *sophrosyne* is an artistic flair for measure and form in the area of morality. As harmony triumphs in the art of the Greeks, it manages to gain momentum also in the calls to virtue.

Happiness and ethics are bound together in many ways, particularly so by the vexation which the memory of a wicked deed excites in the doer. The vexation may turn into bitter regrets or an uneasy conscience. It is true that the guilty conscience was not known prior to Euripides; evidently it presupposes a high degree of introspection.[5] But the belief in the Erinyes is, after all, of great antiquity; it supplied, at least for the spiller of a kinsman's blood, a kind of religious experience which served as well as the modern reaction of horror and loathing at a crime committed. Other feelings which we would also include in the 'guilty conscience' manifested themselves as 'shame', a sensation of discomfort in the presence of others. According to the eudaemonistic theory of ethics the guilty conscience proves that moral conduct may safely be founded on a refined and intelligent understanding of happiness and unhappiness. But then the question arises why it is that a transgression, however profitable, or a sinful pleasure leaves a bitter taste in the agent's mouth. It seems certain that morality is not merely the same thing as the striving for pleasure and profit. The upshot of these reflexions was that those who speculated on the subject of happiness and morality, like those who talked of profit and morality, did not content themselves with the promise of ease and complacency as the rewards of a moral life. Instead they granted virtue the prospect of a permanent 'inner' happiness, and that is simply the assurance of having done no wrong. But notions of this sort do not appear until the days of Socrates. Their preliminary stages are to be traced in the religious concepts of the Orphics and similar sects which promised that all those who had led a pure life would be eligible for a blissful afterlife among the dead. The prize of a virtuous life, they avowed, is lasting happiness. Nevertheless the principal issue, for the Orphics as much as for Socrates, is not the yearning for happiness, but the craving for a 'pure' life. It should be noticed, of course, that neither the Orphics nor Socrates formulated this purity in positive terms; they thought of it as the absence of a taint, which in turn might either be a religious or a properly moral taint. Their expectation that the virtuous life ought to be recompensed with lasting happiness is merely a restatement of the idea which we have already discussed, namely that the wicked ought to be punished; both notions have their origin in the demand that there be justice in the world.

The longing for honour and achievement, the third in our series of motives, seeks to win permanence through fame. For the early Greek, fame is a brand of immortality which has this advantage that it is not beyond the reach of mortal man. Those who toil for *arete* have, therefore, a higher aim than those who search for profit and happiness, whose ken is mostly restricted to the duration of one man's life. Homer and several archaic poets, following an ancient Indo-European idea,[6] declare that the word of the poet allows fame to live on. For is it not true that a name is preserved by grace of the verse which survives beyond its time?

Profit, happiness, and self-assertion, 'egotistic' as they are, need not be immoral. For an ethical life, however, a regard for more than private interests is essential. If self-assertion is to be crowned with fame, its value must be recognized by the community as a whole.

But before we discuss the role of the community in formulating the call to virtue, let us deal with another prohibition. It is clear and self-evident, and definitely moral in nature, although it is not connected with any of the motifs we have mentioned and does not spring from altruistic causes either. It permits us to probe into the relation between morality and private interests, and to find out how much consideration the early Greek believed he owed to his social group. This is the prohibition against lying.

As soon as a child begins to talk he learns that he cannot with impunity say now one thing and then another, or say one thing and do another. A communal life is possible only if any member of the group may trust his fellow-members. With the introduction of the oath a solemn instrument for the procurement of dependable statements was created. In the associations of like-minded men which were formed during the period of the archaic lyric, such as political clubs, religious sects and others, lying, deception and fraud came to be regarded as heinous crimes. For the philosophers, last but not least, the injunction against lying comes to be of special urgency, for thinking requires consistency; one might even say that thinking is a struggle for the elimination of contradictions. Socrates and Plato insist on truthfulness, not only for the philosopher whose reflexion carries him towards knowledge, but for all moral men; for they must base their actions on knowledge. Furthermore they demand consistency of action as well; no one act is to give the lie to another. This is the prelude to what came to be known among the later philosophers as *homologoumenos zen*, the life at harmony with itself. When all is said and done, however, this approach does not lead to a positive definition of goodness or of truth. As in the field of logic so in ethical matters, consistency merely corrects error and falsehood, without providing an answer to the problem of truth or virtue.

The admonition 'Thou shalt not lie' seems self-evident enough, and it was issued many times. But especially during the earliest period it was not taken too seriously. The history of Greek poetry begins with the glorification of the magnificent liar, Odysseus. He does not lie like a child whose speech simply obeys his ideas and desires without the least regard for logic or internal congruity. On the contrary, he lies like a man: he takes great precautions not to be caught in discrepancies. We cannot say that his lying is pre-moral, as if the ugliness of the lie had not yet been discovered. Nor does he place himself beyond the world of good and evil, like the Baron von Muenchhausen whose lively tales suggest that his roots in this world are at best somewhat tenuous. Odysseus is a hero who must be taken at face value, and his lies meet with recognition because they serve just and proper interests. In the scale of values, truth does not occupy the highest position. It must be conceded that even in his own day this lying Odysseus occasioned some misgivings, as is shown by the story of the quarrel over the arms of Achilles which were to be given to the best of the Greeks. Ajax cannot reconcile himself to the decision that they be awarded to Odysseus. The doughty warrior confronts the trickster, and both are found to be one-sided. Odysseus may not be open or straightforward, but Ajax lacks intelligence and agility. It is the particular *arete* of Odysseus that he is always able to look after himself; he lies to his enemies, and also to those who might become his enemies. But he lies not only to secure his own private advantage, but in the interest of the Greeks, of his comrades and his family. In dealing with strangers he deems the lives and the well-being of his friends and relatives more precious than truth. Odysseus clearly formulates his values when he expresses his good wishes to Nausicaa: happy partners in marriage, he says (*Od.* 6.184), are 'a great bane to the foe, but a joy to friends'. Hesiod (*Erga* 353) and Sappho (25.6) repeat this maxim, and Solon prays to the Muses (1.5): Grant me wealth and authority that 'I may thus (!) be pleasant to my friends, and bitter to my enemies' (cf. *Il.* 3.51; Euripides *Medea* 809 f.; Plato *Gorgias* 492 C and *passim*; *Republic* 362 B). This principle had a long life. When the tyrant Hipparchus inscribed his calls to virtue on the herms which he erected along the highways of Attica, he wrote: 'Conduct yourself with a just mind'; and again: 'Do not deceive your friend.' In our eyes this restriction to the friend does not exactly conform with a 'just mind'; is it then permitted to deceive one's enemy? Still, these precepts are not quite as general in their design as we might think; they are addressed to those who travel on the road, chiefly to the peasants who are about to sell their produce on the Athenian market. They must not deceive their fellow-citizens.

Side by side with our earlier concept of morality as profit deferred to the future, we now have a new idea—profit extended to the many. In the circle of one's relatives and friends, the *philoi*, profit becomes a common cause; no one harms his neighbour. This is important enough in any system of ethics, but obviously it is not yet morality's finest flower. For even the beasts operate under such a law, if it is true that one crow will not pick out the eyes of another, and the same code also prevails among criminals (Plato *Republic* 351 C). Of the Cyclopes who do not lead a civilized life Odysseus tells us that each man sits in judgment over his children and women, but that they have no respect for one another (9.114), that they are wicked and fierce and unjust (9.175) and that they disregard the gods (9.275 f.). Life in the primitive group, therefore, in which none but the women and children are 'friends', is a barbaric life. The other Cyclopes are indeed willing to help Polyphemus when he cries to them, but for anyone outside the group they have nothing but murderous contempt; there is no piety from which the wandering stranger might expect protection. It appears, therefore, that even the *Odyssey* demands more from a civilized life than a mechanical response to the dictates of friendship and hostility. The Cyclopes are called 'godless' and 'unjust'; he who feels perfectly free to injure any non-friend does injury to religion and justice. The religious concepts which in the early period so strongly affect the calls to virtue are often the reflexions of ancient taboos. *Aidos*, the feeling of shame, for example, originates as the reaction which the holy excites in a man. In Homer we find a religious element sustaining such sentiments as the respect for parents, reverence for a king, and reverence even for a beggar or suppliants who have no rights but stand under the special protection of the deity. But *aidos* is also the consideration extended to one's equals, and in its secularized form it

borders upon the refined climate of the court and polite
society. Since honour is one of the main conditions for a
moral existence, the respect for this honour, *aidos*, is a
mighty pillar in the structure of civilized humanity. It
perpetuates the authority and the hierarchic order of an
earlier society whose venerable customs were regarded as
sacred, as a work of the gods. Numerous tales deal with the
foundation or dedication of the existing institutions; many
religious commandments plead for the preservation of the
holy. Thus a deep conservatism is the key-note of the calls
to *aidos* and of the injunctions against 'budging' the holy.
The *aidos* of religion is the most powerful agency known in the
early age for imposing inhibitions upon an agent: witness the
action of the goddess who restrained Achilles from indulging
his savage desire and impairing the sacred bonds of reverence.

Besides these prohibitions of religious origin the early
period also knows some positive calls to virtue for the
regulation of human intercourse. The Athenian *bouzygeioi
arai*, for instance, decree that a traveller must be shown
the right way, that a neighbour be given fire if he asks for it,
that a newly-found corpse should be buried, and so forth.
On the whole the Greeks were comparatively chary of pro-
posing that people should shoulder inconveniences for the
purpose of helping others. The commandments which we
have mentioned specify assistance in particular emergencies
only. They are plausible enough, because anyone might
find himself in a similar situation; it is pure self-interest,
therefore, to support such rulings. The principle: '*do ut des*'
applies to all of them in equal force. Certainly the Greeks
did not admit to a universal law which required them to love
their neighbour, or to feeling any great responsibility toward
their fellow-humans. Only on rare occasions, and even then
reluctantly, is motherly love used as a model of ethical
behaviour. In a certain passage of Plato's *Symposium* (207
A), for example, where the notion of *caritas* would have been
most pertinent, the protection which the beasts give to their
young is explained as a longing for immortality, not as a basic
moral reality. Among the Greeks and Romans nobody is
urged to help another except a friend, and with dry satisfaction it is pointed out that the good offices of a friend are
bound to be mutually advantageous.

The desire to harm one's enemy finds its chief obstacle in justice. Justice, or the law, aims to benefit and protect a new universal of its own creation: the State. From the very first, however, this means that justice is restricted to an area within which its benefits can be realized, if necessary, by force. Virtue, on the other hand, presupposes no State. For the good of the commonwealth justice requires that no one harm anyone else by means of deception or violence. In the eyes of the citizen, justice should coincide with gain, or rather, in so far as crimes are punished, injustice with injury. But the use of force, even where punishment is deserved, is still a far cry from true morality; the same is true of the kind of just doing which springs from fear of punishment, and of mere obedience to the law in general.

Although justice fails to achieve what is expected of morality, it has done a great deal to aid and guide men's thinking about ethics. Do not look for your own gain if it means another's loss, do not seek your own happiness at the expense of somebody else's suffering, do not extend your own power to the detriment of others: these and similar moral tenets first impinged on man's conscience by way of the statute law behind which they lay hidden. The statement: 'Do not unto others what thou wouldst not have done unto thee' is self-evident, and need not be supplemented by references to private gain or the profit of the group. It calls for consistency in one's thinking about action, and eclipses all utilitarian considerations. The rule that his own demeanour is to be measured no differently from that of others is for a Greek an integral part of the notion of justice. Justice, *dike*, is the portion due to each member of the group: '*suum cuique*', as the positive juridical maxim puts it. *Dikaiosyne* is the desire to see to it, within one's circle, that each obtains his share, and that there is no trespassing upon alien domains. But how do we determine what portion is due to the individual? The law of property which provides the pattern for this idea of justice confines itself to the protection of ownership; the trespasser is punished, and that is just. In fact, justice, from this point of view, is quite simply 'the wrong which we don't do'.

The truth of the matter is that it was not the concept of justice but that of *arete* which gave rise to the call for positive individual achievement, the moral imperative which the early Greek community enjoins upon its members who in turn acknowledge it for themselves. A man may have purely egotistical motives for desiring virtue and achievement, but his group gives him considerably more credit for these ideals than if he were to desire profit or happiness. The community expects, and even demands, *arete*. Conversely a man who accomplishes a high purpose may convince himself so thoroughly that his deed serves the interests of a supra-personal, a universal cause that the alternative of egotism or altruism becomes irrelevant. What does the community require of the individual? What does the individual regard as universal, as eternal? These, in the archaic age, are the questions about which the speculations on *arete* revolve.

The problem remains simple as long as the individual cherishes the same values as the rest of his group. Given this condition, even the ordinary things in life are suffused with an air of dignity, because they are part of custom and tradition. The various daily functions, such as rising in the morning and the eating of meals, are sanctified by prayer and sacrifice, and the crucial events in the life of man—birth, marriage, burial—are for ever fixed and rooted in the rigid forms of cult. Life bears the imprint of a permanent authority which is divine, and all activity is, therefore, more than just personal striving. No one doubts the meaning of life; the hallowed tradition is carried on with implicit trust in the holy wisdom of its rules. In such a society, if a man shows unusual capacity he is rewarded as a matter of course. In Homer a signal achievement is, as one would expect, also honoured with a special permanence, through the song of the bard which outlasts the deed celebrated and preserves it for posterity. This simple concept is still to be found in Pindar's *Epinicians*. The problem of virtue becomes more complex when the ancient and universally recognized ideal of chivalry breaks down. Already in Homeric times a differentiation sets in. As we have seen in the story of the quarrel over the arms of Achilles, the *aretai* become a subject for controversy. The word *arete* itself contains a tendency toward the differentia-tion of values, since it is possible to speak of the virtues of various men and various things. As more sections of society become aware of their own merit, they are less willing to conform to the ideal of the once-dominant class. It is discovered that the ways of men are diverse, and that *arete* may be attained in all sorts of professions. Whereas aristocratic society had been held together, not to say made possible by a uniform notion of *arete*, people now begin to ask what true virtue is. The crisis of the social system is at the same time the crisis of an ideal, and thus of morality. Archilochus says (fr. 41) that different men have their hearts quickened in various ways. But he also states, elaborating a thought which first crops up in the *Odyssey*: the mind of men is as Zeus ushers in each day, and they think whatever they happen to hit upon (fr. 68). One result of this splitting up of the various forms of life is a certain failure of nerve. Man begins to feel that he is changeable and exposed to many variable forces. This insight deepens the moral reflexions of the archaic period; the search for the good becomes a search for the permanent.

The topic of the virtues is especially prominent in the elegy. Several elegiac poets furnish lists of the various *aretai* which they exemplify by means of well-known myths. Their purpose is to clarify for themselves their own attitudes toward the conflicting standards of life. Theognis (699 ff.) stands at the end of this development; with righteous indignation he complains that the masses no longer have eyes for anything except wealth. For him material gain has, in contrast with earlier views, become an enemy of virtue.

The first to deal with this general issue is Tyrtaeus. His call to arms pronounces the Spartan ideal; perhaps he was the one to formulate that ideal for the first time. Nothing matters but the bravery of the soldier fighting for his country. Emphatically he rejects all other accomplishments and virtues as secondary: the swiftness of the runner in the arena, or the strength of the wrestler, or again physical beauty, wealth, royal power, and eloquence, are as nothing before bravery. In the *Iliad* also a hero best proves his virtue by standing firm against the enemy, but that is not his only proof; the heroic figures of Homer dazzle us precisely because of their richness in human qualities. Achilles is not only brave but also beautiful, 'swift of foot', he knows how to sing, and so forth. Tyrtaeus sharply reduces the scope of the older *arete*; what is more, he goes far beyond Homer in magnifying the fame of fortitude and the ignominy which awaits the coward.

Of the fallen he actually says that they acquire immortality
(9.32). This one-sidedness is due to the fact that the community has redoubled its claim on the individual; Sparta in
particular taxed the energies of its citizenry to the utmost
during the calamitous period of the Messenian wars. The
community is a thing of permanence for whose sake the
individual mortal has to lay down his life, and in whose
memory lies his only chance for any kind of survival. Even
in Tyrtaeus, however, these claims of the group do not
lead to a termite morality. Far from prescribing a blind and
unthinking service to the whole, or a spirit of slavish self-
sacrifice, Tyrtaeus esteems the performance of the individual
as a deed worthy of fame. This is a basic ingredient of *arete*
which, in spite of countless shifts and variations, is never
wholly lost.

As early a poet as Callinus, in the seventh century B.C.,
transforms the motifs of the *Iliad* in a characteristic fashion.
He admonishes the young men of his city not to sit about idly
as if there were peace.

> War contains the whole land (therefore march out against
> the enemy)[7] and even at the moment of death let each man
> once more hurl his spear, for it is honourable and fair
> for a man to fight against the enemy on behalf of his
> country and his children and his wedded wife.   Death will
> come to pass whenever the Fates complete their web for
> him . . . It is not fated for a man to escape death, not
> even if he is descended from immortal fathers. Often someone
> escapes the battle and the noise of the spears and returns
> home, only to meet the doom of death in his house. He,
> however, finds no honour.

To stand up for one's own country, to fight for interests
transcending the welfare of the individual: this is the advice
of Callinus, and it carries special conviction because of the
implication that the family is thereby protected from the
enemy. Such things are, of course, also found in Homer, but
in certain details Callinus ventures farther than Homer.

Hector harangues the Trojans in battle (*Il.* 15.494 ff.):

> Let us fight in a body against the ships of the Greeks; whoever
> among you is hit and falls, let him die. It is not unseemly for
> him to die defending his fatherland. But his wife and his
> children are safe for the future, and his house and blameless
> property, when the Greeks have gone home with their ships.

Hector says: 'It is not unseemly to defend one's fatherland.' Callinus: 'It is honourable and glorious to fight for one's country.' Where Homer speaks of defence, Callinus talks war and loudly proclaims the glory of the battle. Tyrtaeus goes even further (6.1): 'It is a beautiful thing for a brave man to die in the foremost ranks, fighting for his country.' He bestows his praise, not merely on the defence, or on the battle, but on the very death of the hero, and his 'beautiful' is more than 'honourable' or 'glorious'.

Callinus, and to an even greater degree, as we have seen,[8] Tyrtaeus, affirm this heroism for the sake of glory, as a means of warding off ill repute. In this they follow Homer (cf., e.g., *Il.* 5.532; 6.521). But Callinus cites additional reasons why a man should be brave, reasons which are themselves devised in the spirit of the *Iliad*. 'Death will come to pass whenever the Fates decide. Often someone escapes from battle, only to die at home.' This reminds us of words spoken by Hector, but in an entirely different situation. When Hector takes his leave from Andromache before going into the fight he says (*Il.* 6.486):

> Do not sorrow overmuch in your heart. None will send me
> into Hades against the wish of fate (lit.: beyond fate).
> For I say that no one has ever escaped his fate, neither a
> bad man nor a good, once he is born.

There is a very decided difference between the man who, like Hector, ponders his own fighting and his own death and says: everybody must die in the end; and the singer who points to this fate with the purpose of encouraging others to deeds of heroism.

Tyrtaeus who values death for the fatherland as a downright beautiful thing would naturally be inclined to tone down any such reflexion, with its premise that death is something evil and difficult. He warns: 'Let us be brave and fight for this land and die for our children, without heeding our lives' (6.14), or: the brave man 'who has fallen in the foremost line is beautiful' (7.30). Or he actually says: 'Let each man take his shield into the foremost ranks, regarding his life as his foe, and loving death as much as the rays of the sun ' (8.4). The paradoxical phrasing itself indicates what he expects in a man; but that the passage can hardly be meant to be taken in all seriousness is suggested by the lines which follow a little later (8.11): 'Those who remain together and go forth bravely into the hand-to-hand fight and the front of the line, do not die in such numbers.' This thought too is borrowed from Homer. But in the *Iliad* it is in the thick of the battle that the general calls out (5.529; cf. 15.561): 'Be men and take courage. Show respect to each other in the fight, for when men feel this respect more are spared than are killed. Those who flee have neither fame nor strength.' In that critical situation his warning makes good sense; at that moment it really is dangerous to flee. Tyrtaeus, however, uses the same slogan to inspire the soldiers with courage to step forward to the front of the line. What is more, the phrase: 'The brave do not die as often as the cowards' appears after all to imply the admission that death is an evil. Ultimately, when Horace picks up the words of Tyrtaeus (*Odes* 3.2.13): 'It is sweet and honourable to die for the fatherland—death pursues also him who flees . . .',[9] it is only too evident that the ultimate decline of grandeur into bathos is near at hand.

Tyrtaeus, it would appear, is the first to react to the incipient differentiation of the *aretai* and to secure a clear and unequivocal idea of the nature of *arete* as such. What is more important, he tries to find the common bond, the supra-individual unit for which the individual is called into action, and he discovers it in nothing so concrete as the family or the country, but in a more abstract formulation (9.15): 'It is a common good, for the city and for the people, when a man proves himself in battle.' The concept of the State is about to be born.

Outside of Sparta the call to virtue has a different history. It is true, of course, that even in Attica a man was, in time of war, expected to sacrifice himself to his country, if necessary. But Solon in his admonitory elegies allows various virtues to men; instead of discrediting the various forms of *arete* in order to insist on one alone, he assumes from the outset that men pursue their goals along diverse paths. These paths are all equally good or equally bad. Nobody is able to see the end of his road; only Zeus can do that. Solon also reverts to the old theme of Archilochus: man's life is brief, exposed, and dangerous. By enumerating one by one the various pro-

fessions and skills Solon shows that the new society of
citizens is diametrically opposed to the ancient aristocratic
order. The uniform ideal of a ruling class is no longer
acknowledged. This process of differentiation might well
have sapped the vigour of the moral law, and crippled its
authority; Solon banished the danger by combining the ideas
concerning *arete* with the concept of punitive justice. However uncertain the ways of man, says Solon, one thing remains
incontrovertible: injustice is always punished, whether the
blow falls in this generation or not. Solon here blends two
different traditions into one. Archilochus had discerned an
eternal up and down, a great 'rhythm', constituting the basic
pattern of life. In Solon's thought this alternation takes on a
juridical aspect: each crime has its penalty. Archilochus'
saying: 'What has risen must fall again' is qualified by Solon:
'Whatever has risen unjustly must fall again'. Justice is
permanent, and to exercise this justice is the highest type of
arete. The vantage-point from which Solon becomes a
spokesman for justice enables him to see beyond the point
reached by Hesiod or Archilochus. He takes up the struggle
against injustice without being at all affected in his own
person, nor is his indignation due to a wrong done to himself.
He acts in the name of right, not to protect his private
interests, but to defend order and equity in the State. Instead
of impotence or resentment driving him into the arms of a
fictitious commonwealth—as Callicles in the *Gorgias* would
understand the origin of justice—he is propelled by a
profound feeling that everyone deserves his particular share
in the whole, a feeling for the dignity and the significance of
the law of justice. No doubt Solon's notion of justice is as
yet tied to religion. His is a firm belief that the gods punish
injustice, that Athena in particular protects her city, and that
consequently a just action finds its proper, and profitable,
reward. But that he was concerned about justice and nothing
else he was able to prove when he himself came into a position
of power. Solon committed the unprecedented act of re-
nouncing tyranny when it was well within his grasp. This
earned him the charge of weakness and even stupidity: here
was a man who did not dare to accept the noble gift of the
gods—for that is how the people in their naiveté looked upon

power. Solon defends himself against the accusation in a
poem which has in part come down to us (fr. 23):

> I spared the fatherland, nor did I touch power and tyranny,
> but I am not ashamed of it, even though I am said to have
> sullied my fame. With the help of the gods I carried out what
> I had promised; it does not please me to act through the
> violence of tyranny.

And elsewhere (fr. 24.16 ff.) he says: 'Power and justice
have I joined together, and I have written laws in equal
portion for the good and for the bad, fitting the straight
justice for each'. The fact that once upon a time in ancient
Attica a man did not make use of the power which fell to his
lot, but renounced it for the sake of justice, was to be of
immeasurable consequence for the laws and politics of
Greece and Europe as a whole. For Solon himself the
immediate results were disappointing enough. He lived to
see the tyranny which Pisistratus received from the willing
hands of a fickle populace. But the sentiment which inspired
him to put the internal affairs of Athens in order, and which
he broadcast in his poetry for all to hear, has since become an
integral part of politics, in spite of numerous attempts to
abuse it, or to stamp it out: the idea, i.e., that justice is a
permanent entity which stands above men, and that justice,
not violence, is the norm of public affairs. In the Attic state
of the fifth century this concept won a new lease of life, and
found itself raised to a higher power; when the axiom of
justice for all came to be underpinned with the fact of
individual accountability, the final stage of the evolution had
been reached.

In Sparta and Athens, then, the discussion of *aretai*
produces the concepts of state and justice. In Ionia, however,
such writers as Mimnermus and Xenophanes come to totally
different conclusions. To Mimnermus, men are as different
as their sufferings. One is poor, another childless, the third is
sick: the only pleasant things in life are youth and love (frs.
1 and 2). The moral which he distils from this insight is
simple enough: enjoy your life (fr. 7). He deliberately resigns
himself to a life without lasting gain, happiness and
achievement (only the young, he believes, possess 'honour',
fr. 5,—the old man is hated by his children and despised by
women, fr. 1.9), and throws to the winds all thought for the

community. In his own way he becomes as one-sided as Tyrtaeus. Mimnermus discerns no permanent principle guiding our lives; life has lost its firmly stamped character, and since it is brief and transitory, the pleasure of the moment is all that remains to us. In the other writers it was always possible to find at least the seeds of a moral attitude; in Mimnermus they are completely dispensed with. But since he is a real poet he has left us his verses which are more melodious than those of Tyrtaeus or Solon, and he has also bequeathed to us his knowledge of the transitoriness of all beauty. The sweetness of speech which in Homer had served an objective purpose has now become an aim in itself. His insight does not provoke action but illuminates the nothingness of life. Unbelief and formal charm came to be greatly valued at a later period,[10] but they are more consistent with light-hearted pleasantries than with admonitions to virtue.

Xenophanes, like Tyrtaeus, does not hold a brief for those *aretai* which stood in general favour with the Greeks, such as wrestling and boxing and running. Instead he recommends his 'wisdom' as more profitable to the State. It is 'a joy to the city', it 'fattens the bins of the city' and contributes more to a lawfully ordered life than the much-admired athletics (2.19–22). And yet, in spite of the fact that the standard by which he measures *arete* is the gain of the *polis*, the 'common good' as Tyrtaeus had called it, his real moral interest lies along different lines. He realizes that men make their gods in their own image; so he proposes a deity which is not grossly anthropomorphic but, given the limitations of Xenophanes' vocabulary, pure intellect. Xenophanes tests the traditional gods and myths by the touchstone of civic virtue, and rejects them. The intellect is devoid of desires and passions; it alone is permanent, durable, changeless. Thus by celebrating 'wisdom' as the highest *arete* Xenophanes too shows that his choice is determined by the criterion of permanence. Once again, therefore, the search for *arete* has turned out to be the search of a mortal, as the Greeks call man, for immortality.

All these reflexions on the subject of *arete* were supposed to tell us what positive services society exacted from the individual. As it is they have led us far away from the field of ethics, to that of metaphysics. The selfish urges are

overcome most successfully if it can be pointed out that there
is a true, a lasting good; and that ultimately leads us to the
permanent Being.   May we say that these speculations
contain a significant echo of one of the main tenets of the
Olympian religion: that the gods are above all immortal?

Deference to other people's interests, to repeat, was mainly
required in the State, and before the law. As for the legal
prescripts, they were on the whole little else but injunctions
against doing harm to others. In the sphere of the State we
have encountered the commandment to fight for the fatherland, perhaps to die for it. Other appeals for coming to the
assistance of the community are lacking. Altruism is nowhere
called for, nor do we hear that one man ought to provide for
the happiness of another.

Thus there seems to be comparatively little moral substance
in the early Greek calls to virtue. Should we blame the
defective state of our tradition, or the fact that admittedly we
have passed over much that is of lesser consequence? We
suspect that there must be a better reason, and our suspicion
is confirmed if we turn our eyes once more to those exhortations which are based on religion, and to which we have not
yet paid all the attention they deserve.

Over and above the penalties dealt out by the State there
looms the punishment which the gods are expected to visit
upon the wicked. The exact period of time within which the
punishment must be meted out is somewhat elastic. In any
case, as we have seen, the Greek gods make no curt commands, they issue no arrogant threats; they insist on a willing
and understanding heart rather than on blind submission.
Even the eschatological tales concerning culprits in the throes
of torture and believers rewarded with eternal bliss play a
much smaller role among the Greeks than heaven and hell
do in Christian mythology.

In the beginning the moral 'inhibition', too, was a religious
phenomenon. Athena made Achilles restrain his ardour; she
appealed to his understanding by pointing to the profit
involved. *Aidos*, the spirit of reverence which held men back
from rash transgressions was also at first based on religion.
In Homer, however, *aidos* has already severed its ties with
the gods and become simply 'courteous respect'.

Traditionally the good man has honour and happiness

conferred on him; he is, so to speak, likened to the gods. Yet
the Pythian deity warns: know thyself, i.e. know that you are
a man, that an unbridgeable gulf separates you from the gods.
Other sayings from the archaic period point in the same
direction: do not try to climb the brazen sky, do not attempt
to wed Aphrodite. Countless myths express the dangerous
consequences of this *hybris*. The Delphic motto stands out
among the rest because its terms are the most general, and
because it appeals to the understanding. The block or
restriction imposed by a Greek god has never been more
purely or more beautifully expressed; penalty and gain have
dropped out of the field of vision, and the only thing left in
it is understanding.

But this understanding in turn is not without its own share
of problems and difficulties, and it was not long before the
thinkers turned to them. If 'know thyself' means that one
ought to restrict himself to what is human instead of trespassing upon the property of the gods, it is taken for granted
that the power and magnificence of the gods is fully recognized; at the same time there seems to be a presumption that
man strives to obtain a like power and glory. In other words,
the premises of that motto are, on the one hand, an unbroken
faith in the gods, and on the other a naive vitality aspiring, by
means of *arete*, to a godlike happiness. In the course of the
sixth and fifth centuries both the belief in the gods and the
robust confidence in man's own godlikeness came to be
seriously shaken. The belief in the gods underwent a change
which made for greater depth. As the gods began to be
measured by moral standards, and as their true meaning was
identified with the idea of justice, they were raised high above
the human level. Conversely, man examined himself and
found himself less and less competent to think of equalling
the gods. Finally, the recognition that there are various kinds
of *aretai*, and the search for the one true *arete*, spelled the
end of the old optimism and assurance. And yet, this greatest
of all exhortations in early Greece, the Delphic motto, never
lost its force, in spite of the doubt cast upon its premises. It
pointed far into the future, and even Socrates, for whom the
problem of morality bore a totally different complexion, was
able to use it as a fundamental tenet of his ethics.

The figure of Socrates constitutes the turning-point from

the moral thinking of the archaic and classical periods to that of the post-classical and Hellenistic ages. Here and there he is scolded for having destroyed the instinctive optimism and the naive assurance of his predecessors, replacing them with fruitless reflexions. But the truth is that self-examination and uncertainty had started to attack human initiative long before Socrates came upon the scene. Nobody could possibly say that down to the time of Socrates the Greeks had cheerfully relied on the guidance of their instincts, to the exclusion of all other considerations. The moral block becomes operative at a very early stage. Is not its meaning this, that a man does not entrust himself completely to his instincts and his impulses? From the very start the Greeks attempt to bridle their passions with the reins of the understanding and of knowledge. Callicles, in Plato's *Gorgias*, may assert that it is the natural state for the stronger to develop his power freely and to indulge in his desires. But that does not really hold for human beings; such a jungle philosophy could not come into being until the Sophists had abolished all ties of religion and custom by branding them mere conventions. To counteract these aberrations Socrates sought to create a new foundation for morality. And it is new indeed. In pondering the good, Socrates does not train his eyes on the finished achievement, but on the moment when a man has the act before him and is forced to come to terms with it. In the calls to virtue which we have discussed up to now, the precepts owed their validity to the circumstance that the men who issued the calls seemed to be innocent of conflicts or doubts. Socrates, on the other hand, does not play the part of a teacher who knows, but, as he himself put it so poignantly, merely practises the midwife's skill. He assists others in their efforts to bring to light the knowledge which is stored in their own persons. And thus Socrates upholds one of the traditions of tragedy. The tragedians had been the first to interpret human action in the light of an intellectual choice, and to unfurl the standard of the freedom of action. Socrates belongs to the same school; he feels that a man should not act without a full understanding of what he is about, and that each person must organize his own independent search for the good.

When Tyrtaeus, Solon, Xenophanes and Mimnermus put

forward their definitions of the true *arete*, they were no longer
agreed about its nature, but each of them was firmly persuaded of the truth of his position. This persuasion was a
sort of ontological conviction of the permanence and reality
of some fact; either the State, as in the case of Tyrtaeus, or the
eternal law of justice, as proclaimed by Solon, or divine
reason, the vision of Xenophanes—or again the transitoriness
of Mimnermus which permits but a charming poem to
prolong the fleeting happiness of the hour. These writers
would have been hard put to it to understand why Socrates
asks his question: 'what is the good?' anew for each given case.
Heraclitus who drew the balance for the whole period
expresses their stand as follows: the moral task is 'to follow
that which is common to all'—and even for Heraclitus the
common, the universal, is that which endures. The first
business is to understand this universal; that may be difficult,
for the universal may be the imponderable. But once it is
understood, what comes after, the 'consequence' or performance, follows automatically. 'Look upon the end,' focus your
eyes on the goal, says Chilon. Once you have seen it, you only
need *eros kalôn* and *dynamis*, as the archaic age phrases it,[11]
'the love of the beautiful, and the strength to achieve it.'
Responsibility, freedom of action, and self-knowledge have
no function in such a setting.

Socrates does not send out a call to virtue; he teaches it.
He does not endeavour to persuade, but to convince. After
Socrates all exhortations to virtue go by the board; they
become antiquated, no matter how vigorous their after life.
We have rung the curtain on our theme. But seeing that all
the questions concerning virtue have remained in the balance,
let us indicate how the old exhortations find their echoes in
Socrates. For although he is an innovator, the ancient motifs
recur, most likely because they cannot very well be avoided
whenever people turn their minds to the subject of virtue.

Since Socrates has not left us any writings, it is often
difficult to distinguish his property from that of Plato or
Xenophon, the principal recorders of his doctrines. But we
are chiefly interested in the difference between the moral
philosophy created by Socrates and all earlier teachings. It is
thus more important for us to obtain a clear view of that crucial
change than to ascertain the personality of Socrates himself.

I believe that it is possible to fix the point from which Socrates starts out to discuss morality.[12] Euripides' Medea says: 'I know what crimes I am about to commit, but my anger is stronger.' Socrates rejoins: 'As long as a man knows the good, he will do it. All that is necessary is that he has really recognized the nature of the good. Nobody commits a crime voluntarily.'

Socrates' demand is exacting, so exacting indeed that only very few men will be able to carry it out. He asks them to place their passions and impulses completely under the control of the understanding. The historical antecedents to this summons are somewhat as follows. The ancient Homeric contrast between *nous* and *thymos*, between the seeing mind and the (e)motive mind, was already in the archaic age regarded as a counterplay between two forces of the soul, between restrictive understanding and expansive desire. The understanding which operates in the practical, the moral sphere was defined as *sophrosyne*, moderation. Of equal antiquity is the idea that the good must appear as the profitable in order to be amenable to the understanding. And since the one and true gain is virtue, virtue is the object of true knowledge. With his concept of voluntary action, Socrates adopts a vital feature of Attic law, the distinction between voluntary and involuntary deeds.[13] This again involves the element of choice and decision which we have come to know in Attic tragedy. A voluntary action, for Socrates, is an action founded on knowledge, the knowledge, i.e., of loss and gain.

Socrates fixes on the 'decision' as the cardinal point in his examination of ethics. The image which he has in mind is that of a person who comes to a cross-roads and wonders whether to continue to the left or to the right. It was Hesiod who introduced the picture of the two roads into the discussion of virtue, but Socrates imparted to that image the vital function of forcing the traveller into the dire predicament of a choice.[14] We are accustomed to look upon the will as the mainspring of action. But the will, ever straining and champing at the bit, is a notion foreign to the Greeks; they do not even have a word for it. *Thelein* means: 'to be ready, to be prepared for something.' *Boulesthai* is: 'to view something as (more) desirable.' The former denotes a subjective preparedness, a kind of voluntary attitude devoid of specific commitment; the latter refers to a wish or plan (*boule*) aimed at a particular object, i.e. a disposition closely related to the understanding and appreciation of a gain. But neither word expresses a realization of the will, the effective inclination of subject toward object.[15] Besides failing to do justice to the modern notion of the will, neither word describes what Socrates has in mind: the moral edge of the will unsheathed in the act of decision. Aristotle speaks as a follower of Socrates when he says that all action is preceded by *prohairesis*, the 'choice' (*Nic. Eth.* 1139 a 31). In this way the will is concentrated in one point, the choice between two possibilities, and emerges more sharply delineated than is possible in our thinking about the will.[16] Morality, according to this view, is not the good will, but the will, or choice, of the good.[17]

Socrates, then, formulates the search for the good as a choice, as an unequivocal commitment between yea and nay. As a result the discussion of ethics becomes not only very clear in its implications, but also somewhat radical in spirit. By developing his Attic theme of the choice and the search for the desired goal with the tools of Ionic and Western philosophy Socrates underscores this radicalism even further. The good is the gainful; but Socrates does not aim at private profit—that is only apparent gain—but at the 'true' profit. From the earliest period, calculation and reckoning had been part of the quest for gain. Socrates does not take this gain in the sense of ordinary profit, but he nevertheless continues to insist on the need for calculation and understanding. And since his objective is not an apparent gain but true gain, he also demands a true knowledge rather than a semblance of understanding. With this end in view he falls back on the distinctions which Parmenides had set up for judging the external world, the opposites of Being and Appearance, of mere Opinion and genuine Knowledge. He decides against appearance and opinion, and chooses being and knowledge. It should be noted, however, that Parmenides' discrimination between knowledge and opinion differs from that of Socrates because it is based upon the contrast between thinking and sensuous perception, a contrast which is largely irrelevant in a moral context.

In his discussion of happiness, Socrates similarly rejects the false variety and calls for genuine happiness. The latter, in accordance with older concepts, he understands to be the happiness which endures. Lasting happiness cannot be of the body, which is perishable, but must be connected with the soul, for it is immortal. Here Socrates appropriates notions of the religious thinkers, the Orphics and the Pythagoreans. These in turn are based on a distinction between body and soul which was not fully worked out until post-Homeric times. Now Socrates counts all passions and impulses as physical desires, and so because he considers them part of the temporal world which he disparages he takes a more radical stand, theoretically, than those before him who advertised *sophrosyne* as the mistress of the passions. In point of fact, of course, he is no more radical on this score than in any other matter; for in spite of his impressive ability to control himself, and to use his mind as a check on his actions, he could never be called an ascetic.

Sophrosyne was a kind of moral measure, designed to stabilize the harmony of a healthy life. 'Harking to the lead of nature,' as we might say with Heraclitus, it served to keep the parts adjusted to each other. Socrates was firmly persuaded of the truth of Parmenides' theory—gained from an attempt to understand the external world, from the difficulty of conceiving physical motion—that only that which can be thought is permanent. He proceeded to avow that only thinking itself could lay claim to permanence; it did not occur to him to ask whether, or how, the passions and desires might be linked with the permanent, the immaterial—with life, or whatever term might be used. These are questions which Socrates was no more competent to face than those who had preceded him with their calls to virtue. For he takes as his point of departure the radical dilemma of a choice, the sharp cleavage between good and bad. What is more, his good is a teleological concept; it is an end. All this necessarily leads him to the conclusion that there is only one good, but many kinds of evil. And this one good needs to be recognized and known. Who would be rash enough to deny that this doctrine is, in a sense, profoundly true? Whether it is the only method of discussing the problem of virtue is another question again, a question which may surely be raised without at once involving the questioner in the charge that he is on the side of the material world, and against the spirit.

To arrive at a better understanding of virtue, Socrates could not fall back on the computation of profit, for the true profit has nothing in common with the numerical quantities of concrete gain. Nor was he able to use the notion of *sophrosyne* which, after all, has no interest in the 'good' but only in health, harmony, and the concordance of opposites. Again, he must not pursue the path of Parmenides which leads to the Being of the external world. The model which Socrates required for his teleological knowledge had to come from another quarter. He found it—another innovation— in the craftsman. As a carpenter must know a good table before he is able to construct it, so must a man know in advance what is good before he can act properly. Anyone who possesses a mechanical knowledge of some sort will also, as a matter of course, turn out something good. The identification of the good with the profitable is not unconnected with this, and lends its own weight to support the argument.

The Attic word for knowledge, *episteme*, affords a partial explanation why Socrates should have chosen the skill of the craftsman as his model. Unlike the Ionian words denoting knowledge and understanding, which refer only to theoretical cognition, the Attic term also embraces practical connotations. It signifies both knowledge and ability, and is used more particularly to denote experience in manual skills.[18] The direction of Socrates' thinking is, for that reason, given with his language from the first. The nature of his vocabulary enforces a close relation between knowledge and practical interest, between knowledge and ethical thought; and this is in fact the special achievement of Socrates in the history of Greek philosophy. For the earlier philosophers, the thinkers of Ionia and Magna Graecia, were interested chiefly in a theoretical understanding of the external world.

With this concept of a knowledge which parallels the skill of the artisan, Socrates explains the intent, the teleology of human action as follows. The craftsman executes an action of which he has a practical know-how (*epistatai*), which he has learnt as part of his special training, and therefore necessarily understands. Now Socrates demands that the performance of any action ought to be similarly determined by a knowledge of the specific nature of the action. The end, i.e. the good or virtue, is not merely, as in the earlier calls to virtue, an objectively given ideal, but the realization of the 'proper' potential of the agent. The *telos* is no longer an unchangeable universal standard which may be 'seen' by one and all (cf. Chilon's saying: 'See the end'). Instead, it is the product of a methodically acquired knowledge which supplies the needed understanding, and the only way to put it into concrete shape is by means of action. 'To do one's own' is the origin of all moral effort; thus Socrates enlists into his service one of the most fruitful ideas of the ancient discussion of *arete*. For it may be recalled that the early elegists had spoken of the various *aretai* of men. The difference is that he turns his back on social prestige, on glory and honour. He feels that the opinion of others ought to exert no decisive influence on anybody, except perhaps for the judgment of the 'experts', the good and the just. Man is to know himself; such knowledge will enable him to do 'his own'; he must not concern himself with alien matters before he has put his own house in order. Among the pursuits which he rejects under the caption of 'meddlesomeness' we find participation in public affairs. It is true that Socrates' thought is largely formed by his concern for the State. He continually bases his arguments on the allegation that those in charge of the State have no knowledge of the good. Nevertheless he defers the question what is good for the State, nor does he play the role of a reformer, much less a revolutionary, in practical politics. He acknowledges the claims of the State, and he served himself both as a soldier and as an elected officer of the people. He obeys its laws. His attitude towards traditional religion is the same. He does not touch the existing forms no matter how far he has moved beyond them. As long as the good is not genuinely known he preserves a notable respect for the old institutions. Any radical policy of removing the present system because it is bad, and hoping that something better will take its place, is furthest from his thoughts. Upon his own *arete*, however, he imposes the most severe demands, which, in their way, though more profoundly of course, echo the harangues of Tyrtaeus. In Plato's *Apology* (28 B ff.) he says that if one wishes to act properly he must take as little thought of his life as the heroes at Troy, particularly Achilles.

> Wherever a man has taken his place because he has persuaded himself that it is best, or wherever he has been placed by a superior, there, I believe, he ought to stand and accept the risk. He should not think of death or of anything rather than of disgrace.

The stern view which earlier writers from Homer to Tyrtaeus had taken of the notion of *arete*, the idea that *arete* may dictate the sacrifice of one's life, is now extended to cover any kind of moral behaviour, whether freely chosen by the agent or imposed from above. Where the stand is voluntary we read significantly: because he has persuaded himself that it is the right place. Thus persuasion, or knowledge, decides the issue of right and wrong. At the same time, the knowledge of one particular right is true knowledge only if it is founded upon knowledge of the good as such. And here Socrates admitted that he himself had failed to attain his goal. The final conclusion of his wisdom was: I know that I know nothing. And yet his desire to learn remained strong and vigorous. He did not become a sceptic, for in spite of his ignorance he clung to the tenet that virtue can be taught. In the person of Socrates the eternal struggle for wisdom, the searching and pondering which constitutes the proper activity of the philosopher, is supremely in evidence, more so even than in Heraclitus or Parmenides, for they ended up propounding a dogma.

For all this, the philosophizing of Socrates did not remain without fruit. He did more to delimit the 'way' of thinking, the method, than any one of his predecessors. Previously the question: what is virtue? had evoked particular answers such as: bravery, or justice, or wisdom. Socrates came back with the query: what is the common property of these, the common good, which is responsible for bravery, justice and so forth being particular goods? Following his practice of stopping men in the market-place and asking them to define the good, he would again and again, as we are shown in Plato's dialogues, receive particular virtues for an answer. Nobody understood the universal character of the question. So this became the point at which he set the lever; his concern with what we would call the 'concept' constitutes the beginnings of our logic. To-day it goes without saying that the problem of the moral universal is of much greater significance and urgency than the questions raised by such universals as 'horse' and 'man'. In the case of the latter, the problem seems comparatively simple. If we undertake to define 'the' horse in general, we try to obtain a definition which includes within itself all the separate horses given to us by our senses. The definition of 'the' good is another matter. If, at the moment of a decision, I ask: what is the good? I thereby mean something specific that I wish to bring about. But this specific thing is a goal, an objective, and therefore exists only in my mind. Now the general question: what is the good? demands an answer which would determine the good not just for a single situation but for any and all dilemmas. Thus, it appears, I am trying to discover a universal for something which is itself no concrete fact, but merely an object of my thoughts. To appreciate fully the tangled and abstract nature of the problem, let us add the following. The universal meaning of 'horse' is primarily the result of predications: this is (a) horse (cf. below Ch. 10). The 'good' does not emerge from such predications because it does not stand for anything that is empirically given. It grows out of an impasse, at a moment of indecision; thus it is always the product of a question: what is the good? There could be no notion of 'the' good until the old standards of action began to be discredited. Its first bid for recognition appears in the query of the tragic hero who asks: what am I to do? With the question of Socrates: what is virtue? the problem achieves philosophical status. The good is discovered in the search for it; its existence is involved in the commitment which that search carries with it.

If we were to consider to what extent the concept of 'the good' permits of analogies with the concept of the species 'horse', we should immediately find ourselves lost in the labyrinth of Plato's doctrine of ideas. We should also have to face the question whether the transition from one model to another embarrasses philosophical argument, or rather whether it is legitimate at all. Whenever Socrates characterizes the knowledge of the good and the profitable by referring to the know-how of the artisan he creates certain difficulties. For the artisan the good is exemplified by a good table or some such thing, i.e., by an object, but that is not true in the case of the moral agent. Socrates' position becomes even more precarious when he takes Parmenides' distinction between knowledge and mere opinion, which had been evolved in a totally different context, and uses it for his own purposes. He adopts the theories of Parmenides concerning the two types of being, the true and the apparent, and extracts from them a contrast between true and apparent profit. This again he equates with another totally alien distinction, that between transitory and permanent happiness; which, in turn, seem to mean the same thing to him as physical and non-physical happiness. Socrates' quest for virtue is an eminently serious matter, but it bogs down in the quicksands because it aims at a goal which can be reached only with the help of doubtful analogies.

The ancient ideals of the traditional calls to virtue did not survive intact; Socrates absorbed them into his scheme and blended them with one another, as well as with some other notions of pre-Socratic philosophy. And Plato's work continued the trend. Profit becomes true profit—but what is truth in contrast to appearance? Happiness is said to be the happiness of the immortal soul—but what, then, is the soul? Justice has ceased to be what it was for Solon, a mere maintenance of order or an adjustment of claims; it is no longer simply a lack of injustice; instead it has come to mean a positive standard of action—but if so, what is right? Virtue is 'the' good—but what is this universal? Honour and fame are valid only if bestowed by the just—but who are the just? Self-knowledge is no longer rooted in the ideal of a firmly organized caste; gone is the knight who could take comfort from the thought that he was a noble (*aner esthlos*). The State, the religious congregation, *in fine* the community, does not exist whose gain might be acclaimed as an indisputable authority for action. The ego stands lost and alone in the midst of an unknowable universality.

And nevertheless—and this is his special greatness—Socrates does not plunge into the abyss of nihilism. He is firmly anchored and held in place by three things which we already know from the early calls to virtue, but which now stand forth much more clearly as the cardinal forces of morality.

First of all there is the *daimonion*, the divine voice which kept Socrates from doing wrong. This is by and large the same force which we had called an 'inhibition'; it is responsible for justice in the relations of men with each other, and it impedes the doing of harm. But it is not quite the same, for now its nature is that of a revelation, unconditioned and supra-individual. In the second place, there is Socrates' unshaken belief that acting according to one's conviction makes good sense, and that there is nothing more serious and binding than a man's mission to 'achieve' something. This persuasion he sealed with his death. Finally, there is his conviction that man, by virtue of his knowledge, has a share in that reality which is universal and eternal, and that he must recruit his utmost in effort and integrity to attain to that knowledge, even if perfect wisdom is beyond his reach. Only in this way do we stand a chance of breaking through the barriers of our individuality and winning happiness.

This was the message, and the life, of Socrates. No grim fanaticism, no rigid pedantry or disdainful arrogance debased his gospel. He preached it soberly and modestly, with but the faintest trace of a gentle irony, knowing that he, this mortal Socrates, was only one single human being far from perfection, and that his life and his learning were no more than a limited, a very limited quest for the good. But how else could the unlimited reveal itself except in the form of the limited?

CHAPTER 9

FROM MYTH TO LOGIC: THE ROLE OF THE COMPARISON

BEFORE discussing the historical development which leads from the comparisons of myth, and especially from the Homeric simile, to the analogies of science and philosophy, it will be useful to pause briefly for the following question. Where, in the language of ordinary conversation, outside of the precincts of poetry and philosophy, does the comparison of one thing with another occur most frequently ? And, more important yet: Is such a comparison ever a matter of necessity ?

Our habit of referring to the objects in the world around us by means of concrete nouns is itself based on an act of comparison, on the drawing of a parallel. By attaching the name 'horse' to various animals at different times, I equate them in spite of their many distinguishing marks. In the realm of animals, and in that of the plants, no genuine difficulties arise to obstruct this equation; each horse is as much horse as any other, it is a horse in every respect, without allowing the slightest doubt. Other comparisons immediately suggest themselves: donkey and horse resemble each other, notwithstanding the specific distinctions between them. And this leads to a more general definition, such as ungulates, after which there is a more general again: mammals, and so forth. The process may be reversed; by itemizing the specific differentiae it is possible to arrive back at genus and species. Since Plato this has been the regular procedure in logical arguments; a definition includes both the common class and the specific differentiae which distinguish the object from other members of the class.

In the animal and vegetable kingdoms, this method is plausible enough because it is rooted in the very structure of organic nature. In our picture of the world, the family tree and the branches of organic nature correspond to the pattern of the logical method. There is only one difference; in the case of the natural world, any class may be sub-divided into a great variety of groups, each with its specific distinctions. Logic, on the other hand, knows only dichotomy, the division into two; a certain thing either 'is' or 'is not'— *tertium non datur*.

Other areas present a somewhat greater problem. The terms for limbs and similar organic parts, such as hand, or hoof, or leaf, are still fairly precise because of their place in the hierarchy of organic nature; but the Platonic diaeresis cannot be applied to them, or only with profound reservations. When we come to objects made by human hand, the special significance of our terms is much less clear. Chairs or houses resemble each other even less than the leaves and blossoms of plants, and we must always be prepared to encounter some particular piece which cannot be fitted into the general class. Other difficulties arise when we consider such words as river, mountain, or cloud; who would draw the proper line between heap, mound, hill and mountain; between brook, river, and stream; between fog, mist, and cloud?[1]

Finally there are nouns, like water, gold, and wood, which, because we learn nothing from them about the shape of the object, denote a material rather than a 'thing'. The statement: 'This is a table' may refer to the same object as the statement: 'This is wood'; from the point of view of logic, however, they are completely different. True enough, the proposition: 'This is gold' is based on a comparison of a sort; but the query: 'What is gold?' does not point in the same direction as the question: 'What is a horse?' The former, raised as a problem of science, leads to the natural philosophy of the Ionians and their search for the *arche* (beginning, principle), and ultimately to the doctrine of the elements; from the latter we get zoology and its family tree.

Apart from the concrete noun, there are two other types of substantive: the proper noun and the abstract noun. The comparison which underlies the use of proper nouns is a different matter altogether, for the statement: 'This is Socrates' does not have the character of a judgment. It expresses, not a new discovery, but the recollection of something already known;[2] the question: 'Who is Socrates?' calls for prior knowledge rather than recognition. The aim of the question is not *subsumption* under a class, as in the case of the concrete nouns, but an appreciation of the uniqueness of a person, as a particular realization of human possibilities. This still requires factual experience, and thus an act of comparison. But the features compared are attitudes, fortunes, attributes: abstract qualities rather than concrete details. The nouns which denote these abstractions are formed primarily from verbs and adjectives (cf. below); metaphors, also, are called upon to help define abstractions: and here we have yet another type of comparison at work.

We should note that the term *metaphor* is frequently used in situations which do not exhibit the characteristic features of a metaphoric comparison. We take the word 'horn',[3] for example, and, by a figure of speech, apply it to a musical instrument or to the gadget in the hand of the shoe salesman. The reason for this figurative use is the fact that at one time the wind instrument was actually a ram's or bull's horn, and that the earlier name was retained when brass replaced the original material. Similarly a shoe horn was once made of the substance which the designation still recalls. A metaphor of this type reflects the progress of civilization, the accidental substitution of one thing for another. But that is a problem of history, not a problem of speech.

Here is another instance. The verb 'to set' is used to describe the readying of a table for dinner, the correcting of a clock, and the hoisting of sails. Again the responsibility lies with history, and not with the nature of language. For 'to set' means: 'to make sit'. Only if we turn to this basic verb 'to sit' and look at its primary meaning, do we find the key to what was the original metaphor. For if a sail 'sits' in place, or the hands of the clock 'sit' properly, these are expressions which show a figurative use of the verb 'to sit', preserving a close contact with the primary meaning of the word. The actual state of affairs is, therefore, somewhat obscured by the causative 'to set'. In the case of 'set' and 'horn', linguistic development and cultural progress have engendered new word meanings rather than the creation of metaphors. The horn in the orchestra, and the horn in the salesman's hand, are in our minds no longer associated with the original significance of the word 'horn'. Instead the terms have become homonyms, scarcely different from the type represented by the word 'bay', meaning both a 'curved shore' and a 'horse of brown colour'. That the various 'horns' were at first one and the same, and that we are still dimly aware of this etymological identity, is unimportant. Likewise, when I use 'to set' in the various contexts indicated above, I am using different terms, homonyms. But when I say: 'The sail sits', or: 'The hand sits', or: 'A man sits', the verb is always the same, used either in its original sense or *metaphorically*.

From the class of concrete nouns, we may cite such genuine metaphors as: 'The foot of the lamp', or: 'The head of a nail'. The lamp has a foot in as much as it 'stands' on it; its foot does the same service as a real foot. The head of the nail, to be sure, does not have the same function as a real head, but it looks like one ; it is round, its position is at the top, and so forth. The metaphor, then, refers either to a function or to a resemblance[4]—i.e. either to an activity, which is the concern of the verb, or to a property, which is described by an adjective. And this brings us to an important problem: What is the role of the comparison in the use of the verb and the adjective? For although 'foot' and 'head' are substantival metaphors, their significance rests upon definitions which ultimately go back to the verb and the adjective.

Descriptions involving a verb or an adjective also appear to be based on comparisons. Because two activities, or properties, resemble one another, I label both 'to sit' or 'blue'. But this does not mean that 'sit' and 'blue' are general terms covering particular instances, as individual objects are subsumed under a concrete noun. A lion is always completely and unmistakably a lion; all lions are, in this sense, the same; no lion is in any way not-lion. The question is here simply one of yes or no, of being or not-being. 'Blue', on the other hand, may shade off into red or green, one blue may be lighter than another; 'sitting' often borders upon crouching, or leaning, or resting. In these cases, then, ambiguity appears to be an inherent mark of language, more even than in talking of objects like rivers, or mountains, or clouds.[5]

Properties are either pure or mixed. If their degrees or nuances are to be set off against each other, comparisons are needed: white as snow, or, by way of exaggeration: whiter than an egg (Sappho fr. 139),[6] paler than grass (Sappho fr. 2.14), sweet as honey (Homer and later), swift as a horse or a bird (also beginning with Homer). The chief function of these similes, which are fundamental in all languages and in all poetry, is to emphasize the purity or the intensity of an attribute. The Greek lyric employs them, as it does comparisons with gods and heroes, to exalt the man or the woman celebrated in the song.

The relativity of properties is first stated as a fact by Xenophanes (fr. 38): 'If the god had not created pale honey, the figs would be said to be much sweeter.' This inaugurates a new trend which ultimately brought all sensuous perception under the cloud of scepticism (cf. below, chapter 10). As it gained momentum, this trend precipitated all manner of problems, such as the paradox of the heap: should two grains be called 'many'? Or three? Or four?[7]

The first principle by which properties are ordered or understood is the behaviour of our own sensuous perceptions. The eye distinguishes light from dark, it differentiates the whole spectrum from red to violet. In the same fashion the other senses apprehend the variations and gradations within the particular range of which each is the proper judge. Space and time are mediated by the terms 'large' and 'small', a polarity which forms a solid frame of reference for a great many diverse impressions.[8]

Once we leave the adjective and turn to the verb, we are much worse off. In the midst of an immense wealth of possible events, we have specific verbs only for certain typical actions which occur with a high measure of frequency; all others receive their names, rather haphazardly, from them. The infinite multitude of motions and actions, of attitudes and states, is forced into line with an arbitrary violence far surpassing the degree of levelling which we found to exist in the realm of attributes, not to mention objects. Some person either sits or lies; for the numerous stages between these two postures we have no special terms. But even though there might be some doubt about a particular posture, we nevertheless know what we mean by the *real* sitting or the *proper* lying. Sitting and lying—and the same is true of all verbs— are ideal situations which enable us to assess and label those others which resemble them. This ideal character of the verbal predicate has little in common with the purity of a property. A property appears pure by contrast with its opposite, whereas an action finds its perfection in the sureness, the grace, and the appropriateness with which it is performed.

All metaphors may be organized into two categories, depending upon whether they are derived from an adjective or from a verb (there are, of course, certain mixed forms, which we shall discuss later). This system will make it possible for us to inquire into the meaning and the development of these metaphors, and also of the similes. Adjectival metaphors, such as 'sweet' speech or 'sweet' poetry, are of little account in early Greek literature. The notion that a joy is 'light', or 'lofty', or 'ample', and that conversely a pain is 'heavy', 'tense', or 'numb', is occasionally found; happiness is thus represented as a centrifugal, grief as a centripetal movement. But this notion produced only a limited number of adjectival metaphors, and apparently no similes whatsoever. This is in agreement with the general fact that among the early Greeks an actual psychology of moods and emotions was slow to take root.[9] There is, however, one type of adjectival metaphor which is already fully developed in archaic Greek literature, similes and all. The fundamental virtues of beauty, nobility and greatness, prior to being conceived abstractly or pyschologically, are communicated through the image of light (cf. above, chs. 3 and 5). The appearance of virtue is bright; so is that of joy, happiness, and life itself, whereas grief, unhappiness and death are painted dark.[10]

Sappho (fr. 98.6 ff.) praises a distant friend: 'Arignota shines among the Lydian ladies as the moon shines among the stars.'[11] Homer, too, has these images: Achilles is dazzling like the sun, a helmet glitters like a star, Achilles' shield is as bright as the moon or as a fire lit by herdsmen, something is as beautiful as a star, and so forth. In a eulogy by Alcman we read (fr. 1.39 ff.): 'I sing of the light of Agido; I see her like the sun . . .'. The difference between Sappho and her predecessors is that she compares her friend not only with the heavenly body, but also with the other ladies among whom she dwells. Her words strike a faint echo of the Homeric idea that the leader of men is like a bull among cattle (*Il.* 2.480) or a ram among the sheep (*Il.* 3.196); but Homer is interested only in the impression which a scene makes on his eye. The result, in Sappho's lines, is a proportion: Arignota is to the Lydians as the moon is to the stars. An

elaboration of this scheme is to be found at the beginning
of Pindar's first *Olympian* Ode:

> Best of all things is water; but gold, like a gleaming fire
> by night, outshines all pride of wealth beside.
> But my heart, would you chant the glory of games,
> look never beyond the sun
> by day for any star shining brighter through the deserted air,
> nor any contest than Olympia greater to sing.[12]

Basically this conveys the following idea: water is—absolutely
—the best thing (a paradox which after some reflexion turns
out to make profound sense); the contest in Olympia surpasses all other contests as gold surpasses other treasures,
and as the sun outshines the other heavenly bodies. Pindar's
concern with ideals and values induces him to proceed
beyond the light-comparison and to formulate additional
proportions (fr. 106): 'The cleverest hunter among animals
is a Spartan dog from Taygetus; the goats from Scyrus are
best for milking; arms are best obtained from Argos, a
chariot from Thebes, a well-wrought mule cart from Sicily,
island of brilliant fruits.' When things, animals, and men
are alike valued only for their inner virtue and their outward
attraction (cf. also Pindar fr. 234), the result is that their
perfections, their superlatives so to speak, come to be
ranged side by side on one and the same level.[13] The diversity
of the virtues (*aretai*) of various objects and beings is fully
acknowledged (cf. Archilochus and especially Solon), but
Pindar has no interest in starting an inquiry of the 'real
essence';[14] rather he is at pains to discover what is brightest
and best compared with what is less so.

It was this proportional scheme which made the adjectival
metaphor fruitful for the philosophers (Heraclitus) and for
the scientists, particularly the mathematicians. The isolated
adjectival simile and the adjectival metaphor, even where
they are crystallized in a substantive, fail to plumb the depth
of a thing; they do not describe the essence or the function,
but merely the appearance of an object, and this, too, only
in relation to its opposite. Bright is understood as contrasting
with dark, happiness as the reverse of depression. By
referring to part of a nail as its head I make a less significant
statement than if I call somebody the head of a state or if I
speak of the foot of a lamp. The head of a nail is one end—

of a particular shape—in contradistinction to the other; the head of a state is the man who guides its destiny, the foot of the lamp the part on which the lamp stands and supports itself.

For these reasons those metaphors which are based on a sensory impression of similarity are, for our present purposes, relatively unimportant. Designating a piece of paper a 'leaf', or using the same term to describe part of a table, because both are thin, long, and wide: this kind of metaphor may be appropriate, it may be striking, and even witty, but it lacks the element of necessity which would make it philosophically profitable.[15]

Not so the metaphors which spring from the verb. 'The sail sits in place,' or 'The hand of the clock sits on 3 p.m.', are statements which cannot be expressed in any other manner, unless we resort to yet another metaphor. Whenever we describe the motions of dead objects, this anthropomorphism comes into its own.[16] Water runs; the wind blows. This peculiarity of langauge has often been remarked upon; even those verbs which were especially created to denote the movement of inanimate objects, as 'to flow' and 'to waft', contain reminders of this same process of conceiving all activity by analogy with human activity; cf. the river gods and the wind demons of primitive thought.

Last but not least, the verbal metaphors are indispensable for the description of all intellectual and spiritual phenomena. In the Greek language, the ' abstract ' formulation of such matters is worked out before our very eyes, and that gives us an opportunity to trace the development of these metaphors with considerable accuracy. At first the mind is understood by analogy with the physical organs and their functions; the *psyche* is the breath, the air which maintains the life of a man; the *thymos* is the organ of internal (e)motion, and the *nous* is the mind in its capacity as an absorber of images (cf. above, ch. 1). Knowledge (*eidenai*) is the state of having seen; recognition (*gignoskein*) is associated with sight, understanding (*synienai*) with hearing, know-how (*epistasthai*) with practical ability.[17] The 'process', the 'method' and the 'progress' of thought are visualized through the image of a road, as at an earlier time the 'course' of a speech or the 'run' of a poem had originated from a similar picture.[18] In the following historical reflexions we shall often meet with these figurative terms for intellectual matters, particularly since even 'abstract' thought never entirely detached itself from the metaphors, but continued to depend on the crutches of analogy. It will be of philosophical as well as of historical interest to point out the various models upon which the rational explanation of the world came to rely for its terminology.

2

Many of Homer's similes[19] are based upon what we have called 'necessary' metaphors. In *Il.* 11.284 ff. we read that Hector, upon realizing that Agamemnon was leaving the battle, exhorted the Trojans to fight. 'With these words he sought to spur on (*otryne*) the *menos* and the *thymos* of each man.' *Thymos* is the (e)motive mind; *menos* is a function, a power of this *thymos*; we have no word which completely coincides with it, for strength, courage, impulse are only rough equivalents. We might say that it is an 'itch' which allows a man no rest. *Otrynein* means: 'to set a-going;' it applies also to animals, e.g. to dogs (*Il.* 18.584) or to horses (frequently). Our passage continues (292): 'As a huntsman sets the white-fanged dogs upon a wild boar or a lion, so Hector, the son of Priam, set the brave Trojans upon the Achaeans.' The comparison merely continues the metaphor which lies in the phrase: 'to goad the courage'. It is common enough in Homer that the 'motions' of the soul are represented by analogy with animal life. We too speak of 'spurring on', 'bridling', 'taming', or 'baiting' the passions. In fact this is the proper, the appropriate form of describing an action brought to bear upon the emotions. Homer adds a simile in order to bring out more clearly the force of the incident; we need only eliminate it to learn to value its function; without it his account would, in one vital particular, be incomplete and unconvincing. We are inclined to see in such similes chiefly a poetic way of increasing the pathos of a situation; and indeed in later poetry, particularly in Roman literature and in the Romance writings which develop out of them, these comparisons often serve to add colour, dignity, and weight. Homer's similes, too, undoubtedly contribute to the creation of deep feeling, but their principal function is more

direct. They constitute his only mechanism of describing
the essence or the intensity of an event. For if we were to
omit the simile in the lines quoted above, we should read
nothing but: Hector with his words attempted to quicken the
strength and the spirit—pale terms, but they will have to do
—of each man.

The same type of metaphor is to be found in *Il.* 4.421 ff:
Diomedes leaps from his chariot; the bronze of his armour
rings as he sets out (*ornymenou*). As a wave rolls forth
(*ornytai*) in the roaring sea, one after another . . . so the ranks
of the Danaans were set in motion (*kinynto*) . . . each one
commanded by its leader.

Il. 15.615: Hector wanted to breach the ranks of the
warriors, pressing his attack where he saw the largest crowd
and the best arms. But he was unable to disrupt the line . . .
for they endured (*ischon*) like a tower (*pyrgedon*, i.e. arranged
in a square) . . . just as a rock in the sea endures (*menei*)
despite wind and waves.

The source of each of these comparisons is a figuratively
used verb: 'to drive on', 'to rush forth', 'to roll against', 'to
refuse to be broken'. It would be a mistake to suppose that
these similes answer only to the notorious *tertium comparationis*. Their implications may extend far beyond the nucleus
of the explicit comparison; as a matter of fact the art of the
Homeric simile often consists in its wealth of correlations,
in the beauty and the aptness of its less obvious and
more remote implications. But this does not contradict the
fundamental rule that the story—in this case a human action
—requires the comparison to achieve full expression.

If the rock contributes to the understanding of a human
attitude, i.e. if a dead object elucidates animate behaviour,
the reason is that the inanimate object is itself viewed
anthropomorphically; the immobility of the boulder in the
surf is interpreted as endurance, as a human being endures
in the midst of a threatening situation. It appears, therefore,
that one object is capable of casting fresh light upon another
in the form of a simile, only because we read into the object
the very qualities which it in turn illustrates. This peculiar
situation, namely that human behaviour is made clear only
through reference to something else which is in turn explained by analogy with human behaviour, pertains to all

Homeric similes.[20] More than that, it pertains to all genuine metaphors,[21] and in fact to every single case of human comprehension.[22] Thus it is not quite correct to say that the rock is viewed anthropomorphically, unless we add that our understanding of the rock is anthropomorphic for the same reason that we are able to look at ourselves petromorphically, and that the act of regarding the rock in human terms furnishes us with a means of apprehending and defining our own behaviour. In other words, and this is all-important in any explanation of the simile, man must listen to an echo of himself before he may hear or know himself.

Homer's comparison of men with animals is, in the first place, based on some specific activity: the hero rushes upon the enemy as a lion rushes upon the herd. Such comparisons are instructive because the animal is cited for a generic behaviour. The Homeric lion is always a belligerent beast; above all he is known for his fierce attacks, but even on the retreat he remains ever warlike. Where the lion is not extolled as the prototype of noble daring, but is disparaged for his savagery, the criticism presupposes no change in his nature, but only in the way this nature is judged. The lion never acts the part of a slinking cat, much less is he playful. And all the other animals in the similes: the impudent dog, the stubborn ass, the cowardly stag, betray the same constancy of disposition.

Hector, for one, is often likened to a lion. Not only in the attack mentioned above, but in any onslaught against the foe, he exhibits the nature of the king of beasts. Animals, it seems, are naturally adaptable to the characterization of men. It does, however, happen that Ajax is first compared with a lion, and then with a donkey (*Il.* 11.548–57 and 558–65). The idea that some men are of the same order as certain animals is extremely old; but despite some survivals of primitive beliefs among the Greeks, such as animal-shaped gods, animal disguises in cult, and tales about the animal ancestors of certain clans, the crude concepts of a totemic era, if such a one ever existed, had dropped out long before Homer.[23] And yet, Homer's animal similes are more than merely ways of catching a mood or an impression, more than attempts to place an event into greater relief by stressing external similarities. In this respect Homer's approach differs from that of Callimachus who, aptly and beautifully enough, says in his *Hymn to Delos* that Iris crouches by the throne of Hera like a hound of the hunt. When Homer has someone go against his enemies 'like a lion', we must take him at his word. The warrior and the lion are activated by one and the same force; on more occasions than one this force is expressly stated to be the *menos*, the forward impulse. In the epic age the lion, who breaks in upon the herds, is the beast that has the greatest *menos* ; and thus a man who walks 'like a lion' betrays an actual kinship with the beast. The animals of the Homeric similes are not only symbols, but the particular embodiments of universal vital forces; we may compare the role they play in the pictorial art of the 7th century.[24] Homer has little regard for anything except these forces in them, and that is the reason why animals are much more prominent in the similes than in the narrative itself.[25] By themselves, they hold next to no interest for him.

The forces of life are refracted among the beasts; each kind has its own particular shape. And this characteristic distribution induced the writers of the fables, and Semonides whose work is closely related to theirs (cf. below), to elaborate the distinctions between various human types. In one passage of the *Odyssey* which Archilochus subsequently took to heart (*Od.* 18.130 ff.; cf. above, ch. 3) Odysseus says:

> Nothing so feeble is nurtured by the earth as man, among all the beings which breathe and crawl upon the ground. For, while the gods make him thrive, and when his limbs are astir, man does not believe that he will suffer evil afterwards. But when, as it will happen (*dē*), the blessed gods bestow misfortune, he bears that too, unwillingly, with an enduring mind. For the mind (*nous*) of mortal men is as the day which is dispensed by the father of men and gods.

Animals, it appears from this, are less feeble and changeable than human beings, because men's minds and thoughts fluctuate with the decrees of the gods. This, incidentally, is the point where Homer comes closest to a discovery of the soul (cf. above, ch. 3); but his conclusion is that the beast possesses a greater amount of firmness and stability than man.

In the clearly defined, the typical forms wherein nature has allocated her gifts among the beasts, men find the models for gauging their own responses and emotions; they are the mirror in which man sees himself. Rational thought embarks upon the delineation of a character by partitioning it into various properties and forces. And since reason distinguishes between thing and quality, between matter and force, nothing prevents it from ascribing the 'same' quality or power to different characters. The earlier mentality, on the other hand, unaware of these distinctions, is fully absorbed by the totality of the image, and is thus forced to describe peculiarities by means of comparisons. The sentence : 'Hector is as a lion,' besides constituting a comparison, besides focussing the formlessness of human existence against a characteristic type, also signalizes a factual connexion. At least this is true of the older writings. Thus man discovered a solid foundation, not only for his understanding, but for his very existence, in the kinship between himself and the beasts.

Homer's similes assign a role very similar to that of the beasts also to the natural elements. We have already met with the storm, the wave, the rock. These comparisons likewise enable a man to see his real self, by making him turn his attention back upon external nature. Like the descriptions of animals, the pictures of nature are by no means designed only to instil a mood. It is true that wind and rain, sea and river, night and fog, fire and tree each have their own unique appeal. But above all they are regarded as the conductors of fundamental forces such as are alive also in man. Indeed man realizes the forces within him most distinctly when he musters them to combat the corresponding forces outside him.

The *Iliad* relates a war between the Greeks and the Trojans, i.e. an action between men. Consequently it is not surprising that nature, while prominent in the similes, is of little account in the body of the tale. Even in its role as a backdrop to the epic action it is of only minor importance. Similarly, the ordinary things of everyday life, especially those which concern the herdsman and the peasant, are frequent enough in the similes, but rare in the narrative. For the men of whom the poet sings are not those before whom he sings. For the rest, we to-day are well able to appreciate those similes which refer to the joys and sorrows of husbandry, the cares and the hopes of the herdsman, or the labours of the fisherman and the artisan. For usually these evocations of human feelings serve to illustrate yet another human feeling. Again when we read that a crowd sways like a field of grain, that a warrior tumbles down like a poppy fruit, or that arrows bounce back like little winnowed beans, we need no further explanation,[26] since the parallelism is immediately apparent to modern thought.

The similes which relate to an action cannot be entirely separated from those which call attention to an attribute. To cite one example: does the frequent comparison: 'swift as a horse' or 'swift as a bird' refer to a movement or to a property? The latter aspect clearly predominates in such cases as: 'numerous as flowers', 'skin comparable to ivory', 'a dress as delicate as dry onion skin'. But these adjectival comparisons are, as we would expect, less common in epic than they are in lyric poetry; for the epic is not partial to the recording of static situations.

Quite different from the phenomena which we have discussed so far is another type of comparison, the so-called mythical paradigm.[27] Whereas the similes occur in the narrative,[28] the paradigm is found in the speeches.[29] The similes, i.e. those which apply to human behaviour, illustrate the behaviour of a third person or persons; the paradigm helps the speaker to reflect upon himself or to assist another in grasping his circumstances.[30] The aged Phoenix relates to Achilles the story of Meleager (*Il.* 9.527–99) whose wrath brought much misfortune in its wake, and who persisted in his ire until he forfeited the presents that had been offered to him. The purpose of the story is that Achilles should recognize himself in the figure of Meleager. But just because the ethical pattern, the normative aspect, is especially prominent in these cases, we must not take the narrow view that the paradigms, or myth in general, has principally a moral, or even an educational significance.[31] The moral colouring happens to be conspicuous because Homer's men, far from giving themselves over to pure contemplation, are dedicated to action. Reflexion with them usually amounts to a defence of such action, an apology, or a declaration of *nolle contendere*, or the lodging of a claim; and similarly a call for reflexion takes the form of an exhortation, encouragement, or consolation. Still, when Penelope likens her sorrow to the grief of Aedon, she merely takes stock of her own predicament by placing it alongside that of the daughter of Pandareos, without considering the question of morality. In view of its origin from the metaphor, the simile usually refers to one specific activity; but on occasion, especially where animals are used for comparison, the more general, i.e. the generic conduct of the hero also lies within its domain. The mythical paradigm, on the other hand, has this advantage that it allows a more comprehensive glimpse into human behaviour, with all its motives and consequences. To be sure, there are some similes which perform the same service; this happens when Penelope's tears, as Odysseus, unrecognized by her, reminisces about her husband, are compared with melting snow (*Od.* 19.205), or the death of young Euphorbus is likened to the uprooting of a carefully nursed olive tree.[32] But on the whole it can be said that the mythical paradigm is a more suitable instrument for interpreting the fate of man in simple and natural terms.

The paradigm traces its origin from the same need which is also at the root of the animal simile, our need for establishing our place in the world order by means of comparisons, in order to arrive at a tolerable degree of certainty and stability. To-day we still experience the same need, but we prefer to be guided by the facts of experience, or by historical parallels, rather than by legends. Goethe's Antonio says to Tasso when his world is collapsing all around him:

> And when you seem to lose your whole person,
> Compare yourself! Perceive what you are!

Whereupon Tasso answers:

> Your reminder is timely;
> Is there no example of history to help me?
> Shall I not picture some noble man
> Who suffered more than I have ever suffered,
> So that I may compare and find myself?[33]

Like the animal comparison, the mythical comparison is more than just an agent of impersonal information, for man senses a bond of kinship between himself and the mythic personage. Apart from the fact that the heroes form the genealogical link between gods and men, and that the various clans and noble families regard them as their ancestors,

many institutions, too, claim them as their founders. Thus
the ordinary man is impressed with the conviction that he
stands in the stream of a living tradition which springs from
the fountain of a higher life : a conviction which is continually
reinforced by the aetiological legends chanted at the festivals
(cf. above, ch. 5).

The striking generic figures of the Olympian gods had
provided excellent models for human self-cognition (cf.
above, ch. 2), but the momentous legends of the heroic
past supplied an even richer and more varied storehouse
from which to equip a fitting portrayal of human nature.
These tales are an improvement upon the technique of the
simile because they are more flexible in their interpretation,
ever ready to adapt themselves to fresh intellectual standards.
The gods of Homer had cast off their earlier theriomorphic
guise (assuming they had ever gone through such a stage)
and had traversed the long road which leads from the rigid
tyranny of animal necessity to the amiable freedom of human
diversity. Accordingly man, whose cognizance of himself
followed the divine pattern, was released from the dead-end-
street of a fixed design. In their myths, too, which were now
taken out of storage and refurbished into works of great
poetry, we discover a new desire for unfettered fabulation
and innovation. It was that poetry, and finally Attic tragedy,
which through its myths set man on the way to understanding
himself. To make clear the strange interrelation between
myth and human insight into the self—for, to repeat, it is
wrong to see in myth merely a solemn and rather detached
recital of the past—we might do well to adduce an analogy
from more recent times. Rembrandt's scenes of the Old
Testament permit us to trace the course of the artist's own
life, since the ancient stories become real for him only
through the medium of his own experiences; but vice versa
the old figures furnish him with a better approach toward
his own life. Just so the Greeks discovered the human
intellect—by reading it into the myths. The fate of Orestes
makes it possible for Aeschylus to perceive the meaning
of an 'action' in the proper sense of the term; at the same time
he is the first to graft this particular element upon the
ancient myth. As the echo which precipitates man's understanding of himself becomes more human, so does man

himself; as his thought processes become more rational, the secularization of myth follows suit.

Homer's myths reveal two features which anticipate the subsequent enlightenment. For one thing, the reflexions which the myths are designed to assist usually produce a greater sense of humility; the majority of the paradigms teach men to realize their status as men, the limitations upon their freedom, the conditional nature of their existence. They encourage self-knowledge in the spirit of the Delphic motto: 'Know thyself,' and thus they extol measure, order, and moderation. As for the other feature foreshadowing the age of reason, the characters in the paradigms are not demons or bogey-men, but well-known figures with sharply defined contours, either gods or, more often, legendary heroes. Since these figures are tied to a definite locale, and since their genealogy is common knowledge, they stand on the borderline of history or experience; that is, after all, what distinguishes legend and saga from the fairy-tale. It is a characteristic trait of Greek mythology that the motifs of *Maerchen* are always re-moulded into the forms of saga. Saga differs from empirical reality in that it furnishes, along with the facts, also their deeper meaning. The later enlightenment argued that the meaning which emerges from an event is a matter of human interpretation; but in the saga this meaning asserts itself as a valid, a divine component of the tale. In this respect, too, the myth of the Homeric paradigm, and all myth in general, stands half way between the compulsive ideas of the early magic mentality, and the problems and uncertainties of later empirical and historical interpretation.

Neither the primitive magic mentality nor the type of thought which follows scientific lines is able to appreciate the nature of the mythical or, for that matter, the historical paradigm. For, whatever the differences between them, neither approach admits any comparisons which are not based on an absolute identity. This is to say, both in primitive and in scientific thought all equations are patterned on the comparison of concrete nouns: one lion is like another, one piece of gold is the same as another. In primitive thought, a man may be like a god, or like an animal; in the sciences, only that which really 'is' has any validity (cf. below, section 4 of this chapter). But what we find in myth, in poetry, and in history, namely the establishing of precedents for human actions and fortunes, to give them a broader and more universal significance, is rooted in a totally different category of speech.

Just as, among all possible activities, there are a few ideal cases which alone carry a name, and which must serve as our models for defining the countless remaining actions, so there is a limited number of human fates, a few of them historical but most of them fictional, which w﹐ may use as standards in the measuring of men's lives.[34] These archetypal fortunes of the Greek myths are kept alive by the poets, Greek as well as non-Greek, through ever-changing metamorphoses; and even Thucydides, stripped as his history is of all mythical adornments, considers his book permanently valid, because 'these and similar things, as are written here, will always happen again' (1.22).

3

For the purpose of describing the peculiarities of men, Semonides, following in the footsteps of Phocylides, falls back upon the animal simile which he develops into a roster of characters. In his *Tale of Women* he portrays the various types of womanhood by comparing them with animals:

> In the beginning, when God made the mind of woman, he made several distinct types. One he created from the bristly sow. She always has her whole house in complete disorder, everything covered with mud and rolling on the floor. She takes no baths, nor washes her clothes, but just sits among her equally dirty companions and grows fatter and fatter. The second woman God made of the tricky vixen. She is immensely clever, and she never misses a thing, whether it is good or bad. In fact, often she will call a good thing bad, or a bad thing good; and her mood changes from one moment to the next. The third he made of a bitch, always on the go, the spit image of her mother. She wants to hear and know everything that goes on, and while she runs around and looks in all the corners, she never lets up barking, even if she does not see a soul. Her husband may threaten her, or in a fit of rage knock her teeth out with a stone, or coddle her with soft words: there is no stopping her, even if she is in company. She simply has to keep up her senseless yapping.

And so on, down the whole catalogue of beasts, until finally he comes to the bee who typifies the good woman.

In some details Semonides utilizes old beast fables; even before him Hesiod and Archilochus had shaped them to new moral purposes. His special contribution is, it seems, that he tries to exploit the order of the animal kingdom—an order, incidentally, which bears no relation to the classification of zoology—for a systematic survey of women's characters. His use of the animal comparison is, therefore, not designed to throw light on any specific human act. Instead, he builds upon the foundation laid by Homer (cf., e.g., the passages where Hector is likened to a lion) and seeks to describe the permanent nature of a man, his whole character, by setting it off from the other characters. The comparison moves away from the realm of action and into the realm of attributes; motifs characteristic of adjectival comparisons, i.e. those comparisons which concern themselves with a property, begin to occur also in the animal similes which are to illustrate human nature. Thus, Semonides parallels traits which are comparable and yet different; he finds one thing more like this, another more like that: he is on the track of the specific differentiae; for are they not merely another term for property, in contradistinction to the essence? But when all is said and done, Semonides also continues to believe in a factual link between the various animals and the female types. In his view women are descended from the beasts: an echo from the days of magic thinking.

Other extensions of the animal comparison make for a more specialized characterization. Ibycus (fr. 7) comments on Eros who has once more trapped him in his net: 'I tremble before his approach, as a victorious race-horse in his old age boggles at going into the contest with the chariot.' Instead of illustrating a single generic feature, like the speed which Homer's horses typify throughout, this animal comparison is used to emphasize an inner discord, the contrast between passion and age. The comparison serves to express a private sentiment, not a generic fact. Since Sappho had called Eros a 'bitter-sweet animal' (fr. 137), man had learnt from the clash of his own divergent sensations that the individual is a unique being. Ibycus tries to describe this individual contradiction with the picture of an aged courser. Anacreon also, in comparing a saucy but unobliging girl with a young filly, aspires to create a unique character, and the image of which Sappho avails herself to bring into focus an individual fate is similarly rich in its tension : she likens the beautiful maid who was late in finding a husband to an apple high on a tree which the harvesters had not been able to reach.

Whereas the animal comparisons of Semonides show a tendency toward systematization, the images just mentioned serve the opposite end, the understanding of individuality, which in terms of the later evolution of thought was just as important and significant a task. The new thing was that properties, instead of being parcelled out among various subjects, were now concentrated upon one unique figure. And ultimately tragedy, besides laying bare the internal discord within the sensations, also exposed all action as essentially divided against itself, and thus raised a profound problem for man and his world. The tragedians attempted to grasp man as an individual, with all his contradictions and all the conflicts of his nature. Alcibiades' sketch of Socrates, in Plato's *Symposium*, is significant and instructive: his exterior, he says, differs from his inner personality; his aspect is that of a Silenus,[35] but within him there are golden images; his passion contradicts his self-control, 'but what is most surprising, he does not resemble any man, neither the ancient heroes nor a living person. We might compare Brasidas with Achilles, Pericles with Nestor and Antenor and many more. And similarly it is possible to find paradigms for the rest of men.' Socrates, in the opinion of Alcibiades, is 'incomparable' and therefore incomprehensible, and that means: unique and individual. Before the contradictions of his personality, the mythical comparisons which ordinarily, as Alcibiades' words indicate, help to make a man intelligible to his fellows, cannot but fail. And Socrates, it so happens, is the first Greek of whom we possess a faithful portrait bust.

A long and difficult road had to be travelled before such a question as: 'Who is Socrates ?' could be answered. Comparisons paved the way. We have found that, where the object of a question is described by a concrete noun (e.g.: what is a lion?), the comparison does not constitute much of a problem since it is assured of finding a large number of identities. But where the question concerns a proper name, any comparison must seize upon elements which belong to the categories of adjective and verb. The first step is the isolation of a specific activity, by means of the comparison and the 'necessary' metaphor rooted in the verb; then follows a similar definition of the generic attitude; and finally the adjectival comparison, with its range of opposites, makes its contribution to the search. All these conspire together gradually to bring about the characterization of the individual.

But this does not yet exhaust the harvest of fruits which the Homeric simile bestowed upon the history of thought. A second development of the simile takes its start from a concentration on the action and the situation in preference to the agent. The simile then concerns itself with the effect of the action upon a man, or with the logical consequences of an event. The former alternative, particularly in Archilochus and in Sappho, leads to comparisons such as: a storm stirs the heart (Archilochus fr. 67), Eros swoops down upon the soul as the wind upon the oaks on the mountain (Sappho fr. 50; cf. Ibycus fr. 6.6 ff.), wine hits the mind like lightning (Archilochus fr. 77).[36] These expressions indicate a new consciousness of the psyche; the elemental powers of the Homeric similes are described, not so much for the force inherent in them as rather for the state which they cause, for the sorrow, the unrest, the confusion which they entail. A related picture is that of the ship of state rendered helpless by the tempest (Archilochus fr. 7 and 56; cf. also the development of the theme in Alcaeus fr. 46 and 119[37]).

For the evolution of rational thought the other alternative, which begins its career with Solon, is of greater importance. He says (1.13 ff.): Unlawful gain is quickly attended by misfortune. 'The beginning, as with a fire, is at first small, but the end is bad. For the misdeeds of men do not endure for them. But Zeus watches the end of all; suddenly, as the wind in spring scatters the clouds,' and stirs up the bottom of the sea and destroys the works of men 'but soon makes the clear sky reappear ... so also is the vengeance of Zeus ...'[38] In another passage (10.1) he says: 'From the cloud comes the impact of snow and hail, thunder comes from bright lightning; but from great men comes the destruction of the city, and in their ignorance the people lapse into slavery under a tyrant.' Solon adopts the Homeric images of the elemental

powers of nature and expands their scope until they include
new aspects with whose help he is able to say what could not
have been said before. Moreover he sees in these forces not
so much the individual explosions of energy but the universal
necessity which prompts them, not the unique event, but the
continuous condition. And this continuous condition is not,
like the one which Archilochus contemplates, confined to the
present; it is a panorama of eternal dimensions. Thus Solon
gives us our first intimation of the lawfulness of nature, an
insight which places him on the threshold of philosophy.

Solon does not yet say in his own words that there is a
causal nexus in the world of nature and in human fate; the
principle of causation is not yet explicitly stated. But it is
implied in the sequence of natural scenes which illustrate the
order of events in the life of men and the state. The concrete
post hoc is, in its abstract aspect, understood as *propter hoc*.

What is true of the discovery of causality in nature and in
the life of man, is especially true also of the ability of man to
bring his thoughts into a connected order. There, too, the
abstract, the logical, finds only slow recognition. It is only
gradually that causal concatenation takes the place of direct
sensuous accumulation. The importance of comparisons in
this slow emergence of logical thinking has already been
shown in the proportions of Sappho and Pindar. There is
actual proof of this in the first lines of Pindar's oldest poem
(*Pyth.* 10):

> Blessed is Lakedaimon,
> happy Thessaly.   Both have kings of one line
> from Herakles, best in battle.[39]

As in the beginning of the first *Olympian* which we discussed
above ('Best is water . . .') Pindar starts out with an assertion
which is not generally acknowledged, but which, because of
its massive formulation, carries great conviction. As in the
other poem, the beginning consists of an encomium and the
comparison usually associated with it. The second clause
follows without connexion, but despite the absence of any
explicit hint we link the two so as to create the comparison:
Thessaly is fully as happy as Sparta—whose happiness is
well known. The third sentence we construe, again without
being told directly, as an explanation. Thus the three units
which are merely juxtaposed produce a clearly thought out

series of ideas which we might paraphrase as follows: Thessaly is as happy as Sparta, because there too the ancient Doric royal house is in power.

It appears, therefore, that a series of phrases may be logically connected although this connexion is nowhere put into words, and without the speaker himself necessarily having a clear notion of it. In general, then, it is evident that logic may reside in a statement without manifesting itself through forms of its own. Since it is not till very much later that language creates its proper means of expressing logical coherence, the original position of logic in speech is implicit rather than explicit.[40]

Even before the so-called logical thinking came upon the scene, men were able to speak in connected sentences, just as they did not wait for the arrival of rational thought before they began to feel the need for seeking out causes, and for interpreting a series of two events as a necessary sequence of cause and effect. Mythical thought, too, is interested in matters of aetiology; in fact it is of the essence of myth to inquire into origins: the genesis of the world, the sources of natural phenomena, the origin of human beings, of institutions, customs, tools, etc.

The problem is comparable to that of the soul which did, in a certain sense, exist even for Homer, but of which he was not cognizant, whence it did not really exist. Logic, in that same sense, has been in existence ever since men have talked and thought; the reason why it did not, at first, find expression in speech was not that logic did not exist but that it was implicit and understood. As soon, however, as it is discovered, and intrudes into consciousness, human thinking undergoes a radical change, and this mutation is particularly apparent in the comparisons, the images which make up the language.

4

Among the pre-Socratic philosophers, Empedocles is foremost in formulating his comparisons on the pattern of the Homeric similes.[41] Curiously enough, his comparisons also distinctly anticipate some of the methods of the subsequent natural sciences. Thus his writings furnish us with the best evidence for the change from poetry to philosophy. We read (fr. 84.1–11):

> Just as a man, who in a wintry night wants to leave his house,
> lights up the flame of burning fire and prepares a lantern which
> protects the light against winds from all directions, for it
> dissipates the breath of the roaring winds, but the light, which
> penetrates (i.e. through the thin walls of polished horn),[42]
> because it is so much more subtle, illuminates the street with
> untiring rays—just so at that time (when the eye was created)
> the primeval fire hid itself in the round pupil, enclosed in
> membranes and delicate covers, cut through with
> wondrously wrought straight passages, that kept back the depth of
> the water flowing round about; but the fire they allowed to pass
> through to the outside, because it was much more subtle.

With these comparisons Empedocles walks in the footsteps of Homer who also bequeathed to him the literary form in which to expound his doctrine. But he limits his images to the area of the skills and techniques,[43] while Homer takes most of his similes from the sphere of animals, nature, and the life of the herdsmen, the peasants and the fishermen. But even where Homer does use a craft-comparison, it differs from those of Empedocles, in spite of the latter's close emulation. *Il.* 5.902 we read: 'As fig juice quickly curdles milk, swiftly Apollo cured the wound of Ares.' *Od.* 6.232: 'As a skilful man ensheathes silver with gold, Athena poured grace about the head and shoulders of Odysseus.' *Od.* 9.384: 'As someone drills a hole into the plank of a ship with his auger, thus we turned the tree, when we gouged out the eye of the Cyclops.' *Il.* 18.600: 'As the potter makes his wheel go round, just so lightly they danced in a circle.'

The first difference between Homer and Empedocles is that in Homer it is a particular action which is compared with the operation of an artisan or, in the case of the fig juice, with the operation of the substance used by the cheese maker. With a few exceptions, which occur chiefly in the *Odyssey*, this is a fairly general rule. Empedocles starts his comparison in the manner of Homer: 'Just as a man . . . prepares a lantern . . .', but the behaviour of this man is of no significance for the comparison; what matters is the fact that the walls of the lantern permit the light to pass through, but block the air from entering. The Homeric similes, i.e. those that concern themselves with actions rather than properties, are based on metaphors from verbs, and this origin is preserved also in the craft comparisons: Athena *gilds* Odysseus with grace, Odysseus *drills* the trunk into the eye of the Cyclops, the girls *wheel* about in dance, and so forth. The success of these similes is dependent on their ability to describe a slice of life in motion. This is true also of the other similes, as when the attacking Hector is likened to a lion, the enduring hero stands like a rock in the waves, etc.

Empedocles, on the other hand, does not concern himself with this capturing of the brief manifestations of life. All his comparisons are conceived to open our eyes to a physical —or chemical—process, to record a permanent operation. Illustration, i.e. a more or less convincing representation of appearances, is no longer sufficient; instead, the technical model is chosen because it exemplifies the same physical processes as exist in the object which Empedocles is trying to explain. The fact that light, but no air, penetrates the horn shell of the lantern is due to the same physical properties, i.e. the subtle pores, as enable the eye to grant admission to fire, but to contain the water. Empedocles compares the one event with the other, and makes them one; the result is the same uncompromising insistence upon identity which underlies our saying that of two animals each is a lion. True, Empedocles begins the passage with the man who goes out into the cold night; but that is a poetic cocoon which his simile has not yet cast off. In actuality he is not talking about a single man or a particular object or a unique moment, but about a fact which is valid always and everywhere.

The nucleus of Empedocles' similes is a *tertium comparationis*; they make sense only as precise statements of what both units of the comparison have always exactly in common. This meant that the simile was bound to lose its poetic character; and this in spite of the fact that Empedocles continued to deck it out in the glittering ornaments of verse and poetic diction. For Homer, the artistic decoration and elaboration of details, however much objected to by rationalist interpretation, is part and parcel of the simile; for, owing to the mirror function of metaphor, image, and simile —i.e. owing to the fact that one thing cannot be understood in all its concrete vitality except through another—certain unusual features, even if scarcely related to the point of the comparison, may exercise a significant and illuminating role.

In all probability there is only one Homeric simile whose theme is general in nature: the statement of Glaucus that the generations of men wither away like the leaves on the trees.[44] This simile differs from Homer's usual examples both because of its universality and general validity, and also because it relates to a different level of reality. We have said that Homer's similes could be divided into those that derive from an adjectival and those that derive from a verbal metaphor. The leaf-like withering of men obviously involves an activity, but the verb describing it is not, as usually in Homer, one of action. The hero's 'breaking forth', 'goading on', even 'enduring'; the 'gilding' and 'drilling' and 'wheeling' of the technological similes—each of them illustrates a specific human action, through the medium of another such action, either of a man, or an animal, or even an inanimate object viewed anthropomorphically: 'the rock endures', 'the sail sits'. The withering of men and leaves, on the other hand, is no such singular action, but belongs to life itself; it is part of the process of growth and decay which embraces not only men and beasts but also plants. None of the other similes which Homer draws from the vegetable kingdom concern themselves with this organic process. For if a hero falls down like a tree under the blows of the axe, or if he stands fast like an oak in a storm, or if someone glides down like a poppy fruit, the action or suffering of the plant referred to lies outside of the natural scheme of growth and decay.[45]

Both the general character of their content, and the fact that they point to a natural process, puts the comparisons of Empedocles into the same category as this one Homeric simile. But in the case of Empedocles it is never the process of life as a whole which forms the theme of his statements; in his similes, that is, he seems deliberately to pass over those active forces of nature of which, on other occasions, he shows a very keen appreciation. He compares the cosmic mixture of the four elements with the blending of four colours by a painter, or with any other blending of substances. He says: just as fig juice thickens milk (this is based on the above-mentioned Homeric simile), so moisture, added to moisture, may produce a solid; as the baker combines flour and water, so nature allows for combinations; as the sun is reflected on the water, so the celestial light is reflected in the sun; the light of the sun is thrown back by the moon like an echo; the moon revolves about the earth like the felloe of a wheel about its axis; as water remains in a vessel which is swung around, just so the earth does not drop into space because of the quick rotation of the celestial orb; as water which runs across heated pipes becomes warm itself, some springs are hot because they have run over the fiery parts of the earth's core; as the alloying of soft copper and soft tin produces hard bronze, so the mixture of the soft seeds of a horse and a donkey produces a hard substance; the respiration of the skin is compared to the operation of a pipette, the bones of the ear with a ringing bell. These comparisons are not always convincing in every detail, and the reason for this may be that, unlike the Homeric similes, they are not explanations of the actions of men or animals, nor do they concern themselves with the riddle of organic life (as the simile of the withering leaves does), but they represent a third type, based on the verb like the other two, but otherwise entirely different. The theme of this third type of simile is the idea of *motion*.

It appears that the verb falls into three categories, comparable to the three classes into which we had divided the substantive: concrete noun, proper noun, and abstract noun (cf. also below, ch. 10). Empedocles, in his similes, makes use of the category which helps him to construe nature with the minimum of anthropomorphic interpretation: as inanimate nature. His aim is a mechanical explanation of the world; he concentrates upon the pure changes in space and time, and he tries to grasp the particular aspect under which two processes are ultimately identical. Empedocles proves that the identity which could be demonstrated for the area of the concrete noun, particularly between two animate beings, was demonstrable also in the area of the verb, between two different actions. It is Parmenides to whom philosophy owes its emphatic insistence upon the unambiguous identity of 'being' which has been the life-blood of philosophy and the sciences ever since.

After this, the reduction of an event to such physical data is fully accepted as a method of explanation. The Homeric similes, also, had thrown light on what lay concealed, what

could not be comprehended directly.[46] Empedocles adds to
the intelligibility of the explanation by using for his illustrations things which man has made himself, or acts which
man himself performs. In the same spirit, we try to understand the operation of the human eye by studying a photographic camera; man's handiwork appears more plausible to
us than nature's creation. The technical process is less of a
secret to us only because we can repeat it, because we can
subject it to our will. That is why in the technical comparisons of Empedocles recurrence plays such an extensive
role: the mixing of colours, the swinging of a ladle, the use of
a pipette are envisaged in terms of repetition. It is, in the last
analysis, from comparisons of this sort that certain experi-
ments undertaken by the early doctors were descended.[47] If
the impact of Attic-Socratic philosophy had not pushed the
Greek interest in experimentation into the background, the
Homeric simile might have boasted of yet another pro-
ductive heir.

Even before Empedocles formulated these sober equations,
the Ionian nature philosophers had, more simply and more
ingenuously to be sure, produced similar comparisons.
Thales taught that the earth floats on water like a log of
wood. Anaximander and Anaximenes also emphasize the
craft comparisons, but since our knowledge of the actual
words of their writings is defective, the particulars of their
comparisons, and the form in which they proposed them,
are not as clear to us as those of Empedocles.

The comparisons of Heraclitus are fundamentally different.
They never refer to motions, nor to any type of physical or
chemical action. He does not have a single image illustrating
an activity, unless we cite fr. 5 where those who desire to
cleanse themselves of their blood-guilt by means of blood
sacrifices are compared to men who step into mud and
proceed to clean it off with more mud. But in that instance
the comparison illustrates an activity merely in order to
unmask its absurdity.[48]

However, when Heraclitus calls time a child at play (fr. 52),
he implies that time has no proper action of its own. In his
exhortations to extinguish *hybris* like a fire (43), or to fight
for the law as for a wall (44), it is not the manner of extin-
guishing or fighting which forms the point of the comparison

—as it is in the Homeric simile of the beast fighting for its young—but the destructive power of the fire, and the importance of the wall. To understand the thought of Heraclitus, his image of the river is even more instructive (12): 'While we enter the same streams, other and other waters flow by us'. The point of this picture is neither the physical movement of the water, nor the action of the man who enters the river; both the man and his world, both subject and object are equally involved in the idea. The picture embodies the vital correlation which exists between the motion of the water and the man who perceives it. Thus the image revolves about the same problem as Homer's simile of the leaves. The difference is that Homer understands the process of life in a temporal orientation, as decay, while Heraclitus sees it as eternal existence. Over and beyond grasping each living thing in the course of its degeneration, the image characterizes all living matter as such, as something that is always the same and yet always different. Thus the figure which Heraclitus uses approaches a much greater universality. The same is true of the other images which he creates: the harmonious tension of the bow and the lyre (51), the combinations which are at one and the same time complete and incomplete (10), the word of the Delphic god who does not reveal and does not conceal, but gives a sign (93), the physicians who cut and burn and make suffer in order to effect a cure (58), the circle in which beginning and end coincide (103). Heraclitus, too, is serious about the identity of image and object compared, for they are one life; the same tension, same cancellation of contradictions, is revealed in everything, the same *logos* passes through all (cf. 1; 41; 50; 114 etc.), except that the identity itself is, strangely enough, cancelled in its turn, because of the contradictions which it contains. A logic which operates with a proposition such as: 'This is a lion' would not allow that a lion is also a non-lion; but this postulate, repugnant as it is to the basic assumptions of ordinary logic, is accepted by Heraclitus, and emphasized as the real message of his doctrine. The same problem does not exist for Empedocles, because all he tries to explain is motion, i.e. the variations of matter, of inanimate nature. Heraclitus, on the other hand, seeks to explain living nature. Not that the two thinkers were themselves aware of this difference between them; both strove to comprehend the whole of nature, and fire is, for Heraclitus, the living source of all being.

Like Empedocles, Heraclitus also wants to penetrate to an invisible core, to a reality which needs to be uncovered. But the similes of Empedocles, as it were, strive to leave the language of imagery behind, since the process which manifests itself both in the explanatory figure and in the event explained is best defined through the device of an abstract physical law (we should, perhaps, add that the Greeks never really achieved that goal). But the truth which Heraclitus has set himself to unveil cannot be expressed in any other way except through an image. Heraclitus shows us the meaning of the 'necessary' metaphor. We realize that the reality which it expresses lies far below the level of human or animal activity, that it is one with the very roots of our existence. This is the life which cannot be grasped intellectually, by the principle of the excluded middle. It appears to us in the most diverse forms, in which, however, it is always complete; and these forms, in turn, are the only channels through which life may establish contact with man; they are its only means of achieving expression. The naive mind accepts this state of affairs as obvious and natural; it innocently practises its anthropomorphic interpretation of nature, and talks candidly in metaphors. Heraclitus aspires to understand the secret nature of this universal life, divorced from all visible objects.

Beside the images which demonstrate life with all its mysterious contradictions, Heraclitus employs yet another type of comparison. He says (83): 'The wisest man, beside god, appears like an ape, in wisdom, beauty, and all else'. This comparison, unlike those we have discussed, turns upon a property, i.e. it operates with the adjective, not the verb. Various shadings of the beautiful and the wise are linked with one another in the form of a proportion: the beauty of the ape is to that of a man as that of a man to that of the god. Heraclitus frequently introduces comparisons of this sort,[49] either with the same completeness, or merely in the form of hints. Instead of the ape, he will on occasion use a child (70; 79), a sleeper (73), a drunk (117), a deaf man (34), an ox (4), an ass (9), or a pig (13). These proportions are designed to overwhelm the non-thinking man with the enormity of his remoteness from perfection. Comparisons like: 'Fair as a god', 'wise as a god' are common enough in the eulogies of the lyrists, who also use such 'comparative' fancies as: 'Whiter than an egg' (cf. above section 1 of this chapter). But in Heraclitus the proportion serves the end of criticism rather than praise. Even the lyrists had, with a few notable exceptions, envisaged an immense distance between divinity and humankind; in Heraclitus the gulf is even greater. It is almost as if the divinity had become the unknown element in this proportion. This is the scheme from which the logical reasoning by analogy was developed,[50] and in the field of mathematics the 'is as' or 'equals' of these comparisons came to be taken quite literally. The reason for this is that mathematical proportions are based on adjectives of magnitude rather than adjectives of quality (such as: beautiful, or wise) or adjectives which convey the contradictions that worry our senses. The technique of the mathematicians is somewhat like the procedure of Empedocles: he takes a comparison based on a verb metaphor and renders it scientifically unobjectionable by excluding from the event everything that is not motion. Similarly mathematics transforms the comparison based on an adjectival metaphor into a scientific method by operating only with those attributes which are quantitative in character.

Chief among those who formulated the mathematical theory of the proportion were the Pythagoreans. Plato uses proportions for his analogies even in non-mathematical contexts. The question then arises whether the method, if thus transferred, continues to be dependable. For if a comparison is used to prove something, the 'is as' must be taken literally; but there are vast areas of language in which, as we have already shown by various examples, this is obviously impossible.

In the *Gorgias*, Plato sets up the following proportion: Rhetoric is to philosophy as cooking is to medicine. In this equation philosophy is the unknown x which is to be determined. But the formulation of the proportion itself is founded upon certain conceptions which were the products of other analogies. Philosophy and medicine constitute *real* knowledge in contrast to the *apparent* knowledge of rhetoric and cooking. On the other hand, philosophy and rhetoric affect the soul, medicine and cooking the transient body. The distinction between body and soul was one of the findings made in the course of the evolution of Greek thought. It would be intriguing to examine the grounds for assuming the immortality of the soul. But in this context it is more important to ascertain how Plato uses the contrast between genuine and apparent knowledge, the fruit of Parmenides' thought about the external world. For it was Parmenides who realized that only that which is permanent can be thought and grasped by genuine knowledge, while the comprehension of transient life is only a semblance of knowledge. Plato transposes this discovery into his speculation concerning the good, and postulates a permanent good, as opposed to the transient pleasure. But this analogy is not entirely convincing. As an example of that true knowledge which is to correspond to permanent existence, Plato turns to medicine. But that medicine is the knowledge of a good is not susceptible of direct proof; it needs to be explained by means of a further analogy.

The chief model for the knowledge of the good had long, i.e. since Socrates, been the craftsman and his *techne*. A craftsman who fashions a table must know what a good and proper table is, and it is with this image in his mind that he does his work. In this analogy the ethical element which is Socrates' special concern, namely the goal of the action, is an object already known to the mind. Plato retains this equation, and systematically elaborates it: all action culminates in the visible *idea*, which is the highest object of knowledge. Now an *idea* is originally a perfect visible form; cf. the Latin cognate *videre*. Put into grammatical terms, this means that the ideality peculiar to the verb is hardened into a concrete substantival concept, whence it is expected to satisfy more exacting tests of intelligibility.

Later, in the *Meno*, Plato establishes his mathematical definition of knowledge even more firmly; in the *Sophist* he takes the principle of definition and of logical subdivision, so easily carried out in such a field as zoology, and tries to apply it to other areas of thought, and to make it into a universal law. The result was that in the sciences the art of comparing and distinguishing, of combining and separating, came to be reduced to the scheme of diaeresis. Platonic philosophy is full of these transgressive analogies, and indeed every philosophy which strives to explain more than one aspect of the world, which seeks to achieve a comprehensive knowledge, must necessarily perform such *metabaseis eis allo genos*, such trading of models, and analogical leaps. Since Plato was the first to try to erect an integral system of philosophy, to combine into one system the scattered beginnings of earlier writers, he betrays the inherent difficulties more clearly than his followers. Through his writings we learn how those elements which in naive speech are painlessly merged in images and similes, in metaphors and grammatical transformations, become separated by the catalyst of conscious reflexion. We also recognize the strenuous labour which went into the separation of the various strands which make up the complex and ill-defined forms of our speech and thought; for it was necessary to separate them one by one before they could be reunited to form a clear whole.

5

The cleavage between mythical and logical thought is especially striking in the explanation of natural causes, and it is here also that we can trace the historical change from mythical to logical thought at its clearest. What had first been regarded as the deed of a god, or a demon, or a hero, reason presently referred to its sufficient cause. But aetiological myth is not restricted to the explanation of natural processes; beside the phenomena which conform with the causal scheme of natural science, it is especially interested in origins and in life, i.e. matters whose causes are not precisely determined. More than that, myth reaches beyond the confines of the natural world, seeing that the genesis of concepts, feelings, desires, decisions and so forth is also associated with the intervention of the gods. In this respect, therefore, mythical causality controlled a territory which was later, after the discovery of the soul, surrendered to psychological motivation. Furthermore, mythical thought does not limit its activities to the explication of causes; it also serves to make human nature better understood. Thus it is evident that mythical and logical thought are not co-extensive; many aspects of myth remain inaccessible to logic, and many truths discovered by logic were without precedent in myth. Outside of the causal explanation of nature, to speak of a polarity of myth and logic is not quite correct, for the additional reason that myth refers to the content of thought, logic to its form. Nevertheless it is better to retain the two terms, because they effectively describe two stages of human thought. They do not exclude each other completely; there is room, in mythical thought, for much that is logical, and vice versa, and the transition between the two is slow and gradual—in fact no transition is ever fully completed.

Mythical thought is closely related to the thinking in images and similes. Psychologically speaking, both differ from logical thought in that the latter searches and labours while the figures of myth and the images of the similes burst fully-shaped upon the imagination. This brings us to an objective difference: the truth of logical thought is something that requires to be sought, to be investigated, pondered; it is the unknown element in a problem which must be solved with due methodical consideration of the law of contradiction; the result must be accepted by all. The mythical images, on the other hand, reveal to us of themselves their full content and significance, and likewise the figures of the similes speak with a living tongue which needs no interpretation; the listener's understanding is no less direct than the author's acceptance of the gift of the Muse, or his intuition, or whatever expression we might prefer. Mythical thought requires receptivity; logic cannot exist without activity. Logic does not materialize until man has become cognizant of the energy within him, and the individuality of his mind. Logical thought is unimpaired wakefulness; mythical thinking borders upon the dream, in which images and ideas float by without being controlled by the will.

As far as the enlightened intellect is concerned, myth is 'unnatural', and that means above all that it is not free of contradictions. Even Homer is interested in removing flaws from his motivation, and avoids unnatural explanations; the deity does not chose arbitrary ways. The breaking up of the myth, later, begins with the refutation of suspect analogies.

Thus Xenophanes meticulously distinguishes the divine from the human, and refuses to ascribe human properties, much less human vices to the gods. The upshot is that men, and the things formed in their image, are credited with no more than human qualities. Thus Hecataeus unmasks the ancient myths as unnatural because they contradict ordinary experience, and corrects the traditional accounts correspondingly. Aegyptus is said to have had fifty sons? If the truth were known, he had no more than twenty. Heracles fetched the dog of hell? In reality it was a snake who lived underground and bit men to death. The only analogies now admitted are those from controllable experience; nothing must contradict the facts.

The archaic age is characterized by an intense desire to learn. With 'untiring eyes', to use an expression of Empedocles (fr. 86), the Greeks of this period looked around them. For a time their new discoveries and experiences continued to be blended with the luxuriant growth of their myths, but in the end a separation was achieved; thereafter the myths supplied the material for poetry, whereas experience promoted the rising sciences. But just as in Attic tragedy the old delight in variety and colour dwindled before the new interest in intellectual matters, so the enjoyment of the fullness of experience was also swept aside. The philosophers of the classical period tend to accept only those data of experience which can be controlled by thought, which satisfy the tests of repeatability, of identification by comprehension, and of non-contradiction. These tests eliminate much that is life at its powerful best. Strict comparisons, as we have already seen, are possible only within a very limited range of speech; and this meant that under the new dispensation especially the meaning of events was made inaccessible to thought. Within that narrow area the Greeks constructed a solid method of reasoning, by consistently developing the seeds of logic inherent in their speech toward a definite goal. Thus they laid the foundations of their own as well as all modern science. And since in this limited area it was possible to carry out analogies and to make scientific progress with a safe margin of success, this type of thought became the model for achieving the same accuracy in other fields too: cf. the example of Plato. If we were to concentrate more intently upon the question: Which are the categories of speech involved in scientific thought? we might perhaps see our way clear to devise a logic, or two systems of logic, which would do better justice to those matters which do not fall within the province of the sciences.

CHAPTER 10

THE ORIGIN OF SCIENTIFIC THOUGHT

THE linguist who concerns himself with the rise of scientific thinking will have little or no interest in the usefulness of language toward the achievement of scientific insight, or in the objective value and success of scientific terms. More likely he would like to find out what were the elements in ordinary speech which promoted the development of a scientific mentality, and where, in pre-scientific speech, the seeds of that development might be found. He is eager to learn which forms of speech are passed over and eliminated, and what others need to be available so that scientific terms may be forged from them. The linguist, therefore, does not really look at what we might call the objective aspect of his problem, the concrete meaning and the validity of the terms and concepts: that is a field of inquiry which he leaves to the historian of science. For himself, he is interested in language as a vehicle of the human mind, as a tool of the understanding.

Greek is the only language which allows us to trace the true relation between speech and the rise of science; for in no other tongue did the concepts of science grow straight from the body of the language. In Greece, and only in Greece, did theoretic thought emerge without outside influence, and nowhere else was there an autochthonous formation of scientific terms. All other languages are derivative; they have borrowed or translated or got their terms by some other devious route from the Greeks. And it was only with the help of the unique achievement of the Greeks that the other societies were able to progress beyond their own pace of conceptual development.

In Greece, the verbal—and that is to say : the intellectual —seeds of scientific language are of a very ancient date. To take one example: we could scarcely imagine the existence of Greek science or Greek philosophy if there had been no definite article. For how could scientific thought get along without such phrases as τὸ ὕδωρ (water), τὸ ψυχρόν (the cold), τὸ νοεῖν (thought)? If the definite article had not permitted the forming of these 'abstractions' as we call them, it would have been impossible to develop an abstract concept from an adjective or a verb, or to formulate the universal as a particular. As far as the use of the definite article is concerned, Homer's speech is already more advanced than the classical Latin of Cicero. Cicero finds it very difficult to reproduce the simplest philosophical concepts, for no other reason than the lack of an article. To express ideas which to a Greek come easily and naturally, he has to fall back upon circumlocutions: his translation of τὸ ἀγαθόν (the good) is: *id quod* (*re vera*) *bonum est*. Before he can attempt to phrase a philosophical concept without the article, he must borrow the content of the thought. His language, that is, becomes the receptacle of an element of meaning whose expression is more than its own unaided capacities will permit. But, conversely, the language itself must contain within it the rudiments of a future evolution towards a higher stage; and that is what we mean by the 'seeds' inherent in a language.

The definite article is such a seed for the growth of scientific concepts. Its evolution from the demonstrative pronoun, via the specific article, into the generic article was slow and halting.[1] *The* horse, in Homer, is never the concept of a horse, but always a particular horse. This demonstrative use of the article enables Homer to promote an adjective to the status of a noun, as in the case of the superlative: τὸν ἄριστον Αχαιῶν, 'the best of the Achaeans'. In the same way Homer is free to say: τά τ' ἐόντα τά τ' ἐσσόμενα πρό τ' ἐόντα, 'the present, the future, and the past'. The plural number shows that Homer does not yet 'abstract' permanent being, but merely draws together the sum total of all that is now, and distinguishes it from all that will be. Such contrasts occasionally create the impression that Homer had already learnt the generic use of the article: *Il.* 9.320 κάτθαν' ὁμῶς ὅ τ' ἀεργὸς ἀνὴρ ὅ τε πολλὰ ἐοργώς, 'Both the active and the inactive met their doom,' or *Od.* 17.218 ὡς αἰεὶ τὸν ὁμοῖον ἄγει θεὸς ὡς τὸν ὁμοῖον, 'as God always conducts the like to the like.' But these proverbial idioms still refer strictly to an individual, the ὁ points to a single person, even though it is no longer a finger that does the pointing.

Hesiod also lacks the article characteristic of the later scientific concept. Where we would, with Plato, speak of 'the just' (i.e. justice), he says, without the article: δίκαιον, 'a just act' (*Works* 226); or, if he adds the article, he uses the plural τὰ δίκαια, 'the series of individual just acts' (*Works* 217 and 280). In subsequent poetic works the generic article emerges very slowly.[2] Tragedy has it from the outset, especially before an adjective used to denote a virtue or a vice; but even Aeschylus does not yet employ it with abstractions.[3]

While poetry thus maintained a rather reserved stand towards the generic article, in literary prose the generic use of the article was a solidly entrenched fixture from the very beginning. In the day of Aeschylus, Heraclitus speaks of the act of thinking (112; 113), the universal (2; 114) and the *logos* (50). If we compare him with Plato his use of the article is still somewhat sparing.[4] His philosophical thought is, however, entirely dependent upon the generic function of the article; the waxing power of the article is a prerequisite of his abstractions. The article is capable of making a substantive out of an adjective or a verb; and these substantivations, in the field of philosophy and science, serve as the stable objects of our thinking. But the substantives formed in this way do not refer to the same order of things as ordinary concrete nouns; ordinary material things are not the same as the objects of thought created by these substantivations. Neither our term 'substantive' nor the Latin label, originally taken from the Greek, *nomen*, 'name', describes their true nature. Apparently there are three different types of substantive: the proper noun, the concrete noun, and the abstract noun. The proper noun describes only one individual item, and it is, therefore, a closed unit. The concrete noun is quite another matter; it contains within itself a principle of order and arrangement, and this is where we must look for the seed of scientific subsumption and classification. The designation by a concrete noun is the first step on the road to knowledge. The proper noun never produces knowledge, since its object is always one and the same thing which can never be known or understood but only recognized, once it has been seen. To say: 'This is a table' and: 'This is Socrates' is to make two entirely different types of statement. The proper noun is merely a signpost calling attention to an isolated point; its function is to enable

us to affirm something about an individual, e.g.: 'Socrates
has protruding eyes.' The concrete noun, by way of contrast,
has a generic significance; if I want to refer to a single item,
I need to emphasize this by means of a pronoun, by the
specific article, or some similar device.[5]

In primitive speech many things were regarded as persons
and given a proper name, as for instance the famous sword
which was called Excalibur. But it would be incorrect to
conclude that the proper noun was the earliest type of
substantive. We should rather say that the proper noun and
the concrete noun are both forms belonging to the rudimentary stratum of speech, to designate the physical phenomena of the world surrounding man. But the competence of
substantives extends beyond the realm of the physical.
Abstractions, such as 'the universal', 'the act of thinking', are
neither proper nouns, for they do not refer to a unique or
personal object, nor do they, like the concrete noun, comprise
a number of concrete objects. The abstract noun is as
independent a form of the substantive as the concrete or the
proper noun, but it is not as old or indeed as basic as the
other two, for it owes its origin to the development of
thought, and only reaches completion with the generic
definite article.

There are, of course, even in the earliest layers of speech
some seeds of abstractions, nouns which differ somewhat
from concrete nouns or names. Many words which were
later regarded as abstracts began their career as mythical
names. In Homer, e.g., fear appears as a demon, as the
Frightener, the *Phobos*.[6] The extent to which these words
were understood as names, even after their mythic connotation had long worn off, is evident from the use of the article.
Aeschylus, for one, does not use the article in combination
with substantives of the type which Ammann calls *mono-
semantica*, i.e. those nouns which, like proper nouns,
describe something existing only once, as γῆ, ἥλιος, οὐρανός,
σελήνη: earth, sun, heaven, and moon; or which refer to
objects of which the speaker knows only one example: δῶμα,
οἶκος, πόλις, πατήρ, μήτηρ: house, city, father, mother.[7] Nor
does Aeschylus attach the article to abstract nouns. Lessing
once observed that in the language of the German 17th-
century poet Logau the abstract nouns were, by the omission

of the article, given the status of persons. He thought that this was a poetic artifice; in reality the presentation of abstracts as proper nouns had once been the general practice.

Another seed from which the abstract noun developed was the reference to parts of the body where their activities or functions were intended. The statement: 'He has a good head on his shoulders' does not apply to the head as a thing, but to its capacity. In rational speech we would employ an abstract noun: 'He has a good intellect', instead of the functional 'metaphor' (cf. above, ch. 1).

These two ancestors of the abstract noun, the mythical name, and the figurative use of a concrete noun, have as their special area of reference the non-physical—alive, animate, intellectual, dynamic—which ordinarily is not within the reach of the proper or the concrete noun. Both the metaphor and the personification necessarily put an anthropomorphic, or physiognomic, interpretation on the non-physical, i.e. they present it as a product, or an embodiment, of animate reality. Natural science is, however, possible only where the physical is unequivocally distinguished from the non-physical, where a rigid line is drawn between the moved and the mover, between matter and force, thing and property. These distinctions cannot be effected until a reliable and unmistakable method of describing non-physical facts is discovered; and for this, the substantivation of the verb or the adjective is the *sine qua non*. Thus the abstractions of Heraclitus are the prerequisites of scientific thought; that Heraclitus himself did not steer his course toward the sciences, that, on the contrary, he desired to grasp that broader and more vital area which includes both the physical and the non-physical universe, does not upset our argument.

In these substantivations the definite article discharges three functions. First, it delimits and defines the non-concrete. Second, it promotes it to the status of a universal. And third, it re-defines and individualizes this universal so that we may make statements about it. Without exaggerating we might, therefore, say that the generic definite article endows the substantive all at once with the qualities of an abstract, a concrete, and a proper noun. This will become even clearer when we come to examine the way in which the article helped the concrete noun to attain the character of a universal concept.

The demonstrative pronoun from which the article originated confines the concrete noun to the area proper to a name; *hic* or *ille leo* is an individual lion. In a language which has no article, as in Latin, the concrete noun by itself has either a specific or a general force; either: *leo eum aggressus est*, 'the (or: a) lion attacked him', or: *hic leo est*, 'this is a lion'. The formation of the article becomes necessary when the general idea implicit in the concrete noun begins to get the upper hand, and it is felt that the description of a specific individual would require the addition of a specifying agent. As the concrete noun reveals its general character, it becomes more and more apparent that, as the description of a class, it is actually a predicate: οὗτος λέων ἐστίν, 'this is (a) lion'. This is particularly evident in Greek, because the predicate noun never carries the article. The single lion, to which I refer by adding the article, is the object of a statement: 'The lion is old'. Like a name, the concrete noun preceded by the definite article specifies a particular object which *is* lion. Now the generic article has this function that it makes this original statement the object of a new statement. *The* lion, as a scientific concept, comprises the sum total of everything that *is* lion. Thus a new object is posited. 'The lion' differs from 'the lions' or simply 'lions' in that its existence extends beyond the empirical concrete race of lions, and that, in spite of the singular, it comprehends all known or knowable lions. Thus if Cicero translates 'the good' as: *id quod bonum est*, his procedure, though awkward and circuitous, merely reproduces the more direct function of the Greek generic article; the predicate (. . . *bonum est*) is so transformed (*id quod* . . .) that new predications of it are made possible. Only Cicero has to see to it, by adding *re vera* or some similar adjunct, that we do not take his good for an individual good. The universal character of the concept is, therefore, already latent in the concrete noun; that is proved by the fact that the latter may be used as a predicate noun. But this does not yet make it an abstraction. In the statement: *hic leo est* the word *leo* could hardly be said to have an abstract significance. The abstraction is brought about by re-defining the universal through the medium of the article and its demonstrative force, by giving it the quality of a name ('this animal is called lion'), and thus making it into an object of thought. The general concept, we may conclude, absorbs characteristic features of all three types of noun—proper, concrete, and abstract—; we may go so far as to say that rational thought, or logic, is the product of a combination of all three; that is why its nature is so hard to define.

The abstract nouns which owe their existence to the substantivation of adjectives and verbs manifest this transformation of a statement into the object of a statement in just the same way as the more original substantives. That *the* good is that which *is* good we may learn from Cicero's translation; the verb, of course, as always has its proper place in the predicate. Actually the seeds of these substantivations are already apparent in primitive speech, even before the generic article is added to complete the process of abstraction. Prior to recognizing an object as such, I perceive only its property; I say: 'There is blue' or: 'There is something blue'. This is to say, if the fact that I am dealing with a concrete thing is not yet clear to me, I may use the term for a property as a substitute for the noun denoting the object. This substantivation of an adjective is a simple matter because the adjective, at least originally in the Indo-European languages, is inflected like a noun. In fact, the dividing line between noun and adjective is very tenuous.

The germ of the substantivation of the verb is to be looked for in the so-called nominal forms of the verb, the infinitive[8] and the participles. They set the limits for verbal substantivation. If I say: 'He catches (*greift*)' and then ask: 'What is the meaning of "catching (*greifen*)"?' the answer might be: ' "Catching (*das Greifen*)" is an operation of the hands.' Thus the first step toward the formation of an abstraction is made by using the infinitive (in English, the gerund) in the position of predicate noun, to denote a universal. The next step is to add the definite article to the infinitive which is, in turn, transformed into the object of a statement; and this allows for an even more general term, 'operation', to be used as the predicate, which may then be further defined by reference to a specific differentia, 'hands'. The scheme of definition by species and genus with which we are acquainted from the animal kingdom evidently has its place in this context too.

The active participle furnishes a succinct designation of an organ or its function. The hand as the organ of grasping is 'the grasping one (*die Greifende*)', the foot of the lamp is 'the standing one (*das Stehende*)', the soul is 'the thinking one (*das Denkende*)' or 'the moving one (*das Bewegende*)'. The passive participle describes the result of an action, and its importance for the formation of abstract nouns lies chiefly in the province of the intellect, where the result, i.e. the thought, has no existence outside of the action, i.e. separate from the thinking (cf. above, Introduction).

Apart from the infinitive and the participles, which are part of the conjugational system, there are other nominal derivations from the verb, the derivative nouns, whose significance is, however, practically coextensive with that of the verb forms proper. The so-called *nomina agentis*, such as 'grasper', 'thinker' etc. have the same meaning as the active participles; the *nomina acti* such as ῥῆμα 'speech', and μάθημα 'that which is learned' may be reproduced by passive participles; and the *nomina actionis*: πρᾶξις 'action', and σωφρο-σύνη 'moderation' are equivalent to the active infinitives.

In the area of thought and knowledge, action and result are at times linked in a peculiar combination. Those nouns which are derived from verbs occasionally denote, at one and the same time, an organ, its function, and its effect. *Nous* is the image-making mind, but it is also the act of image-making, and finally it is the individual image, the thought (cf. above, ch. 1). *Gnome* is the understanding mind, it is the act of understanding, and the particular result of the understanding, i.e. the knowledge gained.[9] True, as speech became developed philosophically it made for finer distinctions, and finally abstracts, such as *noesis* and *gnosis*, were formed to label these mental activities more precisely. Beginning in the fifth century, verbal nouns ending in *-sis* emerge into prominence, to furnish a more accurate concept of an action. In the course of that century, the immense delight taken in these distinct formulations propagated a multitude of abstracts ending in *-sis*. It became the vogue to paraphrase original verbs by means of the substantives; in Thucydides, for instance, we find γνῶσιν ποιεῖσθαι instead of the simpler γιγνώσκειν. This is the same kind of development which has made the expression: 'To issue a proclamation' more popular than the briefer: 'To proclaim'. The pregnant vitality of the verb is given up in favour of conceptual clarity, and thus a trend whose seeds had existed in primitive speech comes to its full conclusion. The evolution was slow and complex; in the course of it, the verb and the noun were blended into one, and the three basic forms of the noun—name, concrete, and abstract noun—were themselves, as we have shown, poured into the same mould. The new product which the crucible gave forth was the rational, the concept. It needs only to be added that, as regards the history of language, the noun conquered more and more territory, as Herder and Humboldt have already shown.[10]

A similar combination of elements went into the making of the abstract conception of the human mind or spirit, as it was prepared by the lyrists and brought to fruition by Heraclitus. The latter regards it as the crucial trait of the mind that it is a 'common' thing, that it 'passes through everything', and that it 'increases itself' (cf. above, ch. 1). This means that the mind, which was at first looked upon as an organ, i.e. as a concrete object, was now fitted out with attributes which belong to the domain of the adjective or the verb. For it is obviously true of a property that it may be shared by various objects and that it may 'pass' through a variety of things, while spontaneity and self-increase are notions which must be associated with the verb. Tragedy, in the end, acquaints us with a notion of the soul as 'the acting' or 'the moving' thing: the very formulation gives away the origin of the idea, namely the verb. Evidently, therefore, even the nature of the soul cannot be understood except within the framework of the linguistic categories we have been discussing.

It would be an error to suppose that the rational, i.e. the logical expression of thought, is a foreign intruder who pressured his way into language; for it has no home outside language either. We may say, however, that all ways of specifically describing the rational in speech were only gradually explored and opened up. The rational potential contained in the predicate function of the concrete noun had to be brought to the surface by the article whose function it is to particularize a universal; precisely in the same way all other manifestations of the rational had to be revealed to the consciousness by some discovery. At first the rational is merely understood, it has no linguistic categories of its own, and is never witnessed in isolation. By taking up the challenge of further understanding that which is already, i.e. tacitly, understood, the intellect acquires the surprising capacity of retracing its track to itself: the discovery of the mind is at the same time the re-discovery of the mind by itself. In the phrase: 'This is a lion' the rational nexus is implied by the word *is*; the copula 'to be' answers to the logical problem of how the particular and the universal are to be connected. Going back even further, *hic leo*, οὗτος λέων, is understood even without the addition of an *is*. But in this case we encounter a development of linguistic seeds occurring at the Indo-European level; for already in pre-Greek times a verb which signified 'to be available', 'to exist', was also used as a copula. Thus, something that was understood without being expressed came to be regarded under the aspect of *existence*. This made possible the Parmenidean identification of that which is with that which is thought, an identification which depends on our interpreting the *is* in 'this is a lion' as *exists*. And this, in its turn, raised the difficult question what kind of existence may be ascribed to that which is thought, to the universal.

Just as the logical connexion between subject and predicate was at first not specifically set forth, so also the causal connexion between the different parts of speech found, to begin with, no explicit expression. The causal prepositions —διά, *per*, through—originated from terms which designated relations of time and space. These terms contained a causal connotation, but it was at first not brought out as such. Similarly, the causal conjunctions—ὅτι, *quod*, because—are either based on temporal or local notions, or they start out from the purely pronominal associations of two thoughts, i.e. from a mere grammatical co-ordination, whose logical component was only slowly disentangled.

These modes of connecting parts of speech—the copula linking subject and predicate noun, prepositions linking parts of sentences, and conjunctions linking sentences—are the prerequisites of all logical thought. All of them are the product of that strange threefold development which we have already discussed. At first the logical element is merely understood from the context; as a second step, certain words which had at first had a different function came to represent the latent logic; and finally this logic, now overtly expressed, becomes an object of reflexion. But within our thought processes, inevitably tied as they are to the spoken language, the logical relations always remain somewhat mysterious and, in the last analysis, inconceivable. For the simple process of connecting two units with each other is no more at home within the materials of speech than it is to be found beyond its confines; the earliest significant words always refer to something specific, to a particular semantic unit.

Since this logic is a matter of connecting and relating, it is a basic requirement for all rational thought and speech, for the whole of philosophy and all branches of science, regardless of their particular subjects. All thought draws its contents from nouns, verbs, and adjectives; but the mode of the thought, or the type of a science, is determined by the grammatical categories which are employed in the manipulation of the words.

This is especially true in the strict natural sciences, or science par excellence. It is, first of all, concerned with the material things whose nature it wants to explain. Thales says: the origin and nature of things is water. With this he follows up a suggestion of Homer who had declared that Ocean is the origin of the gods (*Il.* 14.201). Only Thales uses a concrete noun in the place of a mythical name. Once before, by Hesiod, an attempt had been made to bring order into the phenomena of the world by including all gods and demons in a genealogical system. But even that attempt to see the world as a systematically arranged pattern had been confined to the use of mythical names. Now Thales transcends beyond the pale of individual things by postulating a common substance in them all. These references to a substance, so very important in early thought, continue to exert their influence in all subsequent speculations of Greek natural philosophy. Earth, water, air and fire are given the position of 'elements'. But soon they begin to lose their concrete character, for they are equated with specific qualities, with the dry and the moist, the cold and the warm. We need only point to medicine to demonstrate the authority with which this doctrine of the elements asserted itself; but it cannot be claimed that it alone sufficed to produce the sciences proper. Anaximenes' statements concerning the rarefication and densification of matter bring us much closer to the threshold of scientific thought; the changing degrees of density, i.e. the variability of any one property, serves to distinguish one substance from another; the difference between things is explained by the differences within a quality. But it is not until we come to Democritus that we find a satisfactory exposition of scientific thought, how it deals with the adjectival properties, and how it arrives at its special perspective and terminology.

That which goes, by and large, under the name of property, i.e. the aspect which an object presents to our attention, which affects our sensations as colour or sound, as temperature or taste, and whose impact derives from a polarity within it: this property is too vital a thing, too Heraclitean, as it were, to provide the material for precise scientific judgments. Its impression upon us is fluid and flexible, depending, as Democritus himself says (B 9), upon the condition in which our bodies happen to be. Colour, sweetness, and bitterness exist only as functions of the *nomos*; objectively speaking, there are only atoms and the void (B 125). Thus he 'throws the qualities overboard' (Diog. Laert. 9.72), or rather reduces them to the forms of atoms, in order to leave dim perception behind and advance to true knowledge (B 11). To Democritus, therefore, what appear to be properties are in reality nothing but a variety of *ideai*, of forms, as he sometimes calls his atoms, arranged in different geometrical positions (B 141; cf. Aristotle *Metaph.* 1.4.985 b 14 ff. = 67 A 6 Diels). The only properties which may be said to exist in actuality are those which can be expressed in terms of space or numbers: large, round, small, parallel, many, few and so forth.

This principle which Democritus was the first to pronounce is well known to us from the modern sciences; sensory perception is eliminated in favour of mathematical measurement. The shadings of a sensation are reduced to the quantitative units of a property, and the variations within a property are brought into relation to a graded system of measurement: thermometer, musical scale, spectrum. Beyond the measuring of distances, of weights and of time the Greeks cannot well be said to have progressed. Only in one direction did they probe further. The Pythagoreans equated the level of musical pitch with the length of a chord. But the Greeks were not interested in observing the infinite transitions within chord and pitch; they were content to record the constant relations responsible for the harmonies, and to use figures—and this is true of all their measurements —as integer numbers. And so this is not very far removed from the axiom of Democritus, that all variations within a quality are based upon the difference between concrete unchangeable shapes. Without entering upon the intricate problem of the ancient concept of number[11] we may safely say that the Greeks had a predilection for explaining qualities in terms of spatial shapes because the latter seemed to them especially suited to represent objective reality. Basically this is the same scientific approach as we find in the modern sciences: the reduction of sense impressions to a mathematically intelligible form. The unscientific metaphysics of Heraclitus, when confronted with the contradictions of sensation, had taken the opposite stand and actually asserted their validity as an integral part of man's experience.[12]

But we have not yet exhausted the categories of the adjective. Apart from the adjectives of sensation, and those of form, quantity and size, there is a third group consisting of the adjectives of evaluation. The former two groups form the point of departure for the scientific thought of Democritus and the philosophy of Heraclitus; adjectives such as 'fair', 'good', 'just' lead us to the problems of Socrates and Plato. The peculiarity of these adjectives is this that they imply a teleological movement toward a single objective. The property which they denote does not lie somewhere between two opposite poles, nor is it to be located along the scale of a progressive comparison. In this case, plurality appears as a gradual defection from the one, the true being. Even in ordinary language the contrast between 'fair' and 'ugly' is not parallel to that between 'warm' and 'cold'; one of the two opposites, namely 'fair', has the distinction of serving as the norm, whereas 'ugly' merely answers to everything that fails to satisfy the test of 'fairness'. These teleological

adjectives are no more accommodating to the system of
scientific concepts than the 'vital' adjectives, for teleological
principles are ever at war with the exact sciences. Science
eliminates them from the phenomenal world, just as it
dismisses the moral element from its consideration of man.
Any consistent materialist should have to set down the
measurable good, i.e. profit, as his goal of action. But
Democritus did not choose this road; he turned off into
another domain, that of psychology, which was related
neither to the sciences nor to ethics proper. He equates the
good with pleasure. Plato also regarded the achievement of
the good as attended by happiness, but there is no doubt
whatever that in his case happiness stands under the control
of ethical ideas. Democritus, conversely, bases the good upon
that which is pleasant to the senses, or, according to our
subdivision, upon an adjectival factor in the realm of sensation. While Plato's good is a goal which always lies just
beyond the present horizon of possibilities, the view of
Democritus is the opposite (B 191): 'Direct your mind to
what is possible, and find satisfaction in the present.' Nor
does he content himself with mere sensation. Whereas
Heraclitus identified life as the tension between two strong
poles of contrast, Democritus says—and we need not doubt
that this is pointed against Heraclitus (B 191): 'Men attain
good cheer through moderation in pleasure and a life well
measured. Want and excess cause a metastasis and produce
great disturbances in the soul. The soul which moves
between distant points is neither stable nor cheerful.' Thus
he seeks happiness through a levelling of the polar tension; he
describes the processes of the soul as motions or fluctuations,
and emphasizes their measuring. His model for the life of
the soul is obviously taken from the realm of physical nature,
and in this he differs immensely from Heraclitus and Plato,
even though they too speak of the motions of the soul, and
the measure of life.

Democritus initiated the view that pleasure is amenable
to a calculus, that it is based upon mechanical motion, or the
lack of such. In this manner he arrives at a purely psychological conception of the sensations, and of ethics. His
famous ethical tenets deal with matters of moral psychology,
a field in which he has much to say that is new and good:

concerning the relation between virtue and the will (62; 89; 79; 257), concerning the conscience (297), modesty (84; 244; 264), repentance (43) and duty (256). But on no occasion does he make an effort, as Socrates and Plato did, to define the good as a goal, or to interpret justice metaphysically as the norm of life, in the manner of Heraclitus. As a psychologist, he trains his sights upon the positive or negative moral sensations, and thus transfers the complex of ethics into a sphere more acceptable to scientific thinking.

Plato is interested chiefly in action, Heraclitus in the soul which is neither active nor in a state of physical motion but alive and 'changing' by virtue of the opposites. Democritus seizes upon the fact of motion, not only in the province of psychology, but even in his contemplation of nature. For according to scientific thought the concrete world whose description relies on the use of verbs is in motion.

This means, first of all, that Democritus understands the verb-aspect of the world as passive rather than active. For, in the view of Democritus, motion is not an act of moving, but the being moved. Since the first whirl of diverse forms was separated from the whole (B 167), all motion has proceeded in accord with necessity: the atoms are 'flung about' in the void (A 58). To conceive all motion passively is tantamount to placing causality at the top of the system: every motion must have its cause. True, in the living organism Democritus postulates soul atoms which actively produce a movement; but that exception is evidently a vestige of mythology and figurative speech. Aristotle draws the logical conclusion of this by distinguishing the intellect from the body as the mover from the moved. The result is that in natural science neither the acting *I* nor the intelligible *you*, but only the concrete *it* has its proper place. In ordinary speech the verb may appear in one of several voices, and in various persons; Democritus knows only one voice of the verb, the passive, and only one person, the third.

It would be possible to show further that natural science allows only one tense. For it is obvious that we can know empirically only what has happened, i.e. past facts, even if those known facts are then transposed into the philosophical present of the *nunc et semper*. But the Greek language has its special rules; in Greek, as is well known, the verb is divided not so much into tenses as rather into aspects of action. This is to say, the actions are, on the basis of the sense impressions they create, partitioned into modes which bear no resemblance to the tenses of our conjugation. In Greek an action is described either as a static condition—the present expresses this aspect—or as an event—the aorist has this function— or as a result—which is put into the perfect. Thus an action is either a durative state: 'He walks' then equals: 'He is walking', a statement in which the activity or the actual motion finds only a minimum of expression. Or an action is a punctive event: 'He steps'; here the activity is prominently expressed, but concentrated in one point. Or again it is nothing but the prior condition of a result: 'He has arrived'. Thus the Greek verb lacks the dynamic obscurity which distinguishes our own usage when we say: 'He walks'; for to our minds the latter expression conveys both a duration and a perpetual renewal of the event. The Greek verb, much better than its English equivalent, succeeds in presenting a clear, transparent picture of the action as it impinges upon the senses.

What effects, we are now ready to ask, did these modes of action exercise upon the role of motion in the natural sciences? Democritus considers motion the result of a motion which once occurred; thus his aspect is that of the perfect. This view, however, fails to grasp motion as such. On the other hand, Heraclitus comprehends motion through the symbol of tension and wave, thus reducing it to the order of phenomena which even in our modern science represent the *ne plus ultra*. But these fail to resolve the physical problem of motion; for tension is of the present: a body held in tension is no less at rest than the arrow in Zeno's paradox. As for the image of the wave, Heraclitus picked it to express the fact of a never-ending supply of fresh impulses. But this merely breaks an action up into a series of individual events, like the running of Achilles which, in that other paradox of Zeno's, falls apart into separate units of action.

Even Aristotle does not yet understand motion in its dynamic nature. In classifying it, he first distinguishes genesis and destruction; but he adds that these are not really motion, since they originate from not-being and again end up in not-being. We agree that this concept would clash with the principles of science,[13] even though the idea of becoming and passing away is very much a part of life and sensation; that is why Heraclitus makes so much of it.

When he comes to his examination of motion proper, Aristotle distinguishes three types: quantitative increase and decrease, qualitative change, and finally *phora*, locomotion (*Phys.* 8. 7). Of these, quantitative and qualitative change do not lend themselves to an exact definition. But we need not enter upon a thorough study of the vexed problems involved in this theory of motion, to realize that Aristotle is here erecting a system of physics which deals only with 'magnitudes and motion and time'. Aristotle has an extraordinarily clear understanding of the nature and limitations of the natural sciences (cf., e.g., *Phys.* 3.4). But he deviates from the modern concept of motion when he sets up his definition: he defines it as a permutation from one being into another being (*Phys.* 5.1). In this formulation the stages prior to and after the motion are fixed as finite magnitudes; motion is merely that which occurs between these two points. This does not, however, tell us anything about that intermediate occurrence. To bridge the distance between the two points, Aristotle introduces the concept of entelechy: motion is the actualization of a possibility. Thus the movable becomes a prerequisite for motion. To explain this, Aristotle refers back to the province of teleological objects, from which Plato also had drawn his paradigms for all things: the process of building is the buildable and the *energeia* of the buildable *qua* buildable (*Phys.* 3.1.201 a 30 ff. and 201 b 7 ff.). We would prefer to define the buildable in terms of the act of building, rather than vice versa. But Aristotle's formulation enables him to reduce motion to a being at rest; the consequence is, of course, that he does not really penetrate to the dynamic process, the actual course of the motion. His interpretation takes its cue from human action. A man finds himself faced with a variety of possibilities, only one of which can in the end attain realization. The real action is involved in the man's concentration upon that one possibility, in his choice —this, incidentally, would correspond to the aorist aspect of the verb; after that, the change itself is regarded as nothing more than a state of being.

The Greeks, then, failed to recognize the irrationality of

motion. Only Zeno came close to it, but he deduced from the
irrationality of what he had found that there could be no
motion. We must conclude that they lacked a genuine
concept of motion. And thus it need not surprise us that
they proposed no laws of motion, except perhaps in terms of
simple periods.

Of all the subjects which to-day are comprised under the
heading of physics, only mechanics and optics achieved a
measure of importance in Greek science;[14] at most we might
add the field of acoustics which was the special preserve of
the Pythagoreans. In these spheres of inquiry, the objective
was to trace only the constant, static relations. In acoustics
the Greek scientists discovered the correspondence between
the pitch of a note and the length of the chord. They did
not, on the other hand, progress to a calculation of pitch on
the basis of vibrations, even though an attempt was made to
connect sounds with underlying motions.[15] In the field of
optics the Greeks did not pass beyond a geometry of light
rays; and their scientific mechanics did not develop beyond
statics.

What we have seen to be true for the substantive and the
adjective, has now been shown to hold for the verb as well.
The formulation of scientific concepts and technical terms is
restricted to the limits set by speech, and this means that it
was geared to the level of development which the Greek
language had reached. It also means that the choice of terms
and concepts was determined by the amount of forms available in the language. All this is, of course, intelligible only
if the forms available in a language are already stamped from
the very first with particular meanings, i.e. if on the strength
of their latent content they channel the beginnings of
scientific thought in a particular direction. Thus the formation of a body of scientific concepts does not emerge *ex nihilo*.
Not that they were already contained in pre-scientific speech,
or that no labour was required to draw them forth. The
real achievement, one that was great and difficult, consisted
in the isolation and the furthering of these seeds, as we have
called them, and this was impossible without a hard struggle
against the other, the unscientific potentialities of early
speech. Even the limitations of the Greek tongue, such as
are evident in the Greek concept of number or in the aspects

of the verb, prove that all forms of speech are meaningful in their own way; they contain a semantic potential which points the way for the hammering out of concepts, but which needs the struggling assistance of thought to emerge into the pure air of knowledge. Speech harbours the seeds of the structure of the human intellect; the growth of human language, and finally the effort of philosophical thinking are necessary to allow that structure to unfold itself fully. The whole edifice of grammar, at least of Indo-European grammar, is organically divided into three parts, and it is this division which conditions the ways of philosophy. For it is responsible for the three genres of poetry: epic, lyric, and drama, which may justly be considered the foundations upon which the three basic categories of philosophy were erected.[16]

The thought of natural science represents only one of the categories with which our speech operates. But its development in human thought has been so purposeful that no other body of concepts, no other terminology has removed itself equally far from the expressions of ordinary language. The Greek tongue is, probably, the only medium in which it can be shown how those concepts grew forth from the soil of speech, and how a good many roots still keep them anchored in that soil. For the Greeks were the first, in the province of natural science, to release the *logos* from language. The same is, however, also true of the other two categories of thinking. Perhaps, therefore, the Greek language will some day enable us to find an answer to the question how philosophy may combine the three separate forms of thinking, and thus regain that ancient unity which naive speech, with its indiscriminate manipulation of the various categories, has never ceased to possess.

THE DISCOVERY OF *HUMANITAS*, AND OUR ATTITUDE TOWARD THE GREEKS

When we are asked what the ancient world means to us, we often turn to the word *humanism* whose associations have, unfortunately, not always been of a congenial nature. Luckily the term is of no importance to our purposes, since it is a very recent coinage, having been created as late as 1808 by a Bavarian school teacher.[1] But the word *humanist*, and the terms *studia humanitatis* and *res humaniores* are much older. It appears as if the 'humane affairs' have been a special concern of classical scholarship. The trouble is that by talking of things 'human' and 'humane' and thus assigning a preferential share of dignity to man, we place ourselves in definite opposition to the practices of classical Greek speech. For with us the aura of solemnity which distinguishes the terms 'humane' and 'humanity' derives from the fact that man is thereby set off against the barbarian, or against the unreasoning beast. But the Greeks of the early and classical periods used the term 'human' in contradistinction to the notion of divinity: the human being is a mortal (*brotos*, *thnetos*) thing, whereas god is immortal (*athanatos*).[2] Man is a frail and feeble being, the shadow of a dream.

For a century and a half, then, our reflexions upon classical antiquity, i.e. upon a period in which the stature of man was rated rather low in the scale, have stood under the aegis of *humanism*. This inner contradiction is indicative of a confusion which cannot be cleared up unless we begin to apply a historical perspective. Our attack will at the start lead us into philological minutiae, but this is unavoidable, if we are not to remain bogged down in the slogans which continually threaten to stop our progress. In the end we shall discover that the contradiction which we have referred to is due to a very definite cause, and that it touches upon some burning questions.

It is sometimes averred that the Greeks in their art did not portray any one man with his accidental traits, but that they represented *man* himself, the idea of man, to use a Platonic expression which is not infrequently used to support the argument. The truth is that such a statement is neither Platonic nor even Greek in spirit. No Greek ever seriously spoke of the idea of man;[3] the one time when Plato uses the expression, in association with the ideas of fire and water, he does so jokingly, and he follows it up with the ideas of hair, of dirt and of filth (*Parm.* 130 C). If we want to describe the statues of the fifth century in the words of their age, we should say that they represent beautiful or perfect men, or, to use a phrase employed in the early lyrics for purposes of eulogy: 'god-like' men. Even for Plato the norm of judgment still rests with the gods, and not with men.

A different view is taken by Plato's contemporary Isocrates. He tries to decide wherein man differs from the animals (15.253 = 3.5) and he seizes in the main upon the power of speech and persuasion, to which the cities, the laws, the arts and skills, in short, all aspects of culture owe their origin. Further (293) he admonishes the Athenians to acquire eloquence through education (*paideia*), 'for you excel all others in that in which man excels the beasts, and the Greeks excel the barbarians: you are better educated (*pepaideusthai*) toward thinking and speaking.'[4] Cicero echoes this (*de inv.* 1.4.5; cf. also *de or.* 1.31; 32–33): 'It seems to me that men differ from animals principally in this that they have the power of speech. Consequently, I think, he who excels other men in the gift in which all men excel the animals has carved out a magnificent achievement.' The characteristic-ally human, the power of speech and education: these are the basic elements of Cicero's humanism, and they are taken straight from Isocrates. Petrarch inherited them from Cicero,[5] and just as Isocrates combined a pride in his being a man with the national pride of a Greek and an Athenian, so Petrarch feels that to be a Roman is to be a man in this specific sense. Both regard themselves as members of the best educated, i.e. of the most eloquent group.

This is not the only instance in which the fourth century shows us how the pride in being a man was connected with the pride in education. Aristippus, for instance, the disciple of Socrates, is said to have remarked:[6] 'I had rather be a beggar than a dunce; the beggar has no money, but the dunce has no humanity (*anthropismos*).' Of the same philosopher it is told that he was once shipwrecked off the coast of Rhodes and, coming upon some geometrical figures drawn in the sand of the beach, exclaimed to his companions:[7] 'Cheer up, I see the traces of men.' Perhaps the most emphatic expression of this attitude is to be found in a quotation which Hermippus ascribes to Thales:[8] 'For these three things I am grateful to fate: first that I was born a man and not a beast, second that I am a man and not a woman, and third that I am a Greek and not a barbarian.' And, conversely, its silliest aspect appears in the story about Stilpon, a philosopher of the days of Alexander the Great (Diog. Laert. 2.115): When Demetrius Poliorcetes asked him after the conquest of Megara to prepare a list of all those things which he lost during the plundering of his house, he answered: nobody was able to carry off my education (*paideia*).[9]

Plato strove after things divine, along the difficult road of philosophy; Isocrates recommended the universal education of the orator as a more useful philosophy; Aristippus taught a hedonistic ethics, and perpetuated the teachings of Socrates in his manner, as one who knew how to enjoy life. Wieland in his novel portrays him not unjustly as a clever man about town whose only concern is with this earthly life. Isocrates derives this new self-assurance of man from the temper of the Attic upper classes of the end of the fifth century, who had seen the sophists proclaim the values of education and rhetoric. Like the philosophy of Socrates and Plato, his doctrine is a product of the Attic enlightenment. The difference between them is this that Plato, the legatee of Socrates, tried to re-establish the belief that outside of the sphere of men there exists some great authority, and that God is the measure of all things.[10] Isocrates, along with the Sophists, takes the opposite view that man is the measure of all things. It should not surprise us that this new autonomy of man at first provoked a feeling of uncertainty and helplessness; we need only think of the moving scenes of Euripides to appreciate how fragile a thing man was considered to be. Nevertheless the fruits of the enlightenment: rhetoric, knowledge, and education, led to a new feeling of accomplishment, which however from the very first carried a distinct stamp of sophistic vanity. Isocrates, like Plato, claims to be teaching philosophy; he draws a firm line between himself and the plebeian pettifoggers, the radical democrats, and the instructors in speech who, being without the benefit of education, have only their own advantage at heart, even if it means using dubious ways. But with equal resolution he turns against the practitioners of casuistry and dialectics who run after useless· arguments; and among these he includes also Plato.

The old aristocracy, believing themselves to be the scions of a divine race, had followed their ancient noble ideals down to the beginning of the fifth century, and had controlled the politics of the city as late as the opening of the Peloponnesian War. In the fourth century this aristocracy had disappeared from the scene of action; their last attempt to defend the ancient prerogatives behind the bulwark of a sophistic education, and to fight the despised mob with a superman morality, had become hopelessly compromised by the thirty tyrants, and had ended in a riot of cruelty. Consequently, the democratic view that all citizens not only have the same rights, but, at least potentially, are of the same worth, spread even among the aristocrats who had come under the influence of the Sophists. Hereafter it is expected of any educated man, despite his pride in his education, in his status as a Greek and an Athenian, to honour the human being as such; for being educated, and to be human, have now become interchangeable terms.

The solidarity of all men was at first acknowledged through the feeling that we are all without exception the same frail mortals, short-lived like the leaves of the forest. But in the fourth century something new was added, and that was sympathy with one's fellow-man. To be sure, even earlier generations had felt the need to help one another and to cherish friendly intercourse. But their acts of kindness had not been based on any appreciation of the virtue and dignity of men. The relevant passages in the *Odyssey*: 'The stranger and the suppliant is as a brother' (8.546) or: 'All strangers and beggars are from Zeus' (6.207) are the outgrowth of a religious commandment to succour the helpless (cf. above, ch. 8). If the disdain of coarseness and crudity was prominent even among the war-lords of the *Iliad*, that was the code of manners of a proud nobility which believed in order and moderation and thus set itself off from the Asiatics (cf. above, ch. 2). It was also a matter of religious conviction, for the gods had furnished the model of such co-operation in a society, and, more important yet, all *hybris*, every transgression of the order is regarded as an infraction of the limits placed on man. The mythical paradigms of the Homeric epic point the moral of self-control and moderation; the man who is conscious of his own frail humanity will not meet his fellow with harshness or insolence (cf. above, ch. 9). Nevertheless, though this attitude prepared the setting for the views of the fourth century, it was not capable, by itself, of evoking a universal sympathy for the dignity of man, or a common love between men. Even the phrase of Antigone: 'I am here, not to deal in hatred, but to deal in love,' refers to the *philoi*, her friends and relatives; one must, as it is often expressed, so shape his life that it is a joy to the *philoi*—and that means of course, that one's enemies may, by the same standard, be injured (cf. above, ch. 8).

Euripides, in his *Medea*, is the first to portray a human being who excites pity by the mere fact of being a human being in torment (cf. above, ch. 6); as a barbarian she has no rights, but as a human being she has. This same Medea is also the first person in literature whose thinking and feeling are described in purely human terms, as the products of a human soul and nothing else. She is a barbarian by birth, but in intellectual attainments, in the power of speech, she is superior to all others. No sooner does man declare his independence of the gods, than he acclaims the authority of the free human spirit and the inviolability of human rights.

How quickly the concept of the dignity of man conquered Attica is to be gathered from the fact that beginning with the relief of Hegeso, i.e. after 420 B.C., or roughly a dozen years after Euripides' *Medea*, Attic grave stelai were displaying the slave girl side by side with her mistress in a position of near-equality, associating the two in the mutual bond of the dignity of man.[11]

When the Peloponnesian War was over, the ancient religious commitment concerning those in need, and concerning one's own social group had lost its compelling force. In its place we now find, in Athens, a stratum of educated men who are, so to speak, inwardly democratized, proud of their own humanity, and willing to recognize the human dignity of each and everybody, regardless of their education.

As in the plays of Euripides, this sentiment becomes particularly strong when a man is shown to be suffering an injustice. Thus we find the formula: 'He who gives false testimony or unjustly thrusts human beings into misfortune,'[12] and the implication is even clearer in Xenophon's statement about king Agesilaus: 'He often told the soldiers not to take revenge upon the prisoners as if they were criminals, but to guard and protect them as human beings.'[13] Xenophon also says of Agesilaus that when he was unable to conquer a city by force, he would win it over through *philanthropy*, through the love of men.[14] The terms *philanthropos* and *philanthropia* are in the fourth century often used to express the idea that a helpless or suffering person is 'also a human being'.[15] Thus Xenophon's Cyrus addresses his soldiery: 'There is an eternal law among men that in a conquered city the inhabitants and their property belong to the conquerors. So if you take what you can you will not commit an injustice, but if you leave something to the victims, your failure to take it will demonstrate your love of men.'[16]

In Xenophon's view, Cyrus is the prototype of the humane ruler, even though his humanity is, as before, based on the notion that good deeds pay off. This view is very common indeed in Greek and Roman discussions of friendship. In the speech just quoted the term *philanthropia* borders upon the province of law; humaneness, as a type of equity recommended by the good general, is contrasted with strict legal practice. But the other passages in which Xenophon mentions the *philanthropia* of Cyrus[17] show that his understanding of the word is not narrowly juridical. Its meaning is that of a friendly sentiment toward others; it includes, for instance, such matters as hospitality and charity. This is the older significance of the word; in the early period it appears especially in connexion with the gods and their benefices to men.[18] In the fourth century philanthropy often denotes the graciousness of a monarch;[19] it is more or less identical with Homer's *philophrosyne*, the noble nature of the man who does not simply follow the inclinations of his *thymos*, but holds it back and tames it (cf., e.g., *Il.* 9. 255), who is *meilichos*, gentle, mild, not *skleros*, harsh, or *authades*, brusque. But more than designating the nature of a man's soul, the term expresses the chivalrous treatment of persons who are of no

particular concern to the man so described. In the same
sense Isocrates enjoins *philanthropia* upon king Philip, and
groups it together with *eunoia*, benevolence (5.114) and
praotes, clemency (5.116). Although the words *philanthropos*
and *philanthropia* are not legal terms, numerous passages in
the orators of the fourth century indicate that the concepts of
benevolence, clemency and *eleos*, compassion soon made
their way into the legal terminology.[20] *Philanthropia* came to
be the comprehensive term for this new concept of *humanity*
or *humanitas*. But since the ancient view of man as a frail and
miserable creature was never completely given up, the 'love
of men' retained a strong admixture of condescension; in
the end the neuter adjective *philanthropon* came to mean:
a tip.[21]

The discovery of this *humanitas* among the Greeks was not
the work of philosophy.[22] In fact, the gracious urbanity of
the new concept forms a definite contrast to the cold severity
of conceptual thought. It springs from the ideals of the
Attic society of the last part of the fifth and the fourth centuries before our era. Its most perfect expression is, therefore,
to be found where that society appears in its purest form: in
the comedies of Menander. His plays are bourgeois spectacles, and yet they portray what was probably the noblest
and most refined society ever to have existed in Europe.
The Attic gentry who appear in these plays are perfectly
natural and at ease with themselves, unruffled by any
pretensions; and still they possess that remarkable firmness
and strength which is the legacy bequeathed to its proud
scions by a noble tradition. Unlike the society of courtiers
who in the archaic period crowded the houses of the tyrants,
or that which a short time after Menander gathered around
the Ptolemies in Alexandria, the people of the New Comedy
form a society of free men. Unhampered by any influences
from within or without, under no compulsion to accept other
men's opinions, the people of Menander exhibit, just before
the collapse of their whole bourgeois structure, a last splendid
flowering of the tender blossom of *humanitas*. Menander's
view of man is, perhaps, most impressively documented by
his famous remark: 'How graceful is a human being, if
indeed he is human' (fr. 761 K.). Here we have the belief in
the worth of man, acquired at the opening of the century,

combined with the sceptical awareness that a human being is not always what he might be.

Unlike Isocrates, Menander does not relate the dignity of his men to their *paideia*, their ability to speak, which distinguishes them from the animals; he is much too refined to deem it necessary to make an exhibit of his education. To shine with quotations from the authors and gnomic saws is, in his eyes, the behaviour of slaves, who thereby, as it were, provide the standard by which Menander wants his citizens measured. The worries which afflict the lives of Menander's men are slight enough, and mostly private; their *philanthropia* is, more often than not, the love of a beautiful hetaera. But though the characters are, on the whole, types rather than unique individuals, the way they differ from each other intellectually, and how they react upon one another, is brought out with consummate charm. These comedies were once lost, and it is only from papyrus fragments found in the past half-century that we have come to know their great artistry. Nevertheless they helped to shape the whole of European social life, through the adaptations which Plautus and Terence made of them. Even among the Romans these drawing-room pieces had an effect far surpassing their merely literary influence. It is, of course, difficult for us to tell what impact they had upon the manners and the speech, and thoughts and feelings of the men who saw them performed. But there is no doubt that, for Cicero, *humanitas* was in great measure that lively freedom, that balanced charm which, as much as a hundred years before the age of Menander, had been a possession of the Attic society which speaks to us from the pages of Plato's dialogues. As a matter of fact, at that time *humanitas* was still associated with a vivid interest in things intellectual; the emphasis on the *human*, on the other hand, was then lacking.

The politically active Romans were, of course, unable to regard the society of Menander as a serious model for imitation; with its confining domesticity, and its slightly weary heroes who are only too happy to relinquish all business to their slaves, it was anything but an inspiring example. So Cicero fortifies his ideal of *humanitas* by once more going back to the early chapter of fourth century Athens, and concentrating his attention, as we have seen, on education and eloquence. And for a Roman, education, or culture, was an even greater achievement than for Isocrates, since even the spontaneous grace of the Attic spirit had to become a matter of education. Moreover Cicero's *humanitas* verges upon *philanthropia*, the amiable, somewhat condescending benevolence which in his thought coincides with the Roman virtue of *clementia*, exactly as the Greeks of the fourth century had coupled *philanthropia* with good will and gentleness. This raises the problem whether the word *humanitas* is to be taken as a translation of *philanthropia*, or whether it derives from *anthropismos*, the term which Aristippus in the anecdote had applied to his cultured humanity. To solve this dilemma it has been suggested that it is necessary to assume the existence of a philosophical doctrine of *humanitas* prior to Cicero, and that the man who formulated it was Panaetius.[23] We are grateful for the observation that Panaetius bases his ethics upon the concept that man is better than the beast, and that we must make an effort to capitalize on this advantage;[24] for this means that Panaetius absorbed into his philosophical system what had first come into open view with Isocrates' pride in his education, the same element which so strongly appealed to Cicero. And yet there remains the question of the name which Panaetius is supposed to have attached to this *humanitas*; for the Greek language contains no one word which would describe at once 'higher humanity' and 'humaneness'. Furthermore, since both concepts were easily available to Cicero in Isocrates and Xenophon's *Cyropaedeia*,[25] we gain little for a better understanding of Cicero's *humanitas* by interpolating the figure of Panaetius. It would be more interesting to find out whether the word *humanitas*, in this sense which was so important to subsequent ages, was already current among the circle of the Scipios; but that we cannot know. In the final analysis it is most likely that the Romans regarded the Greeks who followed the pattern of Menander and Terence as *humani*—the text of Terence surely encouraged this—and referred to their principles of behaviour as *humanitas*, terms which were easily harmonized with Roman aristocratic pride and the Greek concept of education.

In any case, from Cicero onward *humanitas* combines the humane with the humanistic; a special blend of unselfconscious ease and gracious affability is paired with a study of the classical authors who teach the art of speech. The Isocratean and Ciceronian view of humanity that man is a being capable of speech could not but capture the hearts of the Romans. For they had gotten their culture from the great works of Greek literature; not only did the accomplished orators of the time of Cicero learn their lessons from the Greek rhetoricians, but even the poets of the early period received their training from the epic and from tragedy, particularly the latter. As a result Roman writers from the very first inherited an element of playfulness and elegance, for in the world of culture and literature the punches are always pulled. Thus Roman literature inaugurated a strangely independent reign of the spirit, in which rhetoric and pathos joined forces with cultural refinement and elegance. And from Cicero through Petrarch and Erasmus to the age of the baroque, all European culture has borne the impress of this *humanitas*.

But this is only one of the channels through which the influence of antiquity has reached us. Particularly in Germany this concept of the nature of man has never been wholly acceptable. The very first judgment of Luther concerning Erasmus ran: 'In him the human carries more weight than the divine.'[26] Luther attempted to discount the achievement of the European tradition and to find an immediate access to God. This meant that he dispensed with all efforts to reconcile the humane culture of antiquity with the Christian doctrine of salvation. His blunt: 'Here I stand, and stand I must' could not but carry a barbaric note, from the point of view of the wise scepticism and the conciliatory diplomacy of Erasmus.

It was in this same spirit that Winckelmann protested against the rhetoric and the pathos of the baroque, against the spectacular use of ancient figures and motifs for the adornment of opera and auditorium. He pointed to what was genuinely Greek, beyond the Roman mould in which it had been recast, and postulated that the perfect beauty of classical art was indeed divine. Similarly Herder finds his way back to the ancient Greek poetry, and discovers that its beauty was the creation of believing hearts. And it was due to the same trend that the German philologists of the nineteenth century ceased to understand Roman antiquity, that they demoted the Greek orators to the position of historical source material, and that even the theorists of rhetoric excited only their historical interest. This grudging recognition was extended only because, as they averred, every single phenomenon of history deserves the attention of the industrious scholar.

It was thought that Cicero's dialogues, those urbane conversation pieces, could not bear comparison with those of Plato whose dialectic was, after all, a quest for absolute truth. Unlike the other countries in Europe, which were in this sense, too, the heirs of humanism, Germany lacked a society which practised the conventions of a cultured social life. 'In German speech politeness is the same as lying'; honesty and inflexibility were the only recognized virtues, and in their service men derived a special pleasure from unmasking the social conventions and the imposing forms of art, along with the ideologies of political life. Cicero and the humanism regarded as his legacy were hard hit by all this, particularly so because the political tendencies of the nineteenth century accentuated the factual world, technology, national and social affairs. Under their onslaught the Greek studies gave up ground, and Latin also, which till then had served as a propaedeutic to Greek, lost its erstwhile impregnable position.

About the middle of the twenties of the present century, after the first world war, when men began again to consider what values were worth saving in Europe, we entertained doubts whether the traditional forms of humanism were not obsolete. The humanism of Erasmus, it was claimed, had placed too much emphasis on scholarship and learning; the humanism of Goethe was overly aesthetic. What was needed was a new humanism which took account of the whole of man, not only of his thinking and his feeling, but also of his acting. This ethical and political humanism put the concept of *paideia*, of education and culture, in the centre, and thus actually reached back to the sources of the humanism of Isocrates and Cicero. And yet this humanism did not trace its descent from Cicero and Isocrates, but hoped to drink at the common well of all antiquity, particularly Plato, the opposite number of Isocrates, in whose eyes man and his education merited no special status; for he considered God, not man, the measure of all things.

In supporting his self-assurance upon so fragile a foundation as the human being, Isocrates was encouraged to do so by the society in which he lived; it gave him a clear and dynamic concept of the potentialities of human existence. Culture, for him, is not something historical which needs to be conjured up from a distant past; the cultured Athenians of his day present him with a living example of it. Instead of having to summon and admonish his contemporaries to educate themselves, he is able to say with perfect conviction: the things which we possess are the best that man may attain. In a subsequent age Panaetius had to take recourse to the divine *logos* to assert the same values.

Cicero imported his culture from abroad, but even so it fitted well with the established traditions which held together the Roman aristocracy and the state. Petrarch and Erasmus, also, campaigned from prepared positions; in their case it was not the social or political *mise en scène* which shaped their beliefs, but the Christian creed. Winckelmann and Herder, however, had a different approach, for, as we have already stated,[27] they are not primarily concerned with this man-centred *humanitas*; and even in the age of the so-called German idealism, the speculations upon man were still rooted in the belief in an absolute order transcending all men.

Now, however, humanism and *paideia* were no longer built on the substructure of a fixed society or a state, they were no longer bolstered by religious or philosophical convictions. Even rationalism, one of the main supporters of the humanistic tradition, was no longer considered a valid foundation. And what about humaneness and humanity? It would be begging the question to explain them in terms of man, for the nature of man was the most crucial question of them all. An ethical or political humanism should prove its worth through deeds and action, just as the aesthetic humanism had vindicated itself through works of art. It was not sufficient to state: 'Plato's man, and the genuine Greek man, is basically political', for this did not make clear whether man should take a free and active part in the life of the state, or whether he was merely a cog in the political wheel, or whether he should emulate Plato in withdrawing from the hated turmoil of the profane world, and reflecting in isolation upon the idea of a state in which vulgarity was not in control. Instead of political convictions people spoke of a political 'stand'; they pondered, not true justice but an abstract morality, not politics but 'the political', not political decisions but political sentiment, not the role of the politician but the role of political man—in short, the concrete world of specific realities everywhere gave way before the encroachment of a universal *hexis*. The new terms such as the 'forming of men', the 'idea of man', the 'highest norm of culture' lacked any real foundation in fact. Thus this humanism was fated to go the way of any nihilism which masquerades behind the facade of an attitude or stand, whether the stand is heroic or religious. It should have been obvious from the outset that this political humanism was in reality quite unpolitical, or that it could serve any political purpose, which is saying the same thing.[28]

Now, therefore, we are once more confronted by the question: What do we expect of humanism? What do the Greeks mean to us? There is no need for new programmes or the propagation of a new humanism; we shall do much better if we consent to follow the old truths. It is hardly likely that we in Germany shall in the near future lose our stiff-necked pride or our old-fashioned pedantry, nor is it possible that we shall soon form a society such as was established in Athens after her defeat in the Thirty Years' War against Sparta, a society graced with humane wit and world-wise urbanity. In fact we should expect that the times will, if anything, increase our tendency to take things more seriously than other people. Our best course, therefore, will be to concentrate on the *divinum* of the Greeks rather than their *humanum*. This does not mean that we should reintroduce the Greek gods and relapse into a new paganism, but rather that we should focus our attention upon· the gift which those gods bequeathed to the world, and which has remained immortal even though the gods themselves have died. In this way we may perhaps hope to protect ourselves from coarseness and barbarism, without depending upon *humanitas* to sustain our spiritual existence.

The gods are the measure of all things: this dictum signalizes to the Greeks that the world is a cosmos and that everything is controlled by a stable order. It is a concept of nature upon which the Greeks pinned their faith; but more than believing in it, they also attempted to comprehend its principles. The more deeply they probed into the mystery, the clearer it became to them that behind these gods there existed an even more universal plan which controlled the life of man and gave it its meaning. Our European culture may well be said to rest on the discovery of the Greeks that this plan takes different manifestations: to the intellect it appears in the shape of law, to the senses it is beauty, to the active spirit it is justice. The persuasion that truth, beauty and justice exist in the world, even though their appearance is largely hidden, is our ever-present heirloom from the Greeks, and even to-day the power of this conviction is unimpaired.

The classicistic belief that the Greeks are our model must, however, be modified in one important detail. It may be true that classical antiquity should serve as an example for Western thought, for our literature and art, but not in the sense that the works of antiquity, the creations of the artists, the poets, and the philosophers, are absolutely perfect, that they have a timeless validity and that they provide the unchallengeable standards for our own creative activities. This belief has been exploded by the historical scholarship of the last century and a half; classical scholars themselves were instrumental in pointing out the conditional nature of the Greek and Roman cultures. As they penetrated further and further into the ancient world, they began to realize that the most perfect achievements of antiquity had sprung from spiritual roots which to-day strike us as remote and strange. For the greater and the more significant a work is, the more openly it carries the stamp of the spirit of the age; an object of art reflects the contemporary notions of space and shape, a piece of poetry might testify to a religious creed long lost, and the language reveals a conception of human life which lies far behind us on the road which Western man has trod. In the light of this, should we then suggest that only a philistine, a cultural snob, will talk of the timelessness of a work of art? Is it merely a cliché to aver that a great man and his achievement are not subject to the relativity of time? In actual fact, despite the force of its attack, historicism has, in the long run, been unable to destroy our enjoyment of the beauty of classical art. The naive admiration of beauty has not allowed itself to be led astray, and although the classical scholars chose to go along with the historians and to cut themselves free from classicistic sentimentality, they never really gave up their claim that the treasures entrusted to their care were of a very special value. This has, unfortunately, led them into a rather ambiguous situation, and they have spent much labour on the attempt to analyse the peculiarity of their position, in order to find a basis from which to defend their humanism and to vindicate antiquity.

But, we may ask, is there a real conflict between the truth that a great work of art is a product of its age, on the one hand, and its timelessness on the other? It may be suspected that here, as so often in the realm of human thought, a false analogy has been responsible for the creation of a seemingly insoluble problem. Evidently historical progress has been compared with the perfection and elaboration of tools and machinery. In the field of technology that which is obsolete is really dead. An automobile or an aeroplane of our childhood days is a useless and ridiculous object. That which has been overcome, the thing of the past, cannot possibly recover a 'classical' significance. Let us, then, find a better model. In the field of organic nature, too, we speak of development. For instance, we say that the animals are more highly developed organically than the plants. But does this imply that, because there are eagles and lions, the rose is obsolete, useless, and merely comical? On the contrary, is it not true that the flower is the valid, the classical manifestation of something in nature which retains its significance even if higher forms are developed alongside it? To vary a dictum of Ranke, which he used to refer to the ages of history: In the sight of God, the rose is the equal of the lion. That meanings, and values, and developments, are distinct from each other need not be disputed. But they should not, like differing types of machinery, be judged within the narrow gauge of practical effect and measurable profit. The rose falls short of the beasts, but that is what constitutes its special distinction; its perfection is a function of its lack of development; its beauty is a unique thing, possible only in the plant. The beast has acquired its perfection at the expense of the beauty of the flower.

We should add—and this again is true of organic nature as well as of human affairs—that all forms show themselves in their purest state at the point of their origin, before they have undergone the changes which later befall them. The leaf of the fern is more fully formed than that of the higher plants which must relinquish the stage to the glory of the blossom. Similarly certain forms of art, the representations of human beauty and the poetic genres of epic, lyric, and drama found their perfect shape among the Greeks. Their great discovery, the 'naturalness' of existence, has moulded the basic elements of our thought and our artistic feeling, and their philosophers, from Thales to Aristotle, may properly be called the founders of all philosophy; for all modern efforts in this domain are constantly forced to revert to the archetypes of Greek thought. In this way all the questions that were asked by the Greeks have remained our own questions too.

It appears, therefore, that we may speak of a development and even of a progress of the human race, without denying that past ages had their perfection, that theirs was a beauty which is beyond our own grasp, and that perhaps they succeeded even better than we to-day in expressing the very essence of our existence. Nor does this comparison with the organic evolution of life suffice to make clear the meaning of the development of human culture and the significance of Greek antiquity. Man, at least Western man, attempts to steer his future course with a will and a purpose. But since he cannot very well plan in a vacuum, since he must accept the guidance of given facts, he orientates his search along the bearings of his own past. The question: 'What do I want to do?' is in his mind always linked with the further question: 'What am I, and what have I been?' He who wishes to be a German, and primarily a German, must ask himself: 'What were the Teutons?' But if we hope to be Europeans—and such an intent must be implied in our desire to read and write, and to preserve the arts, technology, philosophy—the question which looms before us is: 'What were the Greeks?' And especially if we are dissatisfied with this or that aspect of our modern European culture, we must ask with an added emphasis: 'What was the original form of this culture, at a time when the modern distortions had not yet marred its face?'

There is hardly a soul left to-day who would insist on an imitation of the Greeks. The reason for this is not that the Greeks have lost their prestige, but that the word 'imitation' has lost the meaning which it had before, even in ages of great productivity. In the ancient world, for instance, art was considered an imitation of nature. To-day imitation is regarded as a mere copying, a photographic duplication of reality. Such an imitation, lifeless and stupid, would be the opposite of a true emulation of the Greeks, for it would bring to a stop the very current with which the Greeks have fed and enriched the intellectual life of Europe.

But are we sure we want to imitate the Greeks, and be Europeans in that sense? And if so, why? To give an answer to this last question, the most difficult of them all, it will not do simply to declare that we are Europeans and therefore cannot choose but live in the European tradition. If we carry this tradition merely as one carries a tiring and un-pleasant burden, we would do better to shake it off, to become independent and original. But if our new-found originality is not sustained by a new divine mission, our road must end in crudeness and vulgarity. True, there is that piety of the soul, that love or charity which the Greeks did not yet know; nevertheless, as the past two thousand years have shown, the yearning for justice, for truth, and beauty need not be the devil's work. It too is divine, and we should not be ashamed to call it so. No one who has been frightened by the barbaric forces which threaten all around us will be able to disregard that cultivation of the spirit whose history starts with the Greeks. And in doing so he will centre his eyes, not upon education, nor on *humanitas*, but upon the eternal verities which the Greeks discovered, or which were revealed to them.

But it would be wrong to give the impression that the human and the divine legacy of the Greeks were mutually exclusive, as if we had to choose between the two, as if one was, perhaps, better for one group of people, and the other for another. So let us add in conclusion that there is one respect in which we too must abide by the principle of *humanitas*, even though we may not have the talent which makes men humanists. That is the esteem in which we must hold the dignity of man: a modicum of *humanitas* for which no particular talent is needed. The eternal absolutes which rule over us, especially justice and truth, unhappily often make us forget that the absolute which accedes to our understanding is not entirely absolute after all. On occasion they will even allow us to act as if we were the absolute embodied, to the great sorrow of our fellow-men. At that point, morality turns into dynamite, and the explosion increases in violence as more and more men come to believe that it is their duty to follow the absolute. Finally, when it is agreed that certain institutions have come to represent that absolute, the catastrophe becomes inevitable. Then is the time to remind oneself that each and every human being has his own share of dignity and of freedom. All we require is a little courtesy, a bit of tolerance, and, *o sancte Erasme*, just a dash of your irony.

CHAPTER 12

ART AND PLAY IN CALLIMACHUS

Father Bromius!
Thou art genius,
Century's genius,
Art what inward glow
To Pindar was,
What to the world
Is Phoebus Apollo . . .

Jupiter Pluvius!
Not by the elm tree
Didst thou visit him,
With his brace of doves
In his affectionate arm,
Crowned with the friendly rose,
Playful him, flower-revelling
Anacreon,
Storm-breathing deity!

Not in the poplar grove
On the Sybaris' banks,
Nor at the mountain's
Sunlight-radiant brow
Didst thou seize him
Singing of bees,[1]
Prattling of honey,
Genially beckoning
Theocritus.

When the wheels rattled
Quickly wheel upon wheel around the goal,
Up soared
Victory-flushed
Youths' cracking of whips,
And dust was rolling
As from the mountains
Downward the shower of stones,
Thy soul glowed perils, Pindar,
Heart . . .

WHEN the twenty-two year old Goethe was 'passionately singing to himself this half-nonsense',[2] the *Wanderer's Storm Song*, he probably did not reflect that there was a literary precedent for his distinction between the sublime grandeur of Pindar and the playfulness of Anacreon and Theocritus. And yet the turning-point from the age of the rococo to the era of the 'untutored genius' stands in a significant relation to that other turning-point, in the history of Greek literature, when the contrast between playfulness and pathos was first officially enunciated. Goethe himself, granted that he had been willing to acknowledge this literary debt, could have referred only to the Roman middleman who supplied him with his Greek concept. For the Greek work which may be regarded as his ultimate model has only recently become known through an Egyptian papyrus. It is all the more significant that Goethe in many respects came closer to the spirit of the original than the derivative work with which he was acquainted.

In his poem, Goethe looks at Pindar through the spectacles of a literary tradition rather than with his own eyes. He admits this much himself, for in the following year, in the middle of July 1772, he tells Herder : 'I have now made Pindar my home, and if the splendour of the palace could make a man happy, I should be so.' He goes on to confess: 'Yet I feel what Horace was able to say, what Quintilian praises '. In point of fact the image: 'As from the mountains downward the shower of stones,' is a quotation, or a variation, of Horace's poem (4.2) which has fixed our conception of Pindar since the Renaissance:

> *Monte decurrens velut amnis, imbres*
> *Quem super notas aluere ripas,*
> *Fervet.*

Following this model, the writers of the baroque and the rococo identified Pindar with the grand or sublime style, unfettered by the strict rules of prosody. Again, Goethe's view of Theocritus as the representative of pastoral poetry, and of Anacreon as a light-hearted singer of wine and love, both standing at opposite poles from Pindar, is purely conventional. To cite an example which happens to occur to me : Goldoni says in his *Memoirs* (1.41) about Metastasio's arias, that 'some are written in the spirit of Pindar, others after the manner of Anacreon'. This shows, incidentally, that at that time the name of Anacreon was associated less with the genuine lyrics of the archaic poet than with the so-called Anacreontic poems which were ascribed to him.

But although Goethe fell in with the literary jargon of his time, he went much further. Nor did his readings in Horace, who deprecated his own trifles by comparison with the grandeur of Pindar, set a limit to his thought. In more than one way, Goethe managed to return to an ancient source whence the tradition in which he moved had first sprung up.

Horace, in his ode on Pindar, refuses to celebrate the deeds of Augustus in the solemn accents of a Pindaric song; instead he selects a slender and graceful form. Like other Romans who voice the same idea he thus follows the lead of Callimachus, the father of Hellenistic poetry (cf. above, ch. 6). Both Callimachus and Goethe stood on the threshold of a new age. After more than a century of enlightenment in the course of which the ancient religious beliefs had been dissolved, they had finally become weary of the spirit of rationalism. A new important era of poetry was about to begin. Still, so radically did the rhythm of antiquity differ from the trend of the modern age that Callimachus, and with him his age, decided in favour of a slender delicacy in poetic writing, whereas Goethe, and he too as the leader of his contemporaries, turned in the opposite direction, toward pathos and emotional fervour.

Despite some external similarities, the early Hellenistic age differed greatly in its intellectual situation from the last phase of the eighteenth century. For one thing, it lacked the storm and stress, the revolutionary ardour, of the later period. When, beginning with the third century B.C., after a century of prose writing (cf. above, ch. 6), poetry re-entered the scene with productions of high calibre and great authority, it kept intact the ancient poetic forms, particularly the spoken verse of the archaic period. Its spirit was new, but this newness was not of the sort to be proclaimed as a revelation, or to be championed with impassioned zeal. These Hellenistic poets are, if we may say it in one word, post-philosophical, while the earlier poets are pre-philosophical. The earlier poetry is ever intent to stake out new areas of the mind, and philosophy and science, the rational assimilation of the newly-found material, formed its natural sequel. In the realm of the epic, the heroic sagas furnished the seeds for Ionian historiography, and the theogonies

and cosmologies opened the way for Ionion natural philosophy and its search for the *arche*. The lyric led to
Heraclitus, the drama to Socrates and Plato. But with the
beginning of Hellenistic poetry, the great age of continuous
philosophical creation approached its end. The fourth
century had witnessed the achievements of Plato, Aristotle
and Theophrastus; its close coincides with the foundation of
the two schools of philosophy which were to remain sovereign
in the generations which followed: the Garden of Epicurus
and the Stoa of Zeno. Greek philosophy, that is, had reached
the point which, generally speaking, it was not destined to
surpass. That was the moment when in a new intellectual
centre, in Egyptian Alexandria, the residence of the Ptolemies,
a number of poets, among them Theocritus and Callimachus,
their most important figure,[3] joined together in a circle which
carried poetry to new heights.

These poets are post-philosophical in the sense that they
have ceased to believe in the possibility of mastering the
world by a theoretical control. As against Aristotle who had
credited poetry with a philosophical nature (see above, ch. 5)
they have no use for the universal in poetry, and so they
devote their special attention to details. Callimachus in
particular shows himself to be post-philosophical because he
entertains theories concerning the potentialities of poetry in
his age. This is his innovation in the history of literature; he
lays down his views regarding the art of writing in the form of
programmatic utterances, especially in the lines against his
foes with which he prefaced his longest and most important
work, the *Aitia*. Similar statements appear also in the body
of other works, and finally in a few single epigrams. Callimachus raises the question: What sort of poetry should we
write? This implies that there are various genres of poetry,
and in fact the writers of the period were engaged in the
composition of epic as well as dramatic and lyric poetry.
We consider it only natural, but an earlier age would have
found it hard to understand, that there should be one
' literature ' comprising a number of categories; that the
poet could exercise his own free choice of the genre to which
he wanted to devote his skill.

This first theoretical argument by a poet on behalf of his
own art was, of course, preceded by numerous discussions of

other people's works, such as Aristophanes' biting criticism of
Euripidean tragedy, Plato's reflections on the value of poetry,
the *Poetics* of Aristotle, and many other examples which are
now mostly lost to us. Callimachus readily avails himself of
some of these earlier critiques; his defence of the brevity of
his poetry tallies with the opinion of Aristotle[4], and his
justification of the delicate and unimpassioned style—the
ideal which through Horace remained in force long after him
—is intimately connected with certain motifs in Aristophanes
(cf. above, ch. 6).

Nor were the influences which moulded the thought of
Callimachus restricted to the field of literary criticism. In
the prologue to his *Aitia* (lines 25 ff.) he says that Apollo
warned him at the outset of his poetic undertaking not to take
the broad, much-travelled roads, but to hew out his own path,
however narrow. The notion that man has two roads before
him, and the behest not to take the one which is easy and
populous, but that which is narrow and deserted: this idea
derives ultimately from the *Works and Days* of Hesiod (lines
287 ff.), whence Prodicus took it and worked it into his fable
about Heracles. In Hesiod and Prodicus the narrow path
leads to virtue, the broad avenue to vice; similarly Callimachus decides that the narrow path is the right one, but he
fails to tell us where the two roads lead. This shows that he
has dropped the moral for whose sake the image had originally been invented; even Apollo does not inform him why he
should choose the one path and not the other.

Earlier he had said: a victim should be fat, but a poem
slender. Aristophanes, in his *Frogs*, had taken the opposite
stand and preferred the grand and imposing to the delicate.
Again Callimachus fails to produce a reason such as had
served Aristophanes to justify his opinions. Aristophanes
had rated the grandiose style of Aeschylus higher than the
refined manner of Euripides because, in his view, Euripides
corrupted the people, while Aeschylus instructed them in
noble thoughts. In Callimachus we look in vain for similar
moral evaluations. Once more, therefore, we must ask the
question: What are the motives of Callimachus for the choice
he makes? His answer appears in the words (lines 17 f.):
'Judge my poetry (literally: my wisdom, *sophie*) by its art
(*techne*), not by the Persian cubit.' The only criterion which

he acknowledges is that of his skill, of art itself; the two words *sophie* and *techne* are so closely related as to be practically synonymous; art is to be measured in no terms but its own.

In the earlier period all Greek poetry strove for some meaning lying beyond the limits of the writing itself. Even after poetry, in the course of time, had relinquished more and more of its social function, the poets endeavoured to seize upon a new concrete reality. In the end this objective became progressively more elusive, so that finally the poet abandoned his search to the philosopher. This element in art which points beyond art was, by Aristophanes, narrowed down to the didactic function of poetry. He thus attached to art a moral purpose; it was his way of preserving for poetry a task transcending its own boundaries even though this task was no longer founded in fact. Callimachus gives all that up, and proceeds to gauge art by itself. He addresses himself to a new audience all his own; for while Attic tragedy had still spoken to the mass of the people, Callimachus calls upon a small circle of cultured men to pass judgment on him. Plato's insistence that the experts should do the judging is here applied to a wisdom which is not the knowledge of the ultimate good, but culture, education, and good taste.

The wisdom of Callimachus is, above everything else, a matter of form. He manipulates his verse with the same delicacy and purity of line which Archilochus espoused, but which had been observed neither in the hexameters of the epic nor in the trimeters of drama. His ear is exceptionally sensitive to the effect of sounds, his vocabulary is rich and varied, and he chooses his words with a masterly feeling for cadence and emphasis, constantly reminding the educated reader of some significant reference. His skill in varying his diction, composition, and metrical scheme is unrivalled. Whenever Callimachus speaks of his wisdom, these are the things which he has chiefly in mind; the content is of lesser importance.

He was a scholar; his immense and careful learning is everywhere present in his work. But he did not employ it to write a didactic poem, as might be expected of an artist who cites the example of Hesiod for his art. The only use he makes of his erudition is to introduce a wealth of colourful and interesting material. He is a collector, with a preference for curiosities; he exhibits his wide knowledge less in order to teach his listeners a lesson than to entertain or even confuse them. Instead of talking about things generally known he surprises us by turning up a rare variant, by playing hide-and-seek, guessing-games and all sorts of tricks and pleasantries. His sense of humour provokes him to combine matters which in actuality are entirely unrelated. In his *Hymn to Zeus* he asks the question: Was Zeus born at the Cretan mount Ida or at mount Lycaeus in Arcadia? Since the former version was the one commonly accepted, he naturally decides for the other, far-fetched as it is, and cites in support of his choice the famous words of Epimenides of Crete : 'All Cretans are liars.' And then he scores once more with the remark that the Cretans also show a grave of Zeus, although everybody knows—and this has been skilfully anticipated in the invocation—that Zeus is immortal. His wit, his spirited handling of the sources, is obviously based on a great deal of learning, but this learning is not made to further the case of knowledge; its only service is to bask in its own glory. Later in Seneca, who inherited this amalgamating of myths from Callimachus through the mediation of Ovid, the learning is used to embellish and aggrandize the style; in Callimachus who loathes pathos it is a source of fun and sparkling ingenuity.

In his iambic verses Callimachus brings on the stage the Seven Sages who since the archaic period had, for the Greeks, embodied the ideal of wisdom. Callimachus, however, does not tell any of the numerous stories in which they were shown searching for knowledge, passing just judgment, or doing any of the noble things for which they were famous. In his view, their claim to wisdom is proved by their lack of vanity. The Arcadian Bathycles has left a golden bowl which after his death is to become the property of the wisest man. His son carries it around from sage to sage, each one of them remonstrating that not he, but the next man was the wisest, until ultimately Thales, when the bowl reaches him the second time, dedicates it to Apollo. The reason why Callimachus tells the story is to upbraid the Alexandrian scholars for their quarrels; as far as he was concerned the savants disagreed not because each of them took his convictions and findings seriously, but because they were tainted with pretentiousness and vanity, the congenital vices, as he thought, of the world. In his story about the strife between the olive and the laurel he succeeded once more in taking his stand against pretence and ostentation, two evils which have always lain in wait for those who, without following an objective task, possess enough cleverness and talent to live only for the effect. Of the one and only protection against these vices, self-irony, Callimachus is a past master.

He often stresses the playful nature of his poetry by casting himself in the role of the *ingénu*. The tale of Berenice's lock, for instance, which was sacrificed by the queen on the altar of Aphrodite and thence translated into the sky, is reported by the innocent little lock itself. Ancient myths whose truth he finds hard to credit, and stories invented by himself, he tells with a semblance of childish seriousness. This is one of the most peculiar forms of his wit. In his *Hymn to Delos* he describes how Hera, in her anger at Leto, issues an order to all places in Greece not to offer the unhappy mother a haven for bringing Apollo into the world. All cities, rivers, and mountains are, according to the old religious belief, supposed to possess their own divinities. This is the concept which Callimachus, in his own waggish way, seems to take seriously: no sooner does Leto appear at any one place than the nymphs and demons take to their heels. The result is a general exodus of all localities, until there is no place left for Apollo to be born.

In these poems, and others like them, Callimachus is not just acting the clown. His exaggeratedly ironical pathos is so lively and rich in nuances, and behind it all there is so much genuine joy in the naive and the primitive, so much charm and grace in spite of his raillery, that the finished product is as intriguing as it is hard to puzzle out. He himself calls his poetry ' childish play' (*paizein* and *paignion*). He constructed his slender works 'like a child' (*pais hate*), as the Telchines say of him in the prologue to the *Aitia* (line 6).

Because Callimachus is genuinely filled with the spirit of childhood, he was the first among Greek poets to be able to picture the behaviour of children in true colours, though, of course, with an admixture of irony which guarded him from losing himself entirely to the world of the child. In his

Hymn to Artemis he introduces the goddess as a little girl sitting on the lap of her father Zeus and begging him (lines 6 ff.):

> Please, daddy, let me keep my virginity for ever and let me have many names, so that Apollo cannot keep up with me. And give me arrows and bow—or no, father, I do not ask for a quiver, and I do not want a big bow from you. The Cyclopes will rightaway make the shafts for me, and also a well-curved bow. But allow me to carry torches and to wear a knee-high dress with a bright hem, so I may kill off the wild beasts. Also give me sixty Ocean-daughters for my companions in the dance. . . .

and so she prattles on and produces one request after another. All this furnishes a picture, and in part a very learned picture, of the nature and activities of Artemis. But the way in which Callimachus looks at the little Artemis has something grandfatherly about it; yet he is not sentimental about her, he does not dispense with the superior perspective of the grown-up: he does not become an artificial child himself.

With the same slightly ironical delight in simple and naive things Callimachus relates in his *Aitia* the scurrilous customs of primitive cults, exotic tales, and rare events. With impressive seriousness, and yet not with a wholly straight face, he pours out a wealth of information. If we were to look for a unifying idea, for an intellectual objective or a programme of enlarging the mental horizon of his listeners, we would not find them. Instead we find a keen sense for the colourful variety of all the strange happenings around us, and this sense Callimachus possessed in a greater measure than any Greek writer since the archaic period. It is, however, no longer the genuinely child-like amazement of the earlier writers who took the wonders of life to heart, and who felt themselves sustained by the significant forces which they discovered about them. The amazement of Callimachus is of the head-wagging sort: Isn't life full of odd goings-on?

The world of play, which since the days of tragedy had been part and parcel of all Greek literature, is here blended with mature learning, and it is this genial mixture of youthful emotion and intellectual scepticism which makes for the ripe grace of this distinguished art.

The lack of a concrete objective, and altogether of all higher commitments, is evident also in his love poetry. There the beloved person, and the desire for the happiness of possession, fade into the background, and a new element which merits the label *erotic* in a very modern sense comes to the fore. In one epigram we read this (*ep.* 41) :

One half of my soul has made its getaway. I wonder whether she has once again gone to a boy? And yet, I have so often sent out the order : ' Do not receive the runaway, youths!' . . . She deserves to be stoned to death (i.e., because she is a deserter) and she is in league with wicked Eros; I know that she is on the loose somewhere there.

This love of Callimachus differs from the love which reigned in the earlier works, for in the writers before him it had always been directed to a beloved person; it had been a 'love for somebody', as Plato's Diotima puts it (*Symp.* 199 D). The love of Callimachus, on the other hand, lacks this orientation. A part of his soul has made itself independent, and he does not know where it may have strayed. He is in love without really knowing whom he would love.[5]

Another epigram (*ep.* 31) conveys roughly the following idea: 'The huntsman in the mountains pursues every hare and every deer and delights in the snow. But when he is told: 'There, the animal is hit!' he does not want it. My love is like that: it pursues the fleeing prey, but it hurries past that which is readily available.' This happens to be a rebuff to a boy named Epicydes whom Callimachus addresses in the first line,[6] but at the same time it serves him for a general statement of his view on love. Like the huntsman who is more interested in the sport itself than in his quarry, he devotes more attention to the game of pursuing than to that of catching his object. The two epigrams have this in common that the goal, the direction of the love instinct is declared to be unimportant by comparison with the subjective feeling; in the one case it is the mere impulse, in the other the pleasure of the chase which ranks highest in his scale of values.

Two further epigrams (30 and 43) are rather alike in the point which they are designed to make; on both occasions Callimachus notices that someone else is in love, once because of the expression of his features, and the other time because he fetches a deep sigh. His reaction is: I understand, for I feel the same way. Thus Callimachus chooses to confess his own love via the description of another; but he does not do so in the presence of his beloved, to influence him. In the one case he conveys his sympathy to a rival, and the other epigram is addressed to nobody in particular. The indirect form helps him to avoid the open confession 'I love' with its pathos and inelegance, and to deflect his admission into irony. He creates an impression as if this reminder of his passion were merely a passing comment which he had not really intended.

In the last two epigrams which we have discussed, the playful nature of Callimachus' art manifests itself in the lack of seriousness with which his problem is voiced; in the other two it is shown in the fact that his love exists only for its own sake—and in this it, of course, resembles his art which is only for art's sake. All four epigrams, however, agree in one thing, viz. that love is but the subjective psychological state of being in love, and not the intercession of a deity as it had appeared in Archilochus, Sappho, and even Anacreon. Nor is it the love which we encounter in tragedy, the violent passion which stirs up the innermost soul of a man, nor again the metaphysical search for perfection, as Plato thinks of it. On the other hand, it is decidedly not, as might be expected after all this, a base desire for transitory pleasures of the flesh. Obviously the love of Callimachus is not of the sort to inspire him to ponder the mysteries of god, the world, or human existence. All it does is to make him aware of his own sensibilities.

But in spite of the egocentric character of his poetry, Callimachus does not advance to a genuine self-reflexion or self-analysis. Neither in the field of psychology nor in any other area of the human mind does he deserve to be called an innovator or discoverer, unless we are to regard it as a discovery that he was able to look at himself with a smile and to state : So this is what you are like. By stepping back and viewing himself from a distance, he adds an abstract dimension to his consciousness; but neither Callimachus nor his successors combined this abstractness with sufficient philosophic vitality to make it fruitful as a beginning of new thought.

Callimachus' resolve not to take things too seriously, particularly those matters which exceed the horizon of man, is a sign of post-philosophical exhaustion. If he does take

anything seriously, it is that which is already known. Though
he made merry with the rich literary tradition of Greece
supplied to him by the Alexandrian library, he still retains a
genuinely scholarly interest in the tracing and preserving of
that material. The rules of his sport command him not to
disclose the seriousness and the labour expended on his
research, and not to allow the dust of the library to tarnish
the brilliance of his wit and his fiction. But his poetry would
be unthinkable if he had not had a deep sympathy for learned
studies, or if he had not enjoyed rummaging in old sources.
Among his audience, too, Callimachus expects a wide
acquaintance with tradition; they must understand his
allusions, and show an interest in far-fetched curiosities.
Because he himself moves about with ease and comfort in the
vast halls of learning, so he demands that his public too feel
at home in them. It is only natural that his public can never
be large; his art is decidedly exclusive, choice fare for
connoisseurs.

The language in which he couches his *jeux d'esprit* owes
its light touch to its rhetorical background. It is the birth-
right of Greek rhetoric to incline toward spirited pleasantries,
and to be less interested in content than in form. The
excessive employment of vocal effects for which its founder
Gorgias had striven was soon dropped, for reasons of good
taste rather than from any conviction that the form of speech
ought to be determined by its concrete objective. Euphony
and its stimulus upon the emotions, and a playfully contrived
richness of word relations, i.e. antithesis, anaphora and so
forth, remained the principal goal. The highly developed
prose writing of the fourth century had achieved a perfection
of these stylistic features, and it had demonstrated how they
could be used with discretion. In Callimachus they are less
obvious even than, e.g. in Ovid's *Metamorphoses*, but without
a training in the theory of rhetoric his easy mastery of diction
could not have been accomplished. This is one case, therefore, in which prose exercised a decisive influence upon
poetry. Callimachus is, of course, careful not to adopt the
characteristic traits of that prose, such as the overt expression
of logical connexions; on the contrary, his thought associations are imbued with a kind of Homeric naiveté.

We have seen that in the time of Callimachus the best

minds began to turn away from philosophy and to devote themselves to antiquarian and philological studies, and also to the writing of poetry. Like all earlier attempts of the Greeks to break with the past and to discover new territory, this also was a reaction designed to force a new immediate contact with reality. The philosophers had tried to control the world and life by means of a rational system; the new writers re-discover the great appeal of non-reflective simplicity, and so they turn to the earliest speech of man, to poetry. The cultured men from the big cities are fascinated by primitive customs, by unspoiled manners, by the simple life which is best described by Theocritus, but which also appears in the pages of Herodas and others. But just as in his portrayal of children Callimachus never forgets himself to the point of affecting a false infantility, so also in all other respects he never abandons his irony and his superior wit. Without setting up theories or programmes, he stands for a new, a knowing naiveté; his playfulness stems from the strength of his intellect; it is the genial spirit of one who surveys a lost treasure from the heights of his scepticism rather than weeping sentimental tears.

There were other attempts during his time, as well as the preceding age, to return to an immediate experience of the simple life. The factor which puts Callimachus in a special category is that he does not sacrifice the intellect. He does not want the primitivism of the Cynics; he does not admire the Scythian Anacharsis. Conversely he does not preach culture and humaneness, terms which only too easily betoken a spirit of hollow show and self-applause.

Because Callimachus was on the whole a derivative poet it is not legitimate to speak of him as a discoverer. But his contributions came to be so important for the formation of our European culture that he must be counted among its pioneers. Education or culture is for him tantamount to the faculty of recollection which, aside from cleverly fitting together disparate pieces and thus diverting the listener with surprising effects, enables a man to look down upon the varied manifestations of life with a catholic and sympathetic mind. The cultured man, the scholar, delights in his sensation of standing above the world, without being committed to it. From Callimachus this concept was, through the agency of the Romans, and again primarily through the services of Ovid, handed down to the humanists of the Renaissance. The only difference was that the Romans infused into it the idea of a higher realm of the spirit, of poetry and culture, to which they looked up with a longing admiration. Callimachus lacks this humility; he is too certain of himself, too much at home in his intellectual habitat. His refusal to acknowledge an overall goal of knowledge is matched by his failure to follow any ethical, political, or even simply educational directive. He would be the last to wish to admonish anyone to adopt his cultural convictions. The domain of the spirit in which he dwells is airy and attractive enough to compel the voluntary allegiance of anyone who has a mind for it.

In his *Wanderer's Storm Song* Goethe had contrasted the grand poetry of Pindar with Anacreon and Theocritus. This was not only a declaration of faith in favour of one of the two styles which baroque literary criticism had posited, nor was it merely a renunciation of the rococo literature with which he himself had been identified a little earlier. It was also his break with the heritage of the traditional humanistic creed.

In his *Dichtung und Wahrheit* (2.10) Goethe says he had learned from Herder 'that poetry is a possession of the whole world, of the people, and not just the private property of a few refined, cultured men'. These last words are an exact definition of what poetry had become through Callimachus. Since the Renaissance, this exclusive heirloom had been entered upon and cherished by those educated in the classics; with many variations, and blending with a good many other influences, the tradition may be detected in Ariosto's *Orlando Furioso*, in Pope's *Rape of the Lock*, in Wieland's verse tales, and in Byron's *Don Juan*. Thus we have the paradox that Goethe, in a situation which in many respects resembled that in which Callimachus found himself, turned against the very things which owed their existence to him.

Theocritus and Anacreon—that is, the author of the *Anacreontea*—the playful, genially beckoning Hellenistic poets, are not visited by the deity, not by Zeus (Jupiter), Apollo, or Dionysus (Bromius). Dionysus is 'genius'—behind this we sense the concept of the untutored, the original genius—he is 'what inward glow to Pindar was, what

to the world Phoebus Apollo is.' The 'inward glow' is the
poet's participation in the divine spirit. In a letter dated
Sept. 13th, 1774, written to K. Schmidt, Heinse describes
Goethe himself as a new Pindar: 'Goethe stopped off with
us, a beautiful young man of twenty-five, who from top to
toe is genius and power and strength, a heart full of feeling, a
spirit full of fire with eagle's wings, *qui ruit immensus ore
profundo '*—this being the sequel of Horace's ode on Pindar
from which we quoted above. These words are more significant than similar statements about other poets of the
period who are praised as a new Pindar or, if a lady, as a new
Sappho. Goldoni, for example, says about the *improvvisatore*
Perfetti: 'The poet sang for about fifteen minutes stanzas
in the manner of Pindar. Nothing finer than his song. He
was Petrarch, Milton, Rousseau . . . no, Pindar himself.'
By way of contrast with so affected and banal an application
of historical names, Goethe tries to establish contact with
the original experiences of the artist: 'When the wheels
rattled . . . thy soul glowed perils, Pindar, heart.' True, this
also has little to do with the real Pindar, for that poet nowhere refers to himself as being passionately involved in the
contests which he celebrates, nor does he ever talk of ' victory-
flushed youths' cracking of whips.' What we have is, rather,
a vague concept of Pindar's victory hymns, constructed on
the basis of Horace's simile of the mountain stream, and
brought into line with certain views on the role of 'experience'
in poetry which were current in Goethe's own time.[7]

And yet in one point Goethe's new image of Pindar comes
close to the truth. Goethe emphasizes the religious aspect of
that poetry, following the teaching of Herder that genuine
poetry does not spring from privacy, from refinement or
education, but from the divine. This is the essential difference between Callimachus and Goethe, and between their
two ages, that the reaction against rationalism takes two
different shapes; once it explodes as religious emotion, as
enthusiasm and pathos and dithyrambic excitement, whereas
in Alexandria its manifestation was the *jeu d'esprit*. The
elements which Callimachus introduced into poetry were
those same evils to which Goethe in his day objected, for
rococo poetry was erected on the ideals of good taste and
refined wit. In the age of rationalism the poets had managed

to move closer than ever to the wellspring of the humanistic tradition, to Callimachus.

The new religious fervour of the *Storm and Stress* is no return to the ancient beliefs which had ruled supreme prior to the age of enlightenment. Goethe, to be sure, invokes the classical gods. In taking his leave of the humanistic tradition, he attaches himself to an even older Greek heritage. But what transpired was not the re-establishment of a religious cult, but the creation of an independent secularized faith which traces the divine powers in the workings of nature and in the soul of the individual. Art furnished a very special revelation of these divine forces; and the Greeks were the great artists *par excellence*. That is why Winckelmann was able to find in Homer and in classical sculpture an expression of the divine on earth.[8] This recollection of a distant past whose significance had been temporarily obscured made it possible to overcome rationalism without a recourse to scepticism or sleight-of-hand. In the age of Callimachus, also, new religious needs had come to the fore and sought satisfaction outside the traditional forms of the native cults. This led to the acceptance of Asiatic and Egyptian gods, to an influx of barbaric material which could not but clash with the Greek culture. Wincklelmann, in a later age, was in a position to return to the foundations of European thought. He went outside the seemingly exhausted tradition of religious beliefs, to look for the revelation of the deity in the visible world. And thus he found himself able once more, despite enlightenment and scepticism, to arouse himself and others to an enthusiastic and passionate acclaim of the significant achievements in history and art. Among the Greeks this reversal from playfulness to seriousness was no longer feasible. But Goethe, in his age, repeated that distinction between the grand and the slender art which Aristophanes had been the first to promulgate.

The poetry of the period of *Storm and Stress* is, therefore, not post-philosophical in the same sense as we saw it to be true of Callimachus. In its wake there developed a philosophy which was in many respects opposed to rationalism and which, unlike the philosophy of the enlightenment, succeeded in integrating history in its plan. Another consequence of it was—and here again the contrast with the age of Callimachus is evident—a tremendous upsurge of the historical sciences. This development, whatever other stimuli may have been operative to bring it about, owed its chief impulse to the new approach toward antiquity. Moreover, it was probably due to the new understanding of the Greek world as a historical phenomenon, that in the lyric poetry which at the time overran England and France as well as Germany, self-reflexion did not at once turn into the playful irony of Callimachus; that all poets, however personal the sentiments they expressed, acknowledged their membership in a meaningful world and in a life which in spite of all conflicts deserves to be taken seriously. The romantics may have longed for the age of childhood, they may have yearned for a return to the simple and artless forms of life; at the same time, however, Greek culture was, in some shape or other, their ultimate goal. In the course of the nineteenth century we often find a violent rejection of all things classical, and here we may detect the echoes of certain *Storm and Stress* ideas regarding the primitive genius. But we ought not to overlook the subtle irony of the circumstance that even the raving half-nonsense of the primitive genius is intimately linked with a tradition, a tradition, to boot, which derives from the opposite pole. Let us therefore console ourselves with the knowledge that the tradition of European culture is a reservoir which gives us the strength we need to overcome our spiritual crises. The Greeks did not yet have this reservoir at their disposal; it is all the more imperative that we exploit its energies. In this way, with the help of the Greeks, we shall perhaps be even more successful than they in fighting shy of the wrong turns and blind alleys which hamper our progress.

CHAPTER 13

ARCADIA: THE DISCOVERY OF A SPIRITUAL LANDSCAPE

ARCADIA was discovered in the year 42 or 41 B.C. Not, of course, the Arcadia of which the encyclopedia says: 'The central alpine region of the Peloponnesus, limited off on all sides from the other areas of the peninsula by mountains, some of them very high. In the interior, numerous ridges divide the section into a number of small cantons.' This humdrum Arcadia had always been known, in fact it was regarded as the home of Pelasgus, the earliest man. But the Arcadia which the name suggests to the minds of most of us to-day is a different one; it is the land of shepherds and shepherdesses, the land of poetry and love, and its discoverer is Virgil. How he found it, we are able to tell in some detail, thanks to the researches of Ernst Kapp.[1] The historian Polybius who came from the humdrum Arcadia cherished a great affection for his country. Although there was not much of interest to be related of this land behind the hills, he could at least report (4.20) that the Arcadians were, from the days of their infancy onwards, accustomed to practice the art of singing, and that they displayed much eagerness in organizing musical contests. Virgil came across this passage when he was composing his shepherd songs, the *Eclogues,* and at once understood it to refer to the Arcadian shepherds; for Arcadia was shepherds' country and the home of Pan, the god of the herdsmen, inventor of the syrinx. And so Virgil located the lives and the poetic contests of his shepherds in Arcadia. 'You Arcadians,' he says (10.32), 'who are alone experienced in song.' He mentions two Arcadians 'who are equal in song, and equal to giving response in turn' (7.5). He remarks on mount Maenalus in Arcadia 'which ever hears the love songs of the shepherds and Pan blowing his pipe' (8.23). He calls upon Arcadia to judge a contest between the singers (4.58).[2] The shepherds whom Virgil introduces in his earliest eclogue are not Arcadian but Sicilian (2.21): this setting comes to him from the idylls of Theocritus, the Hellenistic poet who served as the model for all Roman pastoral poetry. Since the shepherds of Theocritus, too, indulged in responsive singing and competitions, Virgil had no difficulty in linking them with the Arcadians of Polybius.

Theocritus who was born in Syracuse had written about the herdsmen of his own country. Meanwhile, however, Sicily had become a Roman province, and her shepherds had entered the service of the big Roman landlords. In this new capacity they had also made their way into Roman literature; witness Lucilius' satire on his trip to Sicily. But they could no longer be mistaken for the shepherds of song and love. Thus Virgil needed a new home for his herdsmen, a land far distant from the sordid realities of the present. Because, too, pastoral poetry did not mean to him what it had meant to Theocritus, he needed a far-away land overlaid with the golden haze of unreality. Theocritus had given a realistic and slightly ironical description of the herdsmen of his country engaged in their daily chores; Virgil regarded the life of the Theocritean shepherds as a sublime and inspired existence. If we look at the beginning of his earliest bucolic poem: 'The shepherd Corydon loved fair Alexis', it has a different ring from anything comparable that Theocritus might have said. In Greek these names were hardened by daily usage; in Virgil they are borrowed words, cultured and strange, with a literary, an exotic flavour, like the names of the mythical heroes which Virgil had drawn from Greek poetry. The effect of this upon the persons of the shepherds was decisive. Later, when Virgil himself had become an example to be followed, the shepherds of European literature were called Daphnis and Amyntas, but they too were awkwardly out of place in the Cotswolds, or the Cornish heath. In the end, when Johann Heinrich Voss by-passed Virgil and re-established Theocritus as his model, he gave the protagonists of his idylls the good German peasant names Krischen and Lene.[3]

Virgil, then, did not aspire to furnish a realistic portrayal of everyday life, but searched for a land which could harbour herdsmen named Corydon and Alexis, Meliboeus and Tityrus, a land which might be a fitting domicile for everything that seems to be implied in such poetic names. In the 10th eclogue, the latest in date of writing, which more than any other pastoral piece by Virgil stresses the Arcadian milieu,

the poet Gallus has been set down in Arcady and there finds
himself in the company of the gods and shepherds. The
Roman god Silvanus and two Greeks, Apollo god of song and
Pan the deity of the Arcadian herdsmen, express their
sympathy with his unhappy love. How would this be possible
in so near and familiar a setting as Sicily? This scene too
has its precedent in Theocritus, but there (1.77 ff.) the gods
Hermes, Priapus and Aphrodite are shown paying a visit to
the mythical shepherd Daphnis, not just to an ordinary
human, much less to an identifiable contemporary of the
writer. Theocritus' scene is mythical, and he keeps that
mythical atmosphere clear of any intrusions. In Virgil's
Arcadia the currents of myth and empirical reality flow one
into another; gods and modern men stage meetings in a
manner which would have been repugnant to Greek poetry.
In actual fact this half-way land is neither mythical nor
empirical; to the Roman Virgil and his Roman public,
Apollo and Pan convey even less of their divinity, as objects
of genuine faith, than they had to Theocritus and his
Hellenistic audience. Arcadia is not an area on the map,
either; even the person of Gallus appears misty and unreal,
which has not, of course, prevented the scholars from trying
to penetrate through the mist and identify the historical
Gallus.

The air of unreality which hangs over Virgil's poems is
thus explained by the fact that he seeks to approximate the
world of Theocritus and that of myth, and that therefore he
manipulates the traditional mythology with a greater licence
than would have been possible for a Greek. The tragedians
of the fifth century, to be sure, had begun to elaborate the
ancient tales and to interpret them anew, but they had
nevertheless maintained the fiction that they were discussing
events of the hoary past. Plato's inventions in the mythical
genre are often no longer connected with the ancient motifs,
but they are always profoundly significant tales, genuinely
mythical in tenor and aim. Callimachus says that when he
first put his writing-tablet on his knees, Apollo gave him
some useful hints for his poetry. But that is obviously a
joke; and when he reports that the lock of Queen Berenice
was placed among the stars, he bases that on the belief of his
time that a great man may after his death be received among

the gods. But nobody, prior to Virgil, seriously shows men of the present in close contact, and on an equal footing, with divine beings.

When the early age, during which the Greeks had accepted myth as history, came to a close the tragic writers and the historians of the fifth century divorced the two fields from each other. Myth retired beyond the world of man, and though at first it retained its old function of providing a standard of explanation and interpretation for human experiences, tragedy turned it into a poetic counterpart of reality. With the emancipation of myth came two important changes. On the one hand the ancient heroes and events were interpreted realistically—the psychological approach to the myths is part of this trend—in order to render them more useful to men in their daily lives; and secondly new dramatic situations were invented to the end of adapting the old myths to the stage. Hellenistic poetry carried the psychological interpretation of mythical characters even further, and it made the setting more naturalistic than ever before; but as against this, it also discovered new aesthetic possibilities for the myths. From these up-to-date versions of the ancient tradition, poetry learned to turn its aesthetic energies into the glorification and embellishment of the objects of commonplace reality. In the end, Theocritus domesticated the Sicilian shepherds and made them acceptable to his sensitive art. Virgil, in a certain sense, set about reversing this order of events, and in fact he finally wound up restoring the grand form of the epic. The *Eclogues* contain the first indications of his role which was to exalt the realistic writing which served as his point of departure, viz. the idylls of Theocritus, by suffusing it with elements of myth. Myth and reality are thus once more joined together, albeit in a manner never before witnessed in Greece.

Virgil arranges the meeting between his friend Gallus and Pan and Apollo because Gallus is a poet. As a poet he is on excellent terms with the Arcadian shepherds; Virgil had transferred his shepherds to Arcadia because the inhabitants of that country, as Polybius had informed him, were especially well versed in song. The shepherds of Theocritus, too, delight in song; but the ancestry of the musical herdsman is older yet. To trace it all the way back, we must turn to the age before Homer, for on the shield of Achilles (*Il.* 18.525) we find shepherds rejoicing in the sound of the syrinx. We have already mentioned the fact that it was the Arcadian deity Pan who was responsible for the invention of this instrument. Bucolic poetry, also, is of an ancient vintage. It appears that, about the year 600 B.C., Stesichorus introduced it into the repertory of Greek literature, with a choral ode in which he told the story of Daphnis. Daphnis was loved by a nymph; but when, in a bout of drunkenness, he became unfaithful to her, he suffered the punishment reserved for him: he was blinded. This account is obviously based on a simple rustic tale, localized in the vicinity of Himera, the city where Stesichorus lived. In his version, as we might expect in a Greek poetic treatment, the folk-tale is changed into a divine myth, for Daphnis is said to be the son—or, according to others, the beloved—of Hermes, and he tends the cattle of Helios. Our information about the poem is, unfortunately, late and imperfect, but we know that an important section of it was a lament for Daphnis. From that time onward the shepherds have been in love, usually without hope of success; either they indulge in their own suffering, or they wring a poetic expression of sympathy from their friends. We cannot say for sure how Stesichorus formulated all this, but it may be supposed that he endowed the pastoral life with some of the subdued lustre which Homer allows to the figure of Eumaeus, the faithful swineherd of Odysseus. The familiar and self-sufficient world of the simple shepherd is rendered in a myth which, though evidently sprung from a folk-tale, is for all that no less real than the myths which tell of heroes and heroic deeds.

More than three hundred years later, Theocritus composes yet another lament for Daphnis. This time it is given out as a song of the Sicilian shepherd Tityrus (7.72), and again as a composition of the herdsman Thyrsis (1.66). Theocritus takes some pains to present a realistic picture of the life led by Sicilian shepherds. But in one respect they are anything rather than country folk: their mood is a literary one. Theocritus engineers a kind of masquerade; he wishes us to recognize poets of his own circle behind the rustic disguise. He adopts the classic motif of the singing and playing shepherd, and develops the scope of the pastoral poem by

voicing the literary themes of the day. All this is done
in a spirit of good-natured jesting; the dissonance between the bucolic simplicity of the pasture and the literary
refinement of the city is never completely resolved, nor was
it ever intended to be, for the whole point of Theocritus'
humour lies in this dissonance. In the lament for Daphnis
we read: 'The trees mourned for him, those which grew along
the Himera river, when he melted away like snow on mount
Haemus or Athos or Rhodope or on the furthest Caucasus.'
This is the speech of the literati, for it is not customary with
shepherds to discuss Haemus or Athos, Rhodope or Caucasus;
it is the grand style of tragedy.

This high-flown diction must not be compared with the
Greek geographical nomenclature with which Horace, who is
our best example for this technique, equips his poems. To a
Roman ear his place names do not convey the parody of
tragedy, but respect for a noble tradition. And that is the
spirit in which Virgil purloined his characters from Theocritus. The Roman poets use these strange-sounding names,
dignified, as they thought, by the Greek passages in which
they had occurred, to add to the stateliness of their speech;
for the Latin tongue has no poetic diction of its own. The
names help to lift the writing to a higher plane of literary art.
As far as the Romans were concerned, if we may venture a
paradox, all these mountains lie in Arcadia, in the land of
Corydon and Alexis, of Pan and Apollo. It would not be
fair to suggest that in the Augustan period such places had
already degenerated into a kind of scenic backdrop for a
poetic stage which may be exchanged at will. But it is certain
that they have nothing whatever to do with any real landscape
outside the theatre, where you might find ordinary, non-
fictional men.

When Theocritus has his shepherds enumerate these
mountains, he creates roughly the same impression as when
Menander puts his quotations from tragedy in the mouths of
uneducated slaves. With deliberate irony he makes his
Sicilian shepherds live above their intellectual means. But
when Virgil read these passages and others like them, he
accepted them in the spirit of the more solemn context from
which they had originally come, as expressions of genuine
feeling. The tension between the real and the literary world

which Theocritus had exploited for its peculiar charms, is brought to nought, and everything shifts back to the even plane of an undifferentiated majesty.

In Theocritus, Daphnis is the shepherd from the myth of Stesichorus. In other works he is just an ordinary herdsman, like Tityrus or Corydon. But he is always either the one or the other. Virgil mentions him already in his earliest eclogue: there he is unquestionably the mythical shepherd (2.26). In two other passages (7.1 and 9.46) he is a common herdsman. But what is his identity in the fifth eclogue? As in other bucolic poems, two shepherds, Menalcas and Mopsus, want to stage a singing contest. They sing of the death and apotheosis of Daphnis, i.e. apparently the Daphnis of the myth. But this Daphnis had been the friend of Menalcas and Mopsus (line 52); thus he also belongs to the immediate environment of the competing herdsmen. Now at the end of the poem we discover that Virgil is using one of the two men as a mask for his own person. Once Virgil had placed his shepherds in Arcadia, it seems, it was but a short step to blend the bucolic with the mythical. This transition was, of course, facilitated by the fact that Theocritus himself had used the figure of Daphnis in both capacities.

In Theocritus, as in Virgil, the shepherds are less concerned with their flocks than they are interested in poetry and love. In both writers, therefore, they are gifted with passion and intellect, but in different ways. Theocritus' herdsmen, notwithstanding their pastoral status, often prove to be urban intellectuals in disguise. Virgil's shepherds, on the other hand—and it is charming to follow the steady progress from eclogue to eclogue—become increasingly more delicate and sensitive: they become Arcadian shepherds. Theocritus, too, stands at a distance from his shepherds; being a man from the city, he looks down upon them partly with a feeling of superiority, partly with an open mind for the straight simplicity of their primitive life. The simplicity is more ideal than fact, and so his shepherds, in spite of all realism, remain fairly remote from the true life in the fields. But this remoteness is as it should be, for a genuine summons back to nature would silence the whole of pastoral poetry; as it turned out, that is exactly what happened in a later age. Above all, these shepherds are not really taken seriously. Their quarrels have

something comical about them; how different from the harsh
wrangling between Eumaeus and Melanthius in the *Odyssey*!
The violent head-on conflicts which we find in tragedy, even
between kings, do not exist in Theocritus, and Virgil goes
even further in smoothing the differences. From Theocritus
on the shepherds display a courtly behaviour, and this court-
liness, or courtesy, remains true of all bucolic poetry. The
rustic life is made palatable to good society by its acquisition
of manners and taste; if there are any embarrassing features
left, the poet neutralizes them by making them appear droll,
by smiling at them. Virgil is even more intent than Theocritus on toning down the crudeness and coarseness of the
shepherds; as a result, he has less occasion to feel superior
to them. Furthermore, while endowing the herdsmen with
good manners and delicate feelings, he also makes them more
serious-minded. But their seriousness differs from that of a
Eumaeus; they have no strength to stand up for their genuine
interests, nor do they ever clash with one another in open
conflict. They are no more conversant with the true elemental passions than the heroes of the *Aeneid* were to be.
And it is significant that in those ages when Arcadian poetry
was in fashion, and when courtly manners were the order of
the day, the *Aeneid* has always been more highly favoured
than the *Iliad* or the *Odyssey*.

Virgil's Arcadia is ruled by tender feeling. His herdsmen
lack the crudeness of the peasant life as well as the over-
sophistication of the city. In their rural idyll the peaceful
calm of the leisurely evening hours stands out more clearly
than the labour for their daily bread, the cool shade is more
real than the harshness of the elements, and the soft turf by
the brook plays a larger role than the wild mountain crags.
The herdsmen spend more time playing the pipe and singing
their tunes than in the production of milk and cheese. All
this is incipient in Theocritus, but the Alexandrian still
shows some interest in realistic detail. Virgil has ceased to
see anything but what is important to him: tenderness
and warmth and delicacy of feeling. Arcadia knows no
reckoning in numbers, no precise reasoning of any kind.
There is only feeling, which suffuses everything with its
glow; not a fierce or passionate feeling : even love is but a
delicate desire, gentle and sad.

Virgil, the discoverer of Arcadia, did not set out to explore new lands. He was no adventurer of the spirit who listens to the call of foreign shores. With utmost modesty he admits that he is proud to have been chosen by the Muse to introduce the Theocritean pastoral among the Romans (6.1). It was not any wish to be an innovator or reformer which caused him to swerve off the path of Theocritus. We must assume that when in his reading of Theocritus he found the grotesque tale of Polyphemus who tried to find a cure for his love in singing, the figure of the Cyclops changed under his very eyes, while he was yet perusing the tale, and turned into a lonely shepherd who voices his longing (*Ecl.* 2). Theocritus says (11.12) that the herds of Polyphemus had to make their way home by themselves in the evenings, because the herdsman forgot all else over his singing. Virgil interprets this as a picture of the golden age when the flocks were able to return to the stables of their own accord, without any herdsman to look after them (4.21). Or again: Virgil has read that during the noon heat lizards sleep in the thornbush. He had found this in Theocritus, where someone expresses his amazement that another person is up and about during that hour, 'while even the lizards take their siesta' (7.22). Virgil has a shepherd who is unhappily in love sing as follows: 'While the flocks seek the cool shade and the lizards hide in the bushes, I must continually sing of my love' (2.8). Thus the sensible beasts have become the happy beasts. Theocritus concludes a jocular prayer to Pan (7.111) with these words: 'If you do not comply with my prayer, I hope you will pasture your flocks during the winter in icy Thrace on the Hebrus, and during the summer among the Ethiopians in the furthest south.' In Virgil, Gallus mourns (10.65 ff.): 'Nor will my unhappy love subside if I drink from the Hebrus in mid-winter or if I plough through the snowfalls of the Thracian winter, nor if I pasture the sheep of the Ethiopians under the sign of Cancer (i.e. in mid-summer).' The drastic punishment threatened to the shepherd's god is transformed into the sorrows of the unhappy lover who roams through the whole wide world and cannot find a hardship extreme enough to free him from his tortures. These subtle changes are numerous; little by little, without drawing our attention to it, Virgil varies the Theocritean motifs. The transformation is so slight that it took a long time before it was noticed how far Virgil had progressed in his *Eclogues* beyond the pleasantries of the Hellenistic poet. He admired and acknowledged the work of Theocritus, he dwelt lovingly on his scenes; but because he read them with the eyes of the new classicistic age, he slowly came back to the classical Greek poetry, with its earnestness, its deep feeling, its drama. Virgil had not intended to be original; he merely re-moulded Theocritus in the image of what he considered to be characteristically Greek. This was the route by which Virgil discovered Arcadia: without searching for it, without proclaiming his arrival; and so we, for our part, have no easy time in discovering that it was he who discovered the land, and what its discovery means to us.

That Virgil, in his *Eclogues*, returned to the spirit of classical art is, first of all, clear from the fact that his poems, unlike those of Theocritus, are not small clippings from the panorama of life, but well-constructed and rounded works of art.[4] Each poem has its climaxes and its lulls; motifs light up and fade out again. Actually, as we might almost expect, this classicistic art is, in such formal matters, more demanding and exact than the classical. The Romans contribute their own native flair for disciplined structural design. Consequently the composition of the poetry written in the classicistic Augustan age is of a special perfection.

This formal beauty of the poem indicates that the work of art has attained to a greater degree of independence. The poem is no longer related to a specific situation or to any one circle of listeners or readers, or to any particular segment of reality. The process of literary creation becomes autonomous; it becomes a realm in itself, an absolute realm, detached from all that is not art and literature. Its perfect form, its grace and its sound, make it what it is. Thus, for the first time in Western literature, the poem becomes a 'thing of beauty', existing only for itself and in itself.

In the course of writing his *Eclogues* Virgil turned with increasing attachment to the severe stateliness of the classical form. But the themes with which he grapples had never been treated by the Greeks. His gradual emancipation from the narrow limits of the Theocritean pastoral does not tempt him to use his eclogues for the description of great deeds or heroic fates. Actually he does not narrate facts or events at all; he is more interested in the unfolding and praising of situations. These situations are not such as had been celebrated in the archaic Greek lyric— particular occasions which help to raise the human spirit above the level of our ordinary existence. On the contrary, it is to a comprehension of this everyday life that Virgil directs his sensitive skill. Arcadia is the land of the gilt-edged weekday. Virgil's sensibility fastens upon the familiar daily activities, the constant traffic with the same routine objects, the peaceful life on the home soil. But this familiarity smacks of nostalgia. His love for the familiar things is a longing rather than happiness. For this is a land in which the mountains and the trees participate in the sorrows of the unhappy lover—a motif which Virgil inherits from the Daphnis myth—, in which animals and men are mutually linked with bonds of friendship and trust, in which the herdsmen sing songs of delicate sentiment. This is a land in which nothing is measured by its practical value, and in which men are not judged by their deeds and achievements. What matters in this poetry is that its creatures appeal to the affections, that they release in us a tender emotion. It is the dawn of a new love.

And yet, the world of pure feeling cannot escape the intrusion of contemporary events. As we read on, Virgil's eclogues contain more and more references to actual happenings. At first glance it might seem odd that topical and political themes should play a much larger role in this remote Arcadian art than in the more realistic works of Theocritus. It has been suggested that we should compare Virgil to the archaic Greek poets, to Alcaeus and Solon; that would mean that in this respect, too, through his admission of politics into the fold of his poetry, Virgil acknowledged the classical Greek authors as his models. But the politics which we encounter in Arcadia is a peculiar brand. Virgil does not venture upon an active participation in the political quarrels of his day, he is not a statesman like Solon, nor a party man like Alcaeus, nor does he recommend a political programme. In his mind, political matters are closely connected with mythical concepts; and here the combining and blending of myth and reality, which is so characteristic of the Arcadian temper, achieves a singularly impressive result.

The first time that Virgil draws contemporary politics into the orbit of his poetry, in the first eclogue, certain very specific legal and social conditions form, as has recently been recognized,[5] the basis of his picture. But the actual plot of the poem—one herdsman wins his freedom, another is driven from his ancestral estate owing to the distribution of land to the veterans—is so deeply coloured with the dye of sentiment that the mere facts recede into the background. That a herdsman is compelled to part from his ancestral plot is seen as a curse of the restless age; that another is enabled to begin a pleasant life in his old age appears as the intervention of a saviour god who has arisen in the great city of Rome and who is putting an end to all the misery and confusion. Whenever Virgil discusses the events of his time, his judgment is controlled by a tender emotion which vibrates throughout Arcadia: the longing for peace and a home. And in the fourth eclogue, where this political yearning is even more prominent, it straightaway reaches out into the golden age and immerses itself in eschatological hopes.

These dreams of the poet place an interpretation upon history which answered to a good many expectations of the age. After the disastrous anarchy of the civil wars the desire for peace was paramount, especially among the better minds of the day. Thus Virgil's poetry reflects a genuine political reality, and it is not without significance that Virgil, at a time when Augustus was only just beginning to make his authority felt in the affairs of Rome, had already voiced that yearning for peace which Augustus was fated to satisfy. In this sense Virgil may be said to have determined to a considerable extent the political ideology of the Augustan age, and his *Eclogues* did indeed exercise an important political and historical function. Most impressive, perhaps, was their influence upon the early works of the second great poet of the Augustan age, upon the *Epodes* of Horace.[6] Still, we should not close our eyes to the fact that certain essential aspects of political action are not considered by Virgil. It is merely the fringes of political reality which he grasps in his hands. When, in the fourth eclogue, he announces his hope that the birth of a certain boy will mean the beginning of a new and blessed era, he is hoping for a miracle. This means that, as a matter of principle, he pays no attention to the fact that politics is grounded in reality, and that it must of necessity resort to force in order to realize its objectives. Political thought thus breaks in two, ideology and *Realpolitik*, with the attendant danger that each of these two will pursue its own journey without paying much attention to the other. Virgil made it possible for those who were themselves not active in politics to engage anew in political thought and poetry. But by its very nature this political poetry could only serve to pave the way for the politically active, to support their policies and to assist them with ideas. For independent plans there was but little scope, much less for opposition.

Once before, among the Greeks, an age of political unhappiness had produced a split between theory and practice. Though Plato began his career with genuine political interests and though his social position and personal inclinations had originally destined him for a political role, he had found no room for his activities in democratic Athens; the prevailing institutions, he felt, led only to gross injustices. With bitter resignation he realized that anyone concerned about justice was out of place in the existing state. So he had removed himself to his Academy, the 'Island of the Blest',[7] where it was possible to dedicate oneself to the rule of justice—even if it was only in thought. Plato was irritated by an element which is inherent in all politics; again and again his mind is agitated by the anti-intellectual obstacles which prevent the perfection of the state: injustice, violence, and lust for power. Deeply worried how he might render those obstacles innocuous, he persists in asking the basic question: What is justice, what is the good, what is the knowledge of these? Thus the Island of the Blest, the philosophy which receives him, permits a life of clear distinctions and sharp reasoning.

Virgil, on the other hand, turns away from this harsh and evil world, he leaves it far behind, and sets out for Arcadia, where he allows no hope, not even any desire to do something about the suffering world, to lighten his sorrow and his despair. If he is striving for a better world, he does so with his emotions, not with his thought or his will. A nostalgic refugee from sombre realities, he places his hopes, not upon a just state, but on an idyllic peace in which all beings will live together in friendship and fraternity, a golden age in which the lion and the lamb will lie down side by side in harmony, in which all opposites are joined and tightly knit in one great love. Only a miracle could bring this about. Later, when he was composing the *Georgics*, he saw this miracle in the achievement of Augustus. Augustus gave back to Italy the gifts of peace, quiet and order. Virgil stepped back into politics in so much as his dreams of Arcadia seemed to have found their fulfilment; Plato, in some ways, softened his criticism of existing institutions, but he never reconciled himself to making his complete peace with political realities. In return, Virgil was always careful not to get involved in the slippery problems of political action; in fact one may presume that they never even penetrated to his dreaming ear.

Even in his last great work, in which political action is more prominently featured, Virgil clings to the standard of his metaphysical hopes in appraising the events of reality. The sufferings and wanderings of Aeneas obtain their significance from the divine guidance which in the end resolves everything into peace and order, and ushers in a golden age. This miraculous direction from above is depicted with the machinery of the early Greek epic. But in the *Iliad* and *Odyssey*, whenever the gods determine an event, they act upon their personal sympathies and antipathies, and their bias is often so pronounced that even in antiquity many took exception to it. That is one of the reasons why Virgil could not afford to adopt the conventional type of divine intercession for his own use. In the *Aeneid* we find the realization of a world scheme to which all things, the gods included, are subservient. Homer too has a Fate, the *Moira*, but it is effective only in so far as the gods cannot prevent mortals from dying; all men must die, even the favourites and the scions of the gods. But Homer knows of no higher plan in accordance with which the gods direct the fortunes of Trojans and Greeks. The gods act precisely as any healthy man with a lively disposition would act; for even the supernatural in Homer is natural. Virgil, on the other hand, has divined a deeper meaning of history; Jupiter's guidance of Aeneas is a prologue to the future development of the Roman Empire, to the glory of the Augustan age.

The dream of the golden age is as old as man's thinking

about the course of the world, no matter whether it springs from a sense of bewilderment, in which case it is remembered as a paradise at the beginning of time, or whether it embodies the ideals of man's positive striving, projected into the end of history. But never before Virgil, either in Greek or Roman literature, had this Utopia been so closely interwoven with historical reality as in the *Aeneid*, or indeed earlier in the *Eclogues*.

In effect, Virgil's relation to the world is lyric; it impels him to seek out that which is dear to him, that to which his delicate senses may respond. But he does not find this in the realities surrounding him, where Sappho, for instance, had found it. He now looks for it in an area beyond the harsh facts of experience, either because the world has become too cruel and impious a place, or, which is the same thing in reverse, because his expectations in spiritual matters have increased. He looks for it in Arcadia; and even the heroic world of the *Aeneid*, with its fulfilment of the desire for order and meaning, bears the stamp of an Arcadian idyll.

The important point about Virgil's art, for the history of thought, is that he initiates an entirely new concept of poetry. Innumerable poets of the West have been the disciples of Virgil. They have viewed the task of literary creation in the light in which it was first approached by Virgil; and that this was of great importance for the nature of their poetry need not be emphasized.

In the tenth eclogue where, as we have already seen, the Virgilian Arcadia appears in its purest colours, the writer introduces his colleague Gallus. The poet alone of all mortals is permitted access to the Arcadian shepherds who are poets themselves. To be sure, not everything that is said by Gallus on this occasion may be used as evidence for Virgil's general conception of the poet and his mission, nor should we scan his lines for proof of what Virgil considered characteristic of the writing of poetry. Indeed, an ancient grammarian tells us that Virgil incorporated entire verses of his friend Gallus in the work. Still, there are a number of statements of which we can assert with some assurance that they are Virgil's own.

When Pan says to Gallus: 'Amor is not affected by the tears of the unhappy lover', the poet answers: 'But you

Arcadians will sing of my suffering. Oh how soft should be
the repose of my bones when your flute speaks of my love.' In
his mind he pictures to himself how happy he might be
here by the cool springs, on the silken turf, in the grove of
Arcadia, if he had his beloved Lycoris to keep him company.
But she has gone off to the war with another. I know of no
passage in the whole of Greek poetry where a man reflects
upon his own death with the same sentimental sensuality.
Ever since Sappho it had been customary among poets to
pray for death to terminate their unhappy love; the tradition
of the dying man consoling himself with the thought that his
name will survive in song is even older. And the notion that
it is the privilege of the dead to be mourned and lamented
by their friends runs far back into the beginning of time.
But that a man should indulge in a contemplation of the
pity which he expects for his distress, and that he should
find satisfaction in this reverie, is unprecedented. Sappho
had sensed an inner urge to be linked with those close to
her in feeling and thought; but this impulse was directed
outward, it clove to the memory of beautiful things, the joint
participation in a festival, for instance, or other similar
experiences. Gallus, quite differently, trains the mirror on
himself, he delights in the knowledge that others will think of
him with some emotion, he dreams of a prestige which he had
never enjoyed even in the happiest hours of his life. This
differs, too, from the attitude of the Greek tragic hero who
openly displays his affliction and appeals for sympathy,
from the feelings of a Prometheus who, nailed to his rock,
exclaims: 'Behold my sufferings'. The tragic character calls
upon witnesses to testify to the injuries he has received in
his struggle with the forces of the world. Instead of revelling
in the sensation of his own tender fragility, he presents himself as an example of the blatant wrongs which will always
occur.

It might be supposed that for this self-indulgence of
Gallus, Virgil used some Hellenistic model which has not
come down to us; and similar objections may well be raised
on other occasions where I have cast Virgil in the role of a
discoverer. True enough, we must always consider the
possibility that a certain motif may have been quite common
in that large body of late Hellenistic literature which is now

almost completely lost. But it is significant that the self-reflexion of Gallus, as so many other Virgilian features, is already foreshadowed in an earlier eclogue by Virgil. In the fifth poem Mopsus says, while singing of the death of Daphnis, that the shepherd had selected his own epitaph (43–44):

> Countrymen, Daphnis is my name :
> The very stars have heard my fame.
> Here in the woods I lived and lie—
> My flock was lovely : lovelier I.[8]

Virgil here follows Theocritus (1.120–21) who had written: 'I am that Daphnis who here pastured his cattle, that Daphnis who watered oxen and cows.' Theocritus' lines are purely factual. It was Virgil who added the references to the speaker's own glory and beauty, the sentimental concentration upon the self, for similar things are not found in Hellenistic poetry,[9] not even in Catullus although he at times indulges in a feeling close to self-pity. The Virgilian Gallus goes to the length of picturing to himself the sad lamentations which others will sing about him. This Arcadian consolation is also an escape from life, an escape into the realm of feeling and pathos. The sensibilities of the poet Gallus are so vulnerable that he is desperately afflicted by the contradiction between his own wistful hopes and the fate which befalls him. He expects his soulful longings to be met with an equal warmth and affection, and this hope is indeed realized in the dreamland of Arcadia, despite the lack of that idyllic bliss which is the shepherd's due.

Next Gallus apostrophizes his far-away love, in verses which are bodily taken from the elegies of the real Gallus. We have here a brilliant cento,[10] which Virgil constructed by lifting from the original distichs certain portions which would fit into his hexameters and still make sense. Thereafter Gallus continues with lines which indubitably are Virgil's own rather than echoes of Gallus' work. This is clear not only from their spirit, but from the fact that they again contain those reminiscences of Theocritus which are so characteristic of the *Eclogues*. Gallus, then, proceeds somewhat as follows: 'I base my verses, i.e. my elegies, on the writings of Theocles of Chalcis,[11] but I shall now compose them in the manner of the Theocritean pastoral. I shall suffer my misfortune in the woods, surrounded by the caves of savage beasts, and I shall cut the name of my beloved into the bark of the trees. In the Arcadian mountains I shall live, among the nymphs, and hunt wild boars.' For Gallus, Arcadian poetry is tantamount to an Arcadian life, a life enacted far away from the turmoil of men.

Centuries earlier, ancient Hesiod had taken his herds up into the desolate mountains and engaged in conversation with the Muses at Hippocrene, the spring of Helicon. But Hesiod was a true herdsman, the deserted mountain crags which he climbs are real, and he is fully convinced that the Muses have summoned him to be their poet. They have appeared to him in person, to assign him his task. He looks upon his shepherd's existence as a hard necessity, not as a romantic occasion to indulge in sentiments. Gallus' desire, in the words which we have cited, to hunt wild boars, is, of course, explained by the fact that the herdsman is also a hunter: Virgil occasionally refers to this in his earlier eclogues (2.29; 3.75; 7.29). But that is not all. For Gallus does not confine himself to the mere wish for a hunt; he tries, by painting a detailed picture of the scene of the chase, the icy mountains, the rocks and the forests, to stir the hearts of his listeners. The hunt, to him, is a remedy for his love. Our tastes would deem this a rather unusual cure. Theocritus' advice that poetry and singing are the only remedies for an unhappy love (11.1 and 17) strikes us as more natural, and no doubt more people have resorted to this latter medicine than to the chase of boars. Actually, Virgil is following in the footsteps of an ancient tradition. Euripides had shown in his *Hippolytus* how Phaedra fell in love with her stepson. He is a huntsman, and so he is not interested in love. Phaedra, in her feverish dreams, imagines herself setting out for the mountains to hunt (215 ff.); only thus, she feels, will she be able to join the object of her passion: a desire which she cannot, of course, confess openly before the chorus. Virgil's transfer of this motif to the Arcadian sorrows of Gallus seems to have been understood at once by the educated Romans. For Seneca, in turn, employs certain elements from this speech of Gallus for the purpose of describing the hunt of Hippolytus in his tragedy *Phaedra* (1-48).

Finally it can be shown that at the conclusion of Gallus'

speech, too, the feelings expressed are magnified and en-
nobled by the introduction of certain motifs from classical
Greek poetry. In these words of Virgil's friend we detect
the same affective quality which distinguishes the pastoral
poems of Virgil more and more from those of Theocritus.
Virgil stresses the element of feeling, he takes it very seriously,
and utilizes the forms and formulas of the classical Greek
poetry to give it voice. We would have known this even
without examining the speech of Gallus. But there is something else, of vital importance, which that speech may teach
us.

What sort of poet does Virgil place before us? What is his
conception of the art of poetry? Whence does the poet draw
his material? He follows his imagination; he gives himself
to his dreams. He savours his thoughts and his longings,
and records them as they come floating through his mind.
Among the Augustan poets, the younger contemporaries of
Virgil, it is quite common that a poet in the stillness of nature
surrenders himself to his feelings, and in our modern age the
creative dream and the artistic imagination are the very
essentials of the poetic personality. It is, therefore, with
some amazement that we should realize that this modern
poet, the poet of fancies and dreams, did not exist until he
saw the light of day in Virgil's Arcadia.

Hesiod, pasturing his flocks and composing his songs on
the lonely slopes of mount Parnassus, does not exert his
imagination, but obeys the inspiration of a deity. This is
not merely a figure of speech, a way of expressing one and the
same truth in two different ways, of seeing it in two perspec-
tives, one religious, the other psychological. No, the facts
themselves are distinct, although in a later epoch the concepts
came to be mixed and confused in various ways. The
message which the Muses impart to Hesiod and which he
conveys to his fellow-men addresses itself directly to the
realities of life; it provides practical suggestions for the work
of the farmer and for upright action, or it explains the divine
powers whose effects are felt in nature and among men. The
Muses command him to announce the future and the past
(*Theog.* 32), and he chooses to tell Perses 'the truth' (*Works*
10). In the fifth century, when this inspiration is no longer
accepted with the concrete simplicity of the older generation,

the task of the poet becomes spiritualized to the point of vagueness. But the poet is, as before, expected to speak of 'what is given'. Even Plato, who in his *Ion* refers to the enthusiasm of the poet as a divine gift, a *theia moira*, regards this inspiration as a means of rousing the audience and transmitting the passion of the poet, not as a creative process in which the objects of the poem are themselves given life.

Invention was not unknown among the makers of tragedy, particularly among the later ones. Euripides, for example, invented Medea's murder of her children. Accordingly, all literary criticism beginning with Aristotle debated to what extent a poet may be permitted to invent his own material; the upshot was that most critics allowed only a limited amount of invention, seeing that the poet was indentured to myth.[12] But invention is not the same as imagination or fantasy. The legendary Euripides, the solitary thinker meditating and composing his scenes in his cave on the seashore, is more like a philosopher than like an Arcadian Gallus indulging in his fancies. Euripides seeks to get to the bottom of certain matters, we might say 'problems', and on occasion he will invent a new situation in order to clarify such a problem. But this invention of new motifs for the sake of creating effective dramatic situations does not rest upon the support of dreams or fancies or feelings; his kind of poetry is essentially indebted to wakeful thinking and reflexion, to a mind both active and conscious of its aims. Nor are the novel creations of the Hellenistic writers to be ascribed either to the ancient inspiration or to Arcadian dreams; they too spring from invention, an invention based on good taste and wit. They are so thoroughly committed to reason as the maker and arbiter of their art that nothing could be less characteristic of their creative skill than the darkly ebbing sub-conscious. The poetic imagination does not exist among the Greeks, except in the realm of the burlesque, as in the comedies of Aristophanes, or in the satyr plays.

In his later poems, the *Georgics* and the *Aeneid*, Virgil did not pursue the path which he had trodden in the *Eclogues*. But some of his younger contemporaries chose to travel the new Arcadian road; especially Tibullus walks as in a dream, and lets images full of feeling and delicate sorrow pass before his vision.

About six hundred years before Virgil, the early Greek lyrists had awoken to the fact that man has a *soul*; they were the first to discover certain features in the feelings of men which distinguished those feelings sharply from the functions of the physical organs, and which placed them at opposite poles from the realm of empirical reality. For the first time it was noticed that these feelings do not represent the intercession of a deity or some other similar reaction, but that they are a very personal matter, something that each individual experiences in his own peculiar fashion, and that originates from no other source but his own person. Further they had found out that different men may be united with one another through their feelings, that a number of separate people may harbour the same emotions, memories, or opinions. And finally they discovered that a feeling may be divided against itself, distraught with an internal tension; and this led to the notion that the soul has intensity, and a dimension of its own, viz. depth. Now everything that we have so far remarked about Virgil's Arcadian world may be summed up by saying that Virgil developed these three basic modes which the early lyric had ascribed to the soul, and interpreted them afresh.

Under Virgil's hands, the spontaneity of the soul becomes the swirling tide of the dream, the creative flux of poetic fancy. The feeling which transcends the individual and forges a link between many men becomes Virgil's longing for peace and his love for his country through which even the beasts and the trees and the mountains are welcomed as fellow-creatures. And finally, the dissonance and depth of the emotions unfold into the conscious suffering of the sensitive man, his awareness that his tender and vulnerable soul lies at the mercy of a harsh and cruel world.

Later on Virgil himself appears to have sensed the futility of pursuing further such an indulgence in the feelings; but the three functions of the soul which he had brought into the open: poetic reverie, unifying love, and sensitive suffering, point far into the future. It was not merely because of his prophecy in the fourth eclogue that Virgil was, in the Middle Ages, regarded as a pioneer of Christianity. His Arcadia is set half-way between myth and reality; it is also a no-man's land between two ages, an earthly beyond, a land of the soul yearning for its distant home in the past. However, in his later years Virgil avoided the regions discovered by him. For in his later poems he acquired a temper of severe manly restraint which led him to draw closer to the classical Greek expressions of feeling and thought; but many a trace of his earlier sensibility remained.

Along with his new understanding of the soul, Arcadia also furnished the poet with a radically new consciousness of his artistic role. Virgil, for his own person, was too modest to boast loudly of his achievement, but in his portrait of Gallus in the tenth eclogue he gives us a general idea of his views on the special function of the poet. The reasons, he hints, why the poet takes his stand among the gods, and why he receives the sympathy of nature, is because his feelings are more profound than those of other men, and because therefore he suffers more grievously under the cruelties of the world. Virgil does not actually spell out these ideas which were to become so important in modern poetry, but even his hinting at them is new. At the beginning of the sixth eclogue Virgil for once formulates a programme of poetic art, but, as is his manner, he is careful not to make too much of himself or his poetry. Following the traces of Callimachus, he refuses to have anything to do with the great epic—later, of course, he was to reverse himself—and he confines himself to the delicate pastime of brief compositions. But in this connexion he accidentally drops a remark which is quite unlike anything that Callimachus ever said; he expresses the hope that his lines, insignificant as their theme is, may be read by someone 'captured by love'. This sympathetic affection is the mark of the poet, and the poet seeks to transmit his compassion to his reader.

Horace is more self-assured. The initial poem of his *Odes*, in which the dignity of the poetic mission is for the first time openly espoused, shows that this dignity has grown from the soil of Virgil's Arcadia:

> But ivy, prize of poets' brows,
> Unites me with the lofty gods;
> And me the grove with cooling boughs
> Withdraws from all the vulgar clods . . .
> If as a bard thou rank'st me high
> My happy head would scale the sky.[13]

The cool grove lies in Arcadia; and it is there, apart from the concourse of ordinary men, that the poet meets with the divine beings of Greek myth. The poet is nearer to the gods: Virgil had already said so in his fifth eclogue. When Mopsus had sung of the death of Daphnis, Menalcas—who at the end turns out to be Virgil himself in disguise—addresses him with the words: 'Divine poet'. In the tenth eclogue Virgil uses the same address in speaking to Gallus. It is the translation of a Homeric phrase. But when Homer calls a singer, or a herald, divine, he merely wants to say that the singer is under the special protection of the gods; the notion that the poet is raised above his fellows by his intellectual and spiritual capacities is quite un-Homeric. But Virgil, the context shows, actually wants us to believe that the poet, by virtue of his poetic art, becomes a super-human creature. In Greek it was possible to refer to Homer as a divine singer,[14] or a legendary shepherd may, in a poem by Theocritus, be addressed: 'Divine Comatas'. But it would have been unthinkable for one poet to apostrophize another in this way. Even in the circle of Catullus, with its ardent cult of friendship and poetry, this exalted note was never struck.

The question why Horace permits the poet, more than anyone else, to be so proud of his work, is not easy to answer, and perhaps it is somewhat indiscreet at that. In this parti-cular poem, placed at the beginning of his *Odes* to announce his general theme, he by and large imitates a scheme common in early Greek poetry; there are also some echoes from Hellenistic literature which are, however, not relevant to the present discussion. According to the ancient scheme, different men are shown striving after differing goals, but the poet has his own more precious ideal. The objectives which Horace envisages for the others: honour, power, wealth, pleasure, are all easy enough to appreciate. But why should he consider it infinitely more impressive to become a celebrated poet? In another equally conspicuous passage, at the begin-ning of his Roman odes, Horace has a second discussion of his poetic role:

> I scorn and shun the rabble's noise.
> Abstain from idle talk! A thing
> That ear hath not yet heard, I sing,
> The Muses' priest, to maids and boys.[15]

This stanza also shows a combination of various traditional

motifs. His reference to himself as a priest of the Muses
harks back to the early Greek conception that the poet is
inspired by the Muses; but no Greek seems to have spoken of
a priest of the Muses. Pindar at times calls himself a prophet
of the Muses, but this means only that he communicates
the divine message of the goddesses. Horace blends this
with notions of the mysteries which must be observed with
an esoteric silence. But does not the priestly cult of the Muses
conflict with his hatred of the people, seeing that the goddesses simply tell the poet what he is to proclaim at large?
And how is it possible for a servant of the Muses to be proud
of his own innovations, if he is but the agent of the Muses'
message?

The early Greek poets are rarely found to boast that they
have produced a song which had never been sung before;
and when they do, the boast does not mean the same thing
as later. Actually, they put themselves in opposition to
other people only when they confront the traditional values
with a new value of their own discovery, i.e. when they pass
judgment on a very specific issue. But this is done without
religious pathos, and without scorn for the common people.
Hesiod is the first in whom we find this pride in his own
knowledge; he feels that he is more discerning than the
'imbeciles and paunches' (*Theog.* 26). Later we encounter it,
more explicitly, in the prose of historians like Hecataeus,
and philosophers like Heraclitus. They demonstrate the
pride of the thinking man who does not accept the foolish
faiths of the mob, but formulates his own truer ideas on the
basis of individual research and meditation. But the more
this self-assurance is coloured by religious notions, as in
Parmenides or Empedocles, the less there is of contempt for
the people. Disparagement of the stupidity of others, as
we have it in Hecataeus, is closely linked with the rationalist
denial of religion.

Callimachus was the first to introduce the proud rejection
of vulgarity into poetry. We now know this chiefly from the
prologue to the *Aitia.* He does not want to travel on the
broad highway thronged by the others, but on his own
paths, however narrow.[16] Callimachus' pride, however, does
not rest upon the enunciation of new ideas or new truths; the
role of the prophet or priest is anything but congenial to his

nature. Rather he is proud of the delicate artistry of his work, of its exquisite form. Is there any common ground between this artistic hauteur and the stentorian voice of the priest? And what about yet another motif which also occurs in the beginning of the Roman ode, the pose of the teacher?[17] That the poet is a teacher of the people was first pronounced in the fifth century B.C., but no Greek ever achieved the magisterial solemnity with which Horace stepped before his youths and maidens, nor had there been a teacher with an equally patrician contempt for the rabble.

Our indiscreet question, why Horace is so proud of his being a poet, receives no answer in these central passages from his writings. Or perhaps we should say that there are too many answers which, if taken seriously, will cancel each other. He feels that he is inspired by the Muses, that he is a keeper of mystic secrets, a herald of new poems, an educator of youth. Apparently no one of these concepts is to be credited whole-heartedly. In Greek poetry they had been fully alive, they had meant all that was implied in them; in Horace their force is greatly impaired. They have become symbols, or metaphors of a sort. Just as we speak of a 'skin like snow', thinking only of the colour of the snow, not of its temperature or its other qualities, likewise the concepts of the Muse, priest, teacher, innovator are not intended in the full sense of each word. But then, we may ask, what is Horace's understanding of his status as a poet? It appears that he will not say, or perhaps he cannot say; the reasons for this would merit a detailed study. All manner of Greek reminiscences help him to present his mission as a grave and noble task. But gravity alone, however solemn, would be an empty gesture; it does not tell us anything about his concrete purpose. If such a purpose really exists, it must obviously be something new and difficult, perhaps even— and the inner contradictions may suggest this—something dubious and problematic. Horace does not speak of Arcadia, but he too envisages a realm to which the poet alone has access and which is closed to ordinary mortals; a place where dignity of intellect, delicacy of soul and bodily beauty thrive and flourish. The poet who seeks this place is a stranger among men. This land in which the Roman poet finds the objects of his striving is the realm of Greek culture and liter-

ature. It follows, of course, that the Greek motifs lose their
ancient contact with reality; the Muses cease to be real
divinities, the priest is no longer a practising priest, the
mystery cult is no longer a genuine worship, and the teacher
has no actual disciples before him. Each image acquires a
metaphorical meaning, and in this land of literary hopes
everything, as in Arcadia, must be taken with a grain of salt.
Myth and reality intrude upon each other; concrete existence
gives way before significance. The heritage of the Greeks is
turned into allegory, and literature is transformed into a
kingdom of symbols.

This uncovers a deep cleavage between the factual and the
significant. The concrete world of experience finds itself
face to face with a new world of art. True, even in Greek
literature allegory and symbols had not been unknown, but
they had been innocuous and unproblematic by comparison.
A Greek writer who speaks of Hephaestus may actually mean
a fire. The evolution of that formula might roughly be
sketched as follows. In an early period it was possible to say:
'Hephaestus destroyed a city', in the firm belief that the god's
fury was in the fire. Then came the enlightenment which
taught that there were no gods, and that Hephaestus
'signified' fire, for only fire was real. In the same fashion it
became possible to 'explain' all other gods. Finally there was
the theory of poetry which stipulated that the writer must
use a picturesque and dynamic style, and that it was more
beautiful and more poetic to use the name Hephaestus rather
than speak of fire. Rationalism on the one hand, poetic
theory and the desire for embellishment on the other, were
responsible for the metonymic use of the names of the gods.

These considerations prevailed also upon Virgil and
Horace, but in one essential the Romans differed from the
Greeks. A Greek poet, so long as he is a believer, recognizes
a reality in the name; for one who has ceased to believe, the
name become a stylistic device or merely poetic play. But
the Romans employ these names to create their Arcadia, the
land of the spirit and of poetry; without the names, the land
could not exist. It is true that the names had already lost
much of their original impact in Attic tragedy; since the myth
is not related, but acted out or played, the gulf between
reality and signification was apparent even then. The drama,

that which is happening on the stage, leads us beyond its own limits to a spiritual meaning; it expounds a problem which cannot be expressed directly. But despite this, the outlines of the mythical figures do not vanish behind a mist of unreality; on the contrary, they stand in the very centre of a grimly tangible plot.

Another reason why the characters of Attic tragedy could never be mere allegories is that they were always accepted as real creatures of flesh and blood. Although the ancient myths are no longer enacted as if they were history pure and simple, and although the straightforward limitation of mythical events was gradually forsaken in favour of an added emphasis upon the intellectual and spiritual sides of the action, the dramatic figures remain with their feet firmly planted on the ground. They are no longer regarded as *real*, but every effort is directed at making them appear *possible*. And as the belief in the reality of the myth dwindled, poetry tried hard to preserve at least a semblance of reality by resorting to the devices of realism and psychology. Allegory, on the other hand, does not insist on this kind of semblance; within its realm, the function of a figure is only to convey one specific meaning. In Virgil the nymphs and the Muses, Pan and Apollo are very close to the level of allegory, for they embody the idyllic life of Arcadia, the peace which fills its pastures and the romantic poetry to which its shepherds are dedicated.

Thus the ancient gods are, so to speak, reduced to the form of *sigla*: they are deprived of their primeval mysterious power, and all that is left to them is an ideality which no longer springs from religious awe but from literary erudition. They have taken on a Utopian quality, embodying the spiritual truths which are not to be found in this world. A similar change in the thinking concerning the gods is indicated in many examples of the classicistic painting and sculpture which flourished in Attica at the time of Virgil. We do not know enough about the Greek literature of this epoch to be able to tell to what extent Virgil was indebted to it in his allegorization of the gods. But what was at least as important was this, that for the Romans the gods and the myths of the Greeks had never been real. They adopted them as part of their cultural heritage from Greek literature and art, and they found in them the world of the spirit which the Greeks had discovered. Among the Romans, therefore, these figures are emphasized chiefly for whatever meaning they may hold for the life of man; they are allegories in the real sense of the word, for they signify something entirely different from what they had originally meant. They are like loan-words taken into another language, which are called upon to translate a strange legacy for the benefit of the heirs and their thoughts and feelings, if such a thing is possible in matters of the mind. The gods become allegories at the very moment when Greek literature gives birth to a literature of the world.

A similar development occurred also in the East. Allegorical interpretation helped Philo to incorporate Greek myth and Greek wisdom into Hellenistic Judaism, and Clement of Alexandria performed the same office for Christianity. Much was accepted, but the religious and philosophical core was rendered harmless by this re-formulation. The world of the Greek spirit was, perforce, a stranger in the cultures which absorbed it, and the allegorical interpretation was needed to permit the Greek heritage to be accepted by nations and ages whose beliefs were in many respects diametrically opposed to Greek thought.

The special importance of Virgil, which distinguishes his accomplishment from the Jewish and the Christian assimilation of Greek culture, and which places him squarely in the Roman tradition leading from Ennius to Catullus, is the fact that he uses the arts, viz. poetry, to channel the Greek heritage into the body of Roman thought. But further than that, his *Eclogues* represent the first serious attempt in literature to mould the Greek motifs into self-contained forms of beauty whose reality lies within themselves. Thus art became 'symbol'. Comparable tendencies do not exist in Greek literature. At most we might establish a certain similarity with the myths of Plato; but even this last comparison serves only to stress the special quality of Virgil's achievement. Plato's myths, too, had been concerned with 'significance' rather than with reality. But they are not self-contained poetry; on the contrary, their objective is to illustrate something else. They refer to a specific argument which Plato would like to express rationally, but for which his language does not suffice. That is why Plato deprecates his myths and calls them mere play. In Greek literature this species of myth-making had no successors.

Arcadia was a land of symbols, far distant from the quarrels and the acrimony of the present. In this land the antique pagan world was permitted to live on without injury to anybody's feelings. Arcadia was so remote that it was no more in danger of clashing with the See of Rome or with the Holy Roman Empire than it had run afoul of the *Imperium Romanum* of Augustus. Only when Europe began to be dissatisfied with the goods handed down to her, and when she took thought upon her own spiritual substance, did Arcadia run into trouble. But that was also the time when the genuine Greece was restored to her rightful place.

NOTES

INTRODUCTION

1. For the 'qualifying' use of metaphor, cf. J. Koenig, *Sein und Denken* (Halle 1937) esp. 222.
2. Cf. ch. 9 below.
3. We take it for granted that if they were cognizant of a thing they said so. This may not be convincing in all cases—cf. ch. 1 note 5 below—but for our present purposes it must suffice.

CHAPTER 1

HOMER'S VIEW OF MAN

1. The word remains in use in Arcadia: λεύσει· ὁρᾷ occurs as a gloss in the excerpt from Diogenianus (Κλειτορίων, line 26) cited by Latte, *Philologus* 80 (1924) 136 ff. Latte also, p. 145, refers to examples from Tegea (*IG* V.2.16.10, cf. XVI.25). We might also mention αὐγάζομαι and λάω = βλέπω, but these words are so rare that very little can be said about their exact meaning; cf. Bechtel, *Lexicologus* 27 and 74.
2. Lehrs, *Aristarch*[3] 86.160.
3. Lehrs, *op. cit.* 86 f. ; Plutarch, *poes. Hom.* ch. 124.
4. Aristarchus believed that γυῖα were the arms and legs: Lehrs, *op. cit.* 119.
5. Apparently even the ancients were aware of this interpretation. When Pindar was a schoolboy he seems to have learnt that χρώς was in many places identical with σῶμα. *Pyth.* 1.55 he says of Philoctetes: ἀσθενεῖ μὲν χρωτὶ βαίνων, 'he came with skin infirm;' although he is acquainted with the concept of the 'living body', and probably even with the word σῶμα in this sense, he avoids it—not only in this passage but throughout—because it lacks the ring of poetic diction. The later commentators of Homer, by their assertion that χρώς is always 'skin', never 'body' (Lehrs, *Quaest. ep.* (1837) 193) imply that others had explained it as 'body'. That Pindar had a concept of the 'body' is further proved by *Nem.* 7.73 where he uses γυῖον in the singular; this also is a poetic substitute for σῶμα.
6. This has been shown by Gerhard Krahmer, *Figur und Raum in der aegyptischen und griechisch-archaischen Kunst* (Halle 1931). Cf. also below ch. 4.
7. To be precise, Homer does not even have any words for the arms and the legs; he speaks of hands, lower arms, upper arms, feet, calves, and thighs. Nor is there a comprehensive term for the trunk.
8. These words have received an excellent and detailed treatment in a Goettingen dissertation by Jacob Boehme, *Die Seele und das Ich bei Homer* (1929). Boehme justly emphasizes that Homer has no term for the whole of a man's mental equipment, for the mind or soul in our sense. The course of ideas followed above was first sketched by me in a discussion of Boehme's book in *Gnomon* 7 (1931) 74 ff. Regarding νόος and νοεῖν, cf. K. von Fritz, *CP* 38 (1943) 79 ff., and 40 (1945) 223 ff.
9. Apollonius 138.17: ῥέθη τὰ μέλη τοῦ σώματος ; schol. *Il.* 22.68: ῥέθη δὲ τὰ ζῶντα μέλη, δι' ὧν ῥέζομέν τι.
10. The scholion cited in note 9 continues: Αἰολεῖς δὲ τὸ πρόσωπον (ῥέθος), καὶ ῥεθομαλίδας τοὺς εὐπροσώπους φασί.
11. Cf. Sappho fr. 33.3 Diehl (all lyric poets will be quoted from this edition, unless otherwise stated); ῥεθομαλίς must have had the same meaning as Theocritus' μηλοπάρειος: 'with a face like an apple'.
12. διὰ γὰρ μυκτήρων ἢ στόματος ἐκπνέομεν (schol. B *Il.* 22.68).
13. We must assume that Homer uses ῥέθη = mouth; there is some evidence for ῥέθος equalling πρόσωπον in Aeolic poetry, though we cannot prove it textually. But the word ῥεθομαλίς lends force to that view, and Sophocles, Euripides, and Theocritus also use ῥέθος for 'countenance'. For modern attempts to explain the word, cf. Schwyzer, *Glotta* 12 (1922) 23.
14. As if by a strange irony, Chrysippus made use of these very blunders to show that Homer was a Stoic in his psychology. He bases his contention on the phrase: πνεῦμά ἐστιν ἡ ψυχὴ κατὰ παντὸς οἰκοῦν τὸ σῶμα (schol. B *Il.* 16.856; cf. also schol. *Il.*

22.68 cited above: δείκνυσι δὲ ὅτι κατὰ παντὸς μέλους τὸ ζωτικὸν καὶ ψυχικόν ἐστιν; with this formulation, cf. Chrys. fr. 785.2.218 v. Arn.: ψυχή ... πνεῦμα λεπτομερές ἐστιν διὰ παντὸς διῆκον τοῦ ἐμψύχου σώματος). These references might be added to v. Arn. fr. 778. Even the etymology ῥέθη τὰ ζῶντα μέλη goes back to Chrysippus, or at least he used it, since it was of special importance to him that the ῥέθη denote the animate limbs. If the passage were not demonstrably late, it would have to be emended, writing μελέων for ῥεθέων.

15. Cf. Boehme, *op. cit.* (note 8) 103.
16. Cf. Boehme, *op. cit.* 103.
17. Cf. Boehme, *op. cit.* 53 and von Fritz, *op. cit.* (note 8) 83. νόῳ probably is not a locative, but an instrumental; cf. Boehme 54.2.
18. Cf. Boehme, *op. cit.* 72.
19. Plato too understands the νοῦς as ὄμμα τῆς ψυχῆς: *Symp.* 219 A, *Rep.* 7.533 D, *Theaet.* 164 A, *Soph.* 254 A. Cf. Buttmann, *Philologus* 97 (1947) 18 f.
20. We may suspect, however, that Plato with his theory of the parts of the soul deliberately echoes Homeric ideas. His use of the concept of the θυμός is purely 'pedagogic'; generally speaking it was in the Calls to Moderation (cf. below ch. 8) that the difference between νοῦς and θυμός was kept alive.
21. Cf. the oldest testimony regarding Pythagoras' doctrine of metempsychosis: Xenophanes fr. 7 Diels, a passage which is perhaps also the oldest certain example of the post-Homeric use of ψυχή. There are other reasons beside this why we should not doubt that Pythagoras used the word in this sense; cf. also Semon. 29.13, Hippon. 42, Sappho 66.8, Alc. 110.34.—For σῶμα in its new significance, cf. also Xenophanes 15.4.
22. Hereafter the fragments of the pre-Socratics are numbered after Diels[6].
23. Cf. now F. Zucker, *Philologus* 93 (1938) 52 ff.
24. Cf. H. Fraenkel, *Homerische Gleichnisse* 55.2. Cf. also expressions like: πυκνὸν ἄχος, ἀδινὰ στενάχειν, μέγα χαίρειν etc.
25. About this, and the beginnings of the later concept in expressions like ὁμόφρονα θυμὸν ἔχοντες cf. *Gnomon* 7 (1931) 84.
26. Cf. above all the expressions upon which Heraclitus appears to have modelled his language: *Il.* 17.139 Μενέλαος μέγα πένθος ἄέξων; 18.110 χόλος ἀέξεται; *Od.* 2.315 καὶ δή μοι ἀέξεται θυμός (passive!); note that the reference is to emotions.
27. Pfister, *RE* s.v. 'Kultus' 2117.33.

CHAPTER 2

THE OLYMPIAN GODS

1. *Pers.* 498. Cf. however Euripides *Med.* 493. Regarding θεοὺς νομίζειν cf. K. Latte, *Gnomon* 7 (1931) 120; J. Tate, *CR* 50 (1936) 3, and *CR* 51 (1937) 3.
2. Cf. W. Rehm, *Griechentum und Goethezeit* (1936).
3. In recent times W. F. Otto has made a notable attempt to describe the religious character of the Olympian pantheon: *Die Goetter Griechenlands* (Bonn 1929; 2nd edition Frankfurt 1934). Cf. also K. von Fritz, *Rev. of Rel.* 9 (1945) 5 ff.
4. The Greeks derive their belief in the existence of God from the order of the universe, while the Christians obtain their revelation of God from the paradox. Cf. Pseud.-Athan. *Quaestiones ad Antiochum* ch. 136 (*Migne* 28.682).
5. Wilamowitz repeatedly said (e.g. *Platon* 1 601) that the natural sciences could not have originated in a milieu in which it was held that the world was created.
6. Concerning 'miracles' in Homer, cf. H. Fraenkel, *Die homerischen Gleichnisse* 30.
7. It is true that for Lucan even the world has lost its meaning; cf. W. H. Friedrich, *Hermes* 73 (1938) 391 ff.
8. Cf. Deichgraeber, *Antike* 15 (1939) 118 f. Regarding the ' naturalness' of the Homeric gods, cf. J. Stenzel, *Platon der Erzieher* 14 ff.
9. The Homeric impulses continue to operate in Hellenistic times; cf. Rodenwaldt, *Abhandl. d. Preuss. Akad.* 1943 n. 13.
10. *The Philosophy of History* (tr. Sibree, revised edition, New York 1944) 50.
11. Plutarch *de recta rat.* 13 says that Pythagoras coined the motto μηδὲν θαυμάζειν as the quintessence of his philosophy; Cicero *Tusc. Disp.* 3.14.30 praises 'nil admirari' as 'praestans et divina sapientia'; Horace *Epp.* 1.6.1 has brought it into general currency. For further passages, cf. Heinze.

CHAPTER 3

THE RISE OF THE INDIVIDUAL IN THE EARLY GREEK LYRIC

1. The lyric fragments are numbered as in the second edition of Diehl's *Anthologia Lyrica*. For the lyrists, cf. R. Pfeiffer, *Philologus* 84 (1929) 137; W. Jaeger, *Paideia* I; H. Gundert, *Das Neue Bild der Antike* I 130. The line of Archilochus cited in the text also echoes *Od.* 4.548 f.

2. The relation between Archilochus and the Homeric passage is disputed; I think that the priority of the Homeric verse is virtually certain. Cf. R. Pfeiffer, *Deutsche Lit. Zeitung* 1928, 2370; P. Von der Muehll, *RE* Suppl. 7, 746.5; H. Fraenkel, *AJP* 60 (1939) 477.

3. Tr. Dorothy Burr-Thompson.

4. An inscription in the Letoon of Delos (E. Bethe, *Hermes* 72 (1937) 201) dates from about the time of Sappho :

κάλλιστον τὸ δικαιότατον, λῷστον δ' ὑγιαίνειν,
πάντων ἥδιστον οὗ τις ἐρᾷ τὸ τυχεῖν.

Beside numerous passages in the lyrics (Pindar, e.g.) the tales about the Seven Sages may also be cited to support our view that the 'highest good' was at this time the subject of a lively debate. The Sages answer such queries as: 'Who is the happiest man?' 'Who is the wisest?' They are not yet concerned with the dilemma of choice; cf. below ch. 8.

5. The significance of Archilochus 22 seems to have been the same; cf. the imitation of *Anacreontea* 7 and Greg. Naz., *ad anim. suam* 84 ff; also Horace, *Epodes* 2 with Heinze's introduction. Another possibility is considered by H. Fraenkel, *Nachr. d. Goett. Ges.* 1924, 81. Similar motifs: Timocr. 1; Pindar, *Paean* 4.15; Horace, *Odes* 1.1 and 1.7.

6. Achilles says to Agamemnon (*Il.* 1.225): you who have the eyes of a dog but the heart of a stag, i.e. an impudent face but a cowardly heart. This, however, is not yet 'tension' (H. Fraenkel, *AJP* 60 (1939) 478) but the juxtaposition of several organs (cf. above ch. 1). It is true, all the same, that the distinction between inward and outward qualities, between Being and Appearance, is about to be formulated.

7. In Homer, κλέπτειν νόον or similar phrases occur only in this description of Aphrodite's magic belt. Usually it is translated 'to deceive', 'to outwit' (cf. schol. D ἠπάτησε etc.), an interpretation which occurs as early as Hesiod,*Theog.* 613 and remains prominent thereafter, particularly in poetry. Archilochus takes its meaning as 'to steal'. The former explanation finds support in φρένας ἠπεροπεύειν (cf. J. Boehme, *Die Seele und das Ich* 48.3); for the latter, which I consider correct, it is possible to refer to such parallels as φρένας ἐξέλετο or ἦτορ ἀπηύρα.

8. I do not quite understand the objection of H. Gundert, *Das Neue Bild der Antike* 1, 136 who remarks: 'Here we see not so much the sufferings of unfulfilled love . . . but the passion itself which with its devastating onslaught makes him suffer.' Earlier Gundert had justly said of Homer: 'There the tension of the"noble spirit" is released in motion and gesture, in immediate action, not in words.' In any event Gundert does not adduce any examples to show that the early lyric writers spoke of the 'suffering' of passion in cases of happy love as well.

9. The last three lines of the poem are lost; probably they contained in one form or another the idea of 'compensation', either: 'since you have won the good fortune of marriage', or: 'since joy and suffering come in turns'.

10. *Od.* 20.57 and 23.343 the word is explained as 'the looser of anxieties' (μελεδή-ματα). Cf. E. Risch, *Eumusia* (Festschr. f. E. Howald) 87 f.

11. This is of course dependent on *Il.* 14.217, the verse mentioned earlier.

12. Cf. *Philologus* 96 (1944) 284.

13. W. Jaeger, *Paideia* 1 (Engl. tr.) 121. H. Gundert, *Das Neue Bild der Antike* 1, 137.2 makes the excellent observation that Archilochus says ὃς μηδίκησε, while Achilles had said *Il.* 1.356: ἠτίμησε. Archilochus' concern is not with class honour, but with justice.

14. W. Jaeger, *Paideia* 1, 121. Cf. *Il.* 2.241.

15. Tr. C. M. Bowra.

16. Cf. also Ibycus fr. 7 and 6.6.

17. Cf. above ch. 1.
18. But cf. our remarks below concerning Sappho and the νοῦς.
19. Fr. 60 καρδίης πλέως: Homer knows the heart as the physical organ which is the seat of courage. *Il.* 10.244 οὐ πέρι μὲν πρόφρων κραδίη καὶ θυμὸς ἀγήνωρ ἐν πάντεσσι πόνοισι, *Il.* 12.247 οὐ γάρ τοι κραδίη μενεδήιος οὐδὲ μαχήμων, *Il.* 16.266 Μυρμιδόνες κραδίην καὶ θυμὸν ἔχοντες, *Il.* 21.547 ἐν μέν οἱ κραδίη θάρσος βάλε. He also has the concept of a man or his φρένες being filled with θάρσος, μένος or ἀλκή. *Il.* 13.60 ἀμφοτέρω πλῆσεν μένεος, *Il.* 17.573 τοίου μιν θάρσευς πλῆσεν φρένας, *Il.* 1.104 μένεος δὲ μέγα φρένες ἀμφὶ μέλαιναι πίμπλαντο, *Il.* 17.499 ἀλκῆς καὶ σθένεος πλῆτο φρένας ἀμφὶ μελαίνας, *Il.* 17.211 πλῆσθεν δ' ἄρα οἱ μέλε' ἐντὸς ἀλκῆς καὶ σθένεος. Archilochus, in substituting the heart for these 'forces', employs the word καρδίη in a more 'abstract' sense than Homeric usage would allow.
20. Cf. H. Fraenkel, *Nachr. d. Goett. Ges.* 1924, 64. Cf. below ch. 5.
21. W. Schadewaldt, *Hermes* 71 (1936) 368.
22. Words like συμπάσχειν, συνασχαλᾶν, συνειδέναι make their first appearance in this period.

CHAPTER 4

PINDAR'S HYMN TO ZEUS

1. Cf. Goethe's remark concerning Pindar below ch. 12 note 7.
2. Cf. also Theognis 15–18.
3. Unfortunately the text is uncertain; cf. Wilamowitz, *Pindaros* 190 f.
4. Cf. Nilsson, *Geschichte der griech. Rel.* I (1941) 411.3.
5. Cf. Plato's *Symposium* 195 C where the rule of Necessity is part of the age *preceding* Zeus.
6. Other sources name Prometheus or Hermes as the god who splits the head of Zeus; cf. Preller-Robert I 189.3.
7. In Empedocles, Harmony is the antithesis of *Neikos*, Contention. In Aeschylus *Prom.* 551 she represents communal organization.
8. Aristides 2.142; cf. Choric. Gaz. 13.1 = fr. 31.
9. The scholia interpret Eur. *Med.* 834 to the effect that Harmonia was made the mother of the Muses, but at the same time they indicate that this version was found nowhere else.
10. Herbert Meyer, *Hymnische Stilelemente* (1933).
11. It should be noted that in contrast to his usual practice Hephaestion does not quote fr. 29 as his model but fr. 30.1.
12. For this contrast, cf. the instances cited above ch. 3.
13. Aristides in his Oration on Zeus fr. 145 quotes from the Pindaric Hymn, and refers to the poem also on other occasions. In his oration he says 13: κοσμήσας μὲν ἄστροις τὸν πάντα οὐρανὸν ὥσπερ ταῖς νήσοις τὴν θάλατταν. He probably had in mind the invocation of Delos in the Hymn to Zeus. Similarly or. 44. 14 (p. 350 K.): ὥσπερ δὲ οὐρανος τοῖς ἄστροις κεκόσμηται οὕτω καὶ τὸ Αἰγαιον πέλαγος ταῖς νήσοις κεκόσμηται.
14. Tr. R. Lattimore.
15. Cf. Hermann Fraenkel, *Die Antike* 3 (1927) 63.

CHAPTER 5

MYTH AND REALITY IN GREEK TRAGEDY

1. Cf. above ch. 3.
2. Su(i)das s.v. οὐδὲν πρὸς τὸν Διόνυσον (3.579 Adl.).
3. Cf. Gorgias fr. 23 Diels.
4. Cf. the beginning of this chapter.
5. Cf. below ch. 9.
6. 'Die Entstehung des griechischen Portraets', *Abh. d. saechs. Akad. d. Wiss. zu Leipzig, Phil. hist. Kl.* 91 (1939) 4. Heft.
7. Cf. Chr. Voigt, *Ueberlegung und Entscheidung, Studien zur Selbstauffassung des Menschen bei Homer,* Diss. Hamburg (Berlin 1933).

8. Schadewaldt, in *Hermes* 71 (1936) 25 f.

9. Antilochus-Athena says to Achilles in Goethe's *Achilleis*: 'Alle Voelker verehren Deine treffende Wahl des kurzen ruehmlichen Lebens.'

10. Goethe, *Maximen und Reflexionen* (1050 Hecker): 'Des tragischen Dichters Aufgabe und Tun ist nichts anderes, als ein psychisch-sittliches Phaenomen, in einem fasslichen Experiment dargestellt, in der Vergangenheit nachzuweisen.'

CHAPTER 6

ARISTOPHANES AND AESTHETIC CRITICISM

1. Lines 1491–5, tr. B. B. Rogers, as will be the following quotations from the *Frogs*.

2. Cf. Max Pohlenz, *Nachr. d. Goett. Ges.* (1926) 142 ff.

3. Cf. *Philologus* 96 (1944) 178 ff. Also Plato *Apol.* 41 A; *Prot.* 316 D; *Ion* 536 B.

4. He connects with this the fact that beginning with Homer the poets always regarded it as understood that 'sweet' poetry delights the listeners; for the writers, however, this pleasure was not necessarily the 'purpose' of poetry. Wilamowitz, *Platon* 1.482 (cf. also 477 f.) maintains that Aeschylus and Pindar wrote their poetry 'with the intention' of educating; but neither poet offers any internal evidence for such a statement.

5. One might suppose a connexion between Aristotle's *Poetics* and Aristophanes' *Frogs* because of the latter's statement (1063) that Euripides dressed his characters in rags for the purpose of exciting pity. This might be related to Aristotle's pity and fear, the emotions which tragedy seeks to arouse. But such a tie-up would be extremely tenuous, for the tragedies themselves make numerous references to pity and fear.

6. In fact they are expressly taken over from that passage; it could be proved that they are designed to meet an objection which none other than Socrates had raised. This is the oldest reliable testimony for the effect which the Socratic discussions had upon ethical speculation: cf. *Philologus* 97 (1947) 125 ff.

CHAPTER 7

HUMAN KNOWLEDGE AND DIVINE KNOWLEDGE AMONG THE EARLY GREEKS

1. Cf. K. Deichgraeber, *RhM* 87 (1938) 19 ff.

2. For comparable data from the Mediterranean region, cf. F. M. Cornford, *JHS* 62 (1942) 6. Cornford's article throws much light on the questions discussed in this chapter.

3. H. Fraenkel, *Hermes* 60 (1925) 185 note 4 and 186 note 1.

4. K. Latte, *Antike und Abendland* 2 (1946) 159.

5. Cf. Latte, *op. cit.* 154.

6. These notions may be found also in later authors. Ibycus 3.23 goes so far as to quote the invocation of the Muses from the *Catalogue of Ships* when he wants to praise the fleet of Polycrates: cf. *Philologus* 96 (1944) 290. Cf. also Pindar, *Paean* 7 b 13: 'For the minds of men are blind if without the Heliconian maidens . . .'

7. Homer invokes the Muses when it is his intention to present a detail which heralds a new development (*Il.* 11.218; 14.508; 16.112), and not, as has been thought, 'when the poet prepares himself to sing of great things'.

8. The address to the herdsmen probably signifies that to begin with the Muses count Hesiod among the rest of the stupid shepherds, only to lift him out of their ranks by awarding him the sprig of laurel.

9. This is taken from the words of *Il.* 1.70 concerning the seer Calchas 'who knew both things that were and that would be and that had been before'. Hesiod line 38 refers this in a very literal sense to the Muses: another indication of the spirit in which Hesiod here speaks of himself.

10. K. Latte, *op. cit.* (note 4) 152 ff. interprets Hesiod's description to the minutest detail, showing how in his mind the Muses are merged with the Nymphs, and how this experience leads him to turn his back on the aristocratic rhapsody of Asia Minor.

11. Concerning this basic feature of the *Theogony*, cf. H. Diller, *Antike und Abendland* 2 (1946) 140 ff.; also Latte 161 f.

12. Cf. Diller, *op. cit.* 141 f.

13. Cf. H. Fraenkel, *op. cit.* (note 3).

14. The continuation of this dictum exhibits a striking turnabout: 'among gods and men the greatest.' This shows how little his discovery means to him in terms of logic. Would he have permitted himself the same slip after reading Parmenides?

15. Concerning the significance of νοεῖν in this fragment, see K. von Fritz, *CP* 40 (1945) 228 f.

16. The curious compound νόου φρενί finds its probable explanation in the fact that νόῳ alone would mean 'intentionally'. Xenophanes needs something in the nature of an organ, and so he uses an organ which is less concretely pictured than others.

17. As K. Reinhardt, *Parmenides* 112 ff. assumes.

18 ἔπος τελεῖν, *Il.* 1.108 etc.

19 *Il.* 19.90. For other passages, cf. H. Gundert, *Pindar und sein Dichterberuf* 113 f. note 63.

20. W. Jaeger, *Paideia* II (English Edition) 33: 'Modern philosophical empiricism is the child, not of Greek philosophy, but of Greek medicine;' cf. also Cornford's essay cited in note 2. For the method of Alcmaeon and the doctors, cf. O. Regenbogen, *Quell. Stud. Gesch. Math.* 1 (1930) 131 ff., and H. Diller, *Hermes* 67 (1932) 14.

21. *Ol.* 6.22 ff., as was pointed out by H. Fraenkel, *Nachr. d. Goett. Ges.* 1930, 154 ff.

22. The text is disputed in many points; line 3 I follow Sextus in reading δαίμονος. δαίμονες would be awkwardly out of place, and to connect the following ἥ with ὁδὸν which is separated from it by four words would seem unduly harsh. Cf. also W. J. Verdenius, *Parmenides* 66 who mentions that Bowra, too, *CQ* 32 (1937) 109 supports δαίμονες. The goddess must have been named previously (in spite of Sextus ἐναρχόμενος . . . γράφει τὸν τρόπον τοῦτον there must have been some introductory words); one might think of *Aletheia* (cf. line 29 and 2 line 4), or perhaps rather of *Peitho* (2 line 4). Meineke's suggestion to read κατὰ πάντ' ἀσινῆ in line 3 (cf. W. Jaeger, *Paideia* vol. 1 p. 177 note 1) does not seem convincing to me. The imperfect forms line 2: πέμπον, line 4: φερόμην and φέρον, line 5: ἡγεμόνευον side by side with the present use in line 1: φέρουσιν and line 3: φέρει convey the impression: they (and I) have done it and are doing it once more.

23. Cf. the detailed analysis by H. Fraenkel, *Nachr. d. Goett. Ges.* 1930 pp. 154 ff.

24. Cf. H. Fraenkel 164 f., Verdenius 12 f.

25. Read ἑκάστοτε . . . παρέστηκεν as Theophrastus has it: Verdenius 6, now also H. Fraenkel, *CP* 41 (1946) 168 f. ἑκάστοτε appears certain because of the fact that several MSS of Aristotle contain it; παρέστηκεν because of the reading of the passage in the *Odyssey* (18.136 f.) which Parmenides used as a model: Verdenius 6, also Fraenkel 172 note 1. Aristotle's παρίσταται appears to be an intrusion from the passage of Empedocles which he had just cited (fr. 108: the reading here is παρίστατο, in contrast with the earlier quotation in the *Metaphysics*; cf. Diels *ad loc.*) and which echoes Parmenides: Verdenius 20 and 27 f. To compare παρίστᾶται with the forms ἔρασαι and ἔραται, Theocr. 1.78 and 2.149 is not permissible, since the latter are obviously based on a misunderstanding of the subjunctive ἔρᾶται Sappho 27a line 4.

26. As a result a man cannot ὀξὺ νοεῖν, as the *Iliad* (3.374) puts it. Cf. also fr. 11.

27. Cf. Xenophanes fr. 24 on the deity, cited above in the text: οὖλος ὁρᾷ, οὖλος δὲ νοεῖ, οὖλος δέ τ' ἀκούει.

28. Socrates' demand, that men should attend first to human affairs and only in the second instance to divine matters, is also involved in the story of Socrates and the Indian cited by Aristoxenus (fr. 53 Wehrli). For the opposite view, cf. Xenophon *Mem.* 1.4, the chapter which W. Theiler, *Zur Geschichte der theologischen Naturerklaerung*, has connected with Diogenes of Apollonia. Cf. also Antisthenes *apud* Themist. περὶ ἀρετῆς, *RhM* 27 (1872) 450, and K. Joel, *Der echte und der xenophontische Sokrates* vol. 2, pp. 212, 479, 864.

29. Examples are cited by E. R. Dodds, *JHS* 65 (1947) 25.

30. Cf. Plato, *Apology* 22 B f. and above all Plato's *Ion*.

CHAPTER 8

THE CALL TO VIRTUE: A BRIEF CHAPTER FROM GREEK ETHICS

1. Schol. A on line 195 says that Athena is φρόνησις.   Cf. Plut. *Coriol.* 32 and schol. A on *Il.* 20.67.

2. For further details, cf. Ch. 5 above.

3. Cf., e.g., the exasperation of Theognis 743.

4. It appears that the word is first found in a newly discovered poem by Alcaeus, 24 B 12: σα]οφρόνην: cf. Diehl, *RhM* 92.13.

5. Cf. F. Zucker, 'Συνείδησις', *Jenaer Akad. Reden* 6 (Jena 1928); also *Gnomon* (1930) 21–30. Regarding Homer *Od.* 14.85 ff., cf. K. Latte, *Antike und Abendland* 2 (1946) 69.

6. This is proved by the phrase κλέος ἄφθιτον, 'imperishable fame', which agrees with early Indo-European poetic diction; cf. A. Kuhn, *Kuhns Zeitschr.* 2 (1853) 467 and J. Wackernagel, *Philologus* 95 (1943) 16.

7. A gap in the text requires some such addition.

8. Instead of summoning the youth he issues a command to the citizens.

9. *'Dulce et decorum est'* evidently means: death in battle is equally desirable for an Epicurean who regards the 'pleasant' as his aim in life, and for the Stoic who regards honour and virtue as his goals. The mention of the Epicurean term 'sweet' (cf. Seneca *ep.* 66.18 and 67.15) is in strong contrast with what follows: 'Death pursues also him who flees', for here death does not appear so very sweet after all.

10. For Callimachus, cf. below ch. 12.

11. H. Fraenkel, *Gnomon* 6 (1930) 13; cf. also Pindar *Ol.* 1.104.

12. Cf. above ch. 6.

13. Cf. K. Latte, *ArchRW* 16 (1920) 268 f.; also C. M. Bowra, *Greek Lyric Poetry* 346.

14. Cf. E. Panofsky, *Herkules am Scheidewege* 45.

15. The same is true of the Greek verbs of 'action': cf. *Philologus* Suppl. 20 Heft 1.17 f.

16. It should also be noted, though there is no need to elaborate on it here, that the Greeks, in speaking of what we would call the 'will', referred it variously to the emotions (θυμός) and to the intellect (νοῦς, γνώμη).

17. Concerning the beginnings of the notion of a 'good will' in Democritus, cf. below ch. 10.

18. Cf. *Philolog. Unters.*, ed. Wilamowitz vol. 29.81.

CHAPTER 9

FROM MYTH TO LOGIC: THE ROLE OF THE COMPARISON

1. cf. below, p. 194.

2. It is understood, of course, that the statement refers to Socrates himself, not to his portrait.

3. Cf. Hans Lipps, *Die Verbindlichkeit der Sprache* (1944) 66 ff. (The following few paragraphs have had to be changed somewhat in translation. In the place of the examples borrowed from Lipps, viz. *Feder* and *sprengen*, I have used the English terms 'horn' and 'set', and built the argument around them, although particularly the verb does not support the argument as strikingly as the German original.—Tr.).

4. Especially a resemblance perceived by the senses, and more particularly by the eye; these metaphors are, therefore, usually of a 'visual' character.

5. The terms for such 'shapeless' objects depend upon certain qualities, particularly upon size; the fluidity of the terms thus shows up the fluidity of the adjectives. The same is true of terms such as : piece, lump, clod, whereby we describe quantities of shapeless matter : a piece of wood, a lump of gold, a clod of earth.

6. For similar exaggeration, cf. also Theocritus 11.2 f., Vergil *Ecl.* 7.37, etc.

7. Cf. above, note 5.

8. For a further discussion of sense perceptions, cf. below, ch. 10.

9. In Greek, moods are construed as 'motions' of the mind rather than as properties. Consequently—and this cannot be more than a mere hint—the verb metaphors play a more prominent role in the illustration of moods than the adjectival metaphors.

10. For the light symbolism of the Greeks, cf. the article φῶς by R. Bultmann, *Kittels Theologisches Woerterbuch zum Neuen Testament,* and *Philologus* 97 (1947) 1 ff.

11. Fr. 4 was originally part of a similar comparison, as is evident from the present tense; contrast fr. 88 and 94.

12. Tr. R. Lattimore.

13. For the influence of this perspective upon the ethnology of Herodotus and Hippocrates, cf. H. Diller, *Wanderarzt und Aitiologe* 82 f. and note 129.

14. Cf. the interpretation of Plutarch, *de tranqu. an.* 13.472 who, in terms almost reminiscent of Goethe, launches an impressive attack against the Stoics.

15. Metaphors such as 'wooden', 'brassy', refer not only to properties, but also to an effect and a mode of reacting. In the present context we need not enter into this at greater detail; but cf. below, section 2.

16. Concerning the onesidedness of this term, cf. below, section 2.

17. *Philol. Unters.* ed. U. v. Wilamowitz, vol. 29.

18. O. Becker, 'Das Bild des Weges und verwandte Vorstellungen im fruehgriechischen Denken', *Hermes* Einzelschr. 4 (1937).

19. The basic book for the Homeric simile is Hermann Fraenkel, *Die homerischen Gleichnisse* (Goettingen 1921). In addition the problem has been further elucidated by Kurt Riezler, 'Das homerische Gleichnis und der Anfang der griechischen Philosophie', *Antike* 12 (1936) 253–71, and by Friedrich Mueller, 'Das homerische Gleichnis', *Neue Jahrb. f. Antike u. deutsche Bildung* (1941) 175–83. For the later development, cf. H. Fraenkel, *AJP* 60 (1939) 478.

20. Cf. H. Fraenkel (above, note 19) 72 f. on the subject of the simile of the Pygmees, and the relevant remarks of K. Riezler (above, note 19).

21. Cf. H. Lipps (above, note 3) 73 f.

22. Cf. *Philol. Unters.* vol. 29, p. 49.

23. Cf. the very cautious judgment of M. P. Nilsson, *Geschichte der griech. Religion* vol. 1 (Munich 1941) 200.

24. Cf. the happy remarks by E. Buschor, *Die Musen des Jenseits* p. 26. For the interpretation of Homer it is of no importance that the Homeric animal comparisons may ultimately be based on magic notions, according to which this or that man really *is* a lion. But it is historically significant that in this context too the verb 'to be' was originally employed with the same rigidity as we have noted above : it referred not only to the being of an object, but also to the capacity of the object (i.e., in this context, of a man or an animal) to serve as the conductor of a force such as *menos.* In fact, it is typical of the magic mentality that its notion of identity is not restricted to the objective existence of a thing, but extends itself to embrace other objects as well, provided they are filled with the same forces, with the same life.

25. The same is true of the natural elements; cf. below.—Fr. Mueller (above, note 19) 181 is right when he says against H. Fraenkel, the living world of the similes should not be taken for a reflexion of the ancient Minoan-Mycenean mentality. But his own assertion, viz. that the narrative exhibits the fixed forms of an older style, while the similes reveal a new mentality, is probably not the last word in this controversy. The Homeric description of animals finds its closest parallel in the so-called orientalizing style. I do not know whether the extant documents allow us to come to a decision, but could it not be that Homer's animal types are also based on a fixed tradition, namely that of the Orient? Cf. F. Dornseiff, *apud* Kroehling, *Greifswalder Beitraege* Heft 5, p. 82 note 8.

26. Riezler (above, note 19) shows in detail how the elaboration of a simile may disclose additional features.

27. Cf. Rob. Oehler, *Mythologische Exempla in der aelteren griechischen Dichtung* (Diss. Basle 1915) and the review of H. Fraenkel, *Gnomon* 3.569.

28. Short similes occur also in the speeches. *Il.* 3.196, e.g., Priam compares Odysseus, whom he does not yet know, with a ram among the sheep.

29. The type of myth which is found in the similes refers to a repetitive event, the earthquake of Typhoeus and the Battle of the Cranes : Fraenkel (above, note 19) p. 73.

30. At least on one occasion a third person is compared with a mythological figure in a speech: *Od.* 2.120 Antinous, in speaking to Telemachus, praises Penelope by comparing her to Tyro, Alcmena and Mycene.

31. Cf. W. Schadewaldt, *Iliasstudien* 142: he says that the paradigm of Meleager, aside from serving as a moral exhortation, also fulfils the purpose of illuminating the fate and revealing the nature of the man.

32. Riezler (above, note 19) pays special attention to these similes.

33. This same truth, that a man comes closer to his own nature by comparing himself to others, is taught in many a tale from the *Arabian Nights*. The motif finds what is perhaps its most artistic expression where King Wird-Chan is alternately swayed by the stories related by his wife and the vizier who hope to give him a better insight into his own conduct with these stories (Night 918–22).

34. Cf. Gottfried Keller in his introduction to *Romeo und Julia auf dem Dorfe* : 'The number of such fables is small, but they constantly appear in a new dress.' Or, more profoundly, Goethe, *Maximen und Reflexionen*, ed. Hecker, p. 1051, immediately after the sentence quoted above, ch. 5 note 10: 'The task of the tragic poet is nothing else but to demonstrate a moral-psychological phenomenon in the past, by using a concrete experiment.'

35. Concerning the significance of this comparison with Silenus, cf. B. Schweitzer, 'Studien zur Entstehung des Portraets bei den Griechen', *Ber. d. Saechs. Akad.* 91 (1939) 4 p. 39.

36. Unfortunately the point of the comparison is not clear in Semonides fr. 12: 'Not even a man who meets a lion, alone on a narrow path among the wooded hills, would have such fear.'

37. That 119 has an allegorical meaning, is to be concluded from the ending: 'Monarchy (we do not want) and we do not want to receive (the tyrants; cf. 48.12; 79.8; schol. 27.4).' This is the end of the poem, as is shown by the fact that the lines which follow in the papyrus project more to the left, a detail which Diehl fails to mention in his edition. But if Heraclitus was, therefore, right in interpreting fr. 119 'allegorically', there is no reason to assume that he made a mistake in fr. 46.

38. On the subject of the comparison, its details and its significance, cf. W. Jaeger, *Paideia* vol. 1 pp. 144 ff. and *Sitz. Ber. Berlin* 1926.79.

39. Tr. R. Lattimore.

40. Cf. H. J. Pos' treatise on 'The Implicit Functions of Language' (Dutch).

41. The similes and the comparisons of the early Greek Philosophers are compiled and discussed by W. Kranz, *Hermes* 73 (1938) 99–122. For the examples from Empedocles, their connexion with Homer and their importance for the natural sciences, cf. chiefly O. Regenbogen, *Quellen und Studien zur Geschichte der Mathematik* vol. 1 (1930) 131 ff., and H. Diller, *Hermes* 67 (1932) 14.

42. Or of animal bladders: cf. *RE* 12.693.

43. Kranz (above, note 41) 107 f.; there is, however, one simile (fr. 101, not fully attested) in which he speaks of a hunting dog.

44. I only mention the fact that the statement, in the context, has a strange air about it (*Il.* 6.146; cf. H. Fraenkel, (above, note 19) p. 41) and that it was not taken as a general truth until Mimnermus fr. 2 and Semonides fr. 29.

45. Similes like that of *Il.* 2.468, from which the Glaucus simile is descended, are quite another matter: the warriors stand there, thousands of men, as the leaves and flowers blossom forth in the spring. This refers to the number of the men, and thus it relates to an adjective.

46. Cf. Diller who treats these images under the heading ὄψις ἀδήλων τὰ φαινόμενα.

47. For this, cf. Regenbogen (above, note 41) and K. von Fritz, *Annals of Mathematics* 46 (1945) 245 ff.

48. It is impossible to tell whether fr. 22, concerning the gold diggers who burrow into the ground but find little gold, was meant to disparage the labours of men or to give an example of industrious striving.

49. Cf. H. Fraenkel, 'A Thought Pattern in Heraclitus', *AJP* 59 (1938) 309, and K. Reinhardt, *Hermes* 77 (1942) 225.

50. Cf. Reinhardt (above, note 49) 226.

CHAPTER 10

THE ORIGIN OF SCIENTIFIC THOUGHT

1. Cf. Kuehner-Gerth, *Grammatik der griechischen Sprache* vol 1, pp. 575 ff. where a wealth of material is collected. Also Arnold Svensson, in *Eranos* 44 (1946) 249–65.

2. E. Lobel, ΛΛΚΑΙΟΥ ΜΕΛΗ LXXIV ff. suggested that the generic use of the article was already known to the Lesbian poets; H. Fraenkel, *Goett. Gel. Anz.* 1928, 276.1 has shown that this is not true of the article before the noun, but it is equally untrue of the article preceding an adjective used as a noun. There also the article specifies a particular thing.

3. For the role of the mythical name as representing an abstraction, cf. below.

4. In fr. 126, for instance, τὰ ψυχρὰ θέρεται, θερμὸν ψύχεται still betrays a 'Hesiodic' outlook: 'All cold things become warm, warm (matter) cools off.'

5. A more detailed discussion of this follows below.

6. For the whole problem, cf. H. Usener, *Goetternamen*, esp. pp. 364 ff. Since φόβος is akin to φόβη, the former was probably, as E. Kapp has suggested, at first the 'hair standing-on-end', or, as a demon, the 'hair-raiser'.

7. Cf. the data collected in Dindorf's *Lexicon Aeschyleum* 235 A. which are, however, neither complete nor systematic.

8. (In the following two paragraphs, I have attempted to convey the purport of the argument by adding, in brackets, the original German terms, wherever it seemed necessary. The chief difficulty which made it impossible to arrive at a straightforward translation is the fact that both Greek and German have the nominal use of the infinitive, whereas in English its place is taken by the gerund, without the article. Since the argument hinges on the presence of the article with the infinitive used as a noun, a construction which does not exist in English, I could do little more than indicate the stages of the argument by means of cross references between my translation and the original.—Tr.)

9. *Philol. Unters.*, 29.32 ff.

10. For the Greek language, this has been shown especially by Diels; cf. *Philol. Unters.* 29.19; also O. Weinreich, *Die Distichen Catulls* 41.

11. Cf. J. Stenzel, *Zahl und Gestalt bei Platon und Aristoteles* 23 ff.

12. Cf. *Hermes* 61.353 ff.

13. Cf. Empedocles B 8, Anaxagoras B 17, Democritus A 37.

14. Cf. J. L. Heiberg, *Geschichte der Mathematik und Naturwissenschaften im Altertum* (Munich 1925), p. 66.

15. Cf., e.g., Aristotle ἐκ τοῦ π. ἀκουστῶν 800 a 1 ff., especially 803 b 34 ff.: αἱ δὲ πληγαὶ γίγνονται μὲν τοῦ ἀέρος ὑπὸ τῶν χορδῶν πολλαὶ καὶ κεχωρισμέναι, διὰ δὲ μικρότητα τοῦ μεταξὺ χρόνου τῆς ἀκοῆς οὐ δυναμένης συναισθάνεσθαι τὰς διαλείψεις, μία καὶ συνεχὴς ἡμῖν ἡ φωνὴ φαίνεται, —i.e. the vibration is again divided into individual impulses. In *Problemata* 1 A. 898 b 26 ff. high pitch is explained as fast, low pitch as slow movement; but there Aristotle is concerned with single disconnected observations. He does not formulate a general exact law, nor does he associate a particular pitch with a particular speed of movement.

16. We have tried to show that of our three categories, one is significant for Democritus, another for Heraclitus, and the third for Plato. The relationship between the three, and the three 'types' of Plato should be obvious. Concerning this division of speech into three categories, Fr. Mauthner has said many instructive things, though with a somewhat different point of view: *Die drei Bilder der Welt, ein sprachkritischer Versuch* (1925).

CHAPTER 11

THE DISCOVERY OF 'HUMANITAS' AND OUR ATTITUDE TOWARD THE GREEKS

1. F. J. Niethammer, *Der Streit des Philanthropismus und des Humanismus in der Theorie des Erziehungsunterrichts unserer Zeit.* Cf. Walter Rüegg, *Cicero und der Humanismus : Formale Untersuchungen ueber Petrarca und Erasmus* (Zurich 1946) 2 ff. —The earliest usage of the word 'humanistic' that has so far been verified dates from the year 1784, while 'humanist', in its Italian form, occurs first in 1538; cf. Rüegg 3 and 129.

2. Rudolf Pfeiffer, 'Humanitas Erasmiana', *Studien der Bibliothek Warburg* 22 (1931)
2 note 3.

3. The following remarks on Plato, Isocrates, Cicero and Aristippus are based on
the researches of E. Kapp; cf. *Goett. gel. Anz.* 1935 pp. 333 ff. I might mention that
the ' idea of man ' is already found occasionally in the writings of German classicism,
as in Wieland's *Agathodaemon* (2.3.58) and, unless my memory deceives me, in Goethe.

4. Cf. 4.47 ff. for similar statements. In 4.50 he says: 'Our city has so far surpassed
the rest of mankind in speech and thought . . . that the name "Greek" designates one
who shares in our education (*paideusis*) rather than a member of our race.'

5. Cf. Rüegg (see above, note 1) 29 and note 4.

6. Diog. Laert. 2.8.70.

7. Vitruvius 6.1.1; cf. Cicero *de rep.* 1.29, and Kapp (see above, note 3) 334.

8. Diog. Laert. 1.33.

9. The prototype of this story is Cicero's tale about Bias who, in a similar situation,
is said to have remarked : *omnia mea mecum porto*. Most probably neither story is
very old (cf., however, Jaeger, *Paideia* 2.70 for another view).

10. Plato, *Laws* 716 C; cf. also *Laws* 497 C and 500 B–D.

11. E. Bielefeldt was kind enough to make this suggestion to me.

12. Andocides 1.7 = Lysias 19.14.

13. Xenophon, *Ages.* 1.21; for this and the preceding reference, cf. Pfeiffer (see
above, note 2).

14. Xenophon, *Ages.* 1.22.

15. Cf. S. Tromp de Ruiter, 'De vocis quae est φιλανθρωπία significatione atque
usu', *Mnemos.* 59 (1932) 271–306.

16. Xenophon, *Cyrop.* 7.5.73.

17. Xenophon, *Cyrop.* 1.2.1 : εἶδος μὲν κάλλιστος, ψυχὴν δὲ φιλανθρωπότατος καὶ φιλομαθέ-
στατος καὶ φιλοτιμότατος. 8.2.1: διὰ παντὸς ἀεὶ χρόνου φιλανθρωπίαν τῆς ψυχῆς ὡς ἠδύνατο
μάλιστα ἐνεφάνιζεν. cf. also 1.4.1; 8.4.71 etc.

18. First found in Aeschylus, *Prom.* 10 f.: ὡς ἂν διδαχθῆ . . . φιλανθρώπου . . . παύεσθαι
τρόπου. 28: τοιαῦτ' ἐπηύρου τοῦ φιλανθρώπου τρόπου. cf. 119: ὁρᾶτε δεσμώτην με δύσποτμον
θεὸν διὰ τὴν λίαν φιλότητα βροτῶν.

19. de Ruiter (see above, note 15) 280 f.

20. de Ruiter (see above, note 15) 285.

21. de Ruiter (see above, note 15) 293; Wilamowitz, *Griechische Tragoedien* 2.27.1.

22. Thus correctly de Ruiter (see above, note 15) 303.

23. R. Harder, *Hermes* 69 (1934) 68–74.

24. Harder (above, note 23) 70. I omit from this discussion the fact that the Stoa
also produced a humanistic tradition whose influence was promoted chiefly by Christianity; for this entails the emergence of new motifs, such as the beginnings of a new
concentration upon inner values, which would have to be discussed within a wider
frame.

25. Cf. Cicero *ad Quintum*, 1.1.23, cited by Harder (see above, note 23) 73.3; for
the immense influence of the *Cyropaedia* upon Cicero and, before him, upon Scipio, cf.
Karl Muenscher, 'Xenophon in der griechisch-roemischen Literatur ', *Philol. Suppl.*
13.2 (1920) 74 and 78.

26. Letter dated March 1st, 1517: *humana praevalent in eo plus quam divina*. For
the fundamental significance of this remark, cf. Pfeiffer (see above, note 2) 20.

27. For details, cf. Rüegg (above note 1) xix ff., and F. Blaettner, 'Das Griechen-
bild Winckelmanns', *Antike und Abendland* 1 (Hamburg 1945) 121 ff.

28. *Goett. Gel. Anz.* 1935, p. 253.

CHAPTER 12

ART AND PLAY IN CALLIMACHUS

1. For this correct reading ('Bienen' instead of 'Blumen') cf. Wilamowitz, *Reden und
Vortraege*⁴ 1.263.

2. *Dichtung und Wahrheit* 3.12.

3. For Callimachus, cf. Wilamowitz, *Hellenistische Dichtung*, and especially also
E. Howald, *Der Dichter Kallimachos von Kyrene* (Erlenbach-Zurich 1943).

4. The fact that the *Aitia* is divided into four books may be connected with the Aristotelian theory that a work of poetry ought not to exceed a certain size. Cf. F. Mehmel, 'Vergil und Apollonios Rhodios, Untersuchungen ueber die Zeitvorstellung in der antiken epischen Erzaehlung', *Hamburger Arbeiten zur Altertumswissensch.* 1.17.

5. Cf. Wilamowitz, *Hell. Dicht.* 1.173.

6. Cf. Wilamowitz, *Hell. Dich.* 2.129.

7. Cf., earlier, Klopstock who speaks of poems which 'abjectly, like Pindar's songs, stagger free from the creative soul' (K. Muncker, *Klopstock* (Stuttgart 1888) 19.532 f. See also K. Burdach, *Deutsche Rundschau* 36 (1910) 254 f.). How different is the tenor of Goethe's later statement, from the year 1827 (*Jub.-Edition* 38.65.29): 'The highest lyric poetry is definitely historical. If one tries to cut out the mythological and historical elements from Pindar's odes, he will find that it means cutting out their very soul ... A true poet who finds as much cause for celebration and praise as he, who can joyfully dwell on family trees and praise the glory of so many rival cities, would unquestionably be able to produce poems of the same quality' (cf. also 37.181.24). By this time the old notions about genius have practically disappeared. In the interim Boeckh had characterized Pindar as follows: 'We consider this the most difficult and the most important task of the interpreter, to explain the purpose of the poet and, as much as that is possible, the condition of the circumstances and the men who gave Pindar his opportunity for writing such poems'; P. A. Boeckh, *Pindari opera quae supersunt* (1821) 2.6.

8. For this, cf. F. Blaettner, 'Winckelmann und die Antike', *Antike und Abendland* 1 (Hamburg 1945) 121–32.

CHAPTER 13

ARCADIA: THE DISCOVERY OF A SPIRITUAL LANDSCAPE

1. In E. Panofsky, '*Et in Arcadia ego*', *Festschrift E. Cassirer*. Cf. *Hermes* 73 (1938) 242.1.

2. Reitzenstein's attempt, in *Epigramm und Skolion* 121 ff., to demonstrate a bucolic poetry in Arcadia prior to Theocritus has already been refuted by E. Panofsky (cf. above, note 1). Cf. the hitherto unprinted dissertation by F. Magnus, *Arkadien* (Hamburg 1945). That Erycius' epigram, *A.P.* 6.96 is based on Virgil's *ecl.* 7.4 is the correct opinion of Norden, *ap.* Cichorius, *Roemische Studien* 306; for details, cf. Magnus.

3. Cf. Eva-Maria Voigt, *Die Antike* 19 (1943) 77.

4. Cf. particularly G. Rohde, '*De Vergili eclogarum forma et indole*' (Berlin 1925) and F. Klingner's studies on Virgil which have now been collected in the volume *Roemische Geisteswelt*; pp. 120 ff. offer a survey of the research done on the *Eclogues* during the past few years.

5. Cf. Liegle, *Hermes* 78 (1943) 209.

6. Cf. *Hermes* 73 (1938) 242.

7. Cf. E. Kapp, *Mnemosyne* ser. 3 vol. 4 (1936–7) 227.

8. Tr. E. V. Rieu (Penguin Classics).

9. Theocritus 3.12: θᾶσαι μὰν θυμαλγὲς ἐμὸν ἄχος is addressed to the loved woman only.

10. This combination of quoted fragments into a new poem is done in imitation of Hellenistic models; cf. O. Crusius, *RE* 3 col. 1931.

11. Cf. *Etymol. Magn.* 327.5; *Suda* s.v. ἐλεγείνειν, 2.241.15 A, and O. Crusius, *RE* 5 coll. 2260 f. For further material on Theocles, cf. W. Ehlers, *Die Gruendung von Zankle in den Aitia des Kallimachos* (Diss. Berlin 1933) 20 note 21.

12. W. Kroll, *Studien zum Verstaendnis der roem. Literatur* (1924) 50 has collected numerous passages from Greek and Roman authors, on the subject of 'invention'. Some of these passages should be examined anew. On p. 62, for example, Kroll mentions the view of Asclepiades of Myrlea (Cicero *de inv.* 1.27 and *auct. ad Her.* 1.13) that metamorphoses are *inventio* (πλάσματα), and remarks that this view 'has the

unquestionable merit of putting the content of tragedy and epic in the category of the imagination'. Against this it must be objected that πλάσματα and *inventio* are not the same thing as the imagination.

13. Tr. anonymous.

14. Cf. e.g., Aristophanes, *Frogs* 1034; Plato, *Ion* 530 B; the epitaph in Alcidamas π. Ὁμήρου; Callimachus, *epigr.* 6.1. In the end the children had to learn in school: Homer is a god, not a mortal; cf. Ziebarth, *Aus der antiken Schule*² no. 26.

15. Tr. C. S. Calverley.

16. Cf. above, ch. 12. For Horace's *odi profanum vulgus*, cf. Callimachus *epigr.* 28: σιχαίνω τὰ δημόσια (other related passages in Christ-Schmid, *Geschichte der griechischen Literatur* 2.1.117.5). It sounds less aggressive; Callimachus refers to vulgarity, Horace to the vulgar mob.

17. Cf. the verse which Diog. Laert. 8.7 attributes to Pythagoras: ὦ νέοι, ἀλλὰ σέβεσθε μεθ' ἡσυχίης τάδε πάντα.

CHAPTER 3

INDEX

A list of ancient authors cited on pp. 1–309. In the case of prominent passages, the specific references have been added in brackets.

A CATALOG OF SELECTED
DOVER BOOKS
IN ALL FIELDS OF INTEREST

A CATALOG OF SELECTED DOVER
BOOKS IN ALL FIELDS OF INTEREST

100 BEST-LOVED POEMS, Edited by Philip Smith. "The Passionate Shepherd to His Love," "Shall I compare thee to a summer's day?" "Death, be not proud," "The Raven," "The Road Not Taken," plus works by Blake, Wordsworth, Byron, Shelley, Keats, many others. 96pp. 5³⁄₁₆ x 8¼.   0-486-28553-7

100 SMALL HOUSES OF THE THIRTIES, Brown-Blodgett Company. Exterior photographs and floor plans for 100 charming structures. Illustrations of models accompanied by descriptions of interiors, color schemes, closet space, and other amenities. 200 illustrations. 112pp. 8⅜ x 11.   0-486-44131-8

1000 TURN-OF-THE-CENTURY HOUSES: With Illustrations and Floor Plans, Herbert C. Chivers. Reproduced from a rare edition, this showcase of homes ranges from cottages and bungalows to sprawling mansions. Each house is meticulously illustrated and accompanied by complete floor plans. 256pp. 9⅜ x 12¼.

                                    0-486-45596-3

101 GREAT AMERICAN POEMS, Edited by The American Poetry & Literacy Project. Rich treasury of verse from the 19th and 20th centuries includes works by Edgar Allan Poe, Robert Frost, Walt Whitman, Langston Hughes, Emily Dickinson, T. S. Eliot, other notables. 96pp. 5³⁄₁₆ x 8¼.   0-486-40158-8

101 GREAT SAMURAI PRINTS, Utagawa Kuniyoshi. Kuniyoshi was a master of the warrior woodblock print — and these 18th-century illustrations represent the pinnacle of his craft. Full-color portraits of renowned Japanese samurais pulse with movement, passion, and remarkably fine detail. 112pp. 8⅜ x 11.   0-486-46523-3

ABC OF BALLET, Janet Grosser. Clearly worded, abundantly illustrated little guide defines basic ballet-related terms: arabesque, battement, pas de chat, relevé, sissonne, many others. Pronunciation guide included. Excellent primer. 48pp. 4³⁄₁₆ x 5¾.

                                    0-486-40871-X

ACCESSORIES OF DRESS: An Illustrated Encyclopedia, Katherine Lester and Bess Viola Oerke. Illustrations of hats, veils, wigs, cravats, shawls, shoes, gloves, and other accessories enhance an engaging commentary that reveals the humor and charm of the many-sided story of accessorized apparel. 644 figures and 59 plates. 608pp. 6⅛ x 9¼.

                                    0-486-43378-1

ADVENTURES OF HUCKLEBERRY FINN, Mark Twain. Join Huck and Jim as their boyhood adventures along the Mississippi River lead them into a world of excitement, danger, and self-discovery. Humorous narrative, lyrical descriptions of the Mississippi valley, and memorable characters. 224pp. 5³⁄₁₆ x 8¼.   0-486-28061-6

ALICE STARMORE'S BOOK OF FAIR ISLE KNITTING, Alice Starmore. A noted designer from the region of Scotland's Fair Isle explores the history and techniques of this distinctive, stranded-color knitting style and provides copious illustrated instructions for 14 original knitwear designs. 208pp. 8⅜ x 10⅞.   0-486-47218-3

Browse over 9,000 books at www.doverpublications.com

ALICE'S ADVENTURES IN WONDERLAND, Lewis Carroll. Beloved classic about a little girl lost in a topsy-turvy land and her encounters with the White Rabbit, March Hare, Mad Hatter, Cheshire Cat, and other delightfully improbable characters. 42 illustrations by Sir John Tenniel. 96pp. 5³⁄₁₆ x 8¼.   0-486-27543-4

AMERICA'S LIGHTHOUSES: An Illustrated History, Francis Ross Holland. Profusely illustrated fact-filled survey of American lighthouses since 1716. Over 200 stations — East, Gulf, and West coasts, Great Lakes, Hawaii, Alaska, Puerto Rico, the Virgin Islands, and the Mississippi and St. Lawrence Rivers. 240pp. 8 x 10¾.
0-486-25576-X

AN ENCYCLOPEDIA OF THE VIOLIN, Alberto Bachmann. Translated by Frederick H. Martens. Introduction by Eugene Ysaye. First published in 1925, this renowned reference remains unsurpassed as a source of essential information, from construction and evolution to repertoire and technique. Includes a glossary and 73 illustrations. 496pp. 6⅛ x 9¼.   0-486-46618-3

ANIMALS: 1,419 Copyright-Free Illustrations of Mammals, Birds, Fish, Insects, etc., Selected by Jim Harter. Selected for its visual impact and ease of use, this outstanding collection of wood engravings presents over 1,000 species of animals in extremely lifelike poses. Includes mammals, birds, reptiles, amphibians, fish, insects, and other invertebrates. 284pp. 9 x 12.   0-486-23766-4

THE ANNALS, Tacitus. Translated by Alfred John Church and William Jackson Brodribb. This vital chronicle of Imperial Rome, written by the era's great historian, spans A.D. 14-68 and paints incisive psychological portraits of major figures, from Tiberius to Nero. 416pp. 5³⁄₁₆ x 8¼.   0-486-45236-0

ANTIGONE, Sophocles. Filled with passionate speeches and sensitive probing of moral and philosophical issues, this powerful and often-performed Greek drama reveals the grim fate that befalls the children of Oedipus. Footnotes. 64pp. 5³⁄₁₆ x 8 ¼.   0-486-27804-2

ART DECO DECORATIVE PATTERNS IN FULL COLOR, Christian Stoll. Reprinted from a rare 1910 portfolio, 160 sensuous and exotic images depict a breathtaking array of florals, geometrics, and abstracts — all elegant in their stark simplicity. 64pp. 8⅜ x 11.   0-486-44862-2

THE ARTHUR RACKHAM TREASURY: 86 Full-Color Illustrations, Arthur Rackham. Selected and Edited by Jeff A. Menges. A stunning treasury of 86 full-page plates span the famed English artist's career, from *Rip Van Winkle* (1905) to masterworks such as *Undine, A Midsummer Night's Dream*, and *Wind in the Willows* (1939). 96pp. 8⅜ x 11.
0-486-44685-9

THE AUTHENTIC GILBERT & SULLIVAN SONGBOOK, W. S. Gilbert and A. S. Sullivan. The most comprehensive collection available, this songbook includes selections from every one of Gilbert and Sullivan's light operas. Ninety-two numbers are presented uncut and unedited, and in their original keys. 410pp. 9 x 12.
0-486-23482-7

THE AWAKENING, Kate Chopin. First published in 1899, this controversial novel of a New Orleans wife's search for love outside a stifling marriage shocked readers. Today, it remains a first-rate narrative with superb characterization. New introductory Note. 128pp. 5³⁄₁₆ x 8¼.   0-486-27786-0

BASIC DRAWING, Louis Priscilla. Beginning with perspective, this commonsense manual progresses to the figure in movement, light and shade, anatomy, drapery, composition, trees and landscape, and outdoor sketching. Black-and-white illustrations throughout. 128pp. 8⅜ x 11.   0-486-45815-6

THE BATTLES THAT CHANGED HISTORY, Fletcher Pratt. Historian profiles 16 crucial conflicts, ancient to modern, that changed the course of Western civilization. Gripping accounts of battles led by Alexander the Great, Joan of Arc, Ulysses S. Grant, other commanders. 27 maps. 352pp. 5⅜ x 8½. 0-486-41129-X

BEETHOVEN'S LETTERS, Ludwig van Beethoven. Edited by Dr. A. C. Kalischer. Features 457 letters to fellow musicians, friends, greats, patrons, and literary men. Reveals musical thoughts, quirks of personality, insights, and daily events. Includes 15 plates. 410pp. 5⅜ x 8½. 0-486-22769-3

BERNICE BOBS HER HAIR AND OTHER STORIES, F. Scott Fitzgerald. This brilliant anthology includes 6 of Fitzgerald's most popular stories: "The Diamond as Big as the Ritz," the title tale, "The Offshore Pirate," "The Ice Palace," "The Jelly Bean," and "May Day." 176pp. 5⅜ x 8½. 0-486-47049-0

BESLER'S BOOK OF FLOWERS AND PLANTS: 73 Full-Color Plates from Hortus Eystettensis, 1613, Basilius Besler. Here is a selection of magnificent plates from the *Hortus Eystettensis*, which vividly illustrated and identified the plants, flowers, and trees that thrived in the legendary German garden at Eichstätt. 80pp. 8⅜ x 11.
0-486-46005-3

THE BOOK OF KELLS, Edited by Blanche Cirker. Painstakingly reproduced from a rare facsimile edition, this volume contains full-page decorations, portraits, illustrations, plus a sampling of textual leaves with exquisite calligraphy and ornamentation. 32 full-color illustrations. 32pp. 9⅜ x 12¼. 0-486-24345-1

THE BOOK OF THE CROSSBOW: With an Additional Section on Catapults and Other Siege Engines, Ralph Payne-Gallwey. Fascinating study traces history and use of crossbow as military and sporting weapon, from Middle Ages to modern times. Also covers related weapons: balistas, catapults, Turkish bows, more. Over 240 illustrations. 400pp. 7¼ x 10⅛. 0-486-28720-3

THE BUNGALOW BOOK: Floor Plans and Photos of 112 Houses, 1910, Henry L. Wilson. Here are 112 of the most popular and economic blueprints of the early 20th century — plus an illustration or photograph of each completed house. A wonderful time capsule that still offers a wealth of valuable insights. 160pp. 8⅜ x 11.
0-486-45104-6

THE CALL OF THE WILD, Jack London. A classic novel of adventure, drawn from London's own experiences as a Klondike adventurer, relating the story of a heroic dog caught in the brutal life of the Alaska Gold Rush. Note. 64pp. 5³⁄₁₆ x 8¼.
0-486-26472-6

CANDIDE, Voltaire. Edited by Francois-Marie Arouet. One of the world's great satires since its first publication in 1759. Witty, caustic skewering of romance, science, philosophy, religion, government — nearly all human ideals and institutions. 112pp. 5³⁄₁₆ x 8¼. 0-486-26689-3

CELEBRATED IN THEIR TIME: Photographic Portraits from the George Grantham Bain Collection, Edited by Amy Pastan. With an Introduction by Michael Carlebach. Remarkable portrait gallery features 112 rare images of Albert Einstein, Charlie Chaplin, the Wright Brothers, Henry Ford, and other luminaries from the worlds of politics, art, entertainment, and industry. 128pp. 8⅜ x 11. 0-486-46754-6

CHARIOTS FOR APOLLO: The NASA History of Manned Lunar Spacecraft to 1969, Courtney G. Brooks, James M. Grimwood, and Loyd S. Swenson, Jr. This illustrated history by a trio of experts is the definitive reference on the Apollo spacecraft and lunar modules. It traces the vehicles' design, development, and operation in space. More than 100 photographs and illustrations. 576pp. 6¾ x 9¼. 0-486-46756-2

CATALOG OF DOVER BOOKS

A CHRISTMAS CAROL, Charles Dickens. This engrossing tale relates Ebenezer Scrooge's ghostly journeys through Christmases past, present, and future and his ultimate transformation from a harsh and grasping old miser to a charitable and compassionate human being. 80pp. 5³⁄₁₆ x 8¼. 0-486-26865-9

COMMON SENSE, Thomas Paine. First published in January of 1776, this highly influential landmark document clearly and persuasively argued for American separation from Great Britain and paved the way for the Declaration of Independence. 64pp. 5³⁄₁₆ x 8¼. 0-486-29602-4

THE COMPLETE SHORT STORIES OF OSCAR WILDE, Oscar Wilde. Complete texts of "The Happy Prince and Other Tales," "A House of Pomegranates," "Lord Arthur Savile's Crime and Other Stories," "Poems in Prose," and "The Portrait of Mr. W. H." 208pp. 5³⁄₁₆ x 8¼. 0-486-45216-6

COMPLETE SONNETS, William Shakespeare. Over 150 exquisite poems deal with love, friendship, the tyranny of time, beauty's evanescence, death, and other themes in language of remarkable power, precision, and beauty. Glossary of archaic terms. 80pp. 5³⁄₁₆ x 8¼. 0-486-26686-9

THE COUNT OF MONTE CRISTO: Abridged Edition, Alexandre Dumas. Falsely accused of treason, Edmond Dantès is imprisoned in the bleak Chateau d'If. After a hair-raising escape, he launches an elaborate plot to extract a bitter revenge against those who betrayed him. 448pp. 5³⁄₁₆ x 8¼. 0-486-45643-9

CRAFTSMAN BUNGALOWS: Designs from the Pacific Northwest, Yoho & Merritt. This reprint of a rare catalog, showcasing the charming simplicity and cozy style of Craftsman bungalows, is filled with photos of completed homes, plus floor plans and estimated costs. An indispensable resource for architects, historians, and illustrators. 112pp. 10 x 7. 0-486-46875-5

CRAFTSMAN BUNGALOWS: 59 Homes from "The Craftsman," Edited by Gustav Stickley. Best and most attractive designs from Arts and Crafts Movement publication — 1903-1916 — includes sketches, photographs of homes, floor plans, descriptive text. 128pp. 8¼ x 11. 0-486-25829-7

CRIME AND PUNISHMENT, Fyodor Dostoyevsky. Translated by Constance Garnett. Supreme masterpiece tells the story of Raskolnikov, a student tormented by his own thoughts after he murders an old woman. Overwhelmed by guilt and terror, he confesses and goes to prison. 480pp. 5³⁄₁₆ x 8¼. 0-486-41587-2

THE DECLARATION OF INDEPENDENCE AND OTHER GREAT DOCUMENTS OF AMERICAN HISTORY: 1775-1865, Edited by John Grafton. Thirteen compelling and influential documents: Henry's "Give Me Liberty or Give Me Death," Declaration of Independence, The Constitution, Washington's First Inaugural Address, The Monroe Doctrine, The Emancipation Proclamation, Gettysburg Address, more. 64pp. 5³⁄₁₆ x 8¼. 0-486-41124-9

THE DESERT AND THE SOWN: Travels in Palestine and Syria, Gertrude Bell. "The female Lawrence of Arabia," Gertrude Bell wrote captivating, perceptive accounts of her travels in the Middle East. This intriguing narrative, accompanied by 160 photos, traces her 1905 sojourn in Lebanon, Syria, and Palestine. 368pp. 5⅜ x 8½. 0-486-46876-3

A DOLL'S HOUSE, Henrik Ibsen. Ibsen's best-known play displays his genius for realistic prose drama. An expression of women's rights, the play climaxes when the central character, Nora, rejects a smothering marriage and life in "a doll's house." 80pp. 5³⁄₁₆ x 8¼. 0-486-27062-9

Browse over 9,000 books at www.doverpublications.com

DOOMED SHIPS: Great Ocean Liner Disasters, William H. Miller, Jr. Nearly 200 photographs, many from private collections, highlight tales of some of the vessels whose pleasure cruises ended in catastrophe: the *Morro Castle, Normandie, Andrea Doria, Europa,* and many others. 128pp. 8⅜ x 11¾. 0-486-45366-9

THE DORÉ BIBLE ILLUSTRATIONS, Gustave Doré. Detailed plates from the Bible: the Creation scenes, Adam and Eve, horrifying visions of the Flood, the battle sequences with their monumental crowds, depictions of the life of Jesus, 241 plates in all. 241pp. 9 x 12. 0-486-23004-X

DRAWING DRAPERY FROM HEAD TO TOE, Cliff Young. Expert guidance on how to draw shirts, pants, skirts, gloves, hats, and coats on the human figure, including folds in relation to the body, pull and crush, action folds, creases, more. Over 200 drawings. 48pp. 8¼ x 11. 0-486-45591-2

DUBLINERS, James Joyce. A fine and accessible introduction to the work of one of the 20th century's most influential writers, this collection features 15 tales, including a masterpiece of the short-story genre, "The Dead." 160pp. 5³⁄₁₆ x 8¼. 0-486-26870-5

EASY-TO-MAKE POP-UPS, Joan Irvine. Illustrated by Barbara Reid. Dozens of wonderful ideas for three-dimensional paper fun — from holiday greeting cards with moving parts to a pop-up menagerie. Easy-to-follow, illustrated instructions for more than 30 projects. 299 black-and-white illustrations. 96pp. 8⅜ x 11. 0-486-44622-0

EASY-TO-MAKE STORYBOOK DOLLS: A "Novel" Approach to Cloth Dollmaking, Sherralyn St. Clair. Favorite fictional characters come alive in this unique beginner's dollmaking guide. Includes patterns for Pollyanna, Dorothy from *The Wonderful Wizard of Oz,* Mary of *The Secret Garden,* plus easy-to-follow instructions, 263 black-and-white illustrations, and an 8-page color insert. 112pp. 8¼ x 11. 0-486-47360-0

EINSTEIN'S ESSAYS IN SCIENCE, Albert Einstein. Speeches and essays in accessible, everyday language profile influential physicists such as Niels Bohr and Isaac Newton. They also explore areas of physics to which the author made major contributions. 128pp. 5 x 8. 0-486-47011-3

EL DORADO: Further Adventures of the Scarlet Pimpernel, Baroness Orczy. A popular sequel to *The Scarlet Pimpernel,* this suspenseful story recounts the Pimpernel's attempts to rescue the Dauphin from imprisonment during the French Revolution. An irresistible blend of intrigue, period detail, and vibrant characterizations. 352pp. 5³⁄₁₆ x 8¼. 0-486-44026-5

ELEGANT SMALL HOMES OF THE TWENTIES: 99 Designs from a Competition, Chicago Tribune. Nearly 100 designs for five- and six-room houses feature New England and Southern colonials, Normandy cottages, stately Italianate dwellings, and other fascinating snapshots of American domestic architecture of the 1920s. 112pp. 9 x 12. 0-486-46910-7

THE ELEMENTS OF STYLE: The Original Edition, William Strunk, Jr. This is the book that generations of writers have relied upon for timeless advice on grammar, diction, syntax, and other essentials. In concise terms, it identifies the principal requirements of proper style and common errors. 64pp. 5⅜ x 8½. 0-486-44798-7

THE ELUSIVE PIMPERNEL, Baroness Orczy. Robespierre's revolutionaries find their wicked schemes thwarted by the heroic Pimpernel — Sir Percival Blakeney. In this thrilling sequel, Chauvelin devises a plot to eliminate the Pimpernel and his wife. 272pp. 5³⁄₁₆ x 8¼. 0-486-45464-9

AN ENCYCLOPEDIA OF BATTLES: Accounts of Over 1,560 Battles from 1479 B.C. to the Present, David Eggenberger. Essential details of every major battle in recorded history from the first battle of Megiddo in 1479 B.C. to Grenada in 1984. List of battle maps. 99 illustrations. 544pp. 6½ x 9¼. 0-486-24913-1

ENCYCLOPEDIA OF EMBROIDERY STITCHES, INCLUDING CREWEL, Marion Nichols. Precise explanations and instructions, clearly illustrated, on how to work chain, back, cross, knotted, woven stitches, and many more — 178 in all, including Cable Outline, Whipped Satin, and Eyelet Buttonhole. Over 1400 illustrations. 219pp. 8⅜ x 11¼. 0-486-22929-7

ENTER JEEVES: 15 Early Stories, P. G. Wodehouse. Splendid collection contains first 8 stories featuring Bertie Wooster, the deliciously dim aristocrat and Jeeves, his brainy, imperturbable manservant. Also, the complete Reggie Pepper (Bertie's prototype) series. 288pp. 5⅜ x 8½. 0-486-29717-9

ERIC SLOANE'S AMERICA: Paintings in Oil, Michael Wigley. With a Foreword by Mimi Sloane. Eric Sloane's evocative oils of America's landscape and material culture shimmer with immense historical and nostalgic appeal. This original hardcover collection gathers nearly a hundred of his finest paintings, with subjects ranging from New England to the American Southwest. 128pp. 10⅝ x 9. 0-486-46525-X

ETHAN FROME, Edith Wharton. Classic story of wasted lives, set against a bleak New England background. Superbly delineated characters in a hauntingly grim tale of thwarted love. Considered by many to be Wharton's masterpiece. 96pp. 5³⁄₁₆ x 8 ¼. 0-486-26690-7

THE EVERLASTING MAN, G. K. Chesterton. Chesterton's view of Christianity — as a blend of philosophy and mythology, satisfying intellect and spirit — applies to his brilliant book, which appeals to readers' heads as well as their hearts. 288pp. 5⅜ x 8½. 0-486-46036-3

THE FIELD AND FOREST HANDY BOOK, Daniel Beard. Written by a co-founder of the Boy Scouts, this appealing guide offers illustrated instructions for building kites, birdhouses, boats, igloos, and other fun projects, plus numerous helpful tips for campers. 448pp. 5³⁄₁₆ x 8¼. 0-486-46191-2

FINDING YOUR WAY WITHOUT MAP OR COMPASS, Harold Gatty. Useful, instructive manual shows would-be explorers, hikers, bikers, scouts, sailors, and survivalists how to find their way outdoors by observing animals, weather patterns, shifting sands, and other elements of nature. 288pp. 5⅜ x 8½. 0-486-40613-X

FIRST FRENCH READER: A Beginner's Dual-Language Book, Edited and Translated by Stanley Appelbaum. This anthology introduces 50 legendary writers — Voltaire, Balzac, Baudelaire, Proust, more — through passages from *The Red and the Black, Les Misérables, Madame Bovary,* and other classics. Original French text plus English translation on facing pages. 240pp. 5⅜ x 8½. 0-486-46178-5

FIRST GERMAN READER: A Beginner's Dual-Language Book, Edited by Harry Steinhauer. Specially chosen for their power to evoke German life and culture, these short, simple readings include poems, stories, essays, and anecdotes by Goethe, Hesse, Heine, Schiller, and others. 224pp. 5⅜ x 8½. 0-486-46179-3

FIRST SPANISH READER: A Beginner's Dual-Language Book, Angel Flores. Delightful stories, other material based on works of Don Juan Manuel, Luis Taboada, Ricardo Palma, other noted writers. Complete faithful English translations on facing pages. Exercises. 176pp. 5⅜ x 8½. 0-486-25810-6

CATALOG OF DOVER BOOKS

FIVE ACRES AND INDEPENDENCE, Maurice G. Kains. Great back-to-the-land classic explains basics of self-sufficient farming. The one book to get. 95 illustrations. 397pp. 5⅜ x 8½. 0-486-20974-1

FLAGG'S SMALL HOUSES: Their Economic Design and Construction, 1922, Ernest Flagg. Although most famous for his skyscrapers, Flagg was also a proponent of the well-designed single-family dwelling. His classic treatise features innovations that save space, materials, and cost. 526 illustrations. 160pp. 9⅜ x 12¼.
0-486-45197-6

FLATLAND: A Romance of Many Dimensions, Edwin A. Abbott. Classic of science (and mathematical) fiction — charmingly illustrated by the author — describes the adventures of A. Square, a resident of Flatland, in Spaceland (three dimensions), Lineland (one dimension), and Pointland (no dimensions). 96pp. 5 9/16 x 8¼.
0-486-27263-X

FRANKENSTEIN, Mary Shelley. The story of Victor Frankenstein's monstrous creation and the havoc it caused has enthralled generations of readers and inspired countless writers of horror and suspense. With the author's own 1831 introduction. 176pp. 5 9/16 x 8¼. 0-486-28211-2

THE GARGOYLE BOOK: 572 Examples from Gothic Architecture, Lester Burbank Bridaham. Dispelling the conventional wisdom that French Gothic architectural flourishes were born of despair or gloom, Bridaham reveals the whimsical nature of these creations and the ingenious artisans who made them. 572 illustrations. 224pp. 8⅜ x 11. 0-486-44754-5

THE GIFT OF THE MAGI AND OTHER SHORT STORIES, O. Henry. Sixteen captivating stories by one of America's most popular storytellers. Included are such classics as "The Gift of the Magi," "The Last Leaf," and "The Ransom of Red Chief." Publisher's Note. 96pp. 5 9/16 x 8¼. 0-486-27061-0

THE GOETHE TREASURY: Selected Prose and Poetry, Johann Wolfgang von Goethe. Edited, Selected, and with an Introduction by Thomas Mann. In addition to his lyric poetry, Goethe wrote travel sketches, autobiographical studies, essays, letters, and proverbs in rhyme and prose. This collection presents outstanding examples from each genre. 368pp. 5⅜ x 8½. 0-486-44780-4

GREAT EXPECTATIONS, Charles Dickens. Orphaned Pip is apprenticed to the dirty work of the forge but dreams of becoming a gentleman — and one day finds himself in possession of "great expectations." Dickens' finest novel. 400pp. 5 9/16 x 8¼.
0-486-41586-4

GREAT WRITERS ON THE ART OF FICTION: From Mark Twain to Joyce Carol Oates, Edited by James Daley. An indispensable source of advice and inspiration, this anthology features essays by Henry James, Kate Chopin, Willa Cather, Sinclair Lewis, Jack London, Raymond Chandler, Raymond Carver, Eudora Welty, and Kurt Vonnegut, Jr. 192pp. 5⅜ x 8½. 0-486-45128-3

HAMLET, William Shakespeare. The quintessential Shakespearean tragedy, whose highly charged confrontations and anguished soliloquies probe depths of human feeling rarely sounded in any art. Reprinted from an authoritative British edition complete with illuminating footnotes. 128pp. 5 9/16 x 8¼. 0-486-27278-8

THE HAUNTED HOUSE, Charles Dickens. A Yuletide gathering in an eerie country retreat provides the backdrop for Dickens and his friends — including Elizabeth Gaskell and Wilkie Collins — who take turns spinning supernatural yarns. 144pp. 5⅜ x 8½. 0-486-46309-5

Browse over 9,000 books at www.doverpublications.com

HEART OF DARKNESS, Joseph Conrad. Dark allegory of a journey up the Congo River and the narrator's encounter with the mysterious Mr. Kurtz. Masterly blend of adventure, character study, psychological penetration. For many, Conrad's finest, most enigmatic story. 80pp. 5³⁄₁₆ x 8¼. 0-486-26464-5

HENSON AT THE NORTH POLE, Matthew A. Henson. This thrilling memoir by the heroic African-American who was Peary's companion through two decades of Arctic exploration recounts a tale of danger, courage, and determination. "Fascinating and exciting." — *Commonweal*. 128pp. 5⅜ x 8½. 0-486-45472-X

HISTORIC COSTUMES AND HOW TO MAKE THEM, Mary Fernald and E. Shenton. Practical, informative guidebook shows how to create everything from short tunics worn by Saxon men in the fifth century to a lady's bustle dress of the late 1800s. 81 illustrations. 176pp. 5⅜ x 8½. 0-486-44906-8

THE HOUND OF THE BASKERVILLES, Arthur Conan Doyle. A deadly curse in the form of a legendary ferocious beast continues to claim its victims from the Baskerville family until Holmes and Watson intervene. Often called the best detective story ever written. 128pp. 5³⁄₁₆ x 8¼. 0-486-28214-7

THE HOUSE BEHIND THE CEDARS, Charles W. Chesnutt. Originally published in 1900, this groundbreaking novel by a distinguished African-American author recounts the drama of a brother and sister who "pass for white" during the dangerous days of Reconstruction. 208pp. 5⅜ x 8½. 0-486-46144-0

THE HUMAN FIGURE IN MOTION, Eadweard Muybridge. The 4,789 photographs in this definitive selection show the human figure — models almost all undraped — engaged in over 160 different types of action: running, climbing stairs, etc. 390pp. 7⅞ x 10⅝. 0-486-20204-6

THE IMPORTANCE OF BEING EARNEST, Oscar Wilde. Wilde's witty and buoyant comedy of manners, filled with some of literature's most famous epigrams, reprinted from an authoritative British edition. Considered Wilde's most perfect work. 64pp. 5³⁄₁₆ x 8¼. 0-486-26478-5

THE INFERNO, Dante Alighieri. Translated and with notes by Henry Wadsworth Longfellow. The first stop on Dante's famous journey from Hell to Purgatory to Paradise, this 14th-century allegorical poem blends vivid and shocking imagery with graceful lyricism. Translated by the beloved 19th-century poet, Henry Wadsworth Longfellow. 256pp. 5³⁄₁₆ x 8¼. 0-486-44288-8

JANE EYRE, Charlotte Brontë. Written in 1847, *Jane Eyre* tells the tale of an orphan girl's progress from the custody of cruel relatives to an oppressive boarding school and its culmination in a troubled career as a governess. 448pp. 5³⁄₁₆ x 8¼.
0-486-42449-9

JAPANESE WOODBLOCK FLOWER PRINTS, Tanigami Kônan. Extraordinary collection of Japanese woodblock prints by a well-known artist features 120 plates in brilliant color. Realistic images from a rare edition include daffodils, tulips, and other familiar and unusual flowers. 128pp. 11 x 8¼. 0-486-46442-3

JEWELRY MAKING AND DESIGN, Augustus F. Rose and Antonio Cirino. Professional secrets of jewelry making are revealed in a thorough, practical guide. Over 200 illustrations. 306pp. 5⅜ x 8½. 0-486-21750-7

JULIUS CAESAR, William Shakespeare. Great tragedy based on Plutarch's account of the lives of Brutus, Julius Caesar and Mark Antony. Evil plotting, ringing oratory, high tragedy with Shakespeare's incomparable insight, dramatic power. Explanatory footnotes. 96pp. 5³⁄₁₆ x 8¼. 0-486-26876-4

CATALOG OF DOVER BOOKS

THE JUNGLE, Upton Sinclair. 1906 bestseller shockingly reveals intolerable labor practices and working conditions in the Chicago stockyards as it tells the grim story of a Slavic family that emigrates to America full of optimism but soon faces despair. 320pp. 5³⁄₁₆ x 8¼. 0-486-41923-1

THE KINGDOM OF GOD IS WITHIN YOU, Leo Tolstoy. The soul-searching book that inspired Gandhi to embrace the concept of passive resistance, Tolstoy's 1894 polemic clearly outlines a radical, well-reasoned revision of traditional Christian thinking. 352pp. 5³⁄₁₆ x 8¼. 0-486-45138-0

THE LADY OR THE TIGER?: and Other Logic Puzzles, Raymond M. Smullyan. Created by a renowned puzzle master, these whimsically themed challenges involve paradoxes about probability, time, and change; metapuzzles; and self-referentiality. Nineteen chapters advance in difficulty from relatively simple to highly complex. 1982 edition. 240pp. 5⅜ x 8½. 0-486-47027-X

LEAVES OF GRASS: The Original 1855 Edition, Walt Whitman. Whitman's immortal collection includes some of the greatest poems of modern times, including his masterpiece, "Song of Myself." Shattering standard conventions, it stands as an unabashed celebration of body and nature. 128pp. 5³⁄₁₆ x 8¼. 0-486-45676-5

LES MISÉRABLES, Victor Hugo. Translated by Charles E. Wilbour. Abridged by James K. Robinson. A convict's heroic struggle for justice and redemption plays out against a fiery backdrop of the Napoleonic wars. This edition features the excellent original translation and a sensitive abridgment. 304pp. 6⅛ x 9¼.
0-486-45789-3

LILITH: A Romance, George MacDonald. In this novel by the father of fantasy literature, a man travels through time to meet Adam and Eve and to explore humanity's fall from grace and ultimate redemption. 240pp. 5⅜ x 8½.
0-486-46818-6

THE LOST LANGUAGE OF SYMBOLISM, Harold Bayley. This remarkable book reveals the hidden meaning behind familiar images and words, from the origins of Santa Claus to the fleur-de-lys, drawing from mythology, folklore, religious texts, and fairy tales. 1,418 illustrations. 784pp. 5⅜ x 8½. 0-486-44787-1

MACBETH, William Shakespeare. A Scottish nobleman murders the king in order to succeed to the throne. Tortured by his conscience and fearful of discovery, he becomes tangled in a web of treachery and deceit that ultimately spells his doom. 96pp. 5³⁄₁₆ x 8¼. 0-486-27802-6

MAKING AUTHENTIC CRAFTSMAN FURNITURE: Instructions and Plans for 62 Projects, Gustav Stickley. Make authentic reproductions of handsome, functional, durable furniture: tables, chairs, wall cabinets, desks, a hall tree, and more. Construction plans with drawings, schematics, dimensions, and lumber specs reprinted from 1900s The Craftsman magazine. 128pp. 8⅛ x 11. 0-486-25000-8

MATHEMATICS FOR THE NONMATHEMATICIAN, Morris Kline. Erudite and entertaining overview follows development of mathematics from ancient Greeks to present. Topics include logic and mathematics, the fundamental concept, differential calculus, probability theory, much more. Exercises and problems. 641pp. 5⅜ x 8½. 0-486-24823-2

MEMOIRS OF AN ARABIAN PRINCESS FROM ZANZIBAR, Emily Ruete. This 19th-century autobiography offers a rare inside look at the society surrounding a sultan's palace. A real-life princess in exile recalls her vanished world of harems, slave trading, and court intrigues. 288pp. 5⅜ x 8½. 0-486-47121-7

Browse over 9,000 books at www.doverpublications.com

THE METAMORPHOSIS AND OTHER STORIES, Franz Kafka. Excellent new English translations of title story (considered by many critics Kafka's most perfect work), plus "The Judgment," "In the Penal Colony," "A Country Doctor," and "A Report to an Academy." Note. 96pp. 5³⁄₁₆ x 8¼. 0-486-29030-1

MICROSCOPIC ART FORMS FROM THE PLANT WORLD, R. Anheisser. From undulating curves to complex geometrics, a world of fascinating images abound in this classic, illustrated survey of microscopic plants. Features 400 detailed illustrations of nature's minute but magnificent handiwork. The accompanying CD-ROM includes all of the images in the book. 128pp. 9 x 9. 0-486-46013-4

A MIDSUMMER NIGHT'S DREAM, William Shakespeare. Among the most popular of Shakespeare's comedies, this enchanting play humorously celebrates the vagaries of love as it focuses upon the intertwined romances of several pairs of lovers. Explanatory footnotes. 80pp. 5³⁄₁₆ x 8¼. 0-486-27067-X

THE MONEY CHANGERS, Upton Sinclair. Originally published in 1908, this cautionary novel from the author of *The Jungle* explores corruption within the American system as a group of power brokers joins forces for personal gain, triggering a crash on Wall Street. 192pp. 5⅜ x 8½. 0-486-46917-4

THE MOST POPULAR HOMES OF THE TWENTIES, William A. Radford. With a New Introduction by Daniel D. Reiff. Based on a rare 1925 catalog, this architectural showcase features floor plans, construction details, and photos of 26 homes, plus articles on entrances, porches, garages, and more. 250 illustrations, 21 color plates. 176pp. 8⅜ x 11. 0-486-47028-8

MY 66 YEARS IN THE BIG LEAGUES, Connie Mack. With a New Introduction by Rich Westcott. A Founding Father of modern baseball, Mack holds the record for most wins — and losses — by a major league manager. Enhanced by 70 photographs, his warmhearted autobiography is populated by many legends of the game. 288pp. 5⅜ x 8½. 0-486-47184-5

NARRATIVE OF THE LIFE OF FREDERICK DOUGLASS, Frederick Douglass. Douglass's graphic depictions of slavery, harrowing escape to freedom, and life as a newspaper editor, eloquent orator, and impassioned abolitionist. 96pp. 5³⁄₁₆ x 8¼. 0-486-28499-9

THE NIGHTLESS CITY: Geisha and Courtesan Life in Old Tokyo, J. E. de Becker. This unsurpassed study from 100 years ago ventured into Tokyo's red-light district to survey geisha and courtesan life and offer meticulous descriptions of training, dress, social hierarchy, and erotic practices. 49 black-and-white illustrations; 2 maps. 496pp. 5⅜ x 8½. 0-486-45563-7

THE ODYSSEY, Homer. Excellent prose translation of ancient epic recounts adventures of the homeward-bound Odysseus. Fantastic cast of gods, giants, cannibals, sirens, other supernatural creatures — true classic of Western literature. 256pp. 5³⁄₁₆ x 8¼. 0-486-40654-7

OEDIPUS REX, Sophocles. Landmark of Western drama concerns the catastrophe that ensues when King Oedipus discovers he has inadvertently killed his father and married his mother. Masterly construction, dramatic irony. Explanatory footnotes. 64pp. 5³⁄₁₆ x 8¼. 0-486-26877-2

ONCE UPON A TIME: The Way America Was, Eric Sloane. Nostalgic text and drawings brim with gentle philosophies and descriptions of how we used to live — self-sufficiently — on the land, in homes, and among the things built by hand. 44 line illustrations. 64pp. 8⅜ x 11. 0-486-44411-2